Lobbying Hitler

Lobbying Hitler
Industrial Associations between Democracy and Dictatorship

Matt Bera

NEW YORK • OXFORD
www.berghahnbooks.com

First published in 2016 by
Berghahn Books
www.berghahnbooks.com

© 2016, 2021 Matt Bera
First paperback edition published in 2021

All rights reserved. Except for the quotation of short passages
for the purposes of criticism and review, no part of this book
may be reproduced in any form or by any means, electronic or
mechanical, including photocopying, recording, or any information
storage and retrieval system now known or to be invented,
without written permission of the publisher.

Library of Congress Cataloging-in-Publication Data

Names: Bera, Matt, author.
Title: Lobbying Hitler: Industrial Associations between Democracy and Dictatorship / Matt Bera.
Description: New York : Berghahn Books, 2016. | Includes bibliographical references.
Identifiers: LCCN 2015025753| ISBN 9781785330650 (hardback : alkaline paper) | ISBN 9781785330667 (e-book)
Subjects: LCSH: Industrial management—Germany—History—20th century. | Executives—Germany—Biography. | Reichert, J. W. (Jacob Wilhelm), 1885– | Lange, Karl, 1889–1955. | Iron industry and trade—Germany—History—20th century. | Steel industry and trade--Germany—History—20th century. | Machinery industry—Germany—History—20th century. | National socialism—Germany—Economic aspects. | Germany—Economic policy—1933–1945.
Classification: LCC HD70.G3 B47 2016 | DDC 338.7/6218092—dc23
LC record available at http://lccn.loc.gov/2015025753

British Library Cataloguing in Publication Data

A catalogue record for this book is available from the British Library

ISBN: 978-1-78533-065-0 hardback
ISBN: 978-1-80073-215-5 paperback
ISBN: 978-1-78533-066-7 ebook

For Michelle. For everything.

Contents

Acknowledgements		viii
List of Abbreviations		ix
Introduction.	Adaptation and Opposition in Democracy and Dictatorship	1
Chapter 1.	Opposition and Adaptation: Reichert and Lange in the Weimar Republic	21
Chapter 2.	Confidence and Complicity: Confronting National Socialist Ideology	62
Chapter 3.	Conflict and Coordination: Creating a National Socialist Economy	110
Chapter 4.	Impotence: Jakob Reichert in the Nazi Wartime Economy	154
Chapter 5.	Indispensability: Karl Lange in the Nazi Wartime Economy	189
Conclusion		220
Glossary		229
Bibliography		231
Index		246

Acknowledgments

As any project naturally depends on the contribution of a large number of people, an honest account of all those who have helped bring this one to fruition would be a substantial undertaking in itself. That said, I would like to particularly thank the colleagues, friends and mentors who read and commented on various iterations of this text, particularly Irmgard Steinisch, Volker Berghahn, Peter Hayes, Wilhelm Bleek and Michelle Braakman. I am also especially grateful for the timely advice provided by James Retallack. I received a great deal of financial, professional and personal assistance from the Canadian Centre for German and European Studies and from John Paul Kleiner in particular, and early research for this project was funded by the German Academic Exchange Service. I would also like to express my thanks for the assistance and warm reception I received from the Bundesarchiv and especially the Hoppegarten branch, as well as the Institut für Zeitgeschichte and Bayerisches Wirtschaftsarchiv in Munich and the Stiftung Rheinisch-Westfälisches Wirtschaftsarchiv in Cologne. I was deeply impressed by the enthusiasm and helpfulness of the Siemens Corporate Archives in Munich, Historisches Archiv MAN in Augsburg and VDMA central office in Frankfurt. Finally, I would like to thank colleagues, peers, friends and students too numerous to name for their input and support. Anything of value in this study undoubtedly stems from the input of all of these people and institutions. Mistakes, omissions and misunderstandings are, of course, my own.

Abbreviations

AIZ	Archiv des Instituts für Zeitgeschichte
	Institute of Contemporary History (Munich)
ADB	Arbeitsgemeinschaft deutscher Betriebsingenieure
	Working Group for German Production Engineers
AVDMA	Arbeitsgemeinschaft der Verbände Deutscher Maschinenbau-Anstalten
	Working Group of Machine Building Associations
AVI	Arbeitsgemeinschaft der Eisenverarbeitenden Industrie
	Working Group of the Iron Working Industry
BAB	Bundesarchiv Berlin
	German Federal Archive, Berlin
BfM	Bevollmächtigter für Maschinenbau
	Commissar for Machine Production
BWA	Bayerisches Wirtschaftsarchiv
	Bavarian Economic Archive
DAF	Deutsche Arbeitsfront
	German Worker's Front
DDP	Deutsche Demokratische Partei
	German Democratic Party
DNVP	Deutschnationale Volkspartei
	German National People's Party
GDBI	Gesamtverband der Deutschen Büroindustrie
	General Association of the German Office Industry
GHH	Gutehoffnungshütte
	(firm)
IRG	Internationale Rohstahlgemeinschaft
	International Crude Steel Agreement
ISC	International Steel Cartel

KPD	Kommunistische Partei Deutschlands Communist Party of Germany
KVP	Konservative Volkspartei Conservative People's Party
MICUM	Inter-Allied Mission for Control of Factories and Mines
NSDAP	Nationalsozialistische Deutsche Arbeiterpartei National Socialist German Workers Party (Nazi Party)
OKW	Oberkommando der Wehrmacht Armed Forces High Command
OSS	Office of Strategic Services
RdI	Reichsverband der deutschen Industrie Reich Association of German Industry
RGI	Reichsgruppe Industrie Reich Group Industry
RVE	Reichsvereinigung Eisen Reich Iron Association
RWM	Reichswirtschaftsministerium Ministry of Economics
R-WW	Stiftung Rheinisch-Westfälisches Wirtschaftsarchiv zu Köln Rhineland-Westphalia Economic Archive Institute
SHA	Staatsarchiv Nürnberg Nuremberg State Archive
SPD	Sozialdemokratische Partei Deutschlands Social Democratic Party
VDEh	Verein deutscher Eisenhüttenleute Association of German Iron Manufacturers
VDESI	Verein deutscher Eisen- und Stahlindustrieller Association of German Iron and Steel Industrialists
VDMA	Verein Deutscher Maschinenbau-Anstalten German Machine Builders' Association
VSt	Vereinigte Stahlwerke AG United Steel
Wigru	Wirtschaftsgruppe business group
WVE	Wirtschaftsvereinigung Eisen German Iron Federation
ZAV	Zusatzausfuhrverfahren Export Promotion Procedure

INTRODUCTION

Adaptation and Opposition in Democracy and Dictatorship

The German merchant firm Wilhelm Grillo found itself in a dilemma in the early days of the tumultuous year 1940. Another firm, Lampe Delta, a Belgian company that produced pocket flashlights, was having difficulty finding a secure supplier of zinc casings for the three-volt batteries its products used and hoped Grillo could put them in touch with a German machine builder that would provide the equipment required to make them in-house.[1] As a merchant, Grillo wondered whether it would be better to find Lampe Delta a producer that would sell them such a machine, or to locate a battery manufacturer that could supply the finished product instead and establish a long-term export relationship. There was nothing really unusual in this request, which was, after all, the sort of question that business people face all the time. But the Germany in which Grillo did business was an ideological and increasingly regulated state that was formally at war with France, the United Kingdom and their allies, even if it had momentarily stalled in a period of 'phoney war'. More was at stake than just Grillo's own business interests.

Looking for guidance, Grillo dispatched a letter to one of the multitudinous semiprivate regulative bodies in the Third Reich, the Pre-inspection Office for Mechanical Apparatus (Vorprüfungsstelle Apparatebau), asking which kind of export – products or productive machinery – would better serve the interests of Germany.[2] The Vorprüfungsstelle Apparatebau panicked. Instead of venturing an answer, it passed the question on to more important organizations. Over the next week the issue was debated through a series of letters and consultations between at least seven separate regulatory offices in two different industries in an effort to answer Grillo's question in an economically and politically acceptable way. Finally, a kind of joint statement was agreed upon after it was discovered that British troops stationed in France used just such a battery for their communication radios, and a circular forbidding the export of either product was released under the cumbersome title 'Concerning the Delivery of Objects, Devices and Machines that are Suitable for the Support of the War Potential of Enemy States or the Increase of the Military or Economic Strength of the Enemy Through the Easing of War Measures Implementation with Respect to Machines for the Production of Pocket Flashlight Batteries, Elements and Dry Elements, and also Lead and Steel Accumulators.'[3] Business in the Third Reich was not a simple matter, and such efforts to reconcile industry, ideology and wartime production could have absurdly complicated results.

The more or less organized wartime economy (particularly in highly cartelized Germany), relied on a variety of methods and institutions regulating business in order to integrate industry into a vast but often confusing and ramshackle machine.[4] In this context, 'support' for the regime required much more than just a change of heart at the ballot box or the introduction of the swastika to company letterhead. Knitting together firms led by men who might at any time be enthusiastic, intimidated, opposed, opportunistic or apathetic required a cadre of managers and organizations who were willing to work within an ideological regime that placed significant limits on the decision-making ability of German entrepreneurs in the name of the state. A stubborn or difficult man in an influential position could thwart – or at least delay and complicate – Nazi aims. One who was more amenable or ambitious could act as a mechanism to ease an industry or firm into the warp and weave of National Socialist regulation.[5] This study examines the process and consequences of adaptation to the National Socialist regime by focusing on the chief business managers (Hauptgeschäftsführer) of two of the most important private industrial organizations that evolved into regulatory bodies during the Third Reich: Jakob Reichert of the Association of German Iron and Steel Industrialists (Verein Deutscher Eisen- und Stahlindustrieller, VDESI) and Karl Lange of the German Machine Builders' Association (Verein Deutscher Maschinenbau-Anstalten, VDMA).

These were not 'ordinary men' in the sense of Christopher Browning's use of the term in his landmark study,[6] but they were something like 'ordinary professional men' who faced a difficult set of choices in a period of enormous change. Like most choices of ours, theirs were not direct life or death decisions. Instead, they were closer to the kinds of decisions so many professionals, businessmen and administrators make on a day-to-day basis and of the small, sometimes familiar steps on the road to violence and barbarism on an unprecedented scale. Rich, full, lengthy personal biographies could be written on either of these two men and their careers, but that is not the purpose of this study. Nor is it to write a comprehensive analysis of the iron and steel or machine-building industries. Instead, it is to compare the choices open to two professional men who represented distinct industries through the organizations they steered, and the consequences of the different paths they chose. These two men had similar jobs, lived and worked in similar social milieus and often crossed paths professionally, even if they were not always on the same side of the negotiating table. Despite these similarities, Lange and Reichert offer a fascinating study in contrasts. Indeed, by the founding of the Federal Republic in 1949 one had killed himself in despair at his own failures while the other was happily integrating into yet another regime.

As the professional representative of the German iron and steel industry, Reichert was an often overbearing, deeply conservative example of the kind of man who helped to bring down the Weimar Republic. Chancellor Gustav Stresemann himself flagged Reichert as evidence of the anti-democratic authoritarianism of heavy industry.[7] Historians on the left have come to identify him as one of 'those furthest right' on the late Weimar political spectrum, and his reputation as an authoritarian representative of the fearsome iron and steel industry led the invading American forces to target Reichert as 'one of the top leaders in the Nazi administration of German business' to be arrested and tried after the war.[8] Despite this imposing reactionary reputation, Reichert stood up to the regime to a surprising degree, though at the cost of his career and eventually his life. Lange, on the other hand, made a reputation for himself in the Weimar years as an economic liberal fully reconciled to the democratic government and willing to compromise with the political left. He was, in effect, a model liberal citizen of the republic who represented a dynamic and practical industry. However, rather than being swept out by National Socialism along with so many others like him, Lange flourished and built himself a small administrative empire in the Third Reich that seemed to defy his record in the republic. The key to these wildly divergent career paths lies in the difference in each man's evaluation of the strengths of his respective industry, its role in the German economy, the long-term interests of his industry and organization, and the level of accommodation with the regime that this prompted.

The stakes are always high when discussing the Nazi period, and the role of business and industry in the rise and rule of the regime has been hotly debated. How and why did business accommodate itself to National Socialism? The answer to this question has helped to determine how a variety of historians understand National Socialist Germany as a whole. The impression that fascism was funded by industry (and heavy industry in particular) was already bolstered in the popular mind by contemporaries like the erudite Stephan Zweig,[9] and as Gerald Feldman pointed out, neither undergraduates nor professional historians express much surprise that business owners and managers would find a way to make money under Hitler.[10] This was also reflected in more theoretical analyses of the period, and by 1935 the Marxists had codified National Socialism before the Seventh Congress of the Third International as the articulation of monopoly capital's dominance over the state.[11] This thesis became the basis of East German historiography and continues to influence some Marxist analysis of the collapse of Weimar and the nature of the Nazi state.[12] This approach was bolstered by the 'almost liturgical' repetition of Max Horkheimer's assertion that 'those who won't discuss capitalism should also stay silent on fascism'.[13]

Although the overtly political nature of GDR historiography isolated its interpretation to a certain degree, the role of industry in the republic's collapse was likewise taken up by the moderate left in the west to explain the ascendance of the Nazis in a highly unstable environment. For them, heavy industrialists' irascible opposition to a democracy that was unwilling to satisfy their whims led them to throw in their lot with the National Socialists by 1933.[14] Dirk Stegmann went considerably further, arguing that heavy industries like Reichert's were searching for an authoritarian solution throughout the Weimar Republic whereas export industries (like Lange's) remained committed to some form of liberal democracy. During the political and economic crisis of the early 1930s, Stegmann argues, heavy industry fulfilled its own aims by backing the National Socialists and 'cementing' the regime in early 1933.[15]

In the early 1980s the discussion of the role of industry in the demise of the democracy exploded into controversy with David Abraham's *Collapse of the Weimar Republic,* in which he argued that the triumph of fascism was the result of the middle class's failure to reconcile the differences between the demands of the liberal export industries and the reactionary heavy industrialists in the context of class struggle.[16] When heavy industry gained the upper hand in industrial politics, it threw its support behind the National Socialists. The dynamic export sector thus became the victim of a powerful, authoritarian heavy industry. Abraham's highly problematic book prompted a number of historians to argue that many, if not most, businessmen had been 'passive, ill-informed bystanders' during the crucial period of the collapse of the republic.[17] To be sure, industrialists failed to use their 'veto power' to oppose the establishment of a National Socialist government, refused to declare a cease-fire on the left and were unable to manage a truce with labour along the lines of the 'Working Community' of 1918.[18] Throughout the economic, social and political chaos that led to the seizure of power, however, the attitudes of industrialists and their representatives towards National Socialism could be better characterized as ambivalent or confused. These men did not have the benefit of hindsight that we enjoy and failed to grasp the severity of the danger facing Germany at least as much as they embraced the destruction of the Weimar Republic.

This challenge was met by an almost equally unhelpful conservative theory of totalitarianism that conflated the NSDAP with a form of Bolshevism that replaced the freedom of the entrepreneur with state control, largely exonerating German business from the collapse of the republic and rise of dictatorship in the process.[19] This narrative of victimization of a group that was threatened with retribution for their actions in the Third Reich was all too convenient for postwar business leaders and provoked a sharp response. Jonathan Wiesen in particular has shown that industry's professed regrets about its own naivety about the Nazis and its failure to stand up to the regime stemmed from a postwar public relations campaign at least as much as their own experience, and does not reflect the willingness of so many businessmen to work with or for the dictatorship.[20]

Although this debate has produced a number of important studies on the relationship between industry as a group and the 'primacy of politics',[21] attention has recently shifted to the decision-making process within firms themselves. Senior scholars working through company archives have produced critical histories that helped to open up a new field of business or company history ('*Unternehmensgeschichte*').[22] This wave of scholarship has thrown light on some of the day-to-day relationships that developed between business and the Nazi state. However, this research has primarily focused on the dramatic tension between the needs of individual firms and the demands of the regime. Managers often found themselves caught between the mundane desire to secure lucrative contracts and the larger immorality and irrationality of Nazi policy.[23] Though these men were seldom ordered to pursue a particular production policy, economic, political and personal pressure weighed heavily on business managers between 1933 and 1945, limiting the options they saw as open to them. This approach has provided important insights but is by nature limited to the experience of the firm in question. It is difficult to apply the findings of these studies to, for instance, assertions that heavy industry was behind an aggressive war of expansion and conquest.[24]

In recent years this discussion has crystallized around the question of businessmen's 'room for manoeuvre' (*Handlungsspielraum*) in the Third Reich. What choice could they reasonably make in a violent dictatorship? This question has opened up a broad interpretive spectrum ranging from Peter Termin's characterization of the Nazi economy as remarkably similar to the planned economy of the Soviet Union on the one hand, to Buchheim and Scherner's assertion that private ownership and decision making was maintained in a 'directed market economy' in which firms and managers continued to make their own choices.[25] Other historians situate themselves along this continuum, although a number of important writers like Hayes and Overy have tended to emphasize the practical constraints and threats businessmen faced.[26] Occasionally this has caused sharp debates over both the structure of the Nazi economy and, more broadly, the culpability of businessmen in the regime.[27]

Nevertheless, these two extremes point to two different but important factors in economic life in this tumultuous period. The strong role of the National Socialist state is difficult to deny. Historians like Overy and Barkai have both emphasized this point, and Abelshauser has gone further to argue that the Nazi state reordered the economy for war so thoroughly that it also set the stage for the postwar economic boom.[28] While Buchheim disputes Abelshauser's characterization of a successful National Socialist economic policy, he also concludes that the state did have a strong impact, albeit through what he refers to as a 'deformed economy'.²⁹ On the other hand, Scherner and Buchheim's interpretation helps to illustrate some of the economic advantages that led businessmen to work with a violent and repulsive regime, and *Unternehmensgeschichte* has also recently come under attack for emphasizing the constraints placed upon businessmen rather than their room for manoeuvre.³⁰ Rather than being forced, businessmen were able to evaluate the relative advantage of various kinds of contracts, and even to use the state to exploit opportunities that could not exist in the Weimar Republic while retaining the right to turn down unprofitable contracts.³¹

Separating economic practice from direct political influence, Mark Spoerer in particular has effectively argued that large portions of the business community saw a substantial rise in profits under the regime.³² More importantly, this was not simply the result of state policy. Entrepreneurs were able to direct investment towards the products that were the most profitable and secure in the context of Nazi aims, leading critics to assert that industry retained much of its influence over the economy during the Third Reich,³³ and even used the regime to accelerate the process of 'modernization' that had lagged behind that of the United States.³⁴ The most critical members of the left were also able to modify their argument to accommodate these findings by noting that industrialists were able to instrumentalize the Nazi regime to achieve their own ends.³⁵ Choice and opportunism dominate this model.

Joachim Streb has pointed out that this debate over a controlled or market economy might be too narrow, and that in practice coercion and opportunism could exist side by side.³⁶ Hayes, for instance, noted that a monstrous regime could be engaged in an inescapable process of 'indirect socialization', while also condemning the venal motives that led businessmen to participate in it.³⁷ Scherner and Buchheim likewise concede that coercion was used in cases like that of Junkers or the Reichswerke Hermann Göring, although they consider these to be normal exceptions rather than the rule.³⁸ This tension between coercion and cooperation has forced business historians to grapple with the line between economics and questions of morality, and consensus remains maddeningly elusive.³⁹

Lange and Reichert's experiences reflect both the push of coercion and pull of opportunism. Although both ran into trouble with the regime soon after 1933, neither seems to have been seriously threatened by dismissal from their positions, much less imprisonment or worse. However, they both confronted a regime that demonstrated its willingness to force their industry in a particular direction through legislation, resource allocation and even expropriation. Just as importantly, each man's authority depended on his ability to meet or mould the needs and policies of the state in a way that was advantageous to his own member firms and acted as a powerful incentive for developing a good relationship with the National Socialists, even if they were worried about the direction of the state. This was complicated enough, and though it might be avoided by industrialists who were simply too busy, self-interested or 'unreflective', Reichert and Lange were professionally responsible for trying to mediate the relationship between their branch of industry and the state.[40]

Machine building and iron and steel production were both key aspects of the German economy, but they differed considerably. The iron and steel industry was slightly larger, representing 10.3 per cent of German net productive value (*Nettoproduktionswert*) compared to 8.2 per cent for machine building in 1927/28.[41] However, machine building was a bigger employer, with 1,220 553 workers compared to 852 690 in iron and steel.[42] Nevertheless, the iron and steel industry was remarkably united, whereas machine building was fragmented. Unlike iron and steel, machine builders tended towards smaller firms that depended on highly skilled (and higher paid) workers.[43] The largest category of firms in Lange's VDMA in 1925 employed an average of a mere 185.2 workers. At least 6,438 members employed fewer than 25 people.[44] These small firms also guarded their independence jealously and did not trust their products to larger organizations. Instead of massive works that turned out a large quantity of standardized products, German machine builders tended to produce specialized tools. U.S. producers assembled single-use machines; German firms tended to favour more complicated 'universal' machines that could be adapted to a variety of tasks, gauges or tolerances in one plant.[45] This fostered a more collaborative relationship with customers but also often resulted in a dizzying array of products offered by each firm, which would frustrate Lange throughout his career. At the same time, Lange's industry and membership encompassed a wide variety of firms that produced everything from typewriters to vehicles and capital production machinery. The heterogeneous nature of the industry itself tended to make cooperation more difficult than in the tightly knit Ruhr iron industry, and before 1914 the VDMA had only managed to bring 226 firms into its organization.[46] The members of this association were also uncomfortable with cartels and marketing associations. Instead, they embraced more flexible organizations that advocated liberal free trade, like the Hanseatic League and Union of Industrialists (Bund der Industriellen).[47] The iron and steel industry in particular was able to use this lack of unity in the machine building industry to put the VDMA in its place when the two industries came into conflict.[48]

In sharp contrast to this competitive cacophony stood iron and steel, an industry characterized by a much smaller number of very large producers and the extraordinary importance of a few powerful firms and industrialists in the Ruhr Valley in particular. Indeed, more than half of all firms in the sector employed more than 1,000 people.[49] This tendency was exacerbated by movement towards massive trusts, cartels, marketing associations and conglomerates in this industry. The massive conglomerate United Steel Works (Vereinigte Stahlwerke) alone produced over 40 per cent of German iron and steel and became the largest firm in the nation upon its creation through the merger of a variety of other large firms in 1926.[50] This new entity and its various management boards brought together the most important German industrialists, led by the 'most important man in the Ruhr', Albert Vögler.[51] This tendency to club together was embodied by the '*Ruhrlade*', a semiformal gathering of the most powerful iron, steel and coal men in the Ruhr Valley to discuss common social and political policy in an intimate, collegial setting.[52] This allowed the iron and steel men to speak with one voice when necessary. They used it to pursue a generally conservative, authoritarian, protectionist project that would place their industry at the centre of German social, economic and political policy.

As chief business managers of formal industrial organizations that represented these two industries, Jakob Reichert and Karl Lange occupy a peculiar place in this picture. The extent to which the German economy approximated 'organized capitalism' might be disputed, but German businessmen in general were inclined to participate in a variety of clubs, associations and cartels that 'stretched like an invisible web across the German economy'.[53] By the Weimar years, this web connected local business networks, via larger sectors of industry, to the 'peak association', the Reich Association of German Industry (Reichsverband der deutschen Industrie, RdI), which provided a forum for German employers as a whole. To a certain extent, these organizations allowed the economic groups they represented to divide resources and markets, share information, coordinate opinions and lobby various levels of government, establishing a set of ground rules for a system that Werner Abelshauser refers to as '*Deutschland AG*'.[54] At the same time, they could be used 'as transmission belts to modify or block political decisions at the top or centre'.[55]

In the 1980s, Eberhard Kolb noted that little work had been done on major industrial organizations after the period of the *Kaiserreich*.[56] With a few notable exceptions, this remains true. Structural studies of industry and politics have tended to lump these organizations together in the camp of 'industry', or more specifically 'heavy industry', in a way that obscures the actions of specific associations or actors.[57] The Reich Association of German Industry is perhaps the most important exception to this rule,[58] but Gerald Feldman and Ulrich Nocken have also published a useful article looking at the organizations of both the iron and steel and the machine-building industry during the 1920s.[59] Beyond this, the field has largely been left to the anniversary *Festschriften* produced by the organizations themselves.[60] With the notable exception of Harold James' work on the banking industry, these tend to lack the critical analysis demanded by the National Socialist period in particular.[61]

Some responsibility for these gaps in scholarship stems from problems with the source material. Much was lost or destroyed in the last chaotic days of the Second World War. This fact also impacts the present study, as the records of the VDMA are particularly difficult to access. Lange himself oversaw the transportation of the organization's files to his own residence in Thuringia as Berlin was pounded by Allied bombs, and it is hard not to wonder how many incriminating documents might have been conveniently lost or forgotten in the chaos. Following the VDMA Festschrift produced by Pohl and Markner, documents still held by the association itself have also strangely disappeared, although much can be reconstructed and expanded upon through the previously unused Bundesarchiv holdings and the archives maintained by private machine building firms. Reichert and the VDESI do not present quite as many difficulties, although today it appears likely that much of the correspondence between Reichert and his mentor Paul Reusch may have been lost in the collapse of the Cologne archive building in 2009. However, Reichert's prolific writing, his work as an editor or member of the editorial staff of *Stahl und Eisen* throughout his career, and his speeches as a Reichstag deputy have generated a substantial historical record. Regardless of their limitations, the extant records for these two key associations appear more complete than for most similar organizations.

A chief business manager of an industrial lobby group was in a tricky position. Unlike the industrialist presidency of each respective organization, their position was not an honorary recognition of work and reputation in the industry. Reichert and Lange were employees of their industries as a whole and were expected to deliver real benefits to their members. They developed policy, negotiated with other organizations and offices of the state, and managed the day-to-day operations of the association. At the same time, they were expected to reflect and represent the interests, opinions and prejudices of industrialists who did not always agree amongst themselves.[62] Theobald Kayser half jokingly defined the business manager as a man who has the

> dignity of an archbishop, self-sacrifice of a missionary, persistence of a tax collector, experience of an economic leader, who works like a coolie, has the tact of a diplomat, eloquence of a minister, general knowledge of a Nobel Prize winner, elastic mind of a politician, health of an Olympic athlete, patience of a nursemaid, smile of a film star and the thick skin of a Hippopotamus.[63]

While this might be more than a little exaggerated, it conveys some of the complexity faced by a chief business manager. 'Success has many authors', one of Reichert's successors observed, but 'a blunder has only one … the business manager'.[64]

Though this strange mixture of bureaucrat, manager, industrialist and sycophant complicates the study of Reichert and Lange, their positions also offer several advantages for the historian. Their work focused attention on the needs, interests and politics associated with their own particular industrial branches. David Abraham rightly drew withering criticism for having neatly divided German industry into two distinct categories of light and heavy industry.[65] Industrialists in Germany in fact wore many hats and could shift the focus of their business practice from mining through to basic production, finishing and shipping as circumstances changed. This was not the case for Lange or Reichert. While they would have been keenly aware of the variety of enterprises that major industrialists participated in, it was ultimately their job to represent one specific aspect of production in Germany. As a result, they and their organizations can provide useful insight into industrial politics that has been separated from both the needs of a particular firm or the confused web of investment across sectors.

One might also easily become lost in a chicken-and-egg argument about the temperament of individuals and the needs and structure of their industry. When did they create policy in their own image, and when were their own ideas determined by the industry they served? At first blush, it is not necessarily surprising that the representative of the iron and steel industry clashed with a regime that sought to intervene in the business of the powerful men he represented. Lange might also be forgiven for dropping a political and economic ideology that conflicted with the new government. We might never know the extent of the turmoil or doubt secreted in the breast of either of these men, but like dependent courtiers, both ultimately had to act in agreement with or flatter the interests, whims or tastes of their masters, even as circumstances changed. However, neither man was simply a cipher, and the 'interests' of these two industries and their member firms were not always clearly articulated. Both men had to make choices in troubled times that would have long-term consequences both for their members and themselves.

Broadly speaking, when it came to collaboration with the National Socialist regime after 1933, both industries had powerful motivations as well as considerable reservations. The iron and steel industry shared a number of important ideas and perspectives with the new government – it stood to benefit from rearmament in particular – but distrusted the interventionist or statist policies of an ideology that they feared might be socialism in disguise. Working in a liberal export dependent industry, machine builders were in a more delicate position and found themselves the target of a good deal of criticism from the Party. After January 1933 a range of responses was also possible in these industries, and the end results were not always clear. Some of the most powerful men in the iron and steel industry embraced National Socialism. Eager to make the best of the situation, Friedrich Flick quickly ingratiated himself to the regime in order to expand his enterprise significantly.[66] The powerful Vögler himself was so deeply entangled in the regime that he killed himself in 1945 to avoid arrest and trial by the victorious Allies.[67] Herman Röchling and Wilhelm Zangen managed to combine successful business careers in cooperation with the regime with administrative positions in the Third Reich. After

1945 a large number of other iron and steel and other industrialists, including Alfried Krupp, were arrested and tried for their actions in National Socialist Germany.[68] There were powerful incentives for Reichert to work closely with a regime that so many of his most important members had allied with. However, this was not the only option open to iron and steel men. Vögler's successor as the head of the massive United Steel, Ernst Poensgen, was cut from different cloth. As the head of this firm and the industrialist president of Reichert's organization, Poensgen opposed many of the changes demanded by the new state and plays a significant part in this narrative. Reichert's friend and mentor, Paul Reusch, also stood up to the regime on several occasions, with significant results.[69] Other iron and steel men were deeply troubled by the regime as well.

Lange faced a similar problem from a different perspective. If his industry had a broad consensus on anything under his guidance during the Weimar years, it was the importance of liberal competition and an enthusiasm for export. After 1933, this meant he would have to betray much of what he and his members had identified as their interests and goals in order to accommodate the regime. After the war Lange was praised for his work, but not every machine builder felt the same at the time. The powerful Maschinenfabrik Augsburg-Nürnberg (MAN), for instance, maintained its distance from the Party (even as it benefited from state contracts), and one of its prominent managers, Otto Meyer, remained married to his Jewish wife throughout the period despite considerable pressure.[70] Joachim Scholtyseck has outlined a possible 'liberal opposition to Hitler' that was in many ways similar to what Lange and the VDMA had advocated in previous years, and Petra Bräutigam has researched opposition to the regime in smaller firms that were not dissimilar to those Lange represented.[71] Even mild-mannered economists with views very similar to those espoused by the VDMA at the University of Freiburg formed a variety of 'circles' that opposed the regime.[72] As this text will demonstrate, not everyone in his industry was satisfied with Lange's behaviour during the regime or wanted to embrace National Socialist ideology as he did.

Lange could not have opposed the regime as obstreperously as Reichert, and Reichert could never have dominated his industry as Lange did by 1940. However, the mix of interests, opinions, values and responses to the rise of National Socialism of the men and the firms they represented meant that neither was doomed to the path he eventually trod. German business adapted to the new regime and then to another total war remarkably quickly, but the process began as an open-ended one; none could have said for sure which path was the correct, or the most profitable, until Reichert, Lange and German industrialists had already embarked on one. Both Reichert and Lange were engaged in a complicated balancing act that weighed ideals, opportunism, fear and some of their members' conflicting demands against each other. Throughout this process they were guided by their own experience and judgement, beliefs and characters, which produced very different consequences. The same characteristics that led contemporaries, the invading Allies and later historians to see Reichert as deeply implicated in the rise and government of the Nazi regime ironically also made him virtually immune to much of National Socialism. The condescending arrogance that he could show to officials or lobbyists outside his industry, stubborn defence of his evaluation of the role of iron and steel in the economy, and unwillingness to compromise made him as reluctant to embrace the new regime as he had been to accept the Weimar settlement, and kept him firmly in Poensgen and Reusch's camp. His faith in the power of the industry he served also made him believe that the regime would be forced to come around to his ideas sooner or later. As a result, he became a surprisingly stout opponent of the National Socialist regime in his own way, even as other members of his own organization were successfully developing more nuanced relationships with the new state.

The opposite is true of Karl Lange. He entered the Third Reich on much shakier footing and had good reason to believe that the new regime would not tolerate much opposition from his industry. In this context, Lange's willingness to reach out across political or economic divides in order to find compromise allowed him to adapt quickly to the new dictatorship, just as it had made him a model business representative throughout much of the Weimar Republic. And whereas Reichert's thorny personality pushed him away from the NSDAP, what had once seemed like Lange's most admirable and reasonable qualities worked to draw him into a brutal and immoral regime.

The first chapter of this study examines roles and experiences the two men had in the years leading up to the triumph of National Socialism that helped to define their response to the new regime in 1933. Reichert met the challenges of the republic as the representative of one of the few surviving power blocs in Germany. The VDESI did not so much adapt to the new state as set itself up in opposition to the compromises that underwrote the establishment of the democracy. Reichert also developed a profound faith in a 'natural' economy that both favoured the German iron and steel industry and supposedly precluded the intrusion of 'politics' into the business world that clashed with the growing National Socialist movement as well as more mainstream political ideas. Lange, on the other hand, took over an organization that incorporated the politics and ethos of the new republic into itself. He accepted organized labour and the political left as legitimate bargaining partners to be engaged in discussion along with heavy industry and the political right, and cultivated a close relationship with the new democratic regime that was consistent with the organization's advocacy of a liberal economic order. Neither of these was an acceptable position in 1933, and both men had to choose how they and their industries would meet the challenge of the new government.

Chapter 2 details the transition to National Socialism and Reichert's and Lange's responses. As in the past, Reichert assumed he would be able to meet the new regime from a position of strength and direct the NS-state in ways that were useful to the iron and steel industry. He assumed National Socialism would have little effect on his own organization and hoped to use the importance of his industry to wring concessions out of the new government even as the traditional conservatism, independence and arrogance of the iron and steel industry alienated him from the regime. Lange did not share Reichert's confidence, and he scrambled to adapt his suspect industry, offering the new regime the almost unconditional support of the machine building industry and shaping his organization to reflect the ethos of the new government.

Chapter 3 examines the broader results of these different approaches to the economic and structural changes that swept Germany as the regime entered a period of massive rearmament after 1936. Lange's early attempt to ingratiate himself opened up new opportunities in the increasingly regulated world of a National Socialist Germany preparing for war. He embraced the new powers and positions he was offered as the leader of an industrial organization in a supposedly 'organic' economy, and integrated even some of the most offensive aspects of a loathsome regime into the functions of his organization. In contrast, Reichert could not shake off the lessons and habits of the previous years despite the increased importance of political connections and the role of the state. His reluctance or inability to take up new responsibilities as demanded by the Nazi state undermined his industry's role in an environment made up more and more of highly competitive organizations squabbling over scarce resources. As a result, Reichert came into conflict with the regime at every turn as he attempted to preserve the old structure of his organization and industry even as the state was trying to coordinate production in preparation for war. This reflected the traditions and interests of his members, but it also shut them out of the developing regulatory system and left the chief business manager under a cloud of suspicion even as Lange was integrated into the machinery of the National Socialist state.

In the emergency atmosphere of the Second World War, these two adaptive strategies bore very different fruit. As Chapter 4 demonstrates, Reichert's consistent attempts to limit the changes to his organization meant that by 1940 he was simply unable to fulfil the demands of the regime even if he wanted to. Not only did Reichert lack the infrastructure to take his members in hand, but he had also failed to accumulate the 'political capital' that would allow him to secure concessions for his members during the war. As a result, the increasingly useless Reichert and his organization were swept aside in the reforms of 1942, to be replaced by a new authoritarian office that would integrate iron and steel into the regulative structure of the Nazi state more thoroughly. Of very little use now to his own members, Reichert's authority vanished. This absence proved to be permanent, and his failure during the Nazi regime cut him out of the councils of power in both his own industry and occupied Germany after 1945 as well. Despairing of his own political impotence and neglect by the industry he had served for so many years, the 62-year-old Reichert slipped into a deep depression before killing himself in early 1947.

Lange, on the other hand, had proven himself a willing and capable administrator in the National Socialist state, one who could marshal the support of his members and was entrusted with ever greater authority as the war progressed. Chapter 5 describes Lange's experience during the war and post war periods. He not only survived Speer's reorganization of 1942 – he prospered. Apparently alone amongst all the old organizational men in German industry, Lange was brought into Speer's system as a trusted, vital regulator. This elevated him far above the industrialists he had formerly represented and placed him at the very centre of production in his industry. It also paid substantial dividends for Lange's members. He was able to draw on his 'political capital' and real decision-making authority to secure benefits for a large number of German machine builders during the war. As a result, it became unthinkable to exclude Lange from the production of machines in Germany. This position persisted to the end of the war and even into the peace: when the VDMA was re-established in 1949, Lange was reinstated in his old job and charged with integrating machine building into yet another political regime.

This study focuses on bureaucratic industrial organizations whose committee reports tended to be rather dry, yet the story is surprisingly distressing. Although the authoritarian, deeply conservative Reichert strangely emerged as a thorn in the side of the Nazi government, he opposed the regime because it clashed with his vision of the iron and steel industry rather than any broader concern with the brutality of National Socialism. This kind of *'resitanz'* made up of arrogance, interest and foot-dragging is not very romantic, and at no time did Reichert take any active steps against the regime or even appear to consider resigning his position to escape it. However, he did put up a surprising and admirable level of resistance. The reaction of the iron and steel industry was even more unpromising: rather than rally around a man who had made considerable sacrifices to stand up for their interests in a hostile environment, his former members came to ignore Reichert as his influence waned, turning instead to men and organizations who had worked more closely with the Nazi regime and could consequently be of more practical use even after the end of the war under a government of occupation. This kind of callous pragmatism does not reflect well on German industry, and it deeply wounded Reichert at a time when he was desperately in need of support, respect and a livelihood.

Lange's case is almost the reverse. Moderate, rational and modest, he was willing to enter the world of negotiation and compromise in a liberal democracy. Yet when the economic and political climate began to change in Germany, Lange shifted with it, demonstrating that the openness to compromise that is so necessary in a republic also allowed him to come to an accommodation with a horrific regime. Like Hendrik Höfgen in Klaus Mann's *Mephisto*, Lange proved quite willing to trade in his former political and economic values after the change of regime. In return, he enjoyed a splendid personal career in the Third Reich and was able to achieve many of his long-term goals for his industry. If Lange was uncomfortable with aspects of the National Socialist state, he, like Höfgen, did not allow this to spoil a productive relationship. Moreover, machine builders seemed to approve of this arrangement. While Reichert languished in isolation, Lange's members rallied around him after the war. This was not simply a question of trading ideals for personal power and profits for his members. Chronology is important here. Lange and his members were engaged in a long game whose terminus remained unknown. His accommodation with the regime risked alienating his own members before it could pay them dividends. The chief business manager initially turned to accommodation out of fear, insecurity and the weakness of his industry. However, this policy yielded tangible results as the state began to turn to industrial lobby groups to regulate the economy, and Lange systematically seized every opportunity to involve himself in the life of the regime. While some of his members began to benefit from this soon afterwards, many did not, and all German machine builders quickly found themselves under a level of regulation that would have been unimaginable in the fractious industry only a few years before. The broader benefits from the spoils of war and higher profits came later and did not extend to everyone in the industry, but they allowed German machine builders to take advantage of the National Socialist regime through Lange and his organization.

Collaboration with a terrible and terrifying state worked. German industry as a body rewarded what worked, not what was consistent, admirable or conscionable. At various times both of these men were free to make some of the choices Buchheim and Sherner have noted, albeit under difficult circumstances, but consequences followed sooner or later. More disturbingly, rewards for collaboration and punishment for resistance came from Reichert and Lange's own members as much as from the state. Businessmen and their firms faced coercion from the state, but they also became an important component of a coercive state that was able to blend threats and opportunity under a monstrous ideology that drew business and industry into its orbit one way or another.

Notes

1. Bundesarchiv Berlin (hereafter BAB) R 9 VIII/4 '*Induschiemie Société de Construction pour L'Industrie Chimique*. (Félix Bruyninckx) an Herrn Direktor Grillo, Firma Wilhelm Grillo Handelsgesellschaft, 8.1.1940'.
2. BAB R 9 VIII/4 'Wilhelm Grillo Handelsgesellschaft GmbH an die Vorprüfungsstelle Apparatebau, 13.1.1940'.

3. BAB R 9 VIII/4 'Aktennotiz, Betr.: Lieferung von Gegenständen, Vorrichtungen und Maschinen, die geeignet sind, das Kriegspotential der Feindstaaten zu mehren und zur Steigerung der militärischen oder wirtschaftlichen Stärke des Gegners bzw. dessen Kriegsführung erleichtern, bezogen auf Maschinen zur Herstellung von Taschenlampenbatterien, Elementen, Trockenelementen, aber auch Blei und Stahlakkumulatoren'.
4. See P. Hayes. 2009. 'Corporate Freedom of Action in Nazi Germany', *Bulletin of the German Historical Institute* 45(Fall), 29–42 and C. Buchheim and J. Scherner. 2009. 'Corporate Freedom of Action in Nazi Germany: A Response to Peter Hayes', ibid., 43–50. For an excellent discussion of the legal constraints applied to the German economy, see the excellent collection of essays in D. Gosewinkel (Ed.). 2005. *Wirtschaftskontrolle und Recht in der nationalsozialistischen Diktatur*, Frankfurt a.M.: Klostermann.
5. See also H. Volkmann. 1981. 'Zum Verhältnis von Großwirtschaft und NS-Regime im Zweiten Weltkrieg', in W. Dlugoborski (Ed.), *Zweiter Weltkrieg und sozialer Wandel*, Göttingen: Vandenhoek & Ruprecht, 88.
6. See C. Browning. 1993. *Ordinary Men: Reserve Police Battalion 101 and the Final Solution in Poland*, New York: Harper Perennial.
7. 'Stresemann's Diary: December 16th, 1925', in E. Sutton (ed.). 1937. *Gustav Stresemann: His Diaries, Letters, and Papers*, vol. 2, London: Macmillan, 364–65.
8. D. Abraham. 1986. *The Collapse of the Weimar Republic: Political Economy and Crisis*, 2nd edn, New York: Holmes & Meier, 205; Donovan Archive, Cornell Law Library. 'Nuremberg Trials', vol. 17, pt. 2, 53.057 'Office of Strategic Services, Research and Analysis Branch. Biographical Report: Reichert, Jakob Wilhelm 16.5.1945', p. 1
9. S. Zweig. 1976. *Die Welt von Gestern: Erinnerungen eines Europäers*, Hamburg: Fischer Taschenbuch Verlag, 259–60.
10. G.D. Feldman. 2003. 'Historische Vergangenheitsbearbeitung: Wirtschaft und Wissenschaft im Vergleich', Max-Planck-Gesellschaft zur Förderung der Wissenschaften e.V. Präsidentenkommission 13, 'Geschichte der Kaiser-Wilhelm-Gesellschaft im Nationalsozialismus', 5–6.
11. J. Caplan. "Afterward" in A. Sohn-Rethel. 1987 *The Economy and Class Structure of German Fascism*, M. Sohn-Rethel, trans. London: Free Association Books, 166.
12. See, e.g., H. Mommsen. 1999. *From Weimar to Auschwitz*, Philip O'Connor, trans., New Jersey: Princeton University Press, 141; Sohn-Rethel, *The Economy and Class Structure of German Fascism*, 89; D. Gluckstein. 1999. *The Nazis, Capitalism and the Working Class*, London: Bookmarks, 37.
13. G.D. Feldman. 1984. 'Aspekte deutscher Industriepolitik am Ende der Weimarer Republik 1930–1932', in G.D. Feldman, *Vom Weltkrieg zur Weltwirtschaftskrise*, Göttingen: Vandenhoek & Ruprecht, 218.
14. See H.A. Winkler. 1975. 'Unternehmerverbände zwischen Ständeideologie und Nationalsozialismus', in H.J. Varain (ed.), *Interessenverbände in Deutschland*, Cologne: Kiepenhauer & Witsch, 228–58. For a discussion of the development of industrial opposition to the Weimar Republic, see M. Schneider. 1975. *Unternehmer und Demokratie: Die freien Gewerkschaften in der unternehmerischen Ideologie der Jahre 1918 bis 1933*, Bonn and Bad Godesberg: Verlag Neue Gesellschaft GmbH. See also F. Neumann. 1981. *Behemoth: The Structure and Practise of National Socialism, 1933–1944*, New York: Oxford University Press, 34; B. Weisbrod. 1979. 'Economic Power and Political Stability Reconsidered: Heavy Industry in Weimar Germany', *Social History* 4(2), 262; B. Weisbrod. 1978. *Schwerindustrie in der Weimarer Republik: Interessenpolitik zwischen Stabilisierung und Krise*, Bielefeld: Peter Hammer Verlag. For a discussion of the Bielefeld School, see R. Fletcher. 1984. 'Recent Developments in West German Historiography: The Bielefeld School and Its Critics', *German Studies Review* 7(3), 451–80.

15. D. Stegmann. 1975. 'Zum Verhältnis von Großindustrie und Nationalsozialismus 1930–1933: Ein Beitrag zur Geschichte der sog. Machtergreifung', *Archiv für Sozialgeschichte* 13, 438–39. Stegmann's work also built on that of Jürgen Kuczynski and Czichon who likewise divided the manufacturing sector into heavy industry and exporters. See A. Barkai. 1990. *Nazi Economics: Ideology, Theory, and Policy*, New Haven, Yale University Press, 12; E. Czichon. 1967. *Wer verhalf Hitler zur Macht? Zum Anteil der deutschen Industrie an der Zerstörung der Weimarer Republik*, Cologne: Pahl-Rugenstein Verlag, 13.
16. Abraham, *The Collapse of the Weimar Republic*, 316. See also D. Abraham. 1980. 'Conflicts within German Industry and the Collapse of the Weimar Republic', *Past and Present* 88(August), 88–128. For an excoriating review of the second edition of Abraham's book, see P. Hayes. 1987. 'History in an Off Key: David Abraham's Second "Collapse"', *Business History Review* 61(3), 452–72.
17. H.A. Turner, Jr. 1985. *German Big Business and the Rise of Hitler*, New York: Oxford University Press, 345; R. Neebe. 1981. *Großindustrie, Staat und NSDAP 1930–1933: Paul Silverberg und der Reichsverband der Deutschen Industrie in der Krise der Weimarer Republik*, Göttingen: Vandenhoeck & Ruprecht, 162–63; Stegmann, 'Zum Verhältnis von Großindustrie und Nationalsozialismus', 433.
18. M. Schneider. 1999. *Unterm Hakenkreuz: Arbeiter und Arbeiterbewegung 1933 bis 1939*, Bonn: Dietz, 126.
19. See, e.g., E. Nolte. 1963. *Three Faces of Fascism*, London: Weidenfeld & Nicholson; Mommsen, *From Weimar to Auschwitz*, 142–43; A.J. Nicholls. 1994. *Freedom with Responsibility: The Social Market Economy in Germany, 1918–1963*, Oxford, Clarendon Press.
20. J.S. Wiesen. 2001. *West German Industry and the Challenge of the Nazi Past, 1945–1955*, Chapel Hill: University of North Carolina Press, 73.
21. For more recent work on the relationship between industry and the state, see R. Overy. 1994. *War and the Economy in the Third Reich*, Oxford: Clarendon Press; A. Tooze. 2007. *The Wages of Destruction: The Making and Breaking of the Nazi Economy*, New York: Viking Penguin.
22. See, e.g., H. James. 2004. *The Nazi Dictatorship and the Deutsche Bank*, Cambridge: Cambridge University Press; G.D. Feldman. 2001. *Allianz and the German Insurance Business, 1933–1945*, Cambridge: Cambridge University Press; L. Gall (ed.). 2002. *Krupp im 20. Jahrhundert: Die Geschichte des Unternehmens vom Ersten Weltkrieg bis zur Gründung der Stiftung*, Berlin: Siedler Verlag. See also P. Hayes. 2004. *From Cooperation to Complicity: Degussa in the Third Reich*, Cambridge: Cambridge University Press; A. Reckendrees. 2000. *Das 'Stahltrust' Projekt: Die Gründung der Vereinigte Stahlwerke A.G. und ihre Unternehmensentwicklung 1926–1933/34*, Munich: C.H. Beck; K.C. Priemel. 2007. *Flick: Eine Konzerngeschichte vom Kaiserreich bis zur Bundesrepublik*, Göttingen: Wallstein Verlag; A. Meyer. 1999. *Hitlers Holding: Die Reichswerke 'Hermann Göring'*, Munich: Europa Verlag; A. Gehrig. 1996. *Nationalsozialistische Rüstungspolitik und unternehmerischer Entscheidungsspielraum: Vergleichende Fallstudien zur württembergischen Maschinenbauindustrie*, Munich: R. Oldenbourg Verlag.
23. For a good example of this, see P. Hayes. 1987. *Industry and Ideology: IG Farben in the Nazi Era*, Cambridge: Cambridge University Press, 343–44.
24. D. Eichholtz. 1969. *Geschichte der deutschen Kriegswirtschaft, 1933–1945*, vol. 1, Berlin: Akademie Verlag, 36–64; D. Eichholtz. 1989. 'Das Expansionsprogramm des Finanzkapitals am Vorabend des Zweiten Weltkriegs', in D. Eichholtz and K. Pätzold (eds), *Der Weg in den Krieg*, Berlin: Akademie-Verlag.

25. P. Termin. 1991. 'Soviet and Nazi Economic Planning in the 1930s', *Economic History Review* 44(1), 573–93; C. Buchheim and J. Scherner. 2006. 'The Role of Private Property in the Nazi Economy: The Case of Industry', *Journal of Economic History* 66(1), 411.
26. J. Streb. 2012. 'Das Nationalsozialistische Wirtschaftssystem: Indirekter Sozialismus, gelenkte Marktwirtschaft oder vergezogene Kreigswirtschaft?' in W. Plumpe and J. Scholtyseck (eds), *Der Staat und die Ordnung der Wirtschaft: Vom Kaiserreich bis zur Berliner Republik*, Stuttgart: Franz Steiner, 61–62.
27. See Hayes, 'Corporate Freedom of Action in Nazi Germany'; Buchheim and Scherner, 'Corporate Freedom of Action in Nazi Germany: A Response to Peter Hayes'; and P. Hayes. 2009. 'Rejoinder', *Bulletin of the German Historical Institute* 45(Fall), 51.
28. See Overy, *War and Economy in the Third Reich*; Barkai, *Nazi Economics: Ideology, Theory, and Policy*; and W. Abelshauser. 1999. 'Kriegswirtschaft undWirtschaftswunder Deutschlands wirtschaftliche Mobilisierung für den Zweiten Weltkrieg und die Folgen für die Nachkriegszeit', *Vierteljahrshefte für Zeitgeschichte* 47(4), 503–38.
29. C. Buchheim. 2001. 'Die Wirtschaftsentwicklung im Dritten Reich. Mehr Desaster als Wunder: Eine Erwiderung auf Werner Abelshauser', *Vierteljahrshefte für Zeitgeschichte* 49(4), 662.
30. See, e.g., Werner Abelshauser, Jan-Otmar Hesse and Werner Plumpe (eds). 2003. *Wirtschaftsordnung, Staat und Unternehmen: Neue Forschungen zur Wirtschaftsgeschichte des Nationalsozialismus*, Essen: Klartext Verlag. The extent of industrialists' room for maneuver, it should be noted, continues to be hotly debated. See Hayes, 'Corporate Freedom of Action in Nazi Germany', 29–42; Buchheim and Scherner, 'Corporate Freedom of Action in Nazi Germany: A Response to Peter Hayes', 43–50; and Hayes, 'Rejoinder', 51.
31. Buchheim and Scherner, 'Corporate Freedom of Action in Nazi Germany: A Response to Peter Hayes'; J. Scherner. 2008. *Die Logik der Industiepolitik im Dritten Reich: Die Investitionen in die Autarkie- und Rüstungsindustrie und ihre staatliche Förderung*, Stuttgart: Franz Steiner Verlag, 20, 21, 284.
32. M. Spoerer. 1996. *Von Scheingewinnen zum Rüstungsboom: Die Eigenkapitalrentabilität der deutschen Industrieaktiengesellschaften 1925–1941*, Stuttgart: Franz Steiner Verlag, 168–70.
33. C. Buchheim and J. Scherer. 2003. 'Anmerkungen zum Wirtschaftssystem des "Dritten Reiches"', in Abelshauser et al., *Wirtschaftsordnung, Staat und Unternehmen*. See also Scherner, *Die Logik der Industriepolitik im Dritten Reich*; C. Gaul. 2004. *Die industriellen Anlageinvestitionen und ihre Steuerung in Deutschland von 1933 bis 1939: Ein Beitrag zur wirtschaftshistorischen Analyse des Verhältnisses von Politik und Ökonomie im Nationalsozialismus*, Hamburg: Verlag Dr. Kovač.
34. See W. Abelshauser. 2003. 'Modernisierung oder institutionelle Revolution? Koordination einer Ortsbestimmung des 'Dritten Reiches' in der deutschen Wirtschaftsgeschichte des 20. Jahrhunderts', in Abelshauser et al., *Wirtschaftsordnung, Staat und Unternehmen*; H. Joly. 2003. 'Ende des Familienkapitalismus? Das Überleben der Unternehmerfamilien in den deutschen Wirtschaftseliten des 20. Jahrhunderts', in V. Berghahn, S. Unger and D. Ziegler (eds), *Die Deutsche Wirtschaftselite im 20. Jahrhundert: Kontinuität und Mentalität*, Essen: Klartext Verlag; and M. von Prollius. 2003. *Das Wirtschaftssystem der Nationalsozialisten 1933–1939: Steuerung durch emergente Organisation und politische Prozesse*, Paderborn: Ferdinand Schöningh.
35. D. Eichholtz. 1999. 'Ökonomie, Politik und Kriegführung: Wirtschaftliche Kriegsplanung und Rüstungsorganisation bis zum Ende der "Blitzkriegsphase"', in D. Eichholtz (ed.), *Krieg und Wirtschaft: Studien zur deutschen Wirtschaftsgeschichte 1939–1945*, Berlin: Metropol Verlag; K.H. Roth. 1999. 'Neuordnung' und Wirtschaftliche Nachkriegsplanung', ibid., 205.

36. Streb, 'Das Nationalsozialistische Wirtschaftssystem', 63.
37. Hayes, *From Cooperation to Complicity,* 19, 114.
38. Buchheim and Scherner, 'The Role of Private Property in the Nazi Economy', 391.
39. For a good example of this process, see Feldman, *Allianz and the German Insurance Business,* x and H. James. 1995. 'The Deutsche Bank and the Dictatorship, 1933-1945', in L. Gall et al. (eds), *The Deutsch Bank, 1870-1995,* London: Wiedenfeld & Nicolson, 282.
40. H. Mommsen. 1998. 'Konnten Unternehmer im Nationalsozialismus apolitisch bleiben?' in L. Gall and M. Pohl (eds), *Unternehmer im Nationalsozialismus,* Munich: C.H. Beck, 70.
41. Weisbrod, *Schwerindustrie,* 34.
42. Statistisches Reichsamt. 1928 *Statistisches Jahrbuch für das Deutsche Reich*. Berlin: Verlag für Sozialpolitik, Wirtschaft und Statistik GmbH. 78.
43. G.D. Feldman and U. Nocken. 1975. 'Trade Associations and Economic Power: Interest Group Development in the German Iron and Steel and Machine Building Industries, 1900-1933', *Business History Review* 49(3), 419.
44. R.A. Brady. 1933. *The Rationalization Movement in German Industry: A Study in the Evolution of Economic Planning,* Berkeley: University of California Press, 155.
45. United States Strategic Bombing Survey. 1947 *No. 54: Machine Tools and Machinery as Capital Equipment,* Equipment Division, 2nd edn, 35-36; T. Siegel and T. von Freyberg. 1991. *Industrielle Rationalisierung unter dem Nationalsozialismus,* Frankfurt a.M.: Campus Verlag, 276.
46. Siegel and Freyberg, *Industrielle Rationalisierung unter dem Nationalsozialismus*; Hans Pohl and Johannes Markner. 1992. *Verbandsgeschichte und Zeitgeschichte: VDMA - 100 Jahre im Dienste des Maschinenbaus, Band I,* Frankfurt a.M.: Maschinenbau Verlag, 371.
47. Pohl and Markner, *Verbandsgeschichte und Zeitgeschichte,* 22; R. Leckebusch. 1966. *Entstehung und Wandlung der Zielsetzung der Struktur und Wirkung von Arbeitgeberverbänden,* Berlin: Dunker Humblot, 148, 50.
48. Pohl and Markner, *Verbandsgeschichte und Zeitgeschichte,* 21.
49. Weisbrod, *Schwereindustrie,* 95.
50. Ibid., 98 and A. Reckendrees. 1996. 'Die Vereinigte Stahlwerke A.G. 1926-1933 und "das Glänzende Beispiel Amerikas"', *Zeitschrift für Unternehmensgeschichte/Journal of Business History* 41(2), 160-61.
51. Reckendrees, *Das 'Stahltrust' Projekt,* 304.
52. See G. Luntowski. 2000. *Hitler und die Herren an der Ruhr: Wirtschaftsmacht und Staatsmacht im Dritten Reich,* Frankfurt a.M.: Peter Lang.
53. William Parker. 1954. 'Entrepreneurship, Industrial Organization, and Economic Growth: A German Example', *Journal of Economic History* 14(4), 382.
54. W. Abelshauser. 2009. 'Eigennutz verpflichtet. Die Verantwortung des Unternehmers in der korporativen Marktwirtschaft', *Geschichte und Gesellschaft* 35(3), 458. See also M. F. Parnell. 1994. *The German Tradition of Organized Capitalism: Self-Government in the Coal Industry,* Oxford: Clarendon Press, viii, 23, 32-33.
55. M. Hayse. 2003. *Recasting West German Elites: Higher Civil Servants, Business Leaders and Physicians in Hesse between Nazism and Democracy: 1945-55,* New York: Berghan Books, 5.
56. E. Kolb. 2005. *The Weimar Republic,* 2nd edn, P.S. Falla and R.J. Park, trans., London: Routledge, 179.
57. See, e.g., Winkler, 'Unternehmerverbände zwischen Ständeideologie und Nationalsozialismus'; Stegmann, 'Zum Verhältnis von Großindustrie und Nationalsozialismus 1930-1933'; Czichon, *Wer verhalf Hitler zur Macht?.* See also F. Blaich. 1979. *Staat*

und *Verbände in Deutschland zwischen 1871 und 1945*, Wiesbaden: Franz Steiner Verlag GmbH.; Hans-Peter Ullmann. 1988. *Interessenverbände in Deutschland*, Frankfurt a.M.: Suhrkamp.
58. See Neebe, *Großindustrie, Staat und NSDAP 1930–1933*; M. Grübler. 1982. *Die Spitzenverbände der Wirtschaft und das erste Kabinett Brüning: Vom Ende der Großen Koalition 1929/30 bis zum Vorabend der Bankenkrise 1931. Eine Quellenstudie*, Düsseldorf: Droste Verlag; D. Kahn. 2006. *Die Steuerung der Wirtschaft durch Recht im nationalsozialistischen Deutschland: Das Beispiel der Reichsgruppe Industrie*, Frankfurt a.M.: Vittorio Klostermann; W. Abelshauser. 2002. 'Gustav Krupp und die Gleichschaltung des Reichsverbandes der Deutschen Industrie, 1933–34', *Zeitschrift für Unternehmensgeschichte* 47(1), 3–26; H. Hartwich. 1967. *Arbeitsmarkt Verbände und Staat, 1918–1933: Die öffentliche Bindung unternehmerischer Funktionen in der Weimarer Republik*, Berlin: Walter de Gruyter.
59. Feldman and Nocken, 'Trade Associations and Economic Power', 418. See also U. Nocken. 1974. 'Inter-Industrial Conflicts and Alliances as exemplified by the AVI-Agreement', in Hans Mommsen et al. (eds), *Industrielles System und politische Entwicklung in der Weimarer Republik: Verhandlungen des Internationalen Symposiums in Bochum vom 12.–17. Juni 1973*, Düsseldorf: Droste Verlag, 693; U. Nocken. 1979. 'Interindustrial Conflicts and Alliances in the Weimar Republic: Experiments in Societal Corporatism', Ph.D. diss. University of California, Berkeley, 57.
60. *Festschriften* on the iron and steel associations and VDMA have been particularly useful to this study. See Pohl and Markner, *Verbandsgeschichte und Zeitgeschichte*, 15; H. Übbing. 1999. *Stahl schreibt Geschichte: 125 Jahre Wirtschaftsvereinigung Stahl*, Düsseldorf: Verlag Stahleisen.
61. See H. James. 2001. *Verbandspolitik im Nationalsozialismus. Von der Interessenvertretung zur Wirtschaftsgruppe: der Centralverband des Deutschen Bank- und Bankiergewerbes 1932–1945*, Munich: Piper Verlag.
62. See also D. von Schmädel. 1968. *Führung im Interessenverband: Probleme der innerverbandlichen Willensbildung*, Berlin: Duncker & Humblot, 88.
63. H. W. Köhler. 1974. *Die stahlwirtschaftlichen Organisationen im Jubiläumsjahr 1974: Ein Beitrag zum Selbstverständnis moderner Verbandstätigkeit*, Düsseldorf: Verlag Stahleisen, 21.
64. Ibid., 22.
65. See, e.g., Hayes, 'History in an Off Key', 456–58.
66. J. Bähr. 2013. 'The Personal Factor in Business under National Socialism: Paul Reusch and Friedrich Flick', in H. Berghoff, J. Kocka and D. Ziegler (eds), *Business in the Age of Extremes*, New York: Cambridge University Press, 153.
67. Luntowski, 'Hitler und die Herren an der Ruhr', 239; N. Frei. 2001. *Karrier im Zweilicht: Hitlers Eliten nach 1945*, Frankfurt: Campus, 314.
68. Frei, *Karrieren im Zweilicht*, 73–130.
69. Bähr, 'The Personal Factor in Business under National Socialism', 154.
70. J. Bähr, R. Banken and T. Fleming. 2008. *Die MAN: Eine deutsche Industriegeschichte*, Munich: C.H. Beck, 285.
71. J. Scholtyseck. 1999. *Robert Bosch und der liberale Widerstand gegen Hitler 1933 bis 1945*, Munich: C.H. Beck, 15; P. Bräutigam. 1997. *Mittelständische Unternehmer im Nationalsozialismus: Wirtschaftliche Entwicklungen und soziale Verhaltensweisen in der Schuh- und Lederindustrie Badens und Württembergs*, Munich: R. Oldenbourg, 16, 338–67.
72. C. Blumberg-Lampe. 1973. *Das Wirtschaftspolitische Programm der 'Freiburger Kreise': Entwurf einer freiheitlich-sozialen Nachkriegswirtschaft Nationalökonomen gegen den Nationalsozialismus*, Berlin: Duncker & Humblot, 15–52.

CHAPTER 1

Opposition and Adaptation
Reichert and Lange in the Weimar Republic

Neither Jakob Reichert nor Karl Lange supported the Nazi Party before 1933 or took any active steps to promote or aid it. They bear none of the direct responsibility for the financing or support of the NSDAP that Turner quantified in *German Big Business and the Rise of Hitler*.[1] Their beliefs, hopes and ideals are a more complicated matter. Reichert in particular shared a number of key ideas with the Party. He distrusted or opposed democracy, aligned himself with the far right in major political debates, mercilessly attacked social democracy and the left in general, and espoused a vision of a 'natural' economy that cut very close to the corporatist 'organic economy'. Lange, on the other hand, became an ever more forceful advocate of the liberal economy and international competition that nourished his industry in the 1920s, while at the same time moving towards authoritarian political solutions. Ironically, both men found themselves at once aiding and opposing the rising tide of National Socialism in Germany by the end of 1932, but for very different reasons. The result was that two of the most important industrial organizations in Germany were both unwilling to preserve the old system and ill adapted for life in the new.

We have a tendency to see the early 1930s as a monumental struggle between the Nazi Party and Weimar democracy. These men did not see things this way. They experienced the crisis years as a dangerous and confusing time in which consensus, or even a compromise, was virtually impossible to achieve on any front. In this context, they each retreated to a very narrow defence of their own industry and interests that was based on their own experiences and ideas in the years leading up to the crisis. The results were positions and arguments that reflected the structure, strengths and needs of the iron and steel or machine building industry, rather than more general aspirations for Germany as a whole. However, the policies and reputations they had each built by the end of 1932 were largely incompatible with the rising National Socialist movement, although for different reasons.

Both Reichert and Lange came from relatively humble backgrounds and rose to positions of considerable respect in German industry. Jakob Reichert was born the son of a Boxberg innkeeper in 1885, and despite spending virtually his entire working life in the iron and steel industry, he initially pursued an education in law and political economy.[2] After completing his doctorate on the *Sparwesen der Stadt Mannheim,* he went to work for the Lower Rhenisch Chamber of Industry and Commerce as a technical assistant before being promoted into its management shortly afterwards.[3] By this time Reichert was already acquainted with the powerful industrialist Paul Reusch, who took an interest in cultivating young men of a variety of backgrounds.[4] Over the course of 1912–13, Reusch helped to shepherd Reichert into his position as chief business manager of the Verein Deutscher Eisen- und Stahlindustrieller in the hope that the 28-year-old lawyer and political economist would help to reinvigorate an organization that had 'fallen asleep'.[5]

Reichert took over the administration of an organization suspended between bureaucratic and personal leadership. The VDESI presided over six regional groups representing the North-West, the East, Central Germany, the North, the South and the South-west.[6] The North-West Group was founded shortly before the others and retained a certain degree of autonomy within the VDESI,[7] but the central office remained predominant and Reichert retained a seat on the management board of the local organization. The remaining regional subsidiaries were more directly subordinated to the central office and Reichert himself served as the business manager of the Northern Group for some time.[8] The VDESI also incorporated the North German Railroad Car Builders Association and the Association of German Shipbuilders as branch groups.[9]

The heterogeneous nature of the VDESI itself and the tendency of large German firms to expand vertically resulted in an organization with an interest in a variety of forms and stages of production in Germany.[10] This necessarily involved the VDESI in a dense network of cartels, syndicates, associations and other groups. Its members were very often members of other organizations as well, and Reichert himself assumed the role of business manager of the Technical Group for Iron Production in the Reich Association of German Industry in 1919, tying him to a larger system of employer lobbyists in the new republic.[11] At the same time, the representatives of a wide variety of organizations often met in joint sessions in order to establish complementary policies.[12]

In this complicated system, the importance of the technical and bureaucratic management of the VDESI was counterbalanced by the extraordinary importance of a few powerful firms and industrialists in the Ruhr Valley in particular. Because of this, the association's day-to-day functioning and formulation of policy required a deft hand capable of remaining aloof from the variety of rivalries and interests within German industry.[13] This constrained

Reichert's freedom to manoeuvre, but he was a consummate courtier, and his ability to negotiate with a number of firms, regions and interests enabled him to cobble together a coherent front for the iron and steel industry.[14] This was a complicated task, but as long as he worked within the limits set by the great iron masters, it allowed him to speak to other interests and the state with the weight of some of the most important men in Germany behind him.

Reichert also kept one foot firmly in party politics throughout the Weimar period. He joined the arch-conservative Deutschnationale Volkspartei (DNVP) and sat in the Reichstag from 1920, serving on the Reichstag Foreign Affairs Committee from 1924.[15] Although he and his colleagues generally shared the traditional authoritarian, nationalist and anti-union outlook of the DNVP and its final leader, Alfred Hugenberg, the relationship between heavy industry and the Party was often strained. Hugenberg himself demonstrated a declining interest in the immediate aims of industry in favour of agriculture and wider nationalist causes.[16] As a result, Reichert and his colleagues in industry, including Paul Reusch, drifted into the relatively moderate wing of the DNVP under Count Westarp.[17] This wing of the Party was more interested than the increasingly radical Hugenberg in a broad bourgeois conservative coalition to counteract the gains of the left.[18] This desire to participate in governance in a productive – if authoritarian – way alienated industry from radicalizing conservatives to a certain extent, and by 1928 it became necessary to secure Reichert's position on the DNVP candidates list through a substantial financial contribution from the most prominent industrialists in the Ruhr through the *Ruhrlade*.[19] Nevertheless, his seat in the Reichstag provided him with a national platform for his political and economic views. It also gave him access to sensitive information, particularly regarding the delicate negotiations over reparations that increased his usefulness to his industry.[20] That said, he was an elected politician who had troubling reservations about democracy itself.

Although Reichert came to deeply regret the policies of the new democratic republic in Germany, he was surprisingly sanguine about the end of the Kaiserreich itself. Unlike many conservatives, he was willing to grant that the change of government and surrender in 1918 were simply the price of extricating Germany from a lost war.[21] However, he had little time for the groups that assumed power under the new republic and blamed a collection of Marxists, socialists and pacifists for the decline of German power in general. For Reichert, the revolution had eliminated all the responsible elements from the German government and left the nation 'leaderless and headless', lacking in any 'inner resolve' (*innerer Halt*).[22] Reichert particularly blamed the social democrats and trade unions for the economic and political instability of the Weimar Republic.[23] He saw social democracy and the left as responsible for almost all the sins of the state. This, he feared, represented nothing less than the beginning of the end for capitalism in Germany,[24] which would ultimately lead to anarchy and revolution.[25] They needed to be stopped, even at the cost of the niceties of democratic representation. He was not alone in this belief. The increase in communist party membership and activity, especially during the depression, alarmed the German middle class, conservatives and authorities alike.[26] The communist party was also seen as much more than a simple political movement, and industrialists in the VDESI saw the threat of revolutionary Marxism lurking behind even such seemingly innocuous activities as sex education societies and child advocacy groups.[27] As a result, Reichert and his colleagues were at least sympathetic to the anticommunist credentials of the NSDAP.[28]

Reichert's attack on the left complemented his distaste for parliamentary democracy, which Hak-Ie Kim in particular argues furnished the basis for an understanding between industry and the National Socialists.[29] At least by the end of the passive resistance movement in the Ruhr in 1923, the collapse of the democratic system in Germany took on an air of inevitability for Reichert, and the VDESI executive called for 'strong men' to seize control of both the government and the economy.[30] Reichert's attacks on the centre-left and even on more moderate conservatives likewise became sharper following the Ruhr occupation and Dawes Plan to settle a new reparations agreement. From then on, he began to include the relatively moderate conservative German People's Party (DVP) in his list of villains along with the Social Democratic and Centre Party, limiting legitimate governing interests in his mind to the weak and undemocratic DNVP.[31] By 1925, Reichert had informed the VDESI that he believed a government based on the parties of the centre was doomed to fail, and Stresemann himself warned that Reichert advised the association that 'nothing else remained but to govern on the basis of Article 48, and not to summon the Reichstag until there are 13 months in the year'.[32] Here was no defender of the democratic republic or the compromise that might make it workable.

Reichert's ideas about the Treaty of Versailles likewise intersected with those of the radical right. Indeed, opposition to the treaty and its effects became a leitmotif of Reichert's career that mixed economics with a pronounced national chauvinism and a certain degree of popular cachet. The treaty was much more than a national humiliation for Reichert and many others on the right. To Reichert, it was the subjugation of Germany by its enemies and resulted in economic, social and even cultural stagnation.[33] At the same time, Reichert feared that German firms were threatened by a wave of 'foreignization' that followed as a result of Versailles and the postwar crisis.[34] His opposition to the treaty also combined the old shibboleth of French repression after their 'victory' in 1918 with dire predictions about a descent into a dreaded 'Bolshevik experiment'.[35] This fear of the political and economic threat posed by France in particular was compounded by a marked nervousness over Germany's military inferiority. Reichert was deeply worried about the military preparations he perceived in the former Entente powers. He saw even the British motivation for the devaluation of the pound and erection of tariff barriers as an attempt to protect their capacity for military expansion.[36] He likewise compared the relative military weakness of Germany to a France that was supposedly 'armed to the teeth'.[37]

Reichert's politics can only be understood through his industry. Large interest groups in any society are apt to equate their own demands with the welfare of the wider polity. While big business and heavy industry are no exception to this, Germany's primary producing industries were particularly guilty of confusing the health of their own enterprise with the state of the nation. The role of coal, iron and steel as the primary elements of an industrial economy particularly encouraged men engaged in producing these products to see themselves as the foundation of a successful, modern economy. Reichert was undoubtedly a nationalist, both by conviction and party affiliation, but his nationalism was inextricably tied to the industry he represented. When he said 'Germany', he usually meant 'iron'.[38] This led Reichert, among others in heavy industry, to assume that he and the VDESI had the right – and the ability – to shape national and international policy, which in turn led him to a curious set of beliefs about politics and economics.

While they did not always agree with the more romantic notions of the imperial elite, heavy industrialists in general admired strong, even authoritarian, leadership over democratic parliamentarism.[39] Despite the changes in the German government following the First World War and the collapse of aristocratic agrarians as a power bloc, heavy industry managed to retain a powerful position in the new Weimar state.[40] In fact, a significant number of industrialists came to believe that only their own cool thinking and participation in the negotiations with organized labour had saved the nation from chaos and Bolshevism as the middle classes 'crept into their mouse holes' when the imperial government collapsed.[41] As a result, Reichert and the men he represented saw themselves as having the right, and perhaps even the obligation, to intervene in state policy in a way no other group could claim, but only if they did so on their own terms.[42] On the one hand, they hoped to have a hand in a strong state that would defend them against other interests and preserve the conditions that guaranteed them a profitable domestic market.[43] On the other, industrialists' respect for an authoritarian government found a corollary in their belief that they must remain '*Herr im Haus*' in their own factories and mines, even dictating legislation that was relevant to their enterprise.[44] This desire to govern their own affairs independently came into direct conflict with the desire for a strong state capable of intervening in economic relationships that could only be reconciled through a certain amount of hypocrisy. Ideally, this 'strong state' would be something that happened to other people.

Reichert's economic ideas went considerably beyond the adoption of theories that were particularly useful to his own industry. Instead, he cobbled together an idiosyncratic view of the world that was built from the ground up on the interests of iron and steel. In some ways, Reichert's economic ideas reflected the importance Friedrich List placed on the concept of the 'National Economy'. List's defence of protective tariffs resonated deeply with iron and steel industrialists who depended on high prices on the domestic market for reliable profits.[45] This was not universal, and Reichert and his assistant, Baare, saw Germany as a special case that required more protection than other states.[46] To this end, Reichert emphasized the importance of breaking the 'free trading influence' on the government in favour of strategic tariffs.[47] By 1932 this concern was developing into a desperate desire for state protection, particularly in light of England's success.[48] Taking the introduction of high British tariffs as a model, Reichert concluded that Germany needed strong iron and steel tariffs simply in order to keep up.[49] This fit in nicely with the rising tide of nationalist, protectionist rhetoric on the far right. Reichert himself framed his appeals for protectionism in the same language, arguing that tariffs must be erected primarily for the benefit of the beleaguered agrarian population, although both Reichert and Baare supported the system of most-favoured nation agreements built during the 1920s that fostered industry while allowing for the import of cheap foodstuffs, and furthermore rejected the turn towards general protectionism or reciprocal trading agreements favoured by declining farmers and Junkers.[50] Heavy industry in general also stood behind General Schleicher's decision to put off import restrictions indefinitely, despite suspicion of much of the rest of his agenda as chancellor.[51] However, Reichert's blending of iron, steel and politics went considerably beyond rationalizing tariffs.

During the Weimar Republic, Reichert came to characterize the European economy as an autonomous system that obeyed a set of 'natural' laws that trumped 'politics' and to view this economy as the site of certain irreducible truths. These laws were not necessarily related to the open-ended competition of liberals following Adam Smith, but were rather a reflection of how he and his industry thought the European economy worked best – particularly for them. Reichert argued that a healthy economy was predicated on an independent iron and steel industry that found its ultimate expression in the Kaiserreich's Ruhr-Lorraine system, which knit German coal and French iron into one (German) resource that was the foundation of the European economy. These 'objective' economic facts were sharply differentiated from politics in his mind. Politicians, Reichert argued, must recognize these laws and shape public policy accordingly.[52] Anything else would cripple the 'natural' economy that alone could deliver stability and prosperity. In practice, Reichert's faith in the 'natural' economy led him to assert that he and his industry should dictate most political policy. For him, the extraordinary advantages of the German producers within the Ruhr-Lorraine industrial system were not simply the result of the historical accident of the settlement of the Franco-Prussian war, but rather the logical expression of the natural relationship between coal and steel.[53] The repatriation of Lorraine to France was thus not only objectionable from the point of view of national pride, it also represented an 'unnatural' attack on the iron production that guaranteed progress and stability in Europe generally.[54] Reparations deliveries were thus both an attack on the German *Volkswirtschaft* and an 'offense against the nature of business'.[55] Reichert thought that sooner or later the French government would have to recognize this fact and come to terms with Germany, regardless of relative military power or legal authority. It would be foolish for the German government to try to reach a political modus vivendi with their neighbours before this happened.[56]

This meant that Reichert was more than willing to lead industry in an attack on political policy aimed at reconciling France and Germany, and the VDESI systematically rejected any postwar settlement that would reflect military and political realities rather than its own interests and 'natural' business relationships, even in the face of the French occupation of the Ruhr in 1923.[57] Indeed, even after the fact that iron and steel industrialists had begun to negotiate with French authorities became public knowledge, Reichert sought to prolong the conflict and refused to believe that his members had accepted an imposed settlement that defied his own economic logic.[58]

Industrialists themselves were forced to swallow their reservations and accept the MICUM agreement with France in the last months of 1923 in order to remain in business, but Reichert was free to continue to agitate against any kind of agreement that subverted the 'natural' economy that favoured German iron and steel. When the introduction of the Dawes Plan in 1924 split opinion in the Reichsverband between moderate industrialists, who supported adoption of the plan as a positive step, and heavy industry in the Ruhr, which rejected any compromise as capitulation,[59] Reichert helped lead the charge against the commission in what would be a dress rehearsal for the campaign against the Young Plan five years later. Drawing his ideas together in a pamphlet with Karl Helfferich, Reichert once again argued that the 'political' nature of the commission precluded a rational settlement of an essentially economic question.[60]

Reichert also found himself called upon to actively ward off the intervention of the state in the early Weimar Republic, but although he proved to be an energetic (and sometimes overzealous) champion of the freedom of the entrepreneur from state controls, he did not seek to replace them with Darwinian competition. Instead, he hoped to replace odious government restrictions on business with profitable private regulation of competition through his own organization. As a result, Reichert helped to block attempts to impose a corporatist structure on the economy from above, and advocated for private associations that would serve the needs of industry, not the state, in a way that would eventually clash with National Socialism.⁶¹ As the leader of the Central Bureau for Export Permits for Iron and Steel, the chief business manager exerted considerable influence over the industry.⁶² Under this control regime, Reichert was ultimately responsible for the approval of all export permits.⁶³ He likewise used his position as a Reichstag deputy to attack Finance Minister Erzberger's export levies and succeeded in securing a 50 per cent reduction for some products.⁶⁴ More importantly, Reichert saw his role on the Export Control Board as that of the guardian of German iron and steel industry profits rather than primarily an agent of the state. This fit in very well with Reichert's belief in the efficacy of 'private regulation'. Moreover, his assertions that the efforts of private associations like his own rather than government policy were responsible for any improvements in Germany since the revolution met with a warm response in the Association of German Industry in particular.⁶⁵ Nevertheless, Reichert's opinion of industrialists' competence to set their own iron prices was also more than a little patronizing.⁶⁶ He feared that export prices would collapse even in iron and steel if his controls were lifted and warned against the 'merchant spirit', recommending instead that 'strict discipline in industry is better than unbridled competition'.⁶⁷ While iron and steel men were happy to allow the state to protect them from outside competition, they were less enthusiastic about the business manager of their organization, who had never 'really sold or handled iron', reviewing their own export contracts.⁶⁸

This incident demonstrated the limits of Reichert's authority in a way that made a lasting impression and likely contributed to his later hesitancy to assume some of the authority offered by the Nazi state. He had begun to stray out of step with his own members and had to be reined in sharply before he could find a way to reinvigorate self-regulation in his industry. He learned his lesson and redirected his efforts towards facilitating the construction of private bodies run by industrialists themselves. For an organizational man like Reichert, the 'cartel-less' period immediately after the First World War was disconcerting.⁶⁹ Luckily, it was relatively short-lived. As the new rentenmark stabilized and French exporters started to enjoy the benefits of inflation, iron and steel industrialists began to look for a means of moderating the business downturn that followed stabilization. Reichert had already called for the establishment of a new international cartel for at least some iron and steel products as early as 1921.⁷⁰ While he was willing to recognize that the fluctuating state of the mark and the state of international relations did not facilitate the development of an international cartel until after the Ruhr crisis, Reichert increasingly emphasized the value of international business co-operation in self-regulation as a way of both maximizing profits and avoiding interference by the state.⁷¹

By 1924, this attitude found a more receptive audience in the business community at home and abroad. An agreement between German manufacturers and the Working Group of the Iron Working Industry (Arbeitsgemeinschaft der eisenverarbeitenden Industrie, AVI) drew them into a formal collaborative structure between 1924 and 1926. For Reichert, this 'civil peace' between primary and secondary producers now allowed the iron and steel industry to pursue its own trade and political aims.[72] The process of re-establishing a network of private regulatory bodies was capped by the conclusion of an International Crude Steel Agreement (*Internationale Rohstahlgemeinschaft*, IRG) on 30 September 1926.[73] This was a substantial success for Reichert's ideas. Indeed, he crowed that this private organ of business regulation had met with the approval of all parties but the communists in the Handelspolitischen Ausschuß,[74] and even some communist theorists greeted the IRG as a step towards the pacifism predicted by Marx.[75] Moreover, Reichert saw the IRG as a starting point on the road towards a more comprehensive private regulation of international trade through an iron and steel cartel or syndicate.[76]

Reichert and the VDESI were also sensitive to attacks on the power of the industrial cartels he was helping to build. The chief business manager interpreted the provisions of the July 1930 Emergency Order (*Notverordnung*), which gave the Ministry of Economics the power to dissolve cartels that refused to lower prices, as a broad attack on the constitutional freedom of coalition for industrialists.[77] He had some reason to be concerned, as manufacturers, and indeed Chancellor Brüning himself, suspected the cartels of undermining other German industries.[78] The political left, liberal press and even the Institute for Economic Research (Institut für Konjunkturforschung) all attacked cartel policies as an unreasonable burden on the German economy in the midst of such an acute crisis.[79] Reichert complained that during the October 1930 meetings of the Reich Economic Council he was overwhelmed by a coalition of merchants and the finishing industry, and took these assaults on the privately organized economy as an attack on capitalism itself.[80] Even as the decline in real prices over the course of 1931 removed the real economic incentive for opposition to restrictions on cartel pricing, the VDESI continued to decry these attacks as an intrusion of party politics into the economy and to question the legality of regulation of the cartels.[81]

As the crisis in iron and steel deepened in 1931, Reichert stuck to his guns.[82] He particularly admired van Hoegarden, a Belgian industrialist who attacked 'the suicidal competitive struggle [that] has gripped the world' and plunged industry into a 'senseless price war'.[83] While Reichert acknowledged the dramatic decline in the price of iron by 1932, he noted that the only exceptions to the general price collapse were products that remained subject to strong international agreements and had not been 'left on the free market'.[84] This, he argued, 'showed the value of an organized world market' and pointed the way out of the economic crisis.[85] For Reichert, private business cooperation that reflected the 'natural' economy was the solution to the depression. Thus, despite being jealous of British tariff policies, the chief business manager of the VDESI was convinced that England and other states could achieve the same levels of success through private international agreements rather than state policies.[86] He took the example of the British Commonwealth and Ottawa agreement as an example that could be applied to private industrial agreements. Its 'strong desire for international co-operation' coupled with a good deal of freedom in tariff and other policies insulated the Commonwealth countries from the cutthroat competitive struggle that unnerved 'association men' like Reichert.[87] At the same time, England organized export associations that acted like syndicates to help keep profits high despite falling prices.[88] Reichert argued that German industry must engage in private negotiations with England in order to establish a similar understanding and to attempt to persuade smaller states that their short-term gains made through dumping were neither sustainable nor reasonable.[89] Authoritarianism was fine for the German state itself, but iron and steel men needed collegial self-regulation to prosper.

Many of Reichert's ideas were self-serving rationalizations of his own organization's role in the welfare of the iron and steel industry. They also insulated him from the rising tide of National Socialism to a surprising degree and led him to defend much of what was left of the Weimar system. Reichert had good reasons for feeling optimistic about the Brüning government in the final days of the republic. The chancellor's policy of deflation and willingness to ignore the Reichstag were very close to his own beliefs. Although he had many criticisms and suggestions for the new government, Reichert had little reason to want to overthrow the state Brüning was creating. In general, the enormous scale of production and primary importance of the iron and steel industry also placed these firms in a better position than most to weather economic downturns. As a last resort, large companies facing actual bankruptcy might appeal to the authorities for aid in order to avoid the social and economic consequences of throwing their large workforces on unemployment benefits. This was in fact the solution that kept the Flick concern solvent during the crisis.[90]

However, the iron and steel industry also entered the Great Depression in the midst of a long-term structural crisis that amplified the effects of the collapse of 1929 and led some of his members to imagine more radical solutions than Reichert was willing to entertain. Commodity prices in general fell victim to a climate of 'relative stagnation' that suppressed prices during the 1920s.[91] This was compounded by the peculiarities of the German iron and steel industry itself. In the postwar period, improvements in labour productivity and efficiency in Germany lagged only behind those of the United States.[92] The world markets' inability to absorb such vast increases in iron and steel production resulted in substantial overcapacity problems by the late 1920s.[93] Blast furnaces in particular needed to be run for long periods of time, and reducing inputs or shutting down to shorten or eliminate shifts was extremely difficult, if not impossible. As a result, it was very hard to cut production meaningfully and still hope to turn a profit once the depression set in earnest.[94]

Despite these problems, Reichert took great pains to argue that overcapacity, rationalization and 'long-term difficulties' were greatly exaggerated compared to the question of external competition, government policy and wages.[95] Nevertheless, he had deep misgivings about the health of his own industry even before the onset of the global economic collapse. He feared that the poor stock showing in iron and steel in 1927 foreshadowed a long downturn that would hit primary producers particularly hard.[96] Moreover, he echoed the powerful Albert Vögler's fears from 1929 that Germany was poised to become a 'crisis centre' that would infect global financial and economic markets.[97] Reichert had good cause for worry. The industry continued to produce below capacity even in the peak year of 1927, and both domestic consumption and production declined significantly thereafter.[98] By 1932, the output of German rolling mills had declined to under 33 per cent of 1927 levels, reaching a low point of just 23 per cent in August.[99] At the same time, imports of rolled products into Germany increased at a much higher rate than those of other states. By 1932, 29 per cent of the structural iron (*Formeisen*) consumed in Germany, for instance, was produced outside the Reich.[100] This difficulty with production and competition was accompanied by a substantial drop in price.[101] By 1932, a rather distressed Reichert acknowledged that the price of iron had never been lower.[102] The decline in profitability and the size of the workforce in the iron and steel industry had a direct effect on the fortunes of the Verein Deutscher Eisen- und Stahlindustrieller itself, and by the end of 1932, the VDESI was forced to revise its budget, cutting it from RM 360,000 in 1930 to RM 200,000 for 1933.[103]

Reichert also drew a direct link between the contemporary economic crisis and the state of German politics. Like many others, he recognized that the depression had led many to question capitalism itself.[104] By late 1931, he was increasingly concerned that the idea that the depression was a final judgement on capitalism was spreading beyond the bounds of the far left into mainstream German society, opening an opportunity that could be exploited by revolutionaries.[105] Something, he thought, had to be done to settle the social and political unrest. His attempts to do something brought him into close contact with the rising tide of right-wing extremism in Germany. Reichert's campaign against the Young Plan in 1929 effectively combined his approach to political and economic questions and exemplifies the significant points of intersection between Reichert and the far right. However, it also denotes some of the growing differences between Reichert and his fellow travellers. The Young Plan was itself a divisive issue for industrialists. While the VDMA supported the plan as the lesser of two evils and the moderate business manager of the RdI, Ludwig Kastl, participated in the expert committee that developed it, many industrialists were highly suspicious of the new reparations schedule.[106] It was strongly opposed by the powerful steel magnates Fritz Thyssen and Albert Vögler, for instance, who were both moving farther to the right, but even so truculent a nationalist as Paul Reusch recognized that little could be done to improve the situation and ordered his agent, Martin Blank, to withdraw from the committee designed to prepare a broad nationalist front against the plan.[107] Reichert, on the other hand, took up the campaign against the Young Plan with unrepentant gusto and, as a bemused DNVP colleague observed, 'revealed himself as a Dawesist' after all.[108] Although Reichert was not a member of the organizing committee that drew together the DNVP, NSDAP, Stahlhelm and other assorted reactionary groups, he threw himself into the campaign against the Young Plan, giving nine public lectures and publishing twenty separate articles on the subject in the last six months of 1929.[109]

Unsurprisingly, the core of Reichert's opposition to the Young Plan was that it represented precisely the sort of political meddling in the 'natural' economy that 'destroyed the course of economic activity (*wirtschaftliche Dinge*) and the natural system of the development of the economy and humanity'.[110] He was particularly alarmed that the demands made on the state treasury by Versailles might encourage the Reich government to turn towards a command economy in order to pay its bills.[111] In increasingly shrill tones, the business manager of the VDESI worried that the plan would lower the standard of living for regular Germans, do nothing to alleviate the burdens of the 'honest taxpayer' and invite civil unrest.[112] He also appealed to the international community, and at least one of his pamphlets was translated into both English and French.[113] Alas, Reichert made a poor populist. Rather than convincing his colleagues, his melodramatic plea to members of the Reichstag to think of their benighted children before adopting the Young Plan brought accusations of demagoguery from other members and a tedious argument over Reichert's understanding of commitment to future generations.[114] At least one of his own party comrades complained that Reichert's long, antagonistic, cliché-ridden speeches were proof of the inferiority of DNVP propaganda.[115]

Despite his vehement opposition to the Young Plan, Reichert did not follow the DNVP's foray further into populist politics in late 1929. Hugenberg's attempt to push through the Reichstag the 'Freedom Law', which included legal penalties for politicians involved in international treaties like the Young Plan, caused considerable strife in the Party and opened up an opportunity for the Nazis to take the lead in opposition to the Young Plan.[116] This went too far even for most heavy industrialists, and Paul Reusch privately referred to the plebiscite on the Freedom Law as a 'great stupidity'.[117] Despite Reichert's public antagonism to the plan, he seems to have shared Reusch's analysis of the plebiscite itself. He did not support Hugenberg and joined with thirteen other DNVP members who refused to vote in favour of the law in the Reichstag on

30 November 1929.[118] Moreover, he ceased publishing and speaking publicly on the subject of reparations and the Young Plan during the weeks that led up to the plebiscite on 22 December.[119] Despite his reputation, Reichert's conservatism had its limits.

The gap between Reichert and the extreme right only widened with the onset of the depression and the increasingly hostile debate over how it might be overcome. At the highest theoretical level, Reichert rejected state intervention in the economy out of hand. In part, this was due to his belief that meaningful state planning was simply too difficult in a modern and populous state like Germany.[120] Reichert's fear and distrust of 'Marxism' in any form also pushed him to reject the state intervention envisioned by the extremist right for fear of creeping socialism. He and many industrialists in the Ruhr retained their faith in capitalism's ability to heal itself, despite the fact that their own brand of capitalism was rather short on open competition or flexibility.[121] The key to overcoming the crisis, he thought, was to allow businessmen a free hand in their own affairs while at the same time granting their opinions more weight in the government itself.[122] Skyrocketing unemployment also allowed Reichert to cast the interests of his members as those of the nation as a whole once again. Political interventions like taxes, insurance contributions, wages and short working hours were, he claimed, to blame for the economic crisis in Germany.[123] At the same time, the growth of the public sector in Germany provided rich fodder for Reichert's speeches and articles.[124]

Reichert's ideas could be reactionary, but they were essentially irreconcilable with National Socialism. The putative 'socialist' aspect of National Socialism unnerved many industrialists who had grown accustomed to thinking in terms of class struggle, however much they might decry the same mentality amongst trade unionists. The vague and populist ideas that characterized the Nazi programme were also treated harshly by ledger-minded managers. Although a few eccentric iron and steel industrialists like Thyssen and Zangen had already embraced National Socialism by 1930, Reichert and many of his colleagues were engaged in what he later called a 'long guessing game' about the upstart party.[125] While Hitler and the Party took pains to appeal to industrialists and big business, the anti-capitalist elements of the Party, with their preference for agriculture, suspicion of international trade and blunders like the publication of the 'Immediate Economic Programme' in early 1932, scared off many industrialists.[126] That said, the discourse of industrial politics moved sharply to the right leading up to the Nazi seizure of power. Max Schlenker, business manager of both the North-West group of the VDESI and the Ruhr-Westphalian industrialists' regional lobby group (the Langnamverein), remained optimistic about the possibility of excluding the Nazis from government, but the speeches of the late 1932 Langnamverein meeting were virtually indistinguishable from many of the ideas of the NSDAP. Fritz Springorum in particular reflected the tone of the radical right in his demands for a 'strong state', *Lebensraum*, rearmament, physical fitness and military service.[127]

The confusion over the depth of the sympathy that heavy industry might have felt for the NSDAP is in large part due to the confused nature of Nazi policies. The Party's unscrupulous willingness to tailor its platform to its audience while simultaneously remaining vague on details constituted an enormous tactical advantage. This 'allowed people to read into it what they wanted and edit out anything they found disturbing'.[128] German businessmen were no more immune to these tactics than other segments of the population. As a result, Nazi economic policy was in a continuous state of flux that allowed a number of businessmen to read their own interests into the Party and leader. As a political economist whose life revolved around his work in iron and steel, Reichert was not a man to be impressed by vague appeals to emotion that did not correspond to clear economic benefits for his members. On the contrary, his single-minded focus on his industry made him more likely to be interested in the minutiae of economic, trade and legal policy. At the same time, Hitler's rejection of the primary role of the economy in the state, his focus on willpower as an economic determinant and his ambivalent attitude towards private property also ran counter to Reichert's long-held beliefs.[129] Reichert may have hoped for a more authoritarian government led by a 'strong man', but this was to be a government that put the economy, and the iron industry in particular, ahead of more abstract notions of state and nation.

If hackneyed hyperbole placed Reichert firmly in the camp of the fears and fearmongering that helped to foster the growth of National Socialism, Reichert and the VDESI themselves shrank from the authoritarian solution that presented itself in the early 1930s. As the Langnamverein emerged as the strongest proponent of an authoritarian solution to the political and economic crisis, Poensgen repudiated these demands and distanced the VDESI from this kind of radicalism in 1931.[130] Reichert himself demonstrated some concern over his own reputation as an authoritarian. By 1932, he was eager to convince his colleagues that his own radicalism had been greatly exaggerated.[131] In private, he admitted that he had mused that the president would have recourse to article 48 in order to govern, but that his opinions were by no means as radical as Stresemann's recently published diary in particular had made them out to be.[132] However, more than a decade of experience in the Reichstag had not turned Reichert into a democrat or *Vernunftrepublikaner*. He continued to be deeply mistrustful of other party politicians, particularly when they took up economic questions, supported the strengthening of the powers of the government despite the absence of a parliamentary majority, and joined the diverse chorus of voices that placed enormous pressure on the Brüning government to do away with parliamentary government altogether.[133]

Nonetheless, as Weimar politics began its descent into violent radicalism, Reichert took concrete steps to preserve an older form of German conservatism against this new threat from the right, unwittingly helping to split the DNVP into two separate groups defined by their differing relation to National Socialism in the process. Westarp and his followers like Reichert in the DNVP hoped to find a balance between fighting the system and practical work with the present government.[134] As the DNVP moved closer to the NSDAP and other radical groups, Reichert and like-minded conservatives left the party in an ill-conceived attempt to create a new movement on the right capable of uniting the bourgeois vote.[135] Reichert's word carried weight in this circle, and Westarp consulted him regularly during the decision-making process.[136] Reinhold Quaatz in particular considered him to be one of the primary intriguers that were already threatening the party by 1929.[137]

These divisions mirrored a larger split in the conservative party. Like Reichert, the dissident conservative group's leader Gottfried Treviranus and his followers were uncomfortable with Hugenberg's turn towards the radical right. Treviranus's circle seceded from the DNVP on 3 December 1929 and declared themselves 'ready to work and fight for their fatherland under the conditions of the present state and contemporary relationships'.[138] Rather than forming a new party, they instead established a loose confederation designed to appeal to Westarp's group in particular.[139] This new People's Conservative Association (Volkskonservative Vereinigung), which was partly financed by Schleicher, was meant to draw traditional conservatives under one roof and avoid falling into the arms of the upstart National Socialists.[140]

This strategy did in fact appeal to Reichert and Westarp. They belonged to the wing of the DNVP that saw governance as a kind of duty and were uncomfortable with Hugenberg's obstructionist approach to the Brüning government despite Reichert's own discomfort with popular democracy.[141] By early April of 1930, Hugenberg was pushing the party to vote against the Brüning government.[142] This provoked Reichert into an open break with Hugenberg. Not only did he vote against him in the Reichstag debates of 12 and 14 April, but he also drafted a circular memorandum to the German National Industrial Committee on 16 April attacking Hugenberg's position.[143]

By July of 1930, the differences between the two wings of the DNVP had become irreconcilable. Westarp left the party, followed by forty-three other party delegates, leaving a rump of only thirty-five left in the old party.[144] Unfortunately, while Reichert and Westarp joined the Volkskonservativen and helped to turn it into a proper party as the Conservative People's Party (Konservative Volkspartei, KVP) on 23 July, most of the dissident DNVP delegates joined other right-wing groups, fragmenting German politics still further.[145] Nevertheless, even Brüning had high hopes that the new KVP would constitute 'a party in which Protestant workers can find a home just as Catholic workers have found a home in the Centre Party'.[146] Reichert's interest in Protestant workers as such is questionable, although his own electoral district of Düsseldorf-Ost was described as a Christian Social 'bastion' and he did maintain contact with the compliant Christian trade unions.[147] However, he and his colleagues in industry were more interested in forming a party that would be able to unite the conservative right with the other bourgeois parties. To this end, Reichert became the chairman of the new party's finance committee and helped secure funds from the Ruhr Valley.[148]

The results of this attempt to establish a new party on the right were disastrous. It garnered only a little over 300,000 votes, earning it just 4 representatives.[149] The DNVP vote was also cut in half as rural farmers abandoned it as well.[150] The National Socialists, on the other hand, increased their share of the national vote from 2.6 per cent in 1928 to 18.3 per cent in 1930.[151] Treviranus himself was brought into the Brüning cabinet and remained there until the collapse of the government in May 1932, but Reichert and his colleagues succeeded in little more than further fragmenting German politics as it sank deeper into crisis. Reichert himself lost his seat in the Reichstag, and with it his voice on the national political stage.

The Westarp group persevered and formed a second loose political organization in an attempt to keep traditional conservatives from moving to the Nazi Party. Reichert was a founding member of this National Political Working Group (Nationalpolitische Arbeitsgemeinschaft) in the summer of 1931.[152] The circle's most important contribution was the establishment and funding of *Letters to Eastern Germany* (*Briefe nach Ostdeutschland*), a publication mailed directly to important or notable individuals two or three times a month that exhorted traditional conservatives to stand by Brüning and Hindenburg.[153] Reichert, Dryander (another former DNVP representative) and Westarp assumed the editorship of these letters.[154] The standard print run was rather modest, averaging only 8,500 copies per month, but during the presidential election of April 1932, they were able to print 20,000 pieces.[155] Although these efforts pale in comparison to the massive propaganda campaigns mounted by the National Socialists or even the Communist Party (KPD), they demonstrate Reichert's and his colleagues' real commitment to a conservative alternative to National Socialism, albeit one based on the authority of notables rather than popular mobilization.

For Reichert, industry's best hope lay in a Great Coalition until the NSDAP gave up their 'half socialist and half foggy-minded (*nebelhaftes*) party programme'.[156] He was also unimpressed by the Day of National Opposition at Bad Harzburg on 11 October 1931 and described a speech by Walter Funk at the Berlin Herrenklub five days later as a 'disappointment'.[157] The chief business manager was pleased by Funk's anti-Marxism, defence of private property and apparent sympathy to cartel policies, but when Reichert rose to grill Funk about the details of party policy on currency, the state budget, taxes and social contributions, he noted that Funk had only the weakest grasp of the relevant questions.[158] The sometimes overbearing business manager then proceeded to pedantically lecture Funk and the NSDAP on the importance of foreign trade and the currency crisis.[159] Hitler's attempt to reach out to industry in his speech to the Düsseldorf *Industrieklub* in 1932 has attracted considerable interest, but the future führer's emphasis on politics over economics in this speech ran directly counter to Reichert's own ideas about the 'natural economy' and business in general.[160] This was not the way to draw even an authoritarian conservative like Reichert into the NSDAP.

The practical implications of Reichert's feelings about the Nazi approach to the economic crisis came home to the organization when the VDESI executive technical committees met for the last time under the Weimar system on 17 November 1932.[161] Rather than pushing the association to urge the government to adopt the same tariffs or move towards the autarky demanded by the radical right, Reichert urged the VDESI to put more faith in private international business agreements that would regulate trade without significant government oversight.[162] This provoked a strong response from Fritz Thyssen, who was a convinced Nazi at the moment.[163] Why, Thyssen wondered, were people like Reichert so concerned about protecting exports when the home economy was threatened?[164] He saw only two viable options: Germany must either devalue its own currency or protect domestic industry through the control of exports and imports. Thyssen dismissed Reichert's fears that government intervention would undermine the German economy and fundamentally questioned the private economy's ability heal itself or rescue Germany from the crisis.[165] Reichert had simply failed to understand the new political situation, as far as Thyssen was concerned. Rationing and import restrictions in Germany would no longer lead to 'state socialism' as the chief business manager feared, but rather to an 'estate economy' (*Ständewirtschaft*) in which industrial groups would regulate trade themselves for the good of both their firms and the nation as a community.[166]

Faced with criticisms that closely reflected Nazi autarkic ideas, Reichert stood his ground and defended his own analysis before the members of his association.[167] He rejected Thyssen's call for a controlled economy as a recipe for economic disaster and the end of business autonomy. This, he argued, would replace the businessman with the bureaucrat.[168] Instead, the self-help and industrial cooperation that he had long advocated would save the iron and steel industry and the industrial economy in general.[169] The great danger that lurked in inviting the state into the private economy must be avoided above all else.[170] Although this was a little rich given the aid extended to the iron and steel industry by the Brüning government, Reichert categorically rejected the intrusion of politics into the economy as he had since 1918, putting him in direct conflict with the Nazi conception of the relationship between state and economy. Over the course of several drafts, the heated exchange between Reichert and Thyssen was all but expunged from the records of the meeting. However, even the published version contained a sharp statement that encapsulated Reichert's argument and warned industrialists not to 'clamour' (*schreien*) for state intervention in trade.[171] Even in late 1932, the VDESI and its members largely agreed with Reichert and decided to forward his report and conclusions to the government despite Thyssen's concerns.

This left Reichert and the VDESI is a curious position on the eve of the Nazi seizure of power. Although he was undoubtedly conservative, even reactionary, the chief business manager found himself out of step with the rising tide of radical politics. Even as the National Socialists called for an autarchic economy that would serve as the handmaiden of a purposeful state, Reichert fought a rearguard action to preserve the power and influence of private regulative bodies like his own. This was an arrogant and selfish position that prevented any real compromise in a polarized political climate, but it set him apart from those furthest to the right in spite of his authoritarian pedigree. Reichert was no democrat, but neither was he a Nazi at the beginning of 1933. This was not a unique problem. Although his circumstances were rather different from Karl Lange's, this position betwixt and between National Socialism and the liberal state was echoed in Lange's efforts in the machine building industry, leaving both men in equally awkward positions by January 1933.

The German Machine Builders Association was in many ways the child of the iron and steel industry, but it had embraced a very different model of capitalism by the end of the Weimar Republic. To counteract the heterogeneous nature of the industry, Lange's predecessor as chief business manager, Friedrich Fröhlich, began to bring a measure of unity to machine building through the VDMA itself, particularly by assembling extensive production, import and export statistics to help guide policy debates.[172] The key to the organization's success, however, lay in the demands of the First World War. The regulatory power acquired by the association made it all but essential for German machine builders to align themselves with the previously neglected organization.[173] As a result, the membership of the association increased dramatically from 246 firms in 1914 to 814 by the end of 1918.[174] The VDMA's central position in the machine building industry continued after the war, when the new government appointed Fröhlich as the head of the Central Office for Export Licensing in late October 1918.[175] The VDMA had managed to bring 90 per cent of the machine building industry under the umbrella of the association by 1923 and could now worry about rogue businesses operating outside of the organization rather than the majority of uninterested owners, but it was still undermined by the fact that it represented a wide variety of smaller producers.[176]

By the time Lange took over the organization it had thus already begun to mature into an important factor in German economic politics. Like Reichert, Karl Lange was the first in his family to enter industry or industrial politics. Born in 1889, he was only four years younger than Reichert, but his experience differed substantially from that of the iron and steel industry representative, making Lange a very different man. Lange's father was the director of a gymnasium in Solingen, but the future chief business manager hoped to pursue a military career. He gave this up in order to enter into an apprenticeship as a merchant in the German textile industry, and in 1912 he left Europe to take up a post with a German trading firm in Uruguay.[177] Lange returned to Germany in 1914 and, unlike Reichert, spent the war years as a soldier, ending his military career as a captain. After the armistice, he secured a position as a representative of the German sheet metalworking industry. By 1923 he was taken on by the VDMA, where he would spend the next thirty years of his life.[178] Less than one year after being hired, the 35-year-old Lange assumed the management of the association. Lange thus brought experience in export and trade (to say nothing of the army and trenches of the First World War) to his post as the representative of the machine building industry.

The organization Lange headed did not harbour the same traditional antagonism towards the political left as the iron and steel industry did. Machine builders lacked the large, impersonal, unskilled workforces and high fixed costs of the massive steel works, so they tended to have better relationships with their employees, were less fearful of the new republic and actively worked towards integrating industry and labour along the lines of the collaboration between industry and labour that helped to see Germany through the collapse of the imperial government.[179] Surprisingly, the association executive even called for the 'reconciliation of individualism with socialism through a press and speaking campaign'.[180] In sharp contrast to the VDESI, Lange and his organization were keenly interested in making settlement that underwrote the republic work.

In theory, Lange managed an organization that was tightly organized into an 'autocratic bureaucracy' along hierarchical lines.[181] The cumbersome 143 technical groups (*Fachgruppen*) were organized into twelve separate groups. Fifty-seven business managers shared responsibility for these organizations, contributing to the fifteen executive committees (*Vorstandsausschüsse*) that helped to steer this massive structure.[182] This cumbersome system invested enormous authority in the professional, bureaucratic management led by Lange, which could potentially give some direction to this confusing structure. These men were responsible for decisions affecting a staggering array of technical and business undertakings. However, following the dismemberment of the wartime export restrictions, Lange's organization lacked the effective authority that the iron and steel industry associations were able to muster. The enormous size and heterogeneity of the membership of the VDMA ruled out any real unanimity of interest or bureaucratic power.[183] This left Lange with a well-ordered organization that was nevertheless unable to really regulate the industry. Lange's answer to the real weaknesses of his organization was to streamline it and emphasize its technical expertise. By 1925, he had whittled the number of employees from 388 down to 77.[184] The number of technical associations was likewise reduced by seventeen between 1924 and 1925.[185] At the same time, Lange strengthened the VDMA Statistical Office by emphasizing the role of reliable data and appointing the exceptionally talented Alexander Rüstow to lead the unit.[186] At the head of a small staff of economists, Rüstow furnished Lange with information that enabled him to emphasize the importance of the machine industry and counter the arguments of heavy industry and the assumptions of the Reich bureaucracy on a wide variety of economic questions.[187]

Lange's own political, moral or economic convictions are difficult to pin down, if indeed they ever existed at all, but he, his staff and the VDMA publicly advocated economic liberalism throughout the period of the Weimar Republic. This suited the structure of the machine industry admirably. The fragmentation and competitiveness of the industry precluded the level of organization of the iron and steel industry and encouraged a greater confidence in its members' own ability to compete on an open market at home and in lucrative foreign markets.[188] This practical spur towards liberalism was supplemented by the work of the VDMA Statistical Office in particular. After his flirtation with socialism, Rüstow became a convinced liberal and increasingly respected economist who would eventually become an important figure in the re-establishment of the German economy after the Second World War as an editor of *Ordo* and contributor to the development of the theories that underwrote the social market economy.[189] In the 1920s Rüstow's cadre of economic analysts, including Wilhelm Utermann, Theodore Eschenberg, Hans Gestrich and Otto Viet, provided the press with a variety of articles and information arguing for a more liberalized trade policy that would help German machine builders compete on the international market.[190] Although the effect of this group is difficult to measure, the work of the VDMA did not go unnoticed, and even Friedrich von Hayek praised the association's defence of a liberal economy during the Weimar Republic and singled it out as one of the few important contributors to broader economic debates outside the halls of academia.[191]

This tendency towards liberalism translated into a number of more overtly political activities. The VDMA did not maintain a representative in the Reichstag as the VDESI did with Reichert, and Lange was not formally affiliated with a particular political party. However, he cultivated relationships with the parties of the centre and moderates on both the left and right, with particular emphasis on the German Democratic Party.[192] Lange was also able to exploit personal access to important representatives of the Centre Party.[193] This rather vague personal influence was supplemented by close relations with the major liberal papers during the 1920s.[194] Though this approach lacked the blunt force of the masters of the iron and steel industry, it also avoided some of the pitfalls of outright propaganda and enabled the VDMA to enter various debates over economic and trade policy through the back door. Indeed, the association's own research and analysis turned up again and again in discussions on policy, allowing it to punch above its weight in the rough and tumble of Weimar politics.[195]

Despite this commitment to the liberal economy, the VDMA still hoped to achieve a far-reaching reconciliation between workers and employers in Germany, but favoured a technocratic solution that sought to combine laissez-faire liberalism with many of the social demands of the left.[196] Whereas this had some of the same aims as later National Socialist ideas about the unity of the *Volk*, the methods were rather different. Lange and his organization seized on the contemporary rationalization discussion as the key to achieving the prosperity and ease that would heal the rift between left and right.[197] It is not particularly surprising that Lange and the VDMA found the rationalization movement seductive. The drive towards more efficient production affected machine building more profoundly than most other industries, and machine builders were at the centre of contemporary rationalization debates.[198] The machine building industry's importance to the rationalization movement also increased the importance of the bureaucratic leadership of the VDMA. A high degree of cooperation was necessary to achieve widespread standardization and efficiencies. To this end, the VDMA seized the initiative by issuing a series of Standards Instruction Letters and attempted to establish Standards Bureaus in most member plants.[199] Unfortunately, these efforts had limited success at best. Many machine builders were suspicious of the VDMA's efforts, and the organization was never able to establish or enforce systematic industrial standards.[200] However, in the absence of other, more successful bodies, Lange was able to portray the VDMA as being in the vanguard of both economic and social progress.[201] This provided the association with a convenient liberal solution to social tension that differentiated it from the more reactionary iron and steel industry, but also might have prepared it for collaboration with the National Socialist government in later years.

This moderation and apparent concern for labour was supplemented by Lange's willingness to reach out to unions and the Social Democrats more directly. The representatives of the finishing industries in general 'looked to the left' during the 1920s, at least in comparison to the iron and steel industry.[202] This does not mean that Lange or his subordinates embraced the ideology of the SPD, much less the KPD, but Lange continued to regard the moderate left as legitimate political actors throughout the Weimar Republic. This was most apparent during industry's tortured attempts to play a role in the formation of a stable coalition government, and had manifested itself even before the more famous Silverberg controversy over cooperation with the SPD.[203] In 1926, the coal magnate and vice president of the RdI, Paul Silverberg, drew bitter criticism from conservative heavy industrialists for suggesting the industry make its peace with the republic and moderate left. However, by that time, the willingness to enter into a practical relationship with labour was old hat to the VDMA, and Rüstow characterized Silverberg's thoughts as simply 'self-evident'.[204]

The political differences between the VDMA and VDESI went well beyond a dispute over the relative merits of particular coalition governments. The chief business managers of each of these organizations held very different views on the general legitimacy of the Weimar state that placed them on opposite sides of the larger political debates of the 1920s. This became evident during the annual assembly of VDMA members on 4 December 1925. During the proceedings, Lange used his own address to his members to lash out at the current government's inability to understand the contemporary economic crisis from a business perspective. Unlike so many of Reichert's outbursts, this did not translate into an attack on democracy itself but focused on ensuring the success of candidates friendly to business and industry, even if they were sometimes to be found on the political left.[205] Reichert, who had been invited to the meeting, was not pleased. He followed Lange's speech with a petulant attack on democratic government itself and argued that Germany required a more autocratic state that would keep elected politicians out of economic affairs.[206]

Whether he spoke for all machine builders or not, in the later years of the 1920s Lange pressed his attack on conservative authoritarian ideas through iron's old political allies in agriculture. For Lange, agricultural interests consistently stood in the way of rational economic policy, particularly in foreign trade.[207] Because industry 'fed' approximately 80 per cent more Germans through the wages paid than did agriculture, he argued, the interests of industry and industrial workers should predominate.[208] Rather than trying to protect an inefficient agricultural sector to feed the nation, Lange favoured using industrial wages and profits to pay for the import of cheaper foodstuffs.[209] Moreover, he scorned the value of agricultural production in a modern state, arguing that farming provided a substandard living.[210] In the hothouse political environment of the late Weimar Republic, this was a provocative attack on a significant portion of the political right. Although the Bismarkian alliance of 'Iron and Rye' had lost much of its potency, it continued to be closely associated with authoritarianism in Germany. His apparent indifference to the national or cultural importance of agriculture also differentiated Lange from the growing *völkische* movement. This was further underlined by the VDMA's attitude towards the campaign against the Young Plan: Lange and the VDMA pragmatically supported the plan as the 'lesser evil'.[211]

Lange also proved to be an extremely adept negotiator.[212] Nowhere was this more evident than in the conclusion of the so-called AVI agreement that tied the iron and steel and machine building industries together. Lange was the catalyst for bringing together representatives of the finishing industries in the AVI, which later lent its name to the final agreement.[213] At its most basic level, this agreement papered over the fundamental conflict over exports and the price of iron. Iron industrialists accepted very tangible concessions, agreeing to refund the difference between world and domestic market prices to the finishing industry in return for support for an iron tariff.[214] Reichert in particular hoped that it would produce a united front that would yoke the finishing industry to his members on a wide variety of issues including wages, social contributions, taxes and international trade in general.[215] Although heavy industry did in fact secure the support of the finishing industry on a number of important social questions, the VDMA proved troublingly independent. Reichert was enraged by what he saw as Lange's attempt to lobby against the iron tariff in 1926.[216] He likewise blamed Lange and the VDMA for a series of articles advocating free trade that furnished the SPD, KPD and German Democratic Party (DDP) with embarrassing technical arguments.[217]

Nevertheless, the practical benefits of the AVI agreement did draw the VDMA closer to the position of heavy industry and muted ideological distinctions. This undermined the association's conciliatory attitude towards labour and its good working relationship with the federal government, particularly by redirecting anger over the price of iron towards the state arbitration system.[218] More spectacularly, Lange himself was drawn into supporting heavy industry during the Ruhr Lockout of 1928 because of the VDMA's obligations under the AVI agreement.[219] The finishing industry was able to remain competitive on the export market and to pass high prices on to domestic customers, but manufacturers were divided over the usefulness of an agreement that undermined their commitment to lower tariffs and free competition.[220] The most unambiguous beneficiaries of the agreement were in fact Lange and the VDMA itself. As the pre-eminent representative of the finishing industry, the association was assigned responsibility for evaluation and administration of rebate claims.[221] Having to apply to Lange in order to receive rebates increased the association's administrative authority substantially and placed the chief business manager at the centre of the export interests in his industry.[222] It was also an early indication that Lange would trade ideology for practical benefits when the opportunity presented itself.

Lange may have seemed like a more moderate, flexible and even likable character than Reichert in the 1920s, but he was also more vulnerable to the pressures of the economic crisis and less confident about his own authority. The international economic crisis that began in 1929 had a profound impact on the firms that made up the German machine building industry. After a period of sustained growth and expansion that peaked in 1928 and 1929, the German machine builders, like so many other industrialists, saw both their sales and profits dry up by the beginning of 1930.[223] In the peak year of 1928, Lange's members sold 3,383,266 tons of product for a total of 3,709,625,000 RM. By 1933, when the very depths of the crisis had already passed, sales had sunk to a mere 993,000 tons and sold at a value of 1,483,080,000 RM.[224] This represented a decrease in sales of over 50 per cent, and the problems faced by the industry were compounded by the fact that the average price per ton of German-made machines dropped by almost 63 RM. Although this was not true of the price of the larger machine tools, which actually increased by over 38 RM per ton, both the total value and weight of this key sector of the industry were cut in half.[225] German exports of finished goods actually fared relatively better than those of other major exporting states, and Germany took the lead in the sale of these products for the first time in 1930, albeit at levels much reduced from those of 1928,[226] but increasing their share in a rapidly contracting global market was cold comfort to ailing machine builders. Domestic sales of machines, which still represented 66 per cent of the industry's total output in 1929, likewise contracted during the crisis, reaching 24.5 per cent of 1928 levels by 1932.[227]

Unlike the great concerns in iron and steel that dominated the VDESI that were 'too big to fail,' the smaller and medium-sized firms in the machine building industry faced the very real prospect of bankruptcy in large numbers.[228] Moreover, smaller firms did not have the luxury of shedding workers in subsidiary shops in order to secure core operations.[229] The travails of the finishing industry were compounded by the fact that iron and steel producers were able to prop up the price of domestic iron through their network of cartels and regulated prices until late 1931.[230] This situation was made even worse by producers' threats to pull out of the AVI agreement, thereby forcing the finishing industry to purchase materials at inflated prices in order to sell goods on a severely deflated international market.[231] The imminent danger of bankruptcy and disgrace led a growing number of small businessmen and manufacturers to turn towards the radical alternative of National Socialism.[232] While this tendency was less pronounced in the machine building industry than, for instance, the cutlery manufacturers around Solingen, a number of VDMA members were attracted to the NSDAP during the depression.[233] Perhaps most notably, Paul Pleiger, the owner of a small machine plant who would later become a major thorn in the side of the iron and steel industry as the head of the state iron works in the Nazi period, joined the NSDAP in 1932 and became *Ortsgruppenleiter* in Sprockhoevel.[234]

This larger turn towards the right was reflected in a shift in the policies of the VDMA itself. Lange laid out the limits of the VDMA's willingness to collaborate with the moderate left during the debate over *Wirtschaftsdemokratie* (economic democracy) in 1929. This would, Lange argued, remove both the voice of the entrepreneur and the worker from business decisions to be replaced by a centralized 'industrial democracy' that would bear little responsibility for the welfare of either the firm or its workers.[235] As a 'modern man who accepts the new hard-won ethic of today out of inner conviction', Lange suggested that economic democracy sounded appealing.[236] 'Does not the rejection of economic democracy', he asked sardonically, 'uncover the black soul of entrepreneurs and capitalism'?[237] He followed these conciliatory gestures with an attack on the left that was considerably more pointed than it had been in the past. He likened the proposed system of economic democracy to that of Soviet Russia and attributed the oppression, poverty and want in what should otherwise be a prosperous nation to precisely the same ideas.[238] By September 1929, Lange was characterizing the threat of economic democracy as a threat to the future of capitalism itself.[239] This kind of alarmist exaggeration was hardly unusual amongst businessmen and industrialists in the Weimar Republic, but for the usually more circumspect VDMA it was heady stuff that represented the beginning of a notable shift towards a policy of confrontation.

This was accompanied by a shift in the VDMA's focus from an emphasis on the effects of high material costs to a widespread criticism of wage levels and the role of trade unions and the state in Germany's economic crisis. By November 1931 Lange had come to acknowledge that the current crisis in Germany reflected the collapse of the international economy. Germany, he argued, was a special case that laboured under particularly unsuitable conditions of its own making.[240] Above all, the VDMA blamed the increase in wages over the course of the 1920s for the current economic crisis.[241] Responsibility for the crisis therefore rested on the shoulders of both the trade unions and an arbitration system that inflated wages beyond levels that could be supported by the market. The market was thus unable to function, and the normal pressure on wages that would accompany unemployment played a 'remarkably small role' in determining contracts.[242] This emphasis on wages made good sense to the VDMA in late 1931. The price of iron, which had previously been so troubling to the machine building industry, had begun to collapse despite the best efforts of iron and steel industrialists and their associations, so it was unsurprising that Lange and the VDMA would turn their attention towards wages instead. In doing so the association moved further from its traditionally conciliatory role to a more open conflict with the trade unions and the relatively labour friendly policies of the Weimar Republic. In the context of the social and political crisis that followed on the heels of the economic collapse, the VDMA took a position that placed it in opposition to the efforts and effects of the parliamentary governments of the late Weimar period. However, unlike heavy industry, Lange and the VDMA hoped that Brüning's extra-parliamentary government would somehow lead to an open, free market economy that would undermine the power of both the state and the cartels.

Lange's increasing defence of economic liberalism, combined with the abandonment of the policy of compromise, closely reflects Alexander Rüstow's developing 'ordoliberalism'. Though Rüstow might only have been groping towards the economic theory that would characterize postwar Germany, he was already envisioning such a combination in a strong state that would oversee 'clean competition' between businesses as an ideal.[243] This version of liberalism fit in very well with the structures and problems of the machine industry on the eve of the economic crisis. However, his way of arguing that the compromises necessary in a state that tried to represent everyone through parliamentary democracy precluded the development of sound economic or social policy was not so different from Reichert's. By 1929, Rüstow was already calling for a 'strong state' that would stand up to the demands of fractious interest groups. Such a state would be led by a chancellor who would enjoy a period of almost dictatorial power that would allow him to rewrite the political compromises of Weimar.[244]

Given Lange's relative reluctance to engage in public politics, it is difficult to ascertain how important Rüstow's ideas were in his relationship with the last governments of the Weimar period. Lange maintained personal contacts with Brüning during his chancellorship,[245] but it is unclear whether he sided with the moderates in the RdI and Chambers of Commerce who opposed Brüning's authoritarian tendencies but supported deflation, or whether he favoured Brüning's turn towards authoritarian government.[246] However, as the economic crisis deepened, the industrialist president of the VDMA, Wolfgang Reuter, joined the chorus of voices calling for a 'strong man' to rule without a parliamentary majority at the RdI meeting of 25 June 1930.[247] For him, the strengthening of the chancellor through the Reichspresident was the last chance to end the crisis in both politics and the economy.[248] The threat that this posed to democracy did not concern Rüstow overmuch, as he saw the foundation of a 'real' democracy as residing in the vague 'unity of state and Volk', which came dangerously close to the ideas of the extreme right.[249] Dieter Haselbach in particular argues that the position of ordoliberals like Rüstow 'can be read as a theoretical legitimation of the presidential governments of the last phase of Weimar'.[250] Indeed, Rüstow deepened his flirtation with authoritarianism through a close relationship with Schleicher throughout the crisis and was considered a strong potential candidate for the post of minister of economics in the last Weimar cabinet.[251]

At a minimum, this is a strong indication that the long-term economic problems of the Weimar Republic and acute crisis of the depression had pushed several of the most senior representatives of the VDMA away from the democratic compromises that had characterized it in the early years of the republic, and towards the motley and growing group of thinkers on the right who no longer had any use for democratic government. That said, Rüstow's calls for a 'strong man' in politics were sometimes confused, and he believed that a limited dictatorship would somehow moderate German politics by undermining the demands of the farthest right as well as the radical left.[252] Stranger still, this turn towards the right was accompanied by an increasingly pugnacious defence of free trade and economic liberalism that infuriated the *völkische* movement and National Socialists, who were calling for varying degrees of protectionism or even autarky.

Lange's solution to the industrial conflicts of the Weimar Republic lay in the establishment of 'organized economic freedom', a concept that appears to have been as unwieldy as its name.[253] It was also as self-serving as Reichert's 'natural economy', though not as exclusive. Lange sadly conceded that a return to the unfettered individualistic liberalism of manchesterism, for instance, was no longer tenable in Germany.[254] However, his own 'organized economic freedom' still sharply restricted the role of the state, leaving the determination of even social questions like economically feasible wages and social contributions to autonomous industrial organizations.[255] On the surface, this looked very much like Reichert's calls for industrial self-regulation that would supplant the role of the state in economic life, but Lange's proposed organization would be significantly weaker than that envisioned by the chief business manager of the VDESI. Lange feared that the relatively extensive cartelization in heavy industry in particular had encouraged a kind of 'collectivism' in industry that undermined its entrepreneurial spirit and practice.[256] The sort of organization Lange saw as necessary to the development of a healthy economy looked, in fact, very much like his own. These associations would provide guidance and assistance to individual firms that would help them compete more effectively, rather than guarantee prices or distribution.[257] In effect, 'organized economic freedom' would look much more free than organized.

In 1930 and 1931, Lange began to lay out a comprehensive defence of the benefits of this liberal economy and to counter the critics of international trade on the radical right. He paid particular attention to the allegation that he and others like him were mere 'export fanatics', unable to appreciate the real cost of international trade to Germany as a nation.[258] International trade relationships showed, Lange countered, that the German export industry's ability to expand was remarkable compared to that of other states.[259] He likewise attacked the assertion that during the crisis Germany was being 'bled white' by excessive imports, instead characterizing foreign goods and investments as a necessary shot in the arm for the German economy.[260] Moreover, he reminded his audience that periods of an active balance of trade generally correspond to poor economic conditions in Germany.²⁶¹ Finally, he warned critics that inland prices were more closely tied to exports than the protectionists cared to admit and that a decline in international trade would be accompanied by a decline in domestic profits as well.²⁶²

These arguments – seemingly made up of equal parts of rational analysis and self-interest – naturally led Lange to argue in favour of a free (or at least more free) trade policy. For Lange, the biggest obstacles to both successful foreign trade and economic recovery were Germany's own trade policies,²⁶³ and he worried about the increase in autarkic ideas amongst members of the Reichstag.²⁶⁴ These arguments culminated in a demand for free trade as a way out of the crisis. 'For years', he argued, 'all rational economists (*Wirtschaftler*) in Europe have fought for the easing of goods traffic between European states'.²⁶⁵ Trade, Lange argued, was the surest way out of the economic (and by implication, political) crisis.

This emphasis on exports led Lange to turn his ire on heavy industry, and he began to lump the practices of producers' cartels in with the evils of the 'political wages' awarded by arbitration committees in an attack that Reichert must have found deeply irritating.²⁶⁶ The president of the VDESI, Poensgen, noted with some dismay that the two industries' efforts to build a common front over the past decade had come to naught, and that the iron and steel and finishing industries were farther apart in 1930 than they ever had been in the past.²⁶⁷ It also brought the VDMA to the attention of radicals on the extreme right.

Writing in the radical journal *Die Tat,* Hans Zehrer penned an attack on the value of international trade that was subsequently picked up by the *Vossische Zeitung* in August 1930.²⁶⁸ In this article, Zehrer followed Werner Sombart, arguing that the era of international trade was inevitably coming to an end, and advocating a return to self-sufficiency.²⁶⁹ This work and similar criticisms of the system of international trade by Hammer and von Thorn in particular were picked up and integrated into National Socialist ideology.²⁷⁰ These National Socialist ideas that 'mixed together anti-capitalist and neo-mercantilist ideas' were a direct challenge to the conception of a liberal economy in the service of international trade expounded by Lange and his organization.²⁷¹ In early 1932 this conflict was brought home to the VDMA through another article in *Die Tat.* Writing as 'Wilhelm Wunderlich', Ferdinand Friedrich Zimmerman attacked Rüstow and the VDMA specifically as 'spiders' forming a liberal bureaucratic elite that lurked behind industrial organizations in the republic.²⁷² The VDMA was singled out as the very 'soul of the export illusion'.²⁷³ Lange met these criticisms with an increasingly weary defence of the value of exports and of free trade.²⁷⁴ However, he also noted with resignation that the widespread belief that 'all nations' in the world had already erected a wall of trade barriers had come to dominate popular thinking in Germany.²⁷⁵ The finishing industry was forced to fight on several fronts.²⁷⁶ On one hand, it faced the undeniable fact that the actions of most governments had made trade between states much more difficult. On the other, it had to contend with protectionist and autarkic feelings at home that further undermined world trade.²⁷⁷

This left the VDMA in a curious position. It had previously occupied the middle ground between the demands of the left and right. In a sense, this reflected the uncomfortable, but often workable, compromises of Weimar democracy. However, as the onset of the depression put pressure on its member firms in the machine building industry, the association began to shuffle awkwardly to the right. Like the representatives of heavy industry, Lange and his organization attacked both the trade unions and the legislation that had enabled the republic to placate the moderate left. This was accompanied by an attack on parliamentary democracy and a turn towards authoritarianism that marked an important departure for Lange and the VDMA and placed the association on the same side of the great political debates of the late Weimar period as the right-wing extremists in heavy industry, the DNVP and even the NSDAP. However, with this political reorientation came an increasing defence of the liberal economy in the face of both the 'organized capitalism' of heavy industry and the increasing demands for autarkic policies from the far right, which made the organization essentially incompatible with the Nazi Party. It thus found itself to be neither fish nor fowl. By abandoning the traditional centre, the VDMA undermined the regime that was most likely to meet its own needs and left itself without any of the major partners that had seen it through previous crises. This strategy likewise undermined the association's role in the political life of the late Weimar Republic, leaving it in a precarious position when the system finally collapsed in 1933. By the time the Nazis seized power, neither the VDMA nor the VDESI was well suited for the changes that were about to sweep Germany. Reichert and Lange would now have to choose which aspects of their own ideas and practices were worth defending in the face of a troubling new regime, and which could be pragmatically dispensed with - or at least shelved for the time being.

Notes

1. Turner, *German Big Business and the Rise of Hitler*.
2. Historischen Kommission bei der Bayerischen Akademie der Wissenschaften. 1982. *Neue Deutsche Biographie*. 13, Berlin: Duncker & Humblot, 313.
3. F. Pudor. 1974. *Männer der frühre deutschen stahlwirtschaftlichen Verbände*, Düsseldorf: Verlag Stahleisen, 33.
4. Staatsarchiv Nürnberg (hereafter SAN) Rep. 502, VI. KV-Anklage Interrogations R 48, 'Erklarung unter Eid, 7.7.1947, Jakob Reichert' 10; SAN Rep. 502, VI. KV-Anklage Interrogations R 48, 'Vernehmung des Dr. Jakob Wilh. Reichert am 17. Mai 1947 von 10:00–11:45', 15; Pudor, *Männer der frühre deutschen stahlwirtschaftlichen Verbände*, 32.

5. Stiftung Rheinisch-Westfälisches Wirtschaftsarchiv zu Köln (hereafter R-WW) Historisches Archiv der Gutehoffnungshütte (hereafter GHH): Nachlass Paul Reusch 400101290/141: Dr J.W. Reichert, Berlin, 'Geschichte der deutschen eisenschaffenden Industrie', 'Reusch an Woltmann 27.1.1948' and GHH Nachlass Reusch 400101222/2 'Reusch an Reichert 8.11.1913' 1.
6. Feldman, 'Industrieverbände und Wirtschaftsmacht', 135.
7. R-WW, GHH: Nachlass Reusch 400101222/2, 'Reusch an Reichert 8.11.1913'; H. Booms, 'Zur Geschichte und Ordnung des Bestandes', in 'Findbücher zu Beständen des Bundesarchivs: Bestand R 13 I, Verein Deutscher Eisen- und Stahlindustrieller/ Wirtschaftsgruppe Eisenschaffende Industrie', Koblenz: Bundesarchiv, Manuskript, 1972 VII, VI; K.H. Pohl. 1976. *Weimars Wirtschaft und die Außenpolitik der Republik, 1924–1926: Vom Dawes-Plan zum internationalen Eisenpakt*, Düsseldorf: Droste, 76.
8. Feldman, 'Industrieverbände und Wirtschaftsmacht', 135.
9. G. D. Feldman. 1977. *Iron and Steel in the German Inflation, 1916–1923*, Princeton: Princeton University Press, 43.
10. Ibid., 44.
11. Feldman and Nocken, 'Trade Associations and Economic Power', 418; Grübler, *Die Spitzenverbände der Wirtschaft und das erste Kabinett Brüning*, 34.
12. A.J Horkheimer and F.C. Langdon. 1968. *Business Associations and the Financing of Political Parties: A Comparative Study of the Evolution of Practices in Germany, Norway and Japan*, The Hague: Martinus Nijhoff, 26.
13. Köhler, *Die stahlwirtschaftlichen Organisationen im Jubiläumsjahr 1974*, 20.
14. Hans Dichgans. 1974. 'Stahl und Politik', *Stahl und Eisen* 94. (21) (*Sonderaufgaben*), 65.
15. Donovan Archive, 53. 057 'Offices of Strategic Services, Research and Analysis Branch. Biographical Report: Reichert, Jakob Wilhelm', 1; Pudor, *Männer der frühre deutschen stahlwirtschaftlichen Verbände*, 33.
16. J.A. Leopold. 1977. *Alfred Hugenberg: The Radical Nationalist Campaign against the Weimar Republic*, New Haven: Yale University Press, 41. See also H. Beck. 2008. *The Fateful Alliance: German Conservatives and the Nazis in 1933, The Machtergreifung in a New Light*, New York: Berghahn Books, 53–69.
17. H. Weiß and P. Hoser (eds). 1989. *Die Deutschnationalen und die Zerstörung der Weimarer Republik: Aus dem Tagebuch von Reinhold Quaatz, 1928–1933*, Munich: R. Oldenbourg Verlag, 33ff.
18. Leopold, *Alfred Hugenberg*, 41.
19. Ibid., 44.
20. J. Reichert. 1922. *Rathenaus Reparationspolitik: Eine kritische Studie*, Berlin: August Scherl GmbH, 21.
21. Ibid., 189.
22. Ibid., 189, 206. For a remarkably similar attack on Hilferding see 'Dr Reichert (DNV)' 1930. *Verhandlungen des Reichstags: Stenographische Berichte und Drucksachen*, Bd. 425. Druck und Verlag der Reichsdruckerei. 96. Sitzung. 26. Juni 1929. 2971–77,2971.
23. 'Dr. Reichert" 1930. *Verhandlungen des Reichstags: Stenographische Berichte und Drucksachen*, Bd. 427. 174. Sitzung. 27. Mai 1930. 5404.
24. BAB R 13/I 104 Bd. 26. 'Aufzeichnung über die am 12. Februar 1931 abgehaltene Sitzung des Hauptvorstandes und des Fachgruppenausschusses', 26.
25. J. Reichert. 1931. 'Der Standpunkt eines deutschen Industriellen in französischer Betrachtung', *Stahl und Eisen* 51(49) (3 December), 1524.
26. R. Evans. 2004. *The Coming of the Third Reich*, New York: Penguin Press, 238–39.
27. Vereinigung für freie Wirtschaft, 'Die marxistische Front', in BAB R 13 I/104 Bd. 26. 191–94.

28. 'Schreiben von Wilhelm Reichert an Friedrich Flick vom 19.10.1931', in Czichon, *Wer verhalf Hitler zur Macht?* 61.
29. H. Kim. 1977. *Industrie, Staat und Wirtschaftspolitik: Die konjunkturpolitische Diskussion in der Endphase der Weimarer Republik 1930–1932/1933*, Berlin: Duncker & Humblot, 209.
30. BAB R 13 I/202, Bd. 19. Heft 2. 'Aufzeichnung über die am 5. Oktober im Gasthof Esplanade abgehaltene Sitzung des Hauptvorstandes und des Fachgruppenausschusses', 184.
31. J. Reichert. 1924. 'Die "unpolitische" Reparationspolitik', in K. Helfferich and J. Reichert, *Das Zweite Versailles*, Berlin: Deutschnationale Schriftvertriebstelle, 26.
32. 'Stresemann's Diary: December 16th, 1925', in Sutton, *Gustav Stresemann*, 364–65.
33. *Verhandlungen des Reichstages*, 135. Sitzung. Marz 6, 1930 Bd. 427. Pp. 4163–70, here 4170.
34. *Verhandlungen des Reichstages*, 96. Sitzung, 26 Juni 1929 Bd. 425. Pp. 2971–77, here 2973; J. Reichert. 1931. 'Die Börsenbewertung führender in- und ausländischer Eisenaktien in den Jahren 1925 bis 1930', *Stahl und Eisen* 51(6) (5 February), 171–72.
35. J. Reichert. 1931. 'Deutsch-französische Aussprache über die Lage der deutschen Industrie', *Stahl und Eisen* 51(42) (15 October), 1297–1299, here 1297, 1298; Reichert, 'Der Standpunkt eines deutschen Industriellen in französischer Betrachtung', 1523–24.
36. BAB R 13/I 105 Bd. 27. 'Aufzeichnung über die am 17. November 1932 abgehaltene Sitzung des Hauptvorstandes und des Fachgruppenausschusses', 6.
37. *Verhandlungen des Reichstags*, 174. Sitzung. 27.5.1930. Bd. 427, pp. 5402–7, here 5407.
38. Eduard Stinnes said the same thing about his father, Hugo, and coal. See E. Stinnes. 1979. 'A Genius in Chaotic Times: A Conversation between E. Stinnes and Andreas Kohlschütter of *Die Zeit*', Bern: OFDAG, CH-3172 Niederwangen, 19.
39. Schneider, *Unternehmer und Demokratie*, 19.
40. Hans-Hermann Hartwich, *Arbeitsmarkt, Verbände und Staat 1918–1933*, 9.
41. G.D. Feldman and I. Steinisch. 1985. *Industrie und Gewerkschaften 1918–1924: Die überforderte Zentralarbeitsgemeinschaft*, Stuttgart: Deutsche Verlags-Anstalt GmbH, 34; A. Gladen. 1974. 'Probleme der staatlichen Sozialpolitik in der Weimarer Republik', in H.J. Varain (ed.), *Interessenverbände in Deutschland*, Cologne: Kiepenheuer & Witsch, 251.
42. Schneider, *Unternehmer und Demokratie*, 19.
43. Ibid., 56; Weisbrod, 'Heavy Industry in Weimar Germany', 249; Pohl, *Weimars Wirtschaft und die Außenpolitik, 1924–1926*, 88.
44. C. Maier. 1975. *Recasting Bourgeois Europe: Stabilization in France, Germany and Italy in the Decade after World War I*, Princeton: Princeton University Press, 58.
45. K. Tribe. 1995. '*Die Vernunft des List*: National Economy and the Critique of Cosmopolitan Economy', in K. Tribe, *Strategies of Economic Order: German Economic Discourse, 1750–1950*, Cambridge: Cambridge University Press, 32–65. 44.
46. BAB R 13/I 104 Bd. 26. 'Aufzeichnung über die am 19. Februar 1930 abgehaltene Sitzung des Hauptvorstandes und des Fachgruppenausschusses', 6.
47. BAB R 13/I 104 Bd.26. 'Aufzeichnung über die am 12. Februar 1931 abgehaltene Sitzung des Hauptvorstandes und des Fachgruppenausschusses', 6.
48. BAB R 13/I 105 Bd. 27. 'Aufzeichnung über die am 17. November 1932 abgehaltene Sitzung des Hauptvorstandes und des Fachgruppenausschusses', 24, 16, 22, 25.
49. BAB R 13/I 104 Bd.26. 'Aufzeichnung über die am 12. Februar 1931 abgehaltene Sitzung des Hauptvorstandes und des Fachgruppenausschusses', 6.
49. BAB R 13/I 105 Bd. 27. 'Aufzeichnung über die am 17. November 1932 abgehaltene Sitzung des Hauptvorstandes und des Fachgruppenausschusses' 16–26, 26.

50. Neebe, *Großindustrie, Staat und NSDAP 1930–1933*, 151, 265 fn. 94; BAB R 13/I 105 Bd. 27. 'Aufzeichnung über die am 17. November 1932 abgehaltene Sitzung des Hauptvorstandes und des Fachgruppenausschusses', 34–35; Michael Wolffsohn. 1977. *Industrie und Handwerk im Konflikt mit staatlicher Wirtschaftspolitik? Studien zur Politik der Arbeitsbeschaffung in Deutschland, 1930–1934*, Berlin: Duncker & Humblot, 85.
51. Kim, *Industrie, Staat und Wirtschaftspolitik*, 222; Neebe, *Großindustrie, Staat und NSDAP 1930–1933*, 151.
52. Reichert, *Rathenaus Reparationspolitik*, 279.
53. BAB R 13 I/ 255 Bd. 1 'Verstädigungsmöglichkeiten zwischen der deutschen und der französischen Eisenindustrie', December 1922, 16.
54. Ibid., 'einer widernatürlichen… Zerreißung der eisenschaffenden Industrie', 16.
55. BAB, R 13 I/255, Bd. 1, 'Die deutsch-französische Interessenverflechtung von Dr. Reichert M.d.R.' (c. 15 March 1923), pp. 175–80, here 176.
56. BAB R 13 I/ 255 Bd. 1 'Verständigungsmöglichkeiten zwischen der deutschen und der französischen Eisenindustrie', December 1922, 23–24.
57. See Feldman, *Iron and Steel*, 92; BAB R 13 I/255 Bd. 1 Pt. 3g. 'Die Verständigungsmöglichkeiten zwischen der deutschen und der französischen Eisenindustrie: Die Stellung der deutschen Eisenindustrie zu den Verständigungsvorschlägen', 250 in BAB pagination. See also Stinnes, 'A Genius in Chaotic Times', 29; G. Feldman. 1997. *The Great Disorder: Politics, Economics and Society in the German Inflation, 1914–1924*, New York: Oxford University Press, 314, 257; M. Hankey. 1972. 'To Lady Hankey, 13.7.1920', in S. Roskill (ed.), *Hankey: Man of Secrets, Vol. II, 1919–1931*, London: William Collins Sons, 178; BAB R 13 I/255 Bd. 1 Pt. 3g. 'Die Verständigungsmöglichkeiten zwischen der deutschen und der französischen Eisenindustrie: Der Vorschlag von Francis Delsi', 246–47, here 57; 'Besprechung über die Währungssanierung, 18. August 1923' in K. Erdmann. 1978. *Die Kabinette Stresemann I und II*. vol. 1, Boppard am Rhein: Boldt, pp. 23–28, here 25.
58. See, e.g., 'Paul Frölich's speech to the Reichstag on Friday, 10 August 1923', 380. Sitzung *Verhandlungen des Reichstags*, Bd. 361. 11805–6; BAB R 13 I/255 Bd. 1. 'Reichert an Reusch, Btr.: Verhandlungen zwischen der deutschen und französischen Industrie. Ihr Schrb. vom 23', 149 in BAB pagination.
59. Weisbrod, *Schwerindustrie*, 274–75.
60. BAB R 13 I/609 *Handakten Dr. J. Reichert, Hauptgeschäftsführer (seit 1913) des Vereins und der Wirtschaftsgruppe mit Vortragsmanuskripten, Aufsätzen, Zeitungsartikeln und Rezensionen, vorwiegend über Fragen der Eisen- und Stahlindustrie*; J. Reichert. 1924. 'Die 'unpolitische' Reparationspolitik', in K. Helfferich and J. Reichert, *Das Zweite Versailles*. Berlin: Deutschnationale Schriftvertriebsstelle, 16–26. 17.
61. See ibid., 100–109; BAB R 8099/580 *Tätigkeit der VDMA in der Revolution. Industrie-organisation (Reichsarbeitsgemeinschaft)*. 'Niederschrift der am Donnerstag, den 12. Juni gehaltenen Aussprache über Sebstverwaltungskörper und Zwangswirtschaft', 50; Reichert, *Rathenaus Reparationspolitik*, 19–26. For Rathenau's own peculiar view of the economy and society, see W. Rathenau. 1918. *Die Neue Wirtschaft*, Berlin: S. Fischer Verlag.
62. BAB R 13/I 615 'Die deutsche Wirtschaft im Weltkrieg 1914–1918', 2; Feldman, *Iron and Steel*, 60; Donovan Archive, 53. 057 'Offices of Strategic Services, Research and Analysis Branch. Biographical Report: Reichert, Jakob Wilhelm', 1; Pudor, *Männer der frühen deutschen stahlwirtschaftlichen Verbände*, 33; C. Böhret. 1975. 'Institutionalisierte Einflußwege der Verbände in der Weimarer Republik', in J. Varain (ed.), *Interessenverbände in Deutschland*, Cologne: Kiepenhauer & Witsch, 218.
63. Feldman and Nocken, 'Trade Associations and Economic Power', 425.

64. Feldman, *Iron and Steel*, 196–97.
65. Reichert, *Rathenaus Reparationspolitik*, 27. See also Jakob Reichert. 1919. *Rettung aus der Valutanot*, Berlin: Zeitfragen-Verlag.
66. Feldman, *Iron and Steel*, 135.
67. G.D. Feldman. 1974. 'Wirtschafts- und sozialpolitische Probleme der deutschen Demobilmachung 1918/19', in Mommsen et al. (eds), *Industrielles System und politische Entwicklung in der Weimarer Republik*, Düsseldorf: Droste Verlag, 626; Feldman, *Iron and Steel*, 206.
68. Feldman, *Iron and Steel*, 205.
69. Ibid., 140.
70. Ibid., 203.
71. Ibid., BAB R 13 I/ 255 Bd. 1 'Verständigungsmöglichkeiten zwischen der deutschen und der französischen Eisenindustrie', December 1922, 17–18; Weisbrod, *Schwerindustrie*, 278.
72. Jakob Reichert. 1936. 'Ein Rückblick auf das zehnjährige Bestehen der internationalen Stahlverbände', *Stahl und Eisen* 26(48), 1432. See also U. Nocken, 'Inter-Industrial Conflicts and Alliances as Exemplified by the AVI-Agreement', 693. The AVI Agreement, an extremely important development in the relationship between iron and steel industrialists and their counterparts in manufacturing, will be addressed further below.
73. Pohl, *Weimars Wirtschaft und die Außenpolitik, 1924–1926*, 233–34, 201; E. Hexner. 1943. *The International Steel Cartel*, Chapel Hill: University of North Carolina Press, 73.
74. Jakob Reichert. 1927. 'Die Festländische Rohstahlgemeinschaft', in *Weltwirtschaftliches Archiv: Chronik und Archivalien*, 25(1927 I), Jena: Gustav Fischer, 355*.
75. Ibid., 340*, Jakob Reichert, 'Ein Rückblick auf das zehnjährige Bestehen der internationalen Stahlverbände', 1432; Hexner, *The International Steel Cartel*, 71; C. Wurm. 1993. *Business, Politics and International Relations: Steel, Cotton and International Cartels in British Politics, 1924–1939*, Cambridge: Cambridge University Press, 15; Reichert, 'Die Festländische Rohstahlgemeinschaft', 371*, 357*.
76. Reichert, 'Die Festländische Rohstahlgemeinschaft', 372*.
77. W. L. Patch, Jr. 1998. *Heinrich Brüning and the Dissolution of the Weimar Republic*, Cambridge: Cambridge University Press, 95; BAB R 13/I 104 Bd. 26 'Aufzeichnung über die am 29. Oktober 1930 abgehaltene Sitzung des Hauptvorstandes und des Fachgruppenausschusses', 4–5.
78. Patch, *Heinrich Brüning and the Dissolution of the Weimar Republic*, 180.
79. BAB R 13/I 104 Bd. 26 'Aufzeichnung über die am 29. Oktober 1930 abgehaltene Sitzung des Hauptvorstandes und des Fachgruppenausschusses', 6.
80. Ibid., 6–7.
81. BAB R 13/I 104 Bd.26. 'Aufzeichnung über die am 12. Februar 1931 abgehaltene Sitzung des Hauptvorstandes und des Fachgruppenausschusses', 23–26.
82. Jacob Reichert. 1931. 'Wirtschaftskrise und Eisenverbrauch', *Stahl und Eisen* 51(22) (28 May), 675.
83. Jacob Reichert. 1932. 'Walzeisen-Weltmarktpreise und internationale Verbände', *Stahl und Eisen* 52(26) (30 June), 634.
84. Ibid.
85. Ibid.
86. Ibid., 636.
87. Jakob Reichert. 1932. 'Das britische Weltreich auf dem Wege zur Selbstversorgung mit Eisen und Stahl', *Stahl und Eisen* 52(45) (10 November), 1094.

88. BAB R 13/I 105 Bd. 27. 'Aufzeichnung über die am 17. November 1932 abgehaltene Sitzung des Hauptvorstandes und des Fachgruppenausschusses', 19.
89. See, e.g., his opposition to Briand in *Verhandlungen des Reichstags*, 174. Sitzung. 27.5.1930. Bd. 427. Pp. 5402–7, here 5504–7; BAB R 13/I 105 Bd. 27. 'Aufzeichnung über die am 17. November 1932 abgehaltene Sitzung des Hauptvorstandes und des Fachgruppenausschusses', 8; BAB R 13/I 105 Bd. 27. 'Aufzeichnung über die am 17. November 1932 abgehaltene Sitzung des Hauptvorstandes und des Fachgruppenausschusses', 26–27.
90. Turner, *German Big Business and the Rise of Hitler*, 254.
91. Weisbrod, *Schwerindustrie*, 31.
92. T. Balderston. 1993. *The Origins and Course of the German Economic Crisis: 1923–1932*, Berlin: Haude & Spencer, 64.
93. Weisbrod, *Schwerindustrie*, 49.
94. Patch, *Heinrich Brüning and the Dissolution of the Weimar Republic*, 179; Weisbrod, *Schwerindustrie*, 56.
95. Jakob Reichert. 1930. 'Die Leistungsfähigkeit der deutschen Stahlindustrie', *Stahl und Eisen* 50(50) (11 December), 1744; BAB R 13/I 104 'Aufzeichnung über die am 12. Februar 1931, 10 Uhr vormittags im Gasthof Esplanade zu Berlin abgehaltene Sitzung des Hauptvorstandes und des Fachgruppenausschusses', 6, 5.
96. BAB R 13/I 104 'Aufzeichnung über die am 12. Februar 1931, 10 Uhr vormittags im Gasthof Esplanade zu Berlin abgehaltene Sitzung des Hauptvorstandes und des Fachgruppenausschusses', 12.
97. Ibid., 13.
98. Reichert, 'Wirschaftskrise und Eisenverbrauch', 672.
99. Statistische Gemeinschaftsarbeit Nordwestliche Gruppe VdESI. 1933 *Statistisches Jahrbuch für die Eisen- und Stahlindustrie 1933*, Düsseldorf: Verlag Stahleisen mbH, 203.
100. Ibid., 197.
101. H. James. 1986. *The German Slump: Politics and Economics 1924–1936*. Oxford: Clarendon Press 156.
102. Reichert, 'Walzeisen-Weltmarktpreise und internationale Verbände', 634.
103. BAB R 13/I 105 Bd. 27 'Aufzeichnung über die am 17. November 1932 , 10 Uhr vormittags im Gasthof Esplanade zu Berlin abgehaltene Sitzung des Hauptvorstandes und des Fachgruppenausschusses', 42.
104. 'Rede von dem Abgeordneten Dr. Reichert, 135. Sitzung 6. März 1930', in *Verhandlungen des Reichstags*, Bd. 427. Pp. 4163–70, here 4168; 'Rede von dem Abgeordneten Dr. Reichert, 174. Sitzung 27. Mai 1930', in *Verhandlungen des Reichstags*, Bd. 427. Pp. 5402–7, here 5402.
105. Jakob Reichert. 1931. 'Wirtschaftssystem, Politik und Arbeitslosigkeit', *Der Arbeitgeber* 23(1 December), 572; 'Rede von dem Abgeordneten Dr. Reichert', 174. Sitzung 27. Mai 1930, in *Verhandlungen des Reichstags*, Bd. 427. Pp. 5402–7, here 5402.
106. Leopold, *Alfred Hugenberg*, 57.
107. Ibid.; Neebe, *Großindustrie, Staat und NSDAP 1930–1933*, 53–54.
108. Weiß and Hoser, *Die Deutschnationalen und die Zerstörung der Weimarer Republik*, 57.
109. Attila Chanady. 1967. 'The Disintegration of the German National People's Party 1924–1930', *Journal of Modern History* 39(1), 84; BAB R 13/I 104 150–1; BAB R 13/I 104 'Aufzeichnung über die am 19. Februar 1930 im Gasthof Esplanade zu Berlin abgehaltene Sitzung des Hauptvorstandes und des Fachgruppenausschusses', 17; 'Rede von dem Abgeordneten Dr. Reichert, 135. Sitzung 6. März 1930', in *Verhandlungen des Reichstags*, Bd. 427. Pp. 4163–4170, here 4163.

110. Reichert, 'Die Börsenbewertung führender in- und ausländischer Eisenaktien in den Jahren 1925 bis 1930', 172; J. Reichert. 1929. 'Dawes-Plan-Erfahrungen und Young-Plan-Aussichten der Deutschen Volkswirtschaft', *Stahl und Eisen* 49(43) (24 October), 1553–54; 'Rede von dem Abgeordneten Dr. Reichert, 96. Sitzung 26. Juni 1929', in *Verhandlungen des Reichstags*, Bd. 425. Pp. 2971–77, here 2973, 2975; BAB R 13/I 104 'Aufzeichnung über die am 19. Februar 1930 im Gasthof Esplanade zu Berlin abgehaltene Sitzung des Hauptvorstandes und des Fachgruppenausschusses', 16; J. Reichert. 1930. 'Die deutsche Wirtschaft unter dem Young-Tributplan', *Stahl und Eisen* 50(21) (22 May), 731.
111. Reichert, 'Wirtschaftssystem, Politik und Arbeitslosigkeit', 573.
112. 'Rezension: Young-Plan, Finanzen und Wirtschaft', *Stahl und Eisen* 50(21), 581; Reichert, '*Dawes-Plan-Erfahrungen und Young-Plan-Aussichten der Deutschen Volkswirtschaft*', 1556; Reichert, '*Die deutsche Wirtschaft unter dem Young-Tributplan*', 732; *Verhandlungen des Reichstags*, 135. Sitzung Marz 6. 1930 Bd. 427. Pp. 4163–4170, here 4168.
113. Reichert, 'Rezension': Young-Plan, Finanzen und Wirtschaft", 581.
114. *Verhandlungen des Reichstags*, 135. Sitzung Marz 6. 1930. Bd. 427. Pp. 4163–70, here 4170. For the dispute with Dernburg in particular over his statements regarding future generations, see *Verhandlungen des Reichstags*, 136. Sitzung, Marz 7 1930. Bd. 427. 434–35 and *Verhandlungen des Reichstags*, 137. Sitzung, 8. März 1930. Bd. 427. 4294–95.
115. Weiß and Hoser, *Die Deutschnationalen und die Zerstörung der Weimarer Republik*, 86.
116. Chanady, 'The Disintegration of the German National People's Party, 1924–1930', 84–85; Leopold, *Alfred Hugenberg*, 70.
117. Leopold, *Alfred Hugenberg*, 63.
118. Weiß and Hoser, *Die Deutschnationalen und die Zerstörung der Weimarer Republik*, 92. See also Chanady, 'The Disintegration of the German National People's Party, 1924–1930', 85.
119. BAB R 13/I 104 'Aufzeichnung über die am 19. Februar 1930 im Gasthof Esplanade zu Berlin abgehaltene Sitzung des Hauptvorstandes und des Fachgruppenausschusses' 17.
120. Reichert, 'Wirtschaftssystem, Politik und Arbeitslosigkeit', 572.
121. Reusch in particular sometimes attacked the over-organization of the German economy, including business, and advocated a return to liberal competition. Kim, *Industrie, Staat und Wirtschaftspolitik*, 146. See also Patch, *Heinrich Brüning and the Dissolution of the Weimar Republic*, 192 and Neebe, *Großindustrie, Staat und NSDAP 1930–1933*, 100–102.
122. *Verhandlungen des Reichstags*, 174. Sitzungen. 27.5.1930. Bd. 427. Pp. 5402–7, here 5404, 5407.
123. See J. Reichert. 1929. 'Die Löhne in der deutschen eisenschaffenden Industrie', *Stahl und Eisen* 49(7) (14 February); Reichert, 'Die Leistungsfähigkeit der deutschen Stahlindustrie'; J. Reichert. 'Frage der Kapitalbildung und Investitionen, insbesondere in der Schwerindustrie', in BAB R 13/I 105 Bd. 27. 257 (RS); J. Reichert. 1931. 'Die Hauptursachen der Arbeitslosigkeit und die Möglichkeit ihrer Überwindung', *Sonderdruck aus Ruhr und Rhein* 31(31 July), 23.
124. Reichert, 'Die Hauptursachen der Arbeitslosigkeit und die Möglichkeit ihrer Überwindung' 23; Reichert, 'Wirtschaftssystem, Politik und Arbeitslosigkeit', 572; *Verhandlungen des Reichstags*, 174. Sitzungen. 27.5.1930. Bd. 427. Pp. 5402–7, here 5403; Reichert, 'Die Hauptursachen der Arbeitslosigkeit und die Möglichkeit ihrer Überwindung', 8.

125. Turner, *German Big Business and the Rise of Hitler*, 142.
126. Barkai, *Nazi Economics*, 36–45.
127. M. Schlenker. 1932. 'Aus dem Fachverein: Gesunde Wirtschaft im starken Staat', *Stahl und Eisen*, 52(49) (8 December), 1226–28.
128. Evans, *The Coming of the Third Reich*, 265.
129. Turner, *German Big Business and the Rise of Hitler*, 72, 81; Barkai, *Nazi Economics*, 26–27.
130. Neebe, *Großindustrie, Staat und NSDAP 1930–1933*, 92–93.
131. BAB R 13 I/105 Bd. 27. 'Reichert an E. Poensgen', 1 June 1932.
132. Ibid.
133. BAB R 13/I 104 Bd. 26 'Aufzeichnung über die am 29. Oktober 1930 abgehaltene Sitzung des Hauptvorstandes und des Fachgruppenausschusses', 4, 8; Patch, *Heinrich Brüning and the Dissolution of the Weimar Republic*, 193.
134. E. Jonas. 1965. *Die Volkskonservativen 1928–1933: Entwicklung, Struktur, Standort und staatspolitische Zielsetzung*, Düsseldorf: Droste Verlag, 24. For the divisions within the DNVP that ultimately led to its division, see L.E. Jones. 2009. 'German Conservatism at the Crossroads: Count Kuno von Westarp and the Struggle for Control of the DNVP, 1928–30', *Contemporary European History* 18, 147–77.
135. See also Beck, *The Fateful Alliance*, particularly 65–70.
136. Weiß and Hoser, *Die Deutschnationalen und die Zerstörung der Weimarer Republik*, 33.
137. Ibid., 43, 69.
138. Jonas, *Die Volkskonservativen 1928–1933*, 20, 56–57.
139. G.R. Treviranus. 1968. *Das Ende von Weimar: Heinrich Brüning und seine Zeit*, Düsseldorf: Econ-Verlag, 285.
140. Ibid.; Jonas, *Die Volkskonservativen 1928–1933*, 58.
141. Jonas, *Die Volkskonservativen 1928–1933*, 79. See also K.J. Mayer. 2006. 'Kuno Graf von Westarp als Kritiker des Nationalsozialismus', in L.E. Jones and W. Pyta (eds), *'Ich bin der letzte Preuße'. Der politische Lebensweg des konservativen Politikers Kuno Graf von Westarp (1864–1945)*, Cologne: Böhlau Verlag GmbH & Cie.
142. Jonas, *Die Volkskonservativen 1928–1933*, 66.
143. Leopold, *Alfred Hugenberg*, 75, 214 fn. 122.
144. Jonas, *Die Volkskonservativen 1928–1933*, 77; Patch, *Heinrich Brüning and the Dissolution of the Weimar Republic*, 99.
145. Jonas, *Die Volkskonservativen 1928–1933*, 77; Patch, *Heinrich Brüning and the Dissolution of the Weimar Republic*, 99.
146. Jonas, *Die Volkskonservativen 1928–1933*, 94; Patch, *Heinrich Brüning and the Dissolution of the Weimar Republic*, 99.
147. Jonas, *Die Volkskonservativen 1928–1933*, 78; W.L. Patch. 1985. *Christian Trade Unions in the Weimar Republic, 1918–1933: The Failure of 'Corporate Pluralism*, New Haven: Yale University Press, 152; *Stahl und Eisen* 48(36), 1260; *Verhandlungen des Reichstages*, 174. Sitzung. 27.5.1930. Bd. 427. Pp. 5402–7, here 5405.
148. Turner, *German Big Business and the Rise of Hitler*, 390; BAB R 13/I 601 'Reichert an Hilmers' (7.4.1934).
149. Jonas, *Die Volkskonservativen 1928–1933*, 88.
150. 'Reichstag Elections 1919–33: Share of votes (%)', in T. Kirk (ed.). 2002. *Cassell's Dictionary of Modern German History*, London: Cassell, 458; Chanady, 'The Disintegration of the German National People's Party, 1924–1930', 90.
151. Kirk, *Cassell's Dictionary of Modern German History*, 458.
152. Ibid., 141.

153. Ibid., 142.
154. Ibid.
155. Ibid., 141.
156. Neebe, *Großindustrie, Staat und NSDAP 1930-1933*, 76, 232 fn. 29.
157. E. Czichon. 1967. 'Reichert an Flick', in *Wer verhalf Hitler zur Macht?* 60.
158. Ibid., 60-61.
159. Ibid., 61.
160. Turner, *German Big Business and the Rise of Hitler*, 208.
161. BAB R 13/I 105 Bd. 27. 'Aufzeichnung über die am 17. November 1932 abgehaltene Sitzung des Hauptvorstandes und des Fachgruppenausschusses'.
162. Ibid., 27.
163. Chanady, 'The Disintegration of the German National People's Party, 1924–1930', 84. See also Fritz Thyssen. 1941. *I Paid Hitler*, Cesar Saerchinger, trans., New York: Hodder and Stoughton. However, this source was produced as an apologia for Thyssen's behaviour before his break with the Nazi Party and should be used with some caution.
164. BAB R 13 I/105 Bd. 27. Draft minutes of the 17 November 1932 VDESI meeting. P. 105 in BAB file.
165. Ibid., 102. BAB R 13/I 105 Bd. 27. 'Aufzeichnung über die am 17. November 1932 abgehaltene Sitzung des Hauptvorstandes und des Fachgruppenausschusses', 27, 34–35.
166. Ibid.
167. BAB R 13 I/105 Bd. 27. Draft minutes of the 17 November 1932 VDESI meeting. P. 112 in BAB file.
168. Ibid., 113.
169. Ibid., 114.
170. Ibid.
171. BAB R 13/I 105 Bd. 27. 'Aufzeichnung über die am 17. November 1932 abgehaltene Sitzung des Hauptvorstandes und des Fachgruppenausschusses', 36.
172. Ibid., 29, 30, 23.
173. Ibid., 35.
174. Feldman and Nocken, 'Trade Associations and Economic Power', 422.
175. Pohl and Markner, *Verbandsgeschichte und Zeitgeschichte*, 36.
176. Feldman and Nocken, 'Trade Associations and Economic Power', 422; BAB R 8099 #3 *Richtlinien für den Aufbau der Maschinenindustrie* (Herr. Ing. Hugo, Vorstand der VDMA) n.d., 112; Feldman and Nocken, 'Trade Associations and Economic Power', 428.
177. Historischen Kommission bei der Bayerischen Akademie der Wissenschaften. 1982. *Neue Deutsche Biographie*. 13, Berlin: Duncker & Humblot, 564.
178. Ibid.
179. BAB R 8099 #3 *Vorstandssitzungen 11.4.1919 und 4.2.1921 VDMA Niederschrift über die Vorstandssitzung des 20. Dec 1920*. 42. and Draft 'Satzung der Arbeitsgemeinschaft für den Deutschen Maschinenbau', 85–88; Nocken, *Inter-industrial Conflicts and Alliances in the Weimar Republic*, 57; Pohl and Markner, *Verbandsgeschichte und Zeitgeschichte*, 49–50; R 8099 #3 *Richtlinien für den Aufbau der Maschinenindustrie* (Herr. Ing Hugo Vorstand der VDMA) n.d., 112.
180. R 8099, #3 *Richtlinien für den Aufbau der Maschinenindustrie* 112.
181. O. Wiskott. 1929. *Eisenschaffende und eisenverarbeitende Industrie: Eine Untersuchung über die Verschiedenartigkeit ihrer Struktur und ihr gegenseitiges Verhältnis*. Bonn: Kurt Schroeder Verlag, 43.
182. Pohl and Markner, *Verbandsgeschichte und Zeitgeschichte*, 62.

183. Ibid., 43, 153.
184. Feldman and Nocken, 'Trade Associations and Economic Power', 428; Pohl and Markner, *Verbandsgeschichte und Zeitgeschichte*, 65.
185. Feldman and Nocken, 'Trade Associations and Economic Power', 433.
186. Ibid.
187. Ibid., 436–37; B. Kulla. 1995. *Die Anfänge der empirischen Konjunkturforschung in Deutschland 1925-1933*, Berlin: Dunker & Humblot, 157; Nocken, *Inter-industrial Conflicts and Alliances in the Weimar Republic*, 509.
188. Brady, *The Rationalization Movement in German Industry*, 153, 168.
189. Ibid., 229; K. Tribe. 1995. 'The Genealogy of the Social Market Economy: 1937–48', in Tribe, *Strategies of Economic Order*, 207; Feldman and Nocken, 'Trade Associations and Economic Power', 436.
190. Feldman and Nocken, 'Trade Associations and Economic Power', 436; Pohl and Markner, *Verbandsgeschichte und Zeitgeschichte*, 66.
191. Pohl and Markner, *Verbandsgeschichte und Zeitgeschichte*, 65–66.
192. Feldman and Nocken, 'Trade Associations and Economic Power', 439; Pohl, *Weimars Wirtschaft und die Außenpolitik, 1924-1926*, 164.
193. Nocken, *Inter-industrial Conflicts and Alliances in the Weimar Republic*, 546; H. Brüning. 1970. *Memoiren: 1918-1934*, Stuttgart: Deutsche Verlags-Anstalt, 380.
194. Feldman and Nocken, 'Trade Associations and Economic Power', 437.
195. See Brady, *The Rationalization Movement in German Industry*, 145 and Balderston, *The Origins and Course of the German Economic Crisis*, 444–49.
196. Nocken, *Inter-industrial Conflicts and Alliances in the Weimar Republic*, 122.
197. Thomas von Freyberg. 1989. *Industrielle Rationalisierung in der Weimarer Republik: Beispiele aus dem Maschinenbau und der Elektroindustrie*, Frankfurt a.M.: Campus Verlag, 309, 314–16, 361–62; M. Schneider. 2005. *Unternehmensstrategien zwischen Weltwirtschaftskrise und Kriegswirtschaft: Die Chemnitzer Maschinenbauindustrie in der NS-Zeit, 1933–1945*, Essen: Klartext Verlag, 123; R.D. Schearer. 1997. 'The Reichskuratorium für Wirtschaftlichkeit: Fordism and Organised Capitalism in Germany, 1918–1945', *Business History Review* 71(4), 572.
198. Brady, *The Rationalization Movement in German Industry*, 148, 153; Schearer, 'The Reichskuratorium für Wirtschaftlichkeit', 580, 583.
199. Brady, *The Rationalization Movement in German Industry*, 150.
200. Ibid., 152, 168.
201. Freyberg, *Industrielle Rationalisierung in der Weimarer Republik*, 360–70.
202. Nocken, *Inter-industrial Conflicts and Alliances in the Weimar Republic*, 621.
203. Pohl, *Weimars Wirtschaft und die Außenpolitik, 1924-1926*, 164.
204. Nocken, *Inter-industrial Conflicts and Alliances in the Weimar Republic*, 452, 170 fn. 148.
205. Ibid., 296–97.
206. Ibid., 294.
207. K. Lange. 1928. 'Industrie und Landwirtschaft', *Maschinenbau* 7(7) (5 April), 301.
208. Ibid., 301.
209. Abraham, *The Collapse of the Weimar Republic*, 179.
210. Lange, 'Industrie und Landwirtschaft', 302.
211. Pohl and Markner, *Verbandsgeschichte und Zeitgeschichte*, 73.
212. Wiskott, *Eisenschaffende und eisenverarbeitende Industrie*, 71.
213. Nocken, *Inter-industrial Conflicts and Alliances in the Weimar Republic*, 94.
214. Nocken, 'Inter-Industrial Conflicts and Alliances as Exemplified by the AVI Agreement', 696.

215. Pohl, *Weimars Wirtschaft und die Außenpolitik, 1924–1926*, 165.
216. BAB, R 13 I/602 'Reichert an Reusch 4.2.1926', 309, 310.
217. Ibid., 310, 311; BAB, R 13 I/602 'Lange an Mayer Etscheit 24.2.1926', 296.
218. Nocken, 'Inter-Industrial Conflicts and Alliances as Exemplified by the AVI Agreement', 699.
219. Ibid.; Nocken, *Inter-industrial Conflicts and Alliances in the Weimar Republic*, 582–83.
220. Nocken, *Inter-industrial Conflicts and Alliances in the Weimar Republic*, 217.
221. Nocken, 'Inter-Industrial Conflicts and Alliances as Exemplified by the AVI Agreement', 696.
222. Wiskott, *Eisenschaffende und eisenverarbeitende Industrie*, 75.
223. Balderston, *The Origins and Course of the German Economic Crisis*, 445.
224. 'Der Absatz der Maschinenfabriken, Apparate und Kesselbauanstalten nach Warenarten', in Statistisches Reichsamt. 1936. *Statistisches Jahrbuch für das Deutsche Reich*, Berlin: Verlag für Sozialpolitik, Wirtschaft und Statistik GmbH, 160.
225. Ibid.
226. K. Lange. 1932. 'Die Bedeutung der deutschen Fertigwarenausfuhr' in *Maschinenbau: Wirtschaftlicher Teil* 11(11) (2 June), 81–82.
227. Balderston, *The Origins and Course of the German Economic Crisis*, 445; James, *The German Slump*, 290.
228. Turner, *German Big Business and the Rise of Hitler*, 195–96.
229. For an example of some of the problems faced by specific small machine firms, see H. A. Turner's discussion of Paul Kleinenwerfer's firm in Turner, *German Big Business and the Rise of Hitler*, 196.
230. James, *The German Slump*, 156.
231. Turner, *German Big Business and the Rise of Hitler*, 199.
232. Nocken, 'Inter-Industrial Conflicts and Alliances as Exemplified by the AVI Agreement', 702.
233. Ibid., 703; Turner, *German Big Business and the Rise of Hitler*, 199.
234. Turner, *German Big Business and the Rise of Hitler*, 201.
235. K. Lange. 1929. 'Wirtschaftsdemokratie oder organisierte Wirtschaftsfreiheit?' *Maschinenbau* 8(12) (20 June), 134, 137.
236. Ibid., 134.
237. 'Enthüllt sich da nicht die ganze schwarze Seele des Unternehmers, des Kapitalisten, wenn er eine Wirtschaftsdemokratie ablehnt?' Ibid., 134.
238. Ibid., 137.
239. K. Lange. 1929. 'Wirtschaftsdemokratische Irrtümer bezüglich der weiterverarbeitenden Industrie', in Deutsche Bergwerks-Zeitung (ed.), *Das Problem der Wirtschaftsdemokratie: Zur Düsseldorfer Tagung des Reichsverbandes der Deutschen Industrie*, Düsseldorf: Industrie Verlag und Druckerei A.G., 78.
240. BAB R 8099/687 'Lohnpolitische Kurvenbilder zur Krisenlage, Nov. 1931' 2. The files formerly contained in the VDMA for this period are extremely fragmentary. This particular set of documents appears to have been a draft report in several sections that were numbered separately. Some of these pages were lost and there is no numbering system overlaid by the Bundesarchiv.
241. BAB R 8099/687 'Preise, Löhne und Arbeitslosigkeit der Deutschen Industrie 1927 bis 1931'; ibid.,'Entwicklung von Tariflohn und Lebenshaltungskosten Januar 1924 bis September 1931', 2; ibid., 'Preise, Löhne und Arbeitslosigkeit der deutschen Industrie 1927 bis 1931'; ibid., 'Entwicklung der Arbeitslosigkeit in Deutschland seit 1927' 3. This critique of wage levels in Germany remains an open question that sparked the heated 'Borchart Debate' in the late 1970s and early 1980s. See, e.g., J. von

Krüdener (ed). 1990. *Economic Crisis and Political Collapse: The Weimar Republic, 1924–1933*, New York: Berg Press; Carl-Ludwig Holtfrerich. 1982. *Alternativen zu Brünings Wirtschaftspolitik in der Weltwirtschaftskrise*, Frankfurter Historische Vorträge, 9, Wiesbaden: Franz Steiner Verlag GmbH.

242. BAB R 8099/687 'Minderung des Gesamtarbeitseinkommens der industriellen Arbeiterschaft seit 1929 durch Arbeitslosigkeit (bzw. Kurzarbeit) und Lohnsenkung'.
243. D. Haselbach. 1991. *Autoritärer Liberalismus und soziale Marktwirtschaft: Gesellschaft und Politik im Ordoliberalismus*, Baden-Baden: Nomos Verlagsgesellschaft, 40–45. See also D. Gerber. 1998. 'Ordoliberalism: A New Intellectual Framework for Competition Law', in *Law and Competition in Twentieth Century Europe: Protecting Prometheus*, New York: Oxford University Press, 233–69; Blumberg-Lampe, *Das Wirtschaftspolitische Programm der 'Freiburger Kreise'*, 57.
244. Ibid., 41.
245. Brüning, *Memoiren*, 380.
246. See Kim, *Industrie, Staat und Wirtschaftspolitik*, 235–36.
247. Grübler, *Die Spitzenverbände der Wirtschaft und das erste Kabinett Brüning*, 128.
248. Haselbach, *Autoritärer Liberalismus und soziale Marktwirtschaft*, 23, 42.
249. Ibid.
250. Ibid., 43.
251. Haselbach, *Autoritärer Liberalismus und soziale Marktwirtschaft*, 328 fn. 280 and Pohl and Markner, *Verbandsgeschichte und Zeitgeschichte*, 74.
252. H. Hömig. 2000. *Brüning: Kanzler in der Krise der Republik. Eine Weimarer Biographie*, Paderborn: Ferdinand Schöningh, 162.
253. K. Lange, 'Wirtschaftsdemokratie oder organisierte Wirtschaftsfreiheit?' 139.
254. Ibid., 140.
255. Ibid.
256. Ibid., 136.
257. Ibid., 139.
258. K. Lange. 1930. 'Bilanz der deutschen Handelspolitik 1925 bis 1929', *Maschinenbau*, 9(1) (2 January), W1.
259. Ibid., W1–2.
260. K. Lange. 1930. 'Zum Thema: Bilanz der deutschen Handelspolitik 1925 bis 1929', *Maschinenbau* 9(3) (6 February), W25; K. Lange. 1931. 'Handelsbilanz und Konjunktur' *Maschinenbau* 10(3) (5 February), W25; K. Lange. 1930. 'Schönheitsfehler der Handelsbilanz?' *Maschinenbau* 9(15) (7 August 1930), W170 (which also appeared in *Wirtschafts- und Export-Zeitung* 25 [28 July]).
261. Lange, 'Handelsbilanz und Konjunktur', W26.
262. K. Lange. 1931. 'Die deutsche Ausfuhr in der Weltwirtschaftskrise', *Maschinenbau* 10(1) (1 January), W2.
263. Lange, 'Zum Thema', W28.
264. Ibid., W3.
265. K. Lange. 1931. 'Deutsch-österreichische Zollunion!', *Maschinenbau* 10(7/8) (16 April), W73.
266. Lange, 'Zum Thema', W27.
267. BAB R 13/I 104 'Aufzeichnung über die am 19. Februar 1930 im Gasthof Esplanade zu Berlin abgehaltene Sitzung des Hauptvorstandes und des Fachgruppenausschusses', 8–9.
268. K. Lange. 1932. 'Die Entwicklung des Welthandels', *Maschinenbau* 11(1) (7 January), W1–W3, here W1.
269. Ibid.

270. J. Block. 1997. *Die Wirtschaftspolitik in der Weltwirtschaftskrise 1929 bis 1932 im Urteil der Nationalsozialisten*, Frankfurt a.M.: Peter Lang, 80.
271. Ibid., 48–49.
272. Haselbach, *Autoritärer Liberalismus und soziale Marktwirtschaft*, 206.
273. Ibid.
274. Lange, 'Die Entwicklung des Welthandels', W1.
275. Lange, 'Die Bedeutung der deutschen Fertigwarenausfuhr', W81.
276. Ibid., W82.
277. Ibid.

CHAPTER 2

Confidence and Complicity
Confronting National Socialist Ideology

After the *Machtergreifung* in January 1933, German industry and its organizations were faced with a new government that threatened the economic order industrialists had come to know. Capitalism, the market and the freedom of the entrepreneur were all openly questioned. From the perspective of industrialists and their organizations, the new state was unpredictable, appeared unstable and was more interested in political and social issues than real business policy. At best, it was unconcerned with the aspirations of industrialists in a capitalist economy. At worst, it might prove to be a species of Marxism, and the party's putative emphasis on the health of the community, work creation and national interest made ledger-minded industrialists more than a little nervous.

The worst of these fears proved unfounded. The new regime demonstrated little interest in upsetting prevailing production structures. It did attempt to 'coordinate' industry and industrial associations as *Wirtschaftsgruppen* (business groups) in 1934–35, but this relied heavily on the traditional structures of industrial organization. The old VDESI and VDMA more or less took the new names Business Group Iron Industry (*Wirtschaftsgruppe Eisenschaffende Industrie*) and Business Group Machine Building (*Wirtschaftsgruppe Maschinenbau*), with few real changes to the organizations' structure or personnel. Following Dietrich Eichholtz and other less ideological historians like Ian Kershaw, Reichert in particular might have been expected to have used the common ideological ground occupied by both the iron and steel industry and the Nazi Party to adapt to the conditions set by the new regime by employing National Socialist ideas, rhetoric and policy to the advantage of his members soon after January 1933.[1] This did not happen. Instead, Reichert met the changes occurring in Germany by seeking to insulate his members behind the protective walls of a powerful and important industry. Lange found himself in a much weaker position. He lacked the complementary ideologies and aims shared by heavy industry and the new government, and found his former liberalism had become a dangerous liability. He also lacked the brute economic strength that the iron and steel men felt they could muster. What he did have was a more flexible organization that was more comfortable with compromise and collaboration than Reichert's. As a result, Lange quickly dropped his old policies and embraced major elements of National Socialism, starting down a road that differed greatly from that of his counterpart in iron and steel.

Was this just about money? Spoerer's assertion that the lure of high profits under the new regime enticed industrialists into support for the Third Reich is problematic in the two cases examined here.[2] Individual firms were eventually able to adapt to or take advantage of the conditions set by the new regime by snapping up Jewish competitors, negotiating exclusive deals with the regime on a 'cost-plus' basis that would have been impossible in a 'normal' economy, or shifting production to armaments.[3] However, in the early years of the regime, the National Socialist government's broader attempts to regulate and direct the German economy threatened to undermine the long-term profitability of the industries represented by Lange and Reichert, but especially machine building. As a good example of a mover and shaker in the liberal, competitive economy hated by the National Socialists, Karl Lange was also personally threatened by the new regime. The future of an industry of highly competitive exporters that produced capital goods that reduced labour inputs or consumer goods that had no place in National Socialist plans was placed in serious jeopardy by the seizure of power in 1933. Iron and steel faced a different set of challenges, and Reichert's members' desire to raise domestic prices was not easily reconcilable with the aims of the Party.

The business managers of the VDMA and VDESI reacted very differently to this new challenge, and their responses reflected the structure and experience of each man and industry. Believing that he, the powerful men he represented and the iron and steel industry were simply indispensable to any regime, Reichert withdrew to what he thought was a position of strength. As a result, he and the VDESI did not really contemplate a fundamental compromise with the ideas or aims of National Socialism. Instead, Reichert worked to push the new regime into adapting to the needs and desires of the iron and steel industry, just as he had done in the Weimar Republic. Lange did not have this luxury. Fearing that he and his industry were particularly vulnerable, he quickly moved to achieve a detente with National Socialist ideology. To achieve this, Lange and the VDMA were willing to both give up the aims and ideals of the industry and participate in some of the more reprehensible discourses of the Party in order to secure a position for themselves in the new regime. This ideological adaptation created the preconditions for their engagement in the Nazi economy in ways that Reichert was not able to match.

The future looked questionable for the iron and steel industry, but Reichert had seen this before. For him and his members, the situation in 1933 was not entirely unlike that in the period following the First World War. In those years, the industry had managed to fend off the threat of the left and avoid fundamental changes in the way industrialists dealt with the state. In spite of the promise that 1918 had seemed to hold for radicals, the iron and steel industry had preserved its independence, not to mention its solvency, and successfully clawed back many of the gains made by labour during the revolution. If the industry had survived intact in 1918, there seemed little reason to believe that it would fare much worse in 1933, particularly given the fact that the industry and new government could agree on more points than had been possible in late 1918. As a result, Reichert tended to underestimate the long-term impact of the Nazi rise to power on both his industry and Germany in general. He assumed that the role of the industry as a primary producer, the number of workers employed by relatively few firms and the traditional unity and organization of the iron and steel men made it a powerful force in any new system of government. No one, he thought, could really ignore the demands of his members without courting total economic collapse. If all went well, the industry might be able to remove old irritants while still maintaining the dominance of powerful firms and the stability and profits of their own self-regulated markets.

There should be no mistake: Many firms in the iron and steel industry profited from employment and armament programmes during the economic boom that Germany experienced before the Second World War. Rearmament demanded vast quantities of iron and steel, and industrialists were finally able to sell everything they were able to make after years of overproduction. The iron industry experienced increased profits which rose from 3.91 per cent to 4.08 per cent in the years leading up to the outbreak of war, but this was relatively modest in comparison to other, more successful industries like shipbuilding, motor vehicles and metalworking.[4] More importantly, iron and steel industrialists in fact believed themselves to have been cheated out of the full benefits of the boom by economic policies peculiar to National Socialism. Under other political circumstances, the German iron and steel industry would have found itself in an ideal position. The National Socialist building programme created an almost insatiable demand for iron and steel.[5] At the same time, industrialists' efforts to limit capacity through national and international cartels and the increasingly acute shortage of iron ore limited the availability of new material.[6] High demand coupled with limited supply should have exerted enormous upward pressure on iron prices, leading to windfall profits in the industry. This was one of the few facets of liberal capitalism that both Reichert and his members could wholeheartedly embrace. But the golden age did not materialize, or at least not in the way that Reichert and his colleagues had envisioned. Though the Nazi regime had few qualms about allowing industrialists to make handsome profits from the armaments boom in particular, it was unwilling to allow rising iron and steel prices to undermine its own plans.

Instead, price controls under National Socialism limited the industry's ability to take advantage of high demand, even as the iron and steel industry found itself paying higher prices for foreign ore.[7] Producers thus found their profitability threatened by having to 'buy high' and 'sell low' at the very moment that they might have made a fortune.

This was clearly not the kind of economic growth that iron and steel industrialists had hoped for, and it did little to overcome producers' reservations about Nazi economics. As the representative of the iron and steel industry as a whole, Reichert was at least as concerned with this structural problem as with the recent success of the more adaptable or rapacious firms. He therefore gave voice to the broader concerns of an industry that demanded maximum profits and flexibility under a regime that hoped to regulate an autarchic economy and ensure a steady supply of cheap steel for armaments and building projects. Thus, although Reichert could afford to be more sanguine than Lange about the viability of his member firms and his own importance as their representative, he had deep concerns about Nazi economics and governance. As a result, he and his organization came into increasing conflict with the National Socialist state. Although the VDESI helped to preserve the independence of its members, as the years progressed its demands resulted in significantly diminishing returns. Moreover, Reichert's complaints and arguments did not just fall on deaf ears: while more pliant representatives of industry were busy flattering or cooperating with the new regime to accumulate the 'political capital' that would allow them influence, Reichert irritated it by sticking to his old saws about private regulation and the role of the entrepreneur.

In the course of one of his interrogations by the U.S. army in 1946, Reichert claimed to have had very little knowledge of the political situation that followed the Nazi seizure of power. He had, he said, turned his attention away from party politics and concentrated on the National Economic Council (*Reichswirtschaftsrat*) instead.[8] While this may have appeared to be only too convenient to his interrogators, there is some truth in Reichert's claim. Both the VDESI and its chief business manager turned inward during the transition to the National Socialist government. By the end of the first year of Nazi rule at the latest, Reichert had clearly recognized that the installation of Hitler in the Chancellery represented a real threat to him and the businessmen he represented.[9] As in the period after the First World War, his chief concern at this time was to see that the iron and steel industry retained as much of its structure and organization as possible. Consequently, his own writing suffered from neglect. He did not publish in *Stahl und Eisen*, for instance, until October 1933, when he nevertheless avoided direct comment on the changes taking place in Germany.[10] This uncharacteristic reluctance to engage in public discussion extended to the VDESI itself. The association did not convene a single meeting of the executive or technical group committees until the end of 1933, preferring instead to allow Reichert and Poensgen to 'work at home,' away from prying or critical eyes.[11]

Although industrial organizations faced nothing like the fate of the trade unions and social democratic or communist parties in the first half of 1933, Reichert and Poensgen had good reasons to be concerned about the new government. One of the first was a change in the peak employers' organization, the Reich Association of German Industry (Reichsverband der deutschen Industrie, RdI) in 1933. The SA occupied the offices of the association on 1 April with Storm Troops demanding that Silverberg, Kastl and a number of other Jewish employees be expelled from the organization immediately.[12] Paul Silverberg, a respected moderate industrialist, was then forced out of the RdI because of his Jewish ancestry.[13] Kastl was even more vulnerable. As the business manager of the association, he had been a prominent critic of more reactionary employers in the Ruhr in particular. Not even the venerable Gustav Krupp could protect the RdI from the ascendant Nazi party.[14] The fact that the new regime could so easily dismiss men as powerful and respected in industrial circles as these was troubling enough. Equally distressing, Kastl's previous 'rejection of the NS movement' was cited by the SA as the grounds for his dismissal even as the party turned its coercive violence against more old-fashioned conservatives.[15] This was an uncomfortable precedent for Reichert, who had also campaigned against the NSDAP, albeit from the traditional right.

This encroachment of the party into industrial politics extended to the VDESI itself. In the spring of 1933 the new government successfully forced the twenty-five-year veteran of the organization Max Schlenker from his position as chief business manager of both the Ruhr regional lobby group the Langnamverein and the North-West Group of the VDESI.[16] This seemed so egregious that the vice president of the VDESI, Fritz Springorum, resigned his presidency of the Langnamverein in protest.[17] Reichert might have had little in common with Kastl save his job title, but the dismissal of Schlenker for political reasons was much more threatening.[18] As a long serving conservative industrial representative with a face disfigured by duelling scars, Schlenker was hardly an example of progressive liberal ideals in business or society. He might, however, serve as an excellent example of the backwards looking conservatives like Reichert and his colleagues in the *Volkskonservative Partei*, and a warning to other traditionalists who had rejected the NSDAP in previous years.[19] Erker and Joly have demonstrated that these purges were short-lived and targeted specific individuals or groups, but they were an unnerving warning to Reichert and the men he represented.[20]

The following summer, Reichert himself had a sobering confrontation with the realities of the new state. In a meeting in 1934 he suggested to the chief business manager of the Bavarian Industrial Association, Dr. Grassmann, that the troublesome Albert Pietzsch was about to be forced out of his offices in the

NSDAP. Pietzsch was a chemical industrialist who had become involved in the Nazi Party very soon after the end of the First World War. He was particularly drawn to the NSDAP left wing's marginal social and economic theories that so worried Reichert and his colleagues.[21] By the early 1930s, Pietzsch had been appointed as Hitler's economic adviser and participated in the drafting of the Law for the Organization of National Labour, the regulations of the German Worker's Front (DAF) and the establishment of labour trustees in Germany.[22] He had also succeeded in raising the ire of industrialists who were unsympathetic to his ideas about the primacy of national interest or political authority over profit.[23] As such, it was hardly surprising that Reichert might take an interest in Pietzsch's career. Moreover, Reichert was right: Pietzsch was closely associated with Strasser, and his star was indeed falling in 1934,[24] although he managed to rehabilitate himself in the eyes of the Party later on. Grassmann passed Reichert's comments on to Pietzsch himself, who promptly launched a suit against Reichert through the Nazi Party court. The Party itself was particularly interested to know which 'important party circles' had leaked this information to Reichert and summoned the chief business manager to explain himself.[25]

Reichert responded to the Party's summons by immediately drafting a series of letters to the president of the Party Court in Munich, to Pietzsch and to Grassmann explaining that it had all been a misunderstanding.[26] Reichert asserted that he had not in fact said that important party members informed him of Pietzsch's imminent fall, but rather had simply speculated that Pietzsch's previous attempt to reconcile Hitler and Strasser had given him a bad odour in the Party.[27] He likewise registered his 'surprise, not to say indignation' that Grassmann had 'put words in his mouth' and left him in such a precarious position.[28] Happily for Reichert, Pietzsch accepted his explanation and blamed Grassmann for the misunderstanding, while Grassmann himself admitted that he might have contributed to the debacle by emphasizing Reichert's excellent contacts and information.[29] Since Pietzsch was satisfied, the Party Court process appears to have gone no further.

Reichert was lucky to have run afoul of the new authorities at such an early date and over such a small matter, for the incident served as a sharp reminder of the new political climate in Germany. His ability to function as the representative of the iron and steel industry turned on his ability to manage contacts and relationships from a wide variety of circles in industry and government. Now it was clear that the semipublic analysis and criticism of politics and policy that had characterized so much of Reichert's earlier career was no longer viable. It was also evidence that the politics and ideology of the Third Reich had already permeated associational politics. Reichert himself seemed shocked that Grassmann had spoken to Pietzsch about the matter at all. Indeed, it took several days, telephone conversations and letters before Reichert was satisfied that it had not been Grassmann himself who had filed the complaint with the Party authorities.³⁰ Reichert could take some comfort in the fact that a colleague had tipped him off about the developing charges,³¹ but even a stillborn suit was clear evidence that party and industrial politics could no longer be safely separated under the new regime.

The ascendancy of the NSDAP also opened the door for the incursion of new men into industrial politics. This was most evident in the changes at the RdI after it had been purged by party members. Kastl was replaced by two 'party men' in the form of Hans von Lucke and Alfred Moeller, and the association itself was reorganized as the Reich Group Industry (Reichsgruppe Industrie, RGI) in June 1933.³² For Reichert, the introduction of these men and their adherence to Nazi doctrine represented a 'revolutionary act,' and in his eyes the former RdI ceased to exist as a representative of industry or employers and would instead function as a representative of the state in industrial politics.³³ This virtually removed the Reichsgruppe from the constellation of private representative organizations like Reichert's and raised the spectre of political appointments in groups like the VDESI.

Men who had previously been shut out also now gained access to Reichert's world for the first time. The chief business manager was particularly incensed to discover that his counterpart in the minor Association of Brandenburg Small Industry (Verein der Märkischen Kleinindustrie), Heinrich Ostermann, had used his NSDAP credentials to go over Reichert's head to complain to the Ministry of Economics about the management of a VDESI subsidiary, the Fittings Association (Fittingsverband).³⁴ Ostermann, who had become a speaker for the NSDAP in 1930, had distinguished himself as a critic of '*Großkapital*' in general and the iron and steel industry in particular.³⁵ Under the new National Socialist regime, he was eventually able to parlay his party contacts into a successful and lucrative career as chief business manager for Business Group Electro-Industry (Wirtschaftsgruppe Elektroindustrie) starting in 1937.³⁶ In the fall of 1933, he took advantage of his party connections and attempted to undermine the terms of the Fittingsverband by taking up the cause of four disgruntled firms. Ostermann charged that the association's current chief business manager, Alms, had favoured particular firms and even given preference to foreigners over German plants.³⁷ Moreover, Ostermann asserted that Nazi policy itself argued against private regulation in the finishing industries.³⁸ He continued to present himself as the 'adviser' to the renegade firms as the discussion became increasingly acrimonious and demanded that Alms resign his position.³⁹

Reichert was personally offended by the accusation that one of the associations attached to the VDESI had behaved unscrupulously. He was even more annoyed that it had been made to the Ministry of Economics (RWM) by the upstart Ostermann. Demanding an explanation, Reichert stepped in to chair the Fittingsverband general membership meeting himself in September

1933.⁴⁰ Over the course of the discussion, Reichert became increasingly angry that an 'outsider' like Ostermann would be able to go 'behind their backs' and cause trouble in business that he could not possibly understand.⁴¹ The chief business manager became enraged when his demands that the firms in question 'have the courage' to speak for themselves were met by silence or petulant griping by members who continued to rely on Ostermann as an interlocutor.⁴² Eventually, Reichert gave up in disgust and left the assembly.⁴³ From that point on, he refused to meet with the firms concerned so long as troublemakers like Ostermann remained involved.⁴⁴ Ostermann, however, was no longer the outsider that Reichert believed him to be. To be sure, he was not a member or administrator of the Fittingsverband itself, but the triumph of National Socialism gave politically connected men with a chip on their shoulder like Ostermann an entry point into the debates and offices from which they had been barred in the past. Political activism and reliability were now beginning to supplant administrative competence and the kind of professional diplomacy that had made Reichert so successful. Instead, a new set of political connections that Reichert did not possess or cultivate became increasingly meaningful in National Socialist Germany.

Thus, even before the new government made any serious attempts to exert its influence over the iron and steel industry, National Socialism had already begun to penetrate the fastness of industrial organization in a way that had not been possible for the political left in the turbulent years after the Great War. For Reichert, the changes in German politics and economic organization clearly called for a change in his and the VDESI's attitude towards National Socialism. Indeed, he was surprisingly candid when questioned during his imprisonment after the war. Industrialists, he noted, felt themselves responsible for not letting their firms 'go to the dogs' under the new regime.⁴⁵ As a result a sort of natural evolution occurred in which the industry began to accommodate itself to the new government.⁴⁶ The same might be said of Reichert and his organization, but to a much lesser degree. The VDESI leadership was encouraged by the fact that both Hitler and Göring made efforts to reach out to industry and assuage some of their fears.⁴⁷ Reichert and his colleagues could not but be pleased by the demise of the Free Trade Unions and Social Democrats, which fulfilled one of the industry's longtime dreams.⁴⁸ He likewise seemed genuinely heartened that unemployment had begun to decline under the new regime.⁴⁹ More importantly, production, prices and profits for the iron and steel industry all reversed their downward spiral and began to creep upwards by as much as 33 per cent for raw iron over the course of the first year of Nazi rule.⁵⁰ These tangible advantages were accompanied by other potential benefits. The *Machtergreifung* held out the possibility of addressing many of the industrialists' demands from the previous decade, if only they could nudge the new regime in the right direction.

Although his postwar interrogators expressed considerable interest in it, Reichert obfuscated the question of the appeal of Nazi organization and the *Führerprinzip* to his own members and organization. Indeed, he claimed he was unable to remember whether or not the industry embraced or wanted it at all.[51] He argued that Ernst Poensgen in particular had no interest in the concept and did not implement it in the VDESI, but Reichert was very clear about the fact that his industry at the very least preferred the *Führerprinzip* to the 'economic democracy' (*Wirtschaftsdemokratie*) of the late Weimar period.[52] His industry had already established an organizational structure that was perfectly acceptable to Reichert by 1919, and he and his colleagues hoped that the establishment of a Nazi 'organic' economy could be made to work to their advantage.[53] In 1933, he hoped to increase the power of his own association, allowing the VDESI to take advantage of the authority of the state while still developing its own policies and wielding the right to block bad or inconvenient ideas without interference from the regime.[54] As a result, he embraced the NSDAP's emphasis on cartels as 'communities of interest' that ensured their importance in the new state, and welcomed its establishment of a Cartel Office, which he thought would rely on industrial organizations and only intervene when requested by associations like his own.[55]

In order to shape the policies of the new regime to suit iron and steel, Reichert and the VDESI bureaucratic leadership entered into 'enthusiastic collaboration' (*lebhaft beteiligt*) with the successor Association of German Industry (Reichsgruppe Industrie), sitting on a variety of committees and reviewing various suggestions for the organization of an organic economy throughout May and June of 1933.[56] Reichert assured his members that during the course of these discussions, he and the VDESI had repeatedly emphasized that Hitler himself had argued in *Mein Kampf* that the freedom of the entrepreneur was essential to an effective, productive economy.[57] He likewise argued that relying on the extant industrial organizations would clearly be the most effective way of organizing production in the state.[58] Other than the fact that its influence would be further entrenched, Reichert's 'organic economy' would thus be virtually indistinguishable from the private industrial organization in the iron and steel industry of the preceding decades. There is no indication that he seriously considered the possibility that the state might expect the VDESI to adapt to Nazi ideas and aims instead.

Reichert did recast the presentation of the interests of the VDESI to conform more closely to Nazi rhetoric, but this was mostly superficial. He and Poensgen both argued that protecting an iron industry (and iron prices) that had come under attack from foreign Marxist 'agitators' (*Hetzern*) after the *Machtergreifung* was analogous to saving German farmers in the name of the *Volk* and nation.[59] He likewise joined in the general chorus of praise for Hitler in an attempt to show the similarities between the new führer's ideas and his own.⁶⁰ Aside from his optimistic interpretation of *Mein Kampf*, Reichert asserted that even Hitler himself agreed on the implausibility of autarky.⁶¹ A man who supposedly possessed the powerful understanding of human nature held by the new chancellor would not, he argued, make the mistake of tampering too much with the German economy or its primary industries.⁶² Reichert contended that the head of the new government was more concerned with the 'spirit' of the economy than with its specific 'form'.⁶³ The iron and steel industry, he implied, reflected this spirit despite all outward appearances. Germany could likewise 'learn something' from Fascist Italy, where they had not rushed things but rather allowed industrial organizations to develop naturally.⁶⁴ Reichert and Poensgen also both took pains to argue that the VDESI was at the disposal of the new government so long as it did not change the association's role in the industry or state. Poensgen urged his members to make use of the material provided by the Ministry of Propaganda in order to combat the putative industrial boycott in foreign states that followed the installation of the National Socialists.⁶⁵ Reichert, for his part, closed his annual report to the association for 1933 with praise for Hitler, what he had been able to achieve, and his faith in the new leader before urging his members to 'exert all their strength, so that things would go better [for the industry] than under the previous system'.⁶⁶ The published version of the minutes concluded with assurances that the German iron and steel industry endorsed the 'new economic spirit' that followed the seizure of power and assured readers that Hitler had the full confidence of the industry and association. They would, Reichert promised, be at the disposal of the new government to work for the good of both *Volk* and economy.⁶⁷

To Reichert and the VDESI, this combination of caution and sycophantic rhetoric seemed to have yielded results after the first year of Nazi rule, and he hoped that the new regime had been tamed through little more than lip service and objective economic reality. He assured his members that the NSDAP that had once espoused outlandish economic ideas was coming to see reason and accept the fact that private economic exchange between nations was a necessity. Even the eccentric National Socialist economist Gottfried Feder had apparently dismissed autarky as implausible.⁶⁸ At the same time, Reichert hoped that the new government spelled the end of press attacks on the iron and steel industry from more liberal-minded industries like Lange's. Indeed, he expressed some surprise that he still had to defend his industry from critics at the annual Friedrich List conference in February 1933, despite the 'new way' that seemed to him to endorse both protectionism and markets regulated by organizations like the cartels of the iron industry.⁶⁹ In order to put a stop to these and similar attacks, particularly a Fall article in Darrés' *Deutsche Agrarpolitik*, Reichert entered into discussions with the Ministry of Propaganda and was promised that the new government would shield the industry in the press.⁷⁰

Reichert's staff also had few concerns about the Ministry of Economics' Action Committee on the Organization of the Organic Economy, which proposed that economic associations adapt to the new regime by implementing the *Führerprinzip*, simplifying the organizational apparatus and 'greening' the management of the associations ('…die Verkleinerung und Verjüngung der maßgebenden Verbandsgremien') by transferring authority to a small cadre of younger men.[71] The VDESI action team associated with the process, made up of the industrialists Poensgen, Boehringer, Hennecke, Raabe, Springorum and Reichert himself, in fact concluded that no changes at all would be necessary for them, and Poensgen assured his members that this would not affect the iron and steel industry at all as they were already sufficiently well organized.[72] Even better, the demand that the organizations represent all producers forced smaller or more independently minded firms into the association.[73] The new government, it seemed, had strengthened the organizational structure of German industry while at the same time doing away with organized labour and the political left. Iron and steel men could ask for little better.

However, one year into the new regime, the state began efforts to reorganize the German economy and industry more seriously. In theory, the old VDESI (along with most other similar organizations) was 'coordinated' into the Business Group Iron Working Industry (Wirtschaftsgruppe Eisenschaffende Industrie) in 1935 and, at least ostensibly, stripped of its capacity as a professional lobby group and pressed into the service of the Third Reich through the Law for the Preparation of the Organic Construction of the Economy of 27 February 1934, which was put into practice through an enabling regulation on 27 December of the same year.[74] Whereas a manager like Lange could use this to retool his organization to meet the new regime, Reichert hoped to minimize changes to little more than window dressing, and even this seemed to be undertaken grudgingly. Lange was quick off the mark, but it would take Reichert and his colleagues another five and a half months of foot-dragging and delay before they at last could announce on 5 May 1936 that the new Wirtschaftsgruppe Eisenschaffende Industrie was up and running.[75] With its transformation into a 'business group' or *Wirtschaftsgruppe* (Wigru), the old VDESI was supposed to become an active participant in the regulation of the German economy charged with seeing a variety of state policies through to implementation.[76] In some ways, the new organization streamlined the old association. Although the Ministry of Economics made the *Wirtschaftsgruppe* responsible for iron and steel production, the eligibility of member firms was both restricted and, like all other *Wirtschaftsgruppen*, compulsory.[77] Rather than a broadly based voluntary organization that netted firms involved in many stages of the production process, the new Wigru was intended to encompass basic iron production along with blast furnace operations, basic steel and rolling mills.[78] At the same time, the subsidiary organizations of the old VDESI were reduced substantially. The regional groups were reduced from six to two organizations (North-West and the Saar) while the *Fachgruppen* were pared down to three primary groups representing iron and steel, stainless steel and Thomas products (*Thomasschlacke*). The property of these former regional and specialty groups then devolved to the central office of the *Wirtschaftsgruppe* in Berlin.[79] Reichert and Poensgen themselves took on the leadership of the technical group for iron and steel production while Wilhelm Steinberg, who had replaced Schlenker, functioned as the chief business manager of the North-West Group and Poensgen served as regional leader.[80] In accordance with the Nazi conception of appropriate hierarchy, the old management board (*Vorstand*) was replaced by an advisory council (*Beirat*).[81] Finally, the new *Wirtschaftsgruppe* was incorporated into Hauptgruppe I of the new RGI along with mining, nonferrous metals and the casting industry.[82]

As in the period before the *Machtergreifung*, iron and steel retained their position as basic elements of production in a modern economy.[83] The central importance of the industry potentially conferred enormous importance on the new Wigru. This was reflected in the fact that Poensgen was also appointed as leader of Hauptgruppe I of the RGI.[84] As a result, the leaders of Wirtschaftsgruppe Eisenschaffende Industrie came to preside over the basic building blocks of the German economy in the Nazi state. The new Wigru was now charged with overseeing the institutions of industrial self-regulation that had developed over the previous decades.

The elimination of most of the regional groups facilitated a more efficient administration of the organization and industry. The central office in Berlin retained control of the most important *Fachgruppen* while Poensgen remained leader of the North-West Group. Berlin also exercised the right to approve communications and briefings emanating from the subsidiary organization.[85] A voluntary Pre-Inspection Office (*Vorprüfungsstelle*) in Düsseldorf was transformed into a semi-official 'Control Office' (*Prüfungsstelle*).[86] The expansion of the Control Office in particular was an expensive undertaking and emphasized the increased 'power of the purse' possessed by the new Wigru. As a result, the association's budget for 1935–36 increased to 350,000 RM. This included 8,000 RM for the RGI and an anticipated 10,000 RM for the Ministry of Economics along with 260,000 RM for the *Wirtschaftsgruppe* itself, representing a 60,000 RM increase over 1933–34.[87] The expansion and staffing of the Control Office a few months after the adoption of this budget required an additional increase of 42 per cent, to be covered by a compulsory increase in member contributions.[88] The following business year (1936–37) saw a further increase of 86,000 RM to cover 150,000 RM for the support of the Control Office, an increase in contributions to the RGI of 40,000 RM and a 43,000 RM increase in the expenditures of the Wigru itself.[89]

This theoretically transformed the Wigru into a powerful organization integrated into a state that demonstrated a notable interest in economic intervention, but the reformed organization was still undermined by its own conception of its role in the German economy. The Party authorities were in fact reluctant to appoint Poensgen, who had not joined the Party, to lead such an important business group. In the event, it took more than a year to finally secure a dispensation from the minister of economics confirming Poensgen to the post.[90] Although iron and steel's central position in the economy increased the importance of the *Wirtschaftsgruppe*, it also left it subject to competing demands in the polycentric structure of National Socialist Germany. As the maker of a basic product that affected so many stages of industrial production, the iron and steel industry was caught between competing interests and a state that was unwilling to allow one industry to cripple its broader plans and policies. The centrality of the industry further drew the attention of a variety of different regulatory bodies. In some cases, this left Poensgen and Reichert at a loss as to whom they were actually responsible, and under what authority. This was particularly true in the case of a dispute over payments from the iron industry for exports in which Poensgen was unable to determine which authority – the RWM, price commissar or Office of the Four Year Plan – was responsible for setting the relevant regulations.[91]

At the same time, the new Wigru self-consciously retained many of the characteristics and practices of the old VDESI. The very establishment of the new Wigru was delayed by Reichert's attempt to consult with his members to ensure that there were no objections to converting the association, and by foot-dragging on the part of the old regional and technical groups who balked at delivering their property to the *Wirtschaftsgruppe*.[92] Despite the Ministry of Economics' mandate to establish a new advisory council (*Beirat*) in place of the old executive structure, the new consultation committee looked remarkably like that of the old VDESI. The new *Beirat* was smaller, but 21 of the 26 industrialists appointed by Poensgen to the first council had served on the VDESI Executive in 1933.[93] In practice, the advisory council also continued to include representatives of the biggest and most important firms in the industry.[94] Reichert complained during his interrogations after the war that *Beirat* members continued to think of themselves as representatives of the individual firms and worked out of self-interest rather than any responsibility to the *Wirtschaftsgruppe* as such, much less to the state in general.[95] The Wigru's chief business manager himself contributed to this impression. Upon its establishment, he and Poensgen assured their members that it would continue holding membership meetings in order to consult with the firms themselves, rather than govern from the top down.[96] This was not the kind of organization the National Socialist government had in mind.

Poensgen also shied away from exercising the authority the RWM had conferred on him through the creation of the *Wirtschaftsgruppen*. Throughout the course of his interrogations following the war, Reichert was very careful to make the point that Ernst Poensgen continued to regard himself as a mediator in the tradition of the VDESI rather than a *Führer* in the National Socialist sense.[97] To a certain extent, this was true of all the leaders of the *Wirtschaftsgruppen,* who were usually chosen by their industry just as they had been in the Weimar era and remained primus inter pares, at least in the eyes of their larger members.[98] Poensgen, however, took this role very seriously. Despite directions from the Ministry of Economics, he insisted on negotiating between firms in order to settle disputes over quotas and construction rather than issuing directives himself, and tried to push Kiegel from the RWM into approving the appointment of a neutral mediator to clear up disagreements.[99] At the same time, he continued to clash with the authorities over the extent to which firms should be compelled to join the variety of organizations set up in the National Socialist state. Poensgen was very clear that, while he would 'try' to adapt to the new conditions, he stood by his position that industrial organizations must be voluntary.[100] While it is not surprising that his opinion had little effect on state policy, he was able to use his own position to retain the tradition of industrial cooperation. Reichert was also careful to note that Poensgen continued to bring representatives of affected firms into meetings with Reichert and his colleagues in order to work out compromise solutions.[101] The leaders of the new *Wirtschaftsgruppe* were not interested in fundamental changes to German industrial organization.

This reluctance to exercise power in the sense expected by the leaders of the National Socialist state was accompanied by a working relationship between the Berlin office and the North-West group of the association that undermined any efforts to centralize and regulate the industry. Although Reichert and the *Wirtschaftsgruppe* theoretically retained the right to approve the work of the regional association, the North-West group began to function as an increasingly autonomous organization. To a certain extent, this was the result of an unwillingness to duplicate work and the continued importance of direct meetings between firms. From its offices in Düsseldorf, the North-West group could deal directly with major industrialists and then forward reports straight to the authorities.[102] However, it also reflected both the central office's reluctance to regulate effectively and what Reichert considered to be the Rhinelander's traditional mistrust of Berlin.[103] In the context of Minister of Economics Schacht's New Plan and, later, the Office of the Four Year Plan, this served to undermine the central organization's authority and utility, as local representatives stepped in to fill the role envisioned for the central office.

The prominence of the Ruhr region and relative independence of the North-West group likewise prevented Reichert from centralizing authority in his own hands the way that Lange was doing in his own organization. Although Reichert retained a role in the appointment of the advisory board of the new Control Office (*Prüfungsstelle*), he let the administration of the office slip away from his personal control.[104] When the voluntary 'Pre-inspection Office' (*Vorprüfungsstelle*) had been set up by the iron and steel industry in Düsseldorf, it was initially headed by the chief business manager of the North-West group. After this organization was elevated to the status of the semi-official *Prüfungsstelle* in 1935, Steinberg stepped down and was replaced by Karl Gerwin, a member of the Steel Works Association (Stahlwerksverband) syndicate's board of directors.[105] This reflected the iron and steel industrialists' tendency to appoint members of their own ranks rather than association bureaucrats to leading positions, but Gerwin was later replaced by his assistant, Philip Greimers.[106] Thus, responsibility for this office passed not only into the hands of an industrialist, but then further into those of another functionary who worked independently from Reichert. This stands in sharp contrast to Lange's policy of keeping close control over the offices and organizations that proliferated in the German economy under National Socialism.

These misgivings and expediencies were complicated by the structure of the organization itself. The central *Wirtschaftsgruppe* was responsible for finance, questions of cartels and marketing, trade and tariff policy, scrap, raw materials and statistics.[107] However, besides strictly regional issues, the North-West group took on responsibility for legal and tax questions, transport, 'social economic' issues, skilled workers and industrial advertising.[108] When an issue covered by the responsibility of the North-West group affected the industry as a whole, they were to include both the Wigru managment and representatives of firms from outside the region.[109] Although this theoretically allowed the central office to oversee and approve discussions made by the regional association, it also granted the local representatives a leadership role in a surprisingly wide variety of issues of importance to the industry as a whole. Disputes between the Wigru management and the regional group were to be settled by Poensgen or referred to member firms.[110] Reichert later complained that, unlike other business groups, his own central office remained relatively small, never numbering more than 100 employees while others employed between four and six hundred.[111] In effect, the *Wirtschaftsgruppe* began its organizational life as a house divided between regional and central offices intended to facilitate cooperation between levels of representation rather than to issue directives from a single authority.

These differences between the theoretical power conveyed on the *Wirtschaftsgruppe* by the Ministry of Economics and its actual reluctance to subordinate other organizations and industrialists was echoed by Reichert's own approach to his new position. As the bureaucratic Wigru leader appointed by the Reich economics minister, Reichert functioned as the day-to-day administrator of the new organization responsible for the administration of iron and steel production.[112] As such, he cultivated an ongoing relationship with authorities like the RWM and price commissar, and state officials consulted him on matters of policy and production.[113] More importantly, both the ministry and, later, the Office of the Four Year Plan initially relied very heavily on Reichert's own statistics and data to direct the increasingly centralized planning of the economy.[114] As economic agencies proliferated in the Third Reich, Reichert was expected to make himself available as an advisor on iron and steel production to new organizations like the reorganized Chambers of Commerce.[115] This brought the chief business manager into close contact with the newly influential men in the German economy. At the same time, it gave him the information necessary to prepare industrialists themselves for briefings with important officials in order to push the regime in appropriate directions.[116] Reichert was also expected to bring his own members to heel to a greater degree than he had done in the past. As noted above, he and Ernst Poensgen were given the joint responsibility of overseeing the formidable iron and steel cartels. His position as chief business manager in an organization that divided quotas, oversaw exports and acted as a mediator between industrialists and an aggressive state gave Reichert considerable regulative authority. He was also expected to see that the industry fully adapted to the political reality of the Third Reich. Despite his own misgivings about the intrusion of politics into the economy, Reichert was expected, for instance, to help see to it that important positions in the iron and steel industry were staffed with 'Party men'.[117]

Despite this, Reichert proved distinctly unwilling to push the limits of his newfound authority and continued to defer to his members as he had done before 1933. When, for instance, Krämer approached Reichert to advise the Reichsstelle about changes to work time and training for youth in iron and steel, Reichert responded by turning to a more traditional committee of industrialists and regional representatives rather than forging ahead as the authorities demanded.[118] Similarly, when the justice secretary expressed concerns that German rolling mills were performing poorly and requested that the matter be investigated, Reichert simply forwarded the request to the technical experts in the Association of German Iron Producers (Verein deutscher Eisenhüttenleute, VDEh) rather than addressing the problem through his own organization.[119] This reluctance to exercise the power vested in him by the state extended to his relationship to the iron and steel marketing organizations – that is, organizations for which he was technically responsible. Rather than acting as an agent of the state overseeing the various arms of the iron and steel industry, Reichert remained a rather passive observer, forwarding requests and reports between the Steel Works Association and the state.[120] He likewise continued to conform to the earlier structures of industrial self-regulation, remaining in the shadow of the leader of his *Wirtschaftsgruppe* to a much greater extent than Lange rather than using his new role to increase his own participation in industrial policy. Thus, while Lange was able to open discussions with Poensgen regarding issues that affected both associations, Reichert remained in the background.[121]

Reichert likewise had little interest in mastering what must have been a staggering number of details that fell to him as a result of the *Gleichschaltung* of the state and economy. The National Socialist state permeated the lives and activities of Germans in the 1930s, but Reichert had little interest in any attempt to co-ordinate the activities of his prickly members. This is particularly evident in his touchy response to the integration of managers and industrialists into a single social insurance plan (*Berufsgenossenschaft*). When the South German Iron and Steel Cooperative Society approached Reichert for his approval of their suggested list of steering committee members, he declined to comment, arguing that this was neither his role nor responsibility.[122] The society's staff were disconcerted by this response. Believing that they required his approval before proceeding, they pointed out that other chief business managers (including Lange) had not presented similar difficulties when their approval was sought.[123] After several letters and phone conversations, Reichert and Baare would go no further than to affirm that they had no objections to any nominations.[124] This unwillingness to immerse himself in the petty quotidian National Socialist life cut Reichert and his organization off from the transformation of the culture of the business community and also extended to matters that would later become more important in German economic life even as Lange and other chief business managers scrambled to push their organizations' responsibility farther along the chain of production.

Reichert and the VDESI thus hoped to ensure that the changes wrought by the National Socialist government were something that happened to other people. However, while he was able to minimize some of the practical changes to his industry's organization, Reichert demonstrated marked reservations about the broader policies of the new government. Unsurprisingly, his analysis and criticism did not take the same public or strident tone that it had during the transition to a republic from 1918 to 1923, but Reichert and the VDESI maintained some distance from the new government of the NSDAP. As is true for many individuals who experienced and participated in the National Socialist regime, some of the most intriguing questions about Reichert's attitudes towards an unquestionably loathsome ideology remain murky. Reichert had made his career mixing politics and economics, but his myopic focus on the economic policies that directly affected the iron and steel industry limited his ability to engage with broader Nazi ideas. At the same time, the nature of the National Socialist regime did not encourage deep or protracted criticism. In his own defence, Reichert noted to his interrogators after the war that one did not stand up to Hitler and his government unless it was 'with a revolver in hand so that you could do yourself in when you landed in a concentration camp.'[125] Nevertheless, Reichert himself did not join the Party and later claimed that in April of 1933 he had entered into an informal agreement with some of his colleagues never to become a member.[126] Rather, he maintained older conservative norms and continued his practice of rewarding speakers or guests of the VDESI with expensive busts of Hindenburg rather than the Nazi paraphernalia coming into vogue.[127] During the VDESI meeting of December 1933, Poensgen was also careful to recognize and praise Schlencker, who had been invited to attend despite having only recently been forced out of the association by the new regime.[128]

As a result, the records left by Reichert, the VDESI and its successor are rather ambiguous about their approach to the Nazi Party itself. On one hand, the *Wirtschaftsgruppe* appeared to publicly embrace the ideology of the new regime. Public meetings adopted many of the symbols, phrases and excuses of the Party itself. The '*Hitler-Gruß*' (Hitler salute) became a common conclusion to Wigru correspondence. The organization pushed its own members into using their private business contacts abroad to combat the foreign 'propaganda' directed against Germany and the Nazi regime.[129]

However, neither the *Wirtschaftsgruppe* nor Reichert himself expressed much enthusiasm for any other of the worst aspects of the regime, and iron and steel industrialists in the old VDESI had little interest in the public show of anti-Semitism that would be embraced by Lange and his organization.[130] Reichert simply had Baare pass on RGI or RWM notices instructing German companies to avoid Jewish firms but avoided comment or active engagement, to say nothing of leadership.[131] Even though both the RGI and RWM grew increasingly petulant about the big cartels' tendency to see the exclusion of Jewish firms and contacts as 'unreasonable' (*unbillig*), the Wigru does not appear to have issued any statements or instructions of its own to encourage anti-Semitism.[132] Reichert's politics might have been reactionary in the Weimar Republic, but there is no evidence that he had any significant connection to the fundamental racism of the new regime. This vague distaste for the regime is difficult to evaluate. His weak defence suggests that the broader social and political questions did not trouble him much, one way or the other. Reichert's relationship to National Socialism must therefore be sought in his approach to Nazi economic, industrial and trade policy. In this context, Reichert and the *Wirtschaftsgruppe* managed to maintain a consistent and even public critique of the Third Reich even after its inclusion in the machinery of the state. While this criticism was understandably more muted under the new regime than in the Weimar Republic, it served to separate Reichert from those more eager to adapt to life after the 'national revolution'.

Reichert did have concerns about the broader economic policies of the regime. Although he was willing to compromise on the role of public spending, Reichert warned against dangerous economic experiments and the high cost of subsidies for public works or employment schemes.[133] His own recipe for job creation and economic recovery was quite different. He demanded freer trade (or at least more international trade at varying levels of tariffs), increased prices for commodities like his own and a greater focus on the private economy as the price of recovery.[134] Reichert likewise nurtured fears about the return of organized labour through the back door. The head of the DAF, Robert Ley, had already floated a 'trial balloon' about bringing employers into his organisation as part of the construction of an organic economy, and Reichert feared that this was an ill-conceived attempt to institutionalize a body along the lines of the failed corporatist Central Working Community (Zentralarbeitsgemeinschaft) of 1918.[135] Aside from Reichert's ingratitude towards an organization that had helped save Germany from collapse fifteen years before, this was a strong indication that he was not entirely convinced that industry had safely come out on top in 1933.[136]

Reichert also worried about the extent to which the new regulations conflicted with his own ideas about regulation and the 'natural economy'. Although the National Socialist emphasis on the role of cartels might have been encouraging, Reichert worried that the plans for their role in an 'organic economy' went too far towards making industrialists and their associations an appendage of the state.[137] To Reichert, the new 'estate structure' should be little more than the traditional organization of his own industry and remain both voluntary and private.[138] He was also notably disturbed by the National Socialist approach to foreign trade. While Reichert was no liberal, he was eager to promote international exchange through the organizations he had helped to build, and his public assertions that the new government had come around to this view were tempered by fears about state regulation of trade.

Reichert remained suspicious of what he still feared were 'socialist' undercurrents in National Socialism. Indeed, the putative transformation of the VDESI into an arm of the state with responsibility for overseeing the well organized cartel structure of the iron and steel industry seemed to have started the industry well on the road to state control already. Various government offices contributed to Reichert's fears. Even as late as 1938, the Office of the Price Commissar still found it useful to alarm Reichert and Poensgen by threatening to socialize their industry.[139] Iron and steel also suffered from an image problem in the new regime. An industry that had developed a high degree of organization specifically designed to keep domestic prices high while undercutting competitors on foreign markets was bound to raise the suspicions of the NSDAP. The Party was in fact particularly sceptical about this industry's reliability in the event of war. In 1935, for instance, a brochure arguing that the iron and steel industry was notable for its lack of effort and extensive profiteering during the First World War circulated amongst the Nazi elite.[140] Reichert hurried to meet with both the author, Captain Schmidt, and other government agencies in order to repair the damage and head off calls for an extraordinary tax to recoup the wartime losses of the state. While he appears to have convinced Schmidt, who agreed to bring Reichert's counterarguments to the führer himself, the chief business manager worried that the industry remained on the wrong side of the regime.[141] Indeed, a little over a year later Reichert noted that even Hitler and Göring were still publicly stating that, of all German producers, the iron and steel industry was particularly unprepared for a war.[142] Both the authorities and the public were also worried about what they perceived to be the declining quality of iron produced by German firms, especially after the spectacular collapse of a bridge at Berlin's Zoologische Garten station in 1936.[143]

More generally, the *Gleichschaltung* of industrial organizations raised expectations in the Party that the 'old traditions and good positions' that had characterized industrial self-regulation would be sacrificed for statist goals.[144] Although he believed that industrial self-regulation still existed in 1935, Chief Business Manager Guth of Reichsgruppe Industrie told Poensgen in no uncertain terms that the assumption of power by the National Socialists had shifted the focus of economic organization towards the interests of the state as a whole.[145] Moreover, Guth argued that this was in line with the development of economic organizations in other states, which he believed had come under state control in 'more and more countries'.[146] This was not the kind of industrial organization that iron and steel industrialists had in mind when they reviewed National Socialist changes in 1934, and it provoked a sharp response from Poensgen and Reichert.

Poensgen expressed his increasing frustration with the intrusion of the state and did not hesitate to accuse the RWM officials of having destroyed the free economy.[147] He even went so far as to threaten to withdraw from discussions affecting industrial organizations if the state was simply going to dictate its own terms.[148] Reichert was more cautious in discussions with state officials, but he continued to push the RWM to defer to industrialists and businessmen and refused to participate in a discussion concerning the establishment of a general export cartel unless the merchants themselves were consulted.[149] He likewise continued to bristle at the suggestion that employers be included in the DAF.[150] Instead, Reichert took his industry's tried and true approach by making industrial organizations look attractive to National Socialism while at the same time defending their independence, ideas and power.

Following the industry's putative *Gleichschaltung* at the beginning of 1935, the chief business manager of the Wirtschaftsgruppe Eisenschaffende Industrie continued to emphasize the essential compatibility of National Socialism and traditional industrial organizations as they already existed, but he was increasingly fighting a rearguard action. Cartels and organizations like his own, Reichert argued, had always had more to do with the medieval collective community that inspired some Nazi thought than with the liberal individualism reviled by the Party.[151] Not only could these organizations comfortably coexist with National Socialism, but voluntary organizations could 'spare the responsible minister[s] some difficult decisions'.[152] Indeed, Reichert asserted that the future prosperity of the iron and steel industry hung on the cooperation between industrial organizations (which could provide expertise and self-regulation) and the state (whose more powerful institutions could regulate imports in particular).[153] The new government's attempt to master and reform the German economy had elicited an equally powerful effort towards self regulation for this common good, he argued, and any further intervention in the private economy was simply unnecessary.[154]

This attempt to fit industrial organizations into the structure of the National Socialist state without making any actual changes was accompanied by an attempt to develop a counterargument that would enable iron and steel industrialists to oppose the state's intervention in the economy. In response to the increasing public pressure being placed on industrial organizations, the Wigru concluded that it was necessary to secure real, rather than simply symbolic, powers of self-regulation.[155] Reichert even went so far as to argue that the Cartel Laws that had irked him so much in 1923 were both friendly to industry and a sufficient tool for protecting the state and 'public good' (*Gemeinwohl*) from abuses.[156] He also made the rather dubious assertion that the cartels themselves had been established out of a desire 'to serve the Fatherland' and could be used in the 'struggle against the individual and emphasis on the communal' espoused by the Party.[157] To him, these organizations continued to represent the best of both worlds by allowing for the coordination desired by the state while also preserving the 'independence and private initiative' of the entrepreneur.[158] He likewise emphasized the greater flexibility of the cartels as compared to the state.[159] More importantly, Reichert fundamentally questioned the state's ability to manage the economy, arguing that intervention in fact made things worse.[160]

Germany's economic health, Reichert argued, still depended on the regulation of trade through private, international cartels and syndicates whose agreements must be left intact and inviolable.[161] He also took aim at the National Socialist alternative of a system of closed trading blocks.[162] Although he asserted that he was not opposed to trading blocks in principle, he sharply criticized attempts to establish such a system for Germany.[163] For a state like Germany, the development of a trading system along the lines of the British Commonwealth was a dangerous chimera.[164] Broader most-favoured-nation agreements, not closed systems organized by the state, had brought Germany back into the world market. Germany should, he thought, decouple the issues of tariffs and trading blocks and raise import duties on specific products (particularly iron and steel) instead of relying on unworkable plans and Hitler's grand but ineffectual threats of retaliation for discrimination against German goods.¹⁶⁵ He also remained highly sceptical of the procedures intended to regulate foreign trade. To him, the state's competence to handle the complexity of foreign trade was highly questionable, and he complained that the programmes intended to subsidize exports had not panned out. In particular, the scrip that acted as a transfer mechanism for the foreign specie that exporters were allowed to retain under Schacht's banking regime was in short supply and threatened to leave the iron and steel industry without sufficient convertible currency.¹⁶⁶ More importantly, the iron and steel industry was denied access to export subsidies because of its participation in the international cartels that Reichert himself had so carefully built and defended.¹⁶⁷

These specific concerns were accompanied by fears of increasing state encroachment on business in general. Apart from the already mounting bureaucratic procedures and potential for conflict, Reichert worried that increased government oversight would undermine private initiative itself.¹⁶⁸ The use of the Ministry of Economics to limit the expansion of plant in particular might appear 'seductive' to iron and steel industrialists who wanted to limit production in order to maintain prices, but Reichert carefully warned his members to look to their own organizations before scurrying off to the state for help.¹⁶⁹ His criticism of the new state was also expressed indirectly in his evaluation of the American National Economic Recovery Act. As in Germany, many American firms had, he argued, demanded the installation of an economic dictator during the crisis. However, American cartels and trusts were now struggling to fend off attacks from a dangerously interventionist state.¹⁷⁰ He asserted that German industry was already sufficiently well organized to have made aggressive economic legislation moot.¹⁷¹

This analysis brought him into more direct conflict with the regime over broader trade and international relations questions. Reichert continued to defend the private international agreements that he hoped would regulate international trade. He was willing to bend so far as to concede that too much attention might have been paid to exports over supplying the home market, but he remained uncomfortable with the National Socialist turn towards protectionism and autarky.¹⁷² This was an ironic position for the primary representative of the German iron and steel industry to find himself in. He, his colleagues and members alike had clamoured for and profited from highly protectionist policies since the latter part of the nineteenth century. However, this had been, to all intents and purposes, a profitable business proposition rather than simple patriotism or a generalized ideology. As a result, Reichert continued to advocate practical measures that would benefit the iron and steel industry by maximizing its profits, and took little interest in autarkic policies that seemed only to serve political ends.¹⁷³ This led Reichert into conflict with the Ministry of Economics when he seemed unable to understand, for instance, why Kiegel would press the German iron and steel industry to purchase German fireproof insulation rather than a cheaper Austrian product.[174] *Geheimrat* Fellinger of the RGI in particular found it necessary to make it clear to Reichert in March of 1936 that international agreements must now be made to serve the practical needs of the state, rather than relying on 'theoretical grounds' like industrial self-regulation or profit for their justification.[175]

Reichert and Poensgen were also deeply concerned about the impact of self-sufficiency on Germany's position on the world market, particularly after both the Reichsbank and Ministry of Economics announced plans to cut direct exports significantly.[176] Reichert in particular worried that the turn towards protectionism would undermine Germany's favourable trade policy and position.[177] Accordingly, he pushed the ministry to grant the iron and steel industry exceptions to trade restrictions, urging it to raise export quotas to countries for which German firms were constantly paying fines for over-export to the various control boards and exchange services, and to establish an export subsidy to England in particular.[178] While this added to the frustration of ministry officials, it also reflected Reichert's tendency to unabashedly place his industry over national goals, even in a National Socialist state.

This self-interest was coupled with a continued faith in international self-regulation as a point of principle. As early as the transitional period between the old VDESI and new Wigru, representatives of the iron and steel industry had clashed with the regime over international cooperation. In November 1934, for instance, Poensgen flatly refused to give up on international cooperation in a discussion with RWM officials.[179] He and Reichert also made efforts to play various state organs against each other by using the RWM's approval of the attempt to bring England into negotiations over the International Steel Cartel (ISC) to pressure the price commissar for concessions.[180] They likewise sought to outflank Kiegel by appealing to more sympathetic branches of the ministry when he rejected Reichert and Poensgen's suggestion that Germany help to establish a new international pipe association.[181]

Even before the new *Wirtschaftsgruppe* had been formally established, Reichert and Poensgen clashed with the increasingly interventionist state more and more often over the issue of exports. During the transition from the old VDESI to the new 'coordinated' body, this conflict centred around the regulation of price and export quantities. On 5 November 1934, the National Socialist government reappointed Carl Goerdeler as Commissar for Price Control (*Reichskommissar für Preisüberwachung*), responsible for overseeing and regulating prices, particularly in primary industries that already possessed their own regulative mechanisms.[182] Eight days after the enactment of a law making the price commissar independent of the Ministry of Agriculture, Goerdeler met with Reichert and Poensgen.[183] Throughout the course of this meeting, the iron and steel representatives argued passionately for an increase in the price of iron. In a rather transparent attempt to restore the traditional export advantage of high domestic prices, Poensgen suggested that lowered iron and steel prices would force industrialists to try to double their exports precisely at a time when dealers would refuse to buy German iron.[184] Better, he thought, to let prices rise and allow iron and steel producers to earn foreign currency for the regime.[185] That same day Poensgen attempted to convince Kiegel and the RWM that price regulation was better left in the hands of the cartels.[186] Reichert's arguments were an even more painful attempt to square the interests of the iron and steel industry with the aims of the regime. He worried that a price decrease would have a negative 'psychological effect' that would undermine the regime and raise the spectre of another economic collapse.[187] Even less convincingly, he argued that the price of iron had no impact on consumption and should thus be exempt from control mechanisms in general. An increase in the price of manure, he asserted, led to a corresponding increase in the price of agricultural products, but a similar increase in the price of iron implements would have no such effect.[188] In this case, Reichert was reduced to literally arguing that iron should not be treated like shit in the Nazi regime.

Goerdeler would have none of it. He was interested in forcing a general decrease in price, and the heavily cartelized iron and steel industry offered him the opportunity to quickly affect the economy by simply converting the private cartels into public regulators.[189] He was therefore eager to get his hands on the old VDESI's production and profit balances for larger firms like United Steel and Krupp.[190] This was not the administration that the iron and steel industry wanted, and the possibility of the state seizing control of the industry by simply taking over the books and functions of the cartels was a chilling prospect. Although the *Wirtschaftsgruppe* was theoretically responsible for oversight of the relevant cartels, it increasingly cut itself out of the machinery of regulation. By late 1935 the Wigru was forwarding reports from the Steel Works Association on to the RWM, forfeiting the tactical advantages of exclusive technical knowledge.[191] Thus, while Reichert noted that by 1935 there was already a good deal of conflict between the cartels and state authorities like the RGI, his own association no longer took the lead or acted as an effective mediator in these disputes as it had done in the past.[192]

Poensgen's tendency to preserve the voluntary character of the old association further contributed to the declining importance of the *Wirtschaftsgruppe*. When the industrialist Florian Klöckner stepped outside of the regulatory system and opened a new sales establishment (*Werkshandel-Niederlassung*) in Munich in early 1936, Kiegel declined to intervene but charged Poensgen and the Wigru with taking the situation in hand and preventing other firms from following suit and opening up the market to unregulated competition.[193] Rather than taking charge in his capacity as leader of Wirtschaftsgruppe Eisenschaffende Industrie as Kiegel had instructed, Poensgen opened negotiations with some of the leading firms and could offer the RWM nothing better than the hope that they would not have opened their own establishments when next they met.[194] Despite the fact that Kiegel continued to lean on the Wigru to resolve the situation, Poensgen eventually turned the matter over to the Steel Works Association, which managed to work out its own agreement between the firms based on the traditional negotiation characteristic of the industry's self-regulating bodies.[195] These actions were not a simple dereliction of duty but rather a means of addressing conflict through the more traditional cartel negotiations possible in the Steel Works Association rather than through a regulative body mandated by the state.

A similar problem presented itself in June of the same year when a number of firms resisted the extension of the committees to regulate exports in the industry. Poensgen himself seemed uncertain of how to proceed in the face of opposition from the firms and rather feebly proposed the appointment of a neutral arbitrator.[196] Uninterested in this kind of bargaining, Kiegel instead proposed the introduction of forced state regulation of iron exports that would require the firms to meet a number of set conditions.[197] Poensgen cautiously endorsed the idea of increased regulations so long as compulsion was limited to an export syndicate. Reichert, however, was even more reluctant and asked that the matter be turned over to the export merchants themselves.[198] This timid approach to the regulation of the large firms in particular was completely in keeping with the tradition of the old VDESI. In the context of an increasingly intrusive state apparatus, it could not but annoy even the sympathetic members of the Ministry of Economics. At the same time, the Wigru's tendency to turn to the RWM when it was unwilling or unable to control its own members became increasingly irritating to the state authorities. Thus, when Poensgen suggested in February 1936 that the Wigru would endorse a compulsory export syndicate if it was intended to prevent new firms from entering the export market, Kiegel expressed his complete indifference to the actual allocation of permits and left the Wigru to solve the problem itself.[199] If the *Wirtschaftsgruppe* was reluctant to regulate its own members in the interest of the state, the state could hardly be expected to regulate the firms in the interest of industrial organization.

Even as Reichert and the Wirtschaftsgruppe Eisenschaffende Industrie failed to live up to National Socialist expectations about the regulation of private industry, their attempts to represent their own members in discussions with the state proved equally disappointing. In his regular meetings with the RWM, Reichert continued to clamour for an increase in iron and steel prices and exemptions from some of the more odious financial burdens imposed by the state.[200] As a result, Reichert began to draw members of the Wigru into his efforts to lobby the state more intensively. By May 1936, the chief business manager had appealed to his members to support his own efforts to pressure the State Railway to waive increased freight rates for the inland transport of ore.²⁰¹ Two months later, he drew his members into the discussion over the limitation of export levies, despite the scepticism of the RWM.²⁰² Reichert hoped to turn this into a semipublic debate in which iron and steel industrialists were encouraged to take part in a discussion that would nevertheless be kept out of the press.²⁰³ The results of these efforts were limited at best. The authorities demonstrated precious little sympathy for the iron and steel industry, and the export levy for 1937 was in fact raised from 50 to 90 million RM.²⁰⁴ Reichert, the *Wirtschaftsgruppe* and the iron and steel industrialists themselves were left to take what comfort they could in small concessions like the decision to limit wage increases in the industry to twice yearly during what had now become a labour shortage.²⁰⁵ More worryingly, repeated clashes with the authorities led to increasingly antagonistic relations between the Wigru and the state. By early 1936, Reichert and his association were actively soliciting members' concerns, needs and complaints to bring up at to meetings with the RWM.²⁰⁶ Although this was completely in keeping with the role of the old VDESI, it significantly undermined the goals and conditions of the *Gleichschaltung* of German industry.²⁰⁷ Moreover, the Wigru's tendency to approach meetings with the RWM bearing a litany of complaints from its members hardly facilitated the effective administration of the German economy. The increasing frustration on both sides was demonstrated in the summer of 1936 in a debate over export figures.

Exports were in fact an intractable problem for the National Socialist regime. It found itself trapped between a desire for self-sufficiency and the need to participate in the international economy in order to secure foreign currency to feed the armaments programme.²⁰⁸ In the case of iron and steel, this left military authorities alarmed at apparently high iron and steel exports while Economics Minister Schacht hoped to increase exports even more, so long as the RWM and Wigru were able to manage permits in a way that would secure foreign currency for the state.²⁰⁹ These conflicting demands contributed to increased tensions. Consequently, when Schacht expressed displeasure that so many iron and steel industrialists were neglecting their 'duty to the *Volkswirt* (people or national economy)' by failing to export sufficient quantities of iron and threatened to hold Poensgen personally responsible, the *Wirtschaftsgruppe* responded by circulating a surprisingly petulant memorandum amongst its members.²¹⁰ The organization conveyed Schacht's concerns; however, it also asserted that the demands of the state, rather than the policy or production of individual firms, had forced producers to put exports on hold, jeopardizing their international connections.²¹¹ The Wigru urged its firms to make a greater effort to export in the future, but placed this suggestion in the context of fulfilling the terms of international cartel agreements rather than any service to the state.²¹²

As in the Weimar Republic, Reichert had hoped to avoid fundamental compromise by pushing the state to adopt or accept his own ideas and enact policies that would specifically benefit his industry, but the Nazi state was a different animal. The National Socialist emphasis on both autarky and competition between states as the basis of economic relations stood in direct contrast to Reichert's approach to international affairs. When this was coupled with his stubborn defence of private self-regulation and industrial organization, Reichert increasingly came to be seen as an opponent of state policy, even though he was more than willing to take advantage of the aspects of Nazi ideology that corresponded to his own ideas (or could at least be made to appear to do so). As a result, he and the successor to the VDESI found themselves outside of the ideological horizons of the new state. Though this did not have direct consequences like imprisonment or unemployment for Reichert, it meant that he failed to build up a store of 'political capital' or goodwill with the National Socialist state that would make him a reliable administrator in the regime in the period between the seizure of power and announcement of the Four Year Plan. This, however, was not the only model open to the managers of the old German industrial organizations.

Karl Lange made a different set of choices after 1933. He and the VDMA lacked the experience and confidence of Reichert and his colleagues, and Lange himself faced a dangerous change in government for the first time. His own members lacked the raw clout of the iron and steel men Reichert represented. He was also the head of an organization with a strong tradition of compromise rather than belligerence. Lacking either the real or perceived strength of Reichert and the iron and steel industry and finding himself in a precarious personal position, Lange quickly moved to appease the Nazi state by rapidly adopting ideas and policies that would conform to the demands and expectations of the new regime. Lange did not just pay lip service to Nazi ideas. He and the VDMA adapted by embracing much of National Socialist thought and pushed their own members to fall in line with the ideas and culture of the new regime, including some of the most unpleasant facets of a brutal ideology. These efforts deeply entangled the German machine building industry in a barbaric regime that had left no doubt about its rejection of the aims and ideals of the old VDMA. As a result, Lange and his organization were able to both survive the transition to a regime that was outwardly hostile to their industry and begin building up a surprising level of trust as a politically and ideologically reliable group.

Unlike Reichert, who might have believed that he could withdraw behind the protective walls of a powerful industry and influential industrialists, Lange saw himself in a far more precarious position and had good reason to feel personally threatened. As noted above, the dismissals of Silverberg and Kastl from their positions in the Reichsverband in April of 1933 were an upsetting precedent, even if they had little to do with Reichert's own political reputation.[213] Lange and the VDMA, on the other hand, had long been identified with the liberal, moderate positions taken by these two early victims of the new government. In March 1933, even before the expulsions in the RdI, the Party ransacked the house of Lange's right-hand man in the VDMA, Alexander Rüstow. Suitably intimidated, Rüstow fled Germany for Istanbul a short time later.[214] This effectively stripped the organization of its primary public champion of liberalism and free trade and sent a pointed message to its chief business manager. The ideological character of the VDMA itself was further changed when the president of the association since 1923, Wolfgang Reuter, retired in January 1934 at the age of 78.[215] In his place, the Ministry of Economics rather than the VDMA itself appointed Otto Sack as the new head of the association. Sack had been a vice president since 1932 and was thus more or less acceptable to the industry. However, he was also already a committed Nazi, and the ministry's intercession was in an unwelcome break with the traditional practices of industrial organizations.[216] In this situation Lange's own position was far from assured.

The advent of the new regime also had an immediate effect on the organization of the machine building industry itself, even within circles that Lange had formerly dominated. Like Reichert, Lange withdrew from public view during the turbulent first months of the new regime. Unlike Reichert, his own break with old habits proved to be more permanent as the primary forums for his old ideas vanished. At the beginning of 1933, the format of the journal *Maschinenbau* was radically altered. Whereas the VDMA, and Lange and Rüstow in particular, had been responsible for the production of an 'economic section' featuring articles on a wide variety of economic, social and political issues, this portion of the journal disappeared completely at the beginning of 1933, and the journal was recast as the official organ of the Working Group for German Production Engineers (Arbeitsgemeinschaft der Deutschen Betriebsingenieure, ADB), which thereafter took responsibility for economic and political content.[217] The ADB immediately took the publication in a new direction, warmly embracing National Socialist ideology and entirely abandoning the ideas of the VDMA. This turned the liberal policy position that Lange and Rüstow had built over the past decade on its head. Now, *Maschinenbau* crowed about the death of liberalism and asserted the 'primacy of politics' and service to state and race above even questions of production and profitability, much less market economics.[218]

This was not just a political or rhetorical problem. The triumph of National Socialism was no less economically unpalatable to German machine builders than to the iron and steel industry in 1933. Mark Spoerer has noted that the German machine building industry did surprisingly well under the Nazi regime, and saw profits increase from 2.10 per cent to 5.81 per cent by 1939.[219] However, these profits came later in the period and were preceded by ideological and practical integration into the Nazi regime. In 1933, the new government appeared to be positively dangerous to the industry. Certain machine exports were still one of the few relatively bright spots in a generally disastrous economic crisis and accounted for no less than 88 per cent of sales in German machine tools when Hitler came to power.[220] The NSDAP's professed aim of autarky was of immediate concern to the industry, particularly given that exports to the hated USSR made up a substantial, if not predominant, portion of German machine sales.[221] Exporters' fears only increased when Hitler himself publicly supported protectionism in the name of the German peasantry over exports in the same speech in which he invoked the Enabling Act.[222] For machine builders, this was not just empty talk. The new government appeared to have a real effect on the industry, and over the course of 1933 exports of machine tools declined from 115.7 million RM in 1932 to 71.1 million RM. While domestic sales did increase by 31.7 million RM, this did not make up for the concurrent decline in exports, and the industry's total output actually sank farther, from 141 to 126.5 million RM under the new regime.[223]

Machine builders in general also suffered from the widespread perception that the spread of labour-saving machines was at least partially responsible for the unemployment crisis in Germany.[224] These ideas permeated German politics down to the local level, and by February 1934 at least one North German mayor had ordered that the industry's ongoing development of labour-saving devices be shut down in his region to fight unemployment.[225] Lange and his organization later claimed to have worked closely with the Nazi Party (particularly the DAF) to prevent a repetition of the Luddite attacks on industrialization ('*Maschinensturm*') of the 1830s.[226] However, while Ley himself rejected this argument, the attempt to limit mechanization in fact pushed Lange and the VDMA into what appears to have been their only significant conflict with the government of the Third Reich.[227] Following the discussion and later implementation of legislation aimed at limiting the use of machines in the cigar industry, the association circulated memoranda in March and July attacking the policy.[228] This did not call the policies of the new regime fundamentally into question, but it shows that Lange and his organization made at least some attempt to defend their industry from attacks by the new regime.

This opposition and the VDMA's long-standing reputation for liberalism were almost disastrous for Lange personally and taught him a lesson about criticizing the regime that he would not forget. On 3 July 1934, the Nazi Party in *Gau* Berlin launched an internal suit against Lange based on the chief business manager's activities over the course of the previous decade.[229] Lange's opposition to the changes in the cigar industry in particular furnished the court with demonstrable evidence of his political unreliability. More disturbingly, the Party charged that Lange's policies and ideas in general were inherently inimical to National Socialism. They argued that he was in fact a proponent of the 'liberal economic and trade policies of the old system,' which had often relied on him for expert advice.[230] Moreover, he had been 'against the National Socialist freedom movement, against the strengthening of the German home market, for international free trade, against German agriculture, for the Dawes and Young Plan, etc.'.[231] For good measure, the Party also charged him with having called the *Führer* a 'psychopath' shortly before his appointment as Chancellor.[232] This was a categorical attack on Lange's role in industrial politics in the years leading up to the seizure of power and a dangerous accusation in the charged atmosphere of the new regime.

These accusations were a serious problem for Lange, particularly because they were, by and large, perfectly true. However, like Reichert, Lange seems to have wriggled out of real danger in 1934. The details of his case are no longer available, but Lange was not prosecuted and the case seems to have been dropped altogether. This can be attributed to the steps Lange took immediately to ingratiate himself into the new National Socialist government. Quickly calculating that the best chance for both his and his organization's survival lay with the new government, Lange threw in his lot with the Party. Despite the strange disappearance of the relevant records, it is clear that Lange joined the NSDAP soon after Hitler's assumption of the chancellorship.[233] At the very least, the chief business manager had become a full Party member by the beginning of July 1934, a fact that ironically allowed for the suit launched against him. The indignant tone of the internal Party suit (*Parteiverfahren*) launched against Lange and its portrayal of the chief business manager as a slippery opportunist taking advantage of the Party's success seems to indicate that his rather quick change of heart after 30 January 1933 raised suspicion amongst National Socialists as well, even if he managed to avoid persecution.[234]

Lange laboured with the zeal of a convert and took a curiously personal role in integrating the VDMA into the ideology and culture of the new governing party despite (or perhaps because of) his long-standing opposition to so many of the NSDAP's policies. While many German firms and organizations contributed to Schacht's 'Adolf- Hitler- Spende' in the weeks leading up to the election of 5 March 1933, the VDMA's two contributions named Lange personally as the donor.[235] Although the first donation of 20,000 RM was clearly drawn on the VDMA's *Maschinenindustrie* account, a larger donation of 30,000 RM on 3 March appears solely in Lange's name.[236] The business managers of German industrial associations did very well for themselves, but it hardly seems possible that Lange had the resources at hand to make such a donation himself. It is much more likely that the funds came from the organization itself, and the fact that Lange alone attached his name to his association's contribution seems to indicate a certain eagerness to change his own reputation in the eyes of the NSDAP that was not shared by other 'association men', or even firm directors.

At the same time, Lange altered his relationship with the troublesome specialized associations attached to the VDMA by very quickly adapting to National

Socialist ideas regarding hierarchy and organization. Thus, when a representative of the Mercedes Büromaschinen- Werke stood for election as president at the founding meeting of the General Association of the German Office Industry (Gesamtverband der Deutschen Büroindustrie, GDBI) on 20 July 1933, Lange stepped in to block his nomination on the grounds that his firm was dominated by foreigners.[237] The following month, the beleaguered Association of German Typewriter Producers (Verband der Deutschen Schreibmaschinenfabrikanten e.V.) met to discuss severing its ties to the VDMA in the hopes of achieving a better profile with the Office Industry Association (Büro-Industrie Verband). Rather than appealing to the traditions of the association or the strength of the current structure as Reichert had done when faced with rebellious firms during this period, Lange responded by drawing on National Socialist ideas. He curtly informed the assembly that 'voluntary ties to this or that organization' were no longer viable and pushed its members into remaining attached to the VDMA through the GDBI.[238] Nazi ideas offered a convenient way around some of the conflicts in his organization, but they also effectively put Lange in the vanguard of the reorganization of industrial associational life and culture that reflected the hierarchical ideas of the Third Reich.

Lange's willingness to adopt new visions of 'leadership' and the role of economic organizations heavily influenced the structure of the old VDMA itself in the early years of the National Socialist regime. Lange and the VDMA greeted the National Socialist *Gleichschaltung* of industrial organizations into 'business groups' (Wigru) as an opportunity to assume effective control over the machine building industry themselves, so they scrambled to establish the new organization as quickly as possible.[239] The RWM regulation establishing Wirtschaftsgruppe Maschinenbau under Hauptgruppe II of Reichsgruppe Industrie was not promulgated until 25 August 1934.[240] However, Lange and his staff managed to have the reformed organization up and running as Wirtschaftgruppe Maschinenbau by the following month, despite the fact that even the chief business manager himself remained unsure of the responsibilities or expenses of the new organization well into the next year.[241] Following the same pattern as the other *Wirtschaftsgruppen* in 1934–35, Lange, the VDMA and its staff, organization and structure were all carried over into the new coordinated economic organization. As a result, the old VDMA was very quickly transformed into an organization designed to regulate and restrict business practice in machine building.

Beginning in late 1934, Lange was able to use the new system to strengthen his own position and that of his organization. Rather than acting as a group that theoretically coordinated a variety of more or less independent firms, the *Wirtschaftsgruppe* absorbed the specialized associations that represented aspects of the industry. Organizations like the relatively new German Office Industry Federation (Gesamtverband der Deutschen Büroindustrie) and the more venerable Precision Tool Association (Deutscher Präzisionswerkzeug-Verband) were immediately incorporated into the *Wirtschaftsgruppe* as *Fachgruppen* (technical groups) or *Unterfachgruppen* (subsidiary technical groups) to deal with the specialized questions in various branches of the industry.[242] This robbed the related organizations of their former independence and made them directly responsible to Lange. This structure was significantly strengthened by the introduction of the *Zusatzausfuhrverfahren* (ZAV) export subsidy programme less than one year later.

By May of 1934, Lange was already pushing for a politically motivated expansion of exports, even if the domestic market offered better opportunities or firms could export only at a loss.[243] Unsurprisingly, smaller firms pushed back, and members of the machine building industry were at the forefront of demands for some kind of export subsidy.[244] This was achieved in mid-1935 with the establishment of the ZAV, which effectively taxed German industry as a whole in order to provide selective subsidies to some key export sectors and firms.[245] As an industry that in the regime's estimation possessed several viable exporting branches, Lange and his new control offices took on the responsibility of allocating subsidies to individual firms.[246] At the same time, although German iron and steel rations for new machines were issued to 'end users' who could then shop their projects around to potential producers, exporters relied on a general fund (*Global-Kontingent*) ultimately administered by the *Wirtschaftsgruppe* to fix their maximum production limits.[247] This significantly expanded the Wigru's role in the lives of its members.

In order to administer the ZAV, a Control Office was established for each business group to oversee prices, licensing requirements and subsidies for exports in particular. Lange himself took over the administration of Prüfungsstelle Maschinenbau as the Reich's representative (*Reichsbeauftragter*), centralizing the new organizations of the machine building industry in his own hands.[248] He also sought to expand the function of his organization and developed the Control Office and *Wirtschaftsgruppe* into a surprisingly extensive organization. It grew to be so large that the entire administrative system of the machine building industry had moved into a complex of four connected buildings by the eve of the Second World War.[249] The Control Office alone required its own building to house all of its 111 employees.[250] This organization, however, further functioned as a central direction agency, overseeing the work of twenty-six separate pre-inspection offices (*Vorprüfungsstellen*) attached to the technical and subsidiary groups.[251]

This allowed Lange to assert enormous influence over the machine building industry as both leader of the Control Office and chief business manager of the *Wirtschaftsgruppe* itself. While maintaining his role at the head of the Wigru's day-to-day operations as the representative and central authority of the machine building industry, he was also able to directly control many of the business relationships between his member firms and the state through the Control Office. Although the organizations associated with The RGI were legally not permitted to function as cartels, by 1936 Lange was pushing the technical groups to do just that; further, he actively encouraged the more specialized *Fachgruppen* to use their close personal connections between the firms and organizations to take up cartel-like functions.[252] As the *Fach-* and *Untergruppen* then reported to Lange, these efforts substantially increased the chief business manager's own responsibility and provide a sharp contrast to Reichert's approach.

Some firms chafed under the demands of Lange's association and tried to avoid the increasingly imperious organization. Siemens & Halske in particular looked to get out of membership in Wirtschaftsgruppe Maschinenbau. In April 1935, the firm's managers tried to extricate themselves from the Wigru by informing it that they no longer regarded themselves as members, considering that machine building constituted a very small part of the firm's operations.[253] The *Wirtschaftsgruppe*, however, would not hear of it and demanded that Siemens & Halske continue to pay for the forty-nine employees who were occasionally employed in machine building.[254] The firm's Vienna subsidiary even expressed scepticism that the Wigru would bother to actually demand the payment of a contribution following the *Anschluss* with Austria at all, as machine building only made up 4 per cent of its sales.[255] However, faced with the *Wirtschaftsgruppe*'s obstinate opposition, the firm chose to go through with plans to give up machine building altogether rather than fight it out with Lange and his subordinates.[256]

National Socialist aims could also stand in for more technical arguments with competing economic organizations when necessary. In the long series of negotiations over the responsibility for the regulation of industrial ovens, for instance, Lange countered the electrical industry's technical and productive arguments by appealing to the RGI's desire to establish an effective organic economy reflecting Nazi ideals.[257] In order to capitalize on this argument Lange pushed for a hearing before the *Reichsgruppe* rather than negotiating with his counterparts in the Business Group for the Electrotechnical Industry (Wirtschaftsgruppe Elektroindustrie).[258] When this failed, the machine builders tried to convince the industry that only a 'weak membership' in Wirtschaftsgruppe Elektroindustrie superseded by full membership in Wirtschaftsgruppe Maschinenbau would fulfil the regulatory aims of the state.[259] These slippery attempts to lay claim to questionable branches of production might have brought him into conflict with other *Wirtschaftsgruppen*, but they also lent Lange's own work a certain dynamism and expanded his influence in the increasingly regulated German economy.

This new-found sympathy for National Socialism extended beyond the structures of Lange's own organization. After 1933, he began to develop and espouse a new approach to economics and the role of the machine industry and its organization in Germany that likewise complemented Nazi aims. The new editors and contributors to *Maschinenbau* saw the triumph of National Socialism in 1933 as the death knell of not only liberalism but capitalism in general.[260] After the war, Lange and his colleagues claimed to have held aloof from these ideas, preserving the nature of the business association of the machine building industry as a 'free organization' that continued to focus on competitive advantage and potential markets for its members.[261] However, though Lange was more circumspect about the death of liberalism than many of his contemporaries, he quickly adapted to the expectations of the regime.

This was an important change in the way Lange saw the role of the Wigru. By January 1935 it had become clear to him that the new *Wirtschaftsgruppe* would cost considerably more to administer than the old VDMA, and he moved to soften the coming blow for his members. However, he also noted that the way the Wigru would spend its money differed greatly from that of the liberal organization of the Weimar era.[262] Many of the firms would effectively see some of their profits redistributed to other companies because, as the chief business manager was careful to point out, the *Wirtschaftsgruppe*'s new watchword would be 'general before personal use'.[263]

Lange's support for the new regime also moved beyond the rejection of the former liberal policies that had become a dead letter into much more disturbing territory. Much of Nazi thought was incompatible with standard economic analysis and behaviour in 1933. A re-evaluation of economic analysis was needed in order to bring it into line with National Socialism.[264] The VDMA contributed significantly to this process amongst the traditionally liberal German machine builders. In the first year of the *Wirtschaftsgruppe*'s existence, the organization demonstrated a marked willingness to act as a bridge between the ideology of the National Socialist regime and its own members. Unlike the former VDESI, Wirtschaftsgruppe Maschinenbau actively encouraged its members to immerse themselves in Nazi business culture. To encourage its members to adapt to the new regime, the association recommended publications like Teubner's *Betriebsgemeinschaft und Betriebsführung* (Corporate Community and Corporate Leadership) and Arnold's *Führerschaft in der Front der Arbeit* (Leadership in the Labour Front) to its members.[265] More intrepid managers were encouraged to take courses in 'leadership' in the National Socialist State.[266] Especially moving or interesting speeches by figures like Göring were made available to members at no cost, and managers were encouraged to motivate their employees to embrace a revived German culture by participating in didactic events like German Book Week.[267] A number of tracts were likewise made available to machine builders to help them to counter the potentially negative impressions their foreign customers might have of Germany under the National Socialist regime.[268] Unsurprisingly, the *Wirtschaftsgruppe* also encouraged its members to support their fellow nationals by, for instance, shipping their goods on German vessels.[269]

To a certain extent, these kinds of statements can be taken as examples of the rhetoric most organizations adopted in the years following the seizure of power in 1933 in order to avoid scrutiny by the party faithful or state offices. However, Wirtschaftsgruppe Maschinenbau also began to take more concrete steps to bring its members into line with National Socialist thought. By May of 1935, the association had already begun to press its members to facilitate the integration of the Saar region by placing their orders there.[270] Lange and his colleagues likewise advised machine builders to endorse Hitler's policy in the Rhineland plebiscite in March 1936[271] and made it clear that members were 'expected' to donate to National Socialist causes like the *Osthilfe*.[272] The Wigru itself was willing to bring National Socialist politics into its own work, denying the Boehringer company a licence to increase exports to Italy on the grounds that the state was politically unreliable, and making the rather dubious claim that the VDMA was responsible for Göring's decision to regulate the movement of workers in Germany.[273]

This support for the National Socialist regime took a more sinister turn when the *Wirtschaftsgruppe* attempted to force its members into severing all ties with Jewish representatives and firms abroad. There is no indication that Lange or his staff directly participated in the 'Aryanization' of German machine plants. However, they did not necessarily have to, as German law effectively took care of this.[274] The relationship between German and foreign firms, merchants and customers was a different question. It is unsurprising that an ideology that demanded the marginalization of Jewish Germans would eventually lead to the exclusion of foreign Jewish contacts, and by 1937 the Ministry of Economics had begun to push German firms into extricating themselves from contracts with such firms wherever possible.[275] However, Wirtschaftsgruppe Maschinenbau's efforts to achieve this same end preceded those of the RWM by several years. Less than five months after the establishment of the new Wigru – before Reichert had even managed to launch his own business group – Lange and his organization had begun to contribute to some of the more odious National Socialist claims about racial characteristics.

At the beginning of February 1935, the association published a relatively lengthy notice in its new organ, *Maschinenbau-Nachrichten*, warning its members to beware of Jewish merchants working in the British Commonwealth, particularly Canada.[276] 'Known Jewish firms,' it charged, had begun buying high-quality German machines and selling them in the Empire under British names. At the same time, it also alleged that Jewish firms were buying low-quality German products and passing them off as the best the Reich had to offer. To the *Wirtschaftsgruppe*, this was clearly an attempt by Jewish firms to undermine the credibility of German industry.[277] The almost paranoid tone of the piece was not entirely out of keeping with the traditions of the VDMA, which in the past had warned its members about shady merchants and middlemen. In fact, the previous edition of *Maschinenbau-Nachrichten* had warned its members about revealing trade secrets to Greek merchants or producers, and the following year it alerted members to its suspicions that a recently founded Belgian trade office was in fact some kind of enemy organization intended to undermine German trade.[278] However, the charges levelled against Jewish merchants were both qualitatively different and more sustained. Whereas the Greek potential for industrial espionage was presented in almost sympathetic terms as stemming from the desire for self-sufficient production, the supposed Jewish transgressions were characterized as simply malevolent. Another account warned of a Jewish representative of a German company who was inexplicably leading foreign customers to other firms.[279] Three months after that the association issued a further warning about a Jewish firm in London that had apparently been embezzling money from the German producers it had represented.[280] In May of 1936, the Wigru also reprinted what it considered to be the relevant details of an American article asserting an extensive Jewish influence on the United States, including the claim that 62 per cent of American property was in the hands of the Jews.[281] This level of engagement with National Socialism went well beyond submissive accommodation and helped to cultivate the pervasive anti-Semitism that characterized the regime.

Lange had thus demonstrated a surprising ability to adapt to the demands and realities of the National Socialist state. Far from the politically suspect manager of an association representing a liberal industry, he had now managed to position himself as a key figure in an organization that broadly reflected Nazi aims and ideologies. By reaching out personally to National Socialism, Lange diffused much of the criticism levelled against him by the new state. He also proved willing to instrumentalize Nazi ideas in a way that Reichert had not in order to protect the structure of his own organization during the transition of 1933. Unlike the chief business manager of the old VDESI, Lange was also able to develop and promote a model of a semi-autarkic economy. Finally, Lange and the VDMA embraced the nationalist and racist aims of the Party while Reichert remained unmoved by 'Nazi culture' or anti-Semitism. The very flexibility that had made Lange and the VDMA good citizens of the Weimar Republic thus ironically allowed them to overcome their past and integrate into the Third Reich by adapting to the climate of the new regime.

As a result, the two organizations took up very different positions in the early years of the Nazi state. While one appeared to embrace the 'new Germany', the other remained aloof and even petulant. Reichert continued to treat the state and its ideology as something to be bargained with, pushed or opposed – just as it had been in the Weimar Republic – but Lange adapted. This allowed Lange to build up a reputation as a reliable servant of the National Socialist state and begin to lay in a store of political capital that could be drawn on in later years. In the final analysis, little might have come from these ideological quibbles and contortions alone. However, Reichert did not just grumble, and Lange was more than just a frivolous weathercock. After 1936, as the state began to gird itself for war, the growing semantic differences between these two men increasingly translated into very different results. In this context, Lange and his association were able to demonstrate that the VDMA was of use to the Nazi state. The VDESI and its successor, on the other hand, were not only politically suspect, but also of less and less practical value to the regime.

Notes

1. Eichholtz, 'Ökonomie, Politik und Kriegsführung: Wirtschaftliche Kriegsplanung und Rüstungsorganisation bis zum Ende der "Blitzkriegphase"', 11; and I. Kershaw. 1993. *The Nazi Dictatorship: Problems and Perspectives of Interpretation*, 3rd edn, London: Edward Arnold, 50.
2. Spoerer, *Von Scheingewinnen zum Rüstungsboom*, 168–70.
3. For an excellent discussion of the variety of business opportunities open to firms under National Socialism, see Scherner, *Die Logik der Industriepolitik im Dritten Reich*.
4. Spoerer, *Von Scheingewinnen zum Rüstungsboom*, 172.
5. Overy, *War and Economy in the Third Reich*, 183–85.
6. BAB R 13 I/605 'RWM Besprechung, 16.1.1936'.
7. BAB R 13 I/601 'RWM Besprechung, 17.4.1937', 4.
8. SAN Rep. 502, VI KV-Anklage Interrogations R 48, 'Vernehmung des Jakob Reichert 11.11.1946', 4.
9. See, e.g., BAB R 13 I/106 Bd. 28 'Aufzeichnung über die am 7. Dezember 1933 abgehaltene Sitzung des Hauptvorstandes und des Fachgruppenausschusses', Draft of Reichert's *Jahresbericht*, p. 76.
10. J. Reichert. 1933. 'Das Neue Wettbewerbsgesetz der amerikanischen Eisen- und Stahlindustrie', *Stahl und Eisen* 53(40) (5 November), 1031–34.
11. BAB R 13 I/106 'Aufzeichnung über die am 7. Dezember 1933 abgehaltene Sitzung des Hauptvorstandes und des Fachgruppenausschusses', 4.
12. M. Broszat. 1981. *The Hitler State: The Foundation and Development of the Internal Structure of The Third Reich*, J. Hiden, trans., London: Longman, 164.
13. Neebe, *Großindustrie, Staat und NSDAP 1930–1933*, 189.
14. Werner Abelshauser, 'Gustav Krupp und die Gleichschaltung des Reichsverbandes der Deutschen Industrie, 1933-34', 3–26.
15. Neebe, *Großindustrie, Staat und NSDAP 1930–1933*, 194; Beck, *The Fateful Alliance*, 219–52.
16. Neebe, *Großindustrie, Staat und NSDAP 1930–1933*, 187; BAB R 13 I/106 'Aufzeichnung über die am 7. Dezember 1933 abgehaltene Sitzung des Hauptvorstandes und des Fachgruppenausschusses', 4; Übbing, *Stahl schreibt Geschichte*, 132.
17. Neebe, *Großindustrie, Staat und NSDAP 1930–1933*, 187; BAB R 13 I/106 'Aufzeichnung über die am 7. Dezember 1933 abgehaltene Sitzung des Hauptvorstandes und des Fachgruppenausschusses', 3.
18. Übbing, *Stahl schreibt Geschichte*, 132.

19. For a photo of Schlenker, see ibid., 112. For the conflict between traditional conservatives and the Nazi Party in 1933, see Beck, *The Fateful Alliance*, 114–73.
20. P. Erker. 1999. *Deutsche Unternehmer zwischen Kriegswirtschaft und Wiederaufbau: Studien zur Erfahrungsbildung von Industrie-eliten*, Munich: Oldenbourg Verlag; H. Joly. 2000. 'Kontinuität und Diskontinuität der industriellen Elite nach 1945', in D. Ziegler (ed.), *Großbürger und Unternehmer: Die deutsche Wirtschaftselite im 20. Jahrhundert*, Göttingen: Vandenhoek & Ruprecht, 58.
21. P. Gohle, 'Vita', in *Albert Pietzsch, Industrieller und Wirtschaftsfunktionär. Präsident der Reichswirtschaftskammer. Nachlass 1874–1957 (1991) Bestanddsignatur: ED 458*, Archiv des Instituts für Zeitgeschichte, München (hereafter AIZ), http://www.ifz-muenchen.de/archiv/ed_458.pdf, 1999, 5. For Strasser's curious political and economic ideas, see D. Silverman. 1998. *Hitler's Economy: Nazi Work Creation Programs, 1933–1936*, Cambridge, MA: Harvard University Press, 51–52; James, *The German Slump*, 350; Barkai, *Nazi Economics*, 40–48; P. Stachura. 1983. *Gregor Strasser and the Rise of Nazism*, London: Allen & Unwin.
22. Stachura, *Gregor Strasser and the Rise of Nazism*, 6; AIZ, Albert Pietzsch; Industrieller und Wirtschaftsfunktionär. Präsident der Reichswirtschaftskammer; Nachlass 1874–1957 (1991), amtliches Schriftgut, Manuskripte, Geschaeftsunterlagen, Spruchkammerakten, persönliche Unterlagen. ED 458, Band 1, Mitgliedschaft in der NSDAP 1927/30-1945/ Stab Stellvertreter des Führers: Beauftragter für Wirtschaftsfragen 1933–1936. 'Pietzsch an den Stellvertreter des Führers 11.4.1934'.
23. See A. Pietzsch. 1933. 'Grundsätzliche Betrachtungen über Volkswirtschaft', supplement to *Der Arbeitgeber* 22(15 November). For a later example see AIZ Nachlass Pietzsch, ED 458 Bd. 2 Beirat der Deutschen Reichsbahn/Reichswirtschaftskammer 'Wirtschaftslenkung durch den Staat (Denkschrift 1938)'. For Pietzsch's relationship to industrialists, see IAZ. ED 458 Bd. 1. 'Pietzsch an den Stellvertreter des Führers, 21.8.1935'.
24. BAB R 13 I/602 'Grassmann an Reichert, 6.8.1934'.
25. BAB R 13 I/602 'NSDAP Oberstes Parteigericht an Reichert, 1.8.1934'.
26. BAB R 13 I/602 'Reichert an daß Oberste Parteigericht der NSDAP, z. Hd. des Herrn Vorsitzenden Walther Buch, 3.8.1934', 'Reichert an Grassmann, 3.8.1934', and 'Reichert an Pietzsch, 3.8.1934'.
27. BAB R 13 I/602 'Reichert an daß Oberste Parteigericht der NSDAP, z. Hd. des Herrn Vorsitzenden Walther Buch, 3.8.1934'.
28. BAB R 13 I/602 'Reichert an Grassmann, 3.8.1934'.
29. BAB R 13 I/602 'Pietzsch an Reichert, 6.8.1934'; BAB R 13 I/602 'Grassmann an Reichert, 6.8.1934'; R 13 I/602 'Reichert an Grassmann, 8.8.1934'.
30. BAB R 13 I/602 'Reichert an Grasmann, 6.8.1934'.
31. BAB R 13 I/602 'Ungewitter an Reichert bei Baier, 23.7.1934'.
32. SAN Rep. 502, VI KV-Anklage Interrogations R 48, 'Vernehmung des Jakob Reichert 18.6.1947', 4–5; Neebe, *Großindustrie, Staat und NSDAP 1930–1933*, 195.
33. SAN Rep. 502, VI KV-Anklage Interrogations R 48, '"Vernehmung des Jakob Reichert 18.6.1947"', pg. 5, 2.
34. BAB R 13 I/601 'Reichert an die Fima Bänninger GmbH, R. Hooste & Co, Gustav Gerhardis, Gußstahlwerke Wittman AG, 26. 9. 1933', 1.
35. SAN Rep. 502, VI KV-Anklage Interrogations R 48, 'Vernehmung des Jakob Reichert 11.11.1946', 12.
36. The RWM itself was shocked to learn that Wirtschaftsgruppe Elektroindustrie hoped to offer Ostermann a staggering 70,000 RM per year. In the interest of maintaining an effective hierarchy, the RWM capped Ostermann's salary (and that of other *Haupt-*

geschäftsführer) at 36,000 RM, the same salary paid to the chief business manager of Reichsgruppe Industrie. BAB R 3101 9090 'RWM Vermerk 27.8.1937' and 'Der Leiter der Reichsgruppe Industrie an RWM 9.9.1937'.
37. BAB R 13 I/601 'Alms an Ostermann 3.10.1933'.
38. BAB R 13 I/601 'Ausführung auf der Mitgliederversammlung des Fittingsverbands am 30. Sept. 1933', 2.
39. BAB R 13 I/601 'Ostermann an Alms 29.9.1933'; BAB R 13 I/601 'Reichert an die Firma Bänninger GmbH, R. Hooste & Co, Gustav Gerhardis, Gußstahlwerke Wittman AG, 26.9.1933', 1.
40. BAB R 13 I/601 'Reichert an die Firma Bänninger GmbH, R. Hooste & Co, Gustav Gerhardis, Gußstahlwerke Wittman AG, 26.9.1933', 1.
41. BAB R 13 I/601 'Ausführung auf der Mitgliederversammlung des Fittingsverbands am 30. Sept. 1933', 1, 3, 6.
42. Ibid., 5, 6.
43. Ibid., 7.
44. BAB R 13 I/601 'Reichert an A. Hilger, Dr. Bührer, Dr. Alms. 21.10.1933'.
45. SAN Rep. 502, VI KV-Anklage Interrogations R 48, 'Vernehmung des Jakob Reichert 11.11.1946', 11.
46. Ibid.
47. Ibid.
48. See Evans, *The Coming of the Third Reich*, 357–58.
49. BAB R 13 I/106 'Aufzeichnung über die am 7. Dezember 1933 abgehaltene Sitzung des Hauptvorstandes und des Fachgruppenausschusses', 17.
50. J. Reichert. 1934. 'Wiederaufstieg der deutschen Eisen- und Stahlindustrie im Jahre 1933', *Stahl und Eisen* 54(1) (4 January), 12.
51. SAN Rep. 502, VI KV-Anklage Interrogations R 48, 'Vernehmung des Jakob Reichert 18.6.1947', 3.
52. SAN Rep. 502, VI KV-Anklage Interrogations R 48, 'Vernehmung des Jakob Reichert 3.7.1947', 3–4; SAN Rep. 502, VI KV-Anklage Interrogations R 48, 'Vernehmung des Jakob Reichert 18.6.1947', 3.
53. SAN Rep. 502, VI KV-Anklage Interrogations R 48, 'Vernehmung des Jakob Reichert 18.6.1947', 3.
54. BAB R 13 I/106 'Aufzeichnung über die am 7. Dezember 1933 abgehaltene Sitzung des Hauptvorstandes und des Fachgruppenausschusses', 19; SAN Rep. 502, VI KV-Anklage Interrogations R 48, 'Vernehmung des Jakob Reichert 18.6.1947', 2.
55. BAB R 13 I/106 'Aufzeichnung über die am 7. Dezember 1933 abgehaltene Sitzung des Hauptvorstandes und des Fachgruppenausschusses', 14–15.
56. BAB R 13 I/106 Bd. 28. 'Organisationsfragen: (berufsständischer Aufbau der Industrie)' prepared for the 7.12.1933 meeting of the VDESI, 1.
57. BAB R 13 I/106 'Aufzeichnung über die am 7. Dezember 1933 abgehaltene Sitzung des Hauptvorstandes und des Fachgruppenausschußes', 19.
58. Ibid.
59. BAB R 13 I/106 'Aufzeichnung über die am 7. Dezember 1933 abgehaltene Sitzung des Hauptvorstandes und des Fachgruppenausschusses', Draft of Poensgen's Address, 20; J. Reichert. 1933. 'Deutschlands Stellung in der Weltwirtschaft', *Stahl und Eisen* 53(32) (10 August), 835; BAB R 13 I/106 'Aufzeichnung über die am 7. Dezember 1933 abgehaltene Sitzung des Hauptvorstandes und des Fachgruppenausschusses', Draft of Reichert's *Jahresbericht*, 44, 47.
60. See Reichert, 'Wiederaufstieg der deutschen Eisen- und Stahlindustrie im Jahre 1933', 12.

61. Reichert, 'Deutschlands Stellung in der Weltwirtschaft', 835.
62. BAB R 13 I/106 'Aufzeichnung über die am 7. Dezember 1933 abgehaltene Sitzung des Hauptvorstandes und des Fachgruppenausschusses', Draft of Reichert's *Jahresbericht*, 75.
63. BAB R 13 I/106 'Aufzeichnung über die am 7. Dezember 1933 abgehaltene Sitzung des Hauptvorstandes und des Fachgruppenausschusses', 20.
64. BAB R 13 I/106 'Aufzeichnung über die am 7. Dezember 1933 abgehaltene Sitzung des Hauptvorstandes und des Fachgruppenausschusses', Draft of Reichert's *Jahresbericht*, 74–75.
65. BAB R 13 I/106 'Aufzeichnung über die am 7. Dezember 1933 abgehaltene Sitzung des Hauptvorstandes und des Fachgruppenausschusses' Draft of Poensgen's Address, 20.
66. BAB R 13 I/106 'Aufzeichnung über die am 7. Dezember 1933 abgehaltene Sitzung des Hauptvorstandes und des Fachgruppenausschusses', Draft of Reichert's *Jahresbericht*, 75–76.
67. BAB R 13 I/106 'Aufzeichnung über die am 7. Dezember 1933 abgehaltene Sitzung des Hauptvorstandes und des Fachgruppenauschusses', 20.
68. BAB R 13 I/106 'Aufzeichnung über die am 7. Dezember 1933 abgehaltene Sitzung des Hauptvorstandes und des Fachgruppenausschusses', Draft of Reichert's *Jahresbericht*, 50–51.
69. Ibid., 42–43.
70. Ibid., 48–49.
71. BAB R 13 I/106 Bd. 28. 'Organisationsfragen: (berufsständischer Aufbau der Industrie)' prepared for the 7 December 1933 meeting of the VDESI, 2.
72. Ibid., 3; BAB R 13 I/106 'Aufzeichnung über die am 7. Dezember 1933 abgehaltene Sitzung des Hauptvorstandes und des Fachgruppenausschusses', 4–5.
73. BAB R 13 I/106 Bd. 28. 'Organisationsfragen: (berufsständischer Aufbau der Industrie)', prepared for the 7 December 1933 meeting of the VDESI, 2.
74. R-WW, GHH Nachlass Paul Reusch 400101222/4 'Reichert an Wirtschaftsgruppe Eisenschaffende Industrie, Rundschreiben #998, 3.4.1935'.
75. R-WW, GHH Nachlass Paul Reusch 400101222/4 'Reichert und Poensgen an die Herren Mitglieder, Vorsitzenden und Mitglieder des Hauptvorstande, und die Gruppen des Vereins, Mitglieder der Nordwest-, Süd- usw. Gruppen, 10.5.1935'.
76. SAN, Vernehmung des Dr. J.W. Reichert. Interrogation # 724. 4.2.1947, p. 2; G. Greer. 1925. *The Ruhr-Lorraine Industrial Problem: A Study of the Economic Interdependence of the Two Regions and their Relation to the Reparation Question*, New York: The Macmillan Company, 32.
77. R-WW, GHH 40010222/4 'Reichert an die Wirtschaftsgruppe, Rundschreiben #998. 3.4.1935'.
78. BAB R 13 I/617 'Beiratsitzung 29.3.1935I'.
79. R-WW Nachlass Paul Reusch 40010222/4 'Reichert an die Wirtschaftsgruppe, Rundschreiben #998. 3.4.1935'.
80. BAB R 13 I/240 'Mitglieder-Verzeichnis November 1935'.
81. BAB R 13 I/617 'Reichert an den Herrn Führer der Hauptgruppe I der gewerblichen Wirtschaft 10.12.1934'.
82. BAB R 12 I/214 'Reichsgruppe Industrie: Dienstverteilung in der Geschäftsführung 1.4.1935'.
83. Greer, *The Ruhr-Lorraine Industrial Problem*, 25.
84. R-WW GHH, Nachlass Paul Reusch, 400101290/42, Ernst Poensgen, 'Hitler und die Ruhrindustriellen: Ein Rückblick' c. 1946, 7.
85. SAN Rep. 502, VI KV-Anklage Interrogations R 48, Interrogation #323, 'Vernehmung des Dr. J.W. Reichert, 18.11.1946', 6.

86. R-WW, GHH Nachlass Paul Reusch, 400101222/4 'Reichert an die Mitglieder des Beirats der Wirtschaftsgruppe, 11.7.1935'.
87. BAB R 13 I/617 'Reichert an Poensgen, 19.3.1935'.
88. R-WW, GHH Nachlass Paul Reusch, 400101222/4 'Reichert an die Mitglieder des Beirats der Wirtschaftsgruppe, 11.7.1935'.
89. BAB R 13 I/ 619 'Beiratssitzung 9.7.1936'.
90. R-WW GHH, Nachlass Paul Reusch, 400101290/42, Ernst Poensgen, 'Hitler und die Ruhrindustriellen: Ein Rückblick' c. 1946, 7.
91. BAB R 13 I/602 'RWM Besprechung 23.4.37', 1.
92. R-WW GHH Nachlass Paul Reusch, 400101222/4 'Reichert und Poensgen an die Herren Ehrenmitglieder, Vorsitzenden und Mitglieder des Hauptvorstandes, 10.5.1935' and 'Baare an die Herren Mitglieder des Ausschusses der Fachgruppe der eisenschaffenden Industrie, 27.4.1935'.
93. Cf. BAB R 13 I/105 'Aufzeichnung über die Sitzung des Hauptvorstandes und Fachgruppenausschusses, 17.11.1932', 23; R 13 I/617 'Reichert an die Herrn Führer der Hauptgruppe I der gewerblichen Wirtschaft 10.12.1934'; and 'Reichert und Baare an E. Poensgen 12.2.1935'.
94. SAN, Rep. 502, VI KV-Anklage Interrogations R 48, Interrogation #323. 'Vernehmung des Dr. J.W. Reichert, 18.11.1946', 3.
95. SAN, Rep. 502, VI KV-Anklage Interrogations R 48, Interrogation #724, 'Vernehmung des Dr. J.W. Reichert 4.2.1947', 4.
96. R-WW, GHH Nachlass Paul Reusch 4001222/4 'Reichert und Poensgen an die Herren Ehrenmitglieder, Vorsitzenden und Mitglieder des Hauptvorstands, an die Gruppen der Wirtschaftsgruppe, 10.5.1935'.
97. See, e.g., SAN Rep. 502, VI KV-Anklage Interrogations R 48, 'Erklärung unter Eid, 3.7.1947', 3.
98. Greer, *The Ruhr-Lorraine Industrial Problem*, 32.
99. BAB R 13 I/605 'RWM Besprechung, 6.2.1936' and 'RWM Besprechung 4.6.1936', 5.
100. R-WW, GHH Nachlass Paul Reusch 400101290/32b 'Poensgen an Guth, 22.2.1936'.
101. SAN, Rep. 502, VI KV-Anklage Interrogations R 48, Dr. J.W. Reichert 'Erklärung unter Eid, 3.7.1947', 3.
102. SAN, Rep. 502, VI KV-Anklage Interrogations R 48, Interrogation #323. 'Vernehmung des Dr. J.W. Reichert, 18.11.1946', 6-7.
103. Ibid., 7.
104. R-WW, Nachlass Otto Wolff Abt. 77, Nr. 285 Fasz. 4. 'Siedersleben an Reichert 6.5.1944'.
105. R-WW, GHH Nachlass Paul Reusch 400101290/42 'Reichert an alle Mitglieder, 24.7.1935'.
106. BAB R 9 XI/2 'Anschriften: der Prüfungsstelle und Vorprüfungsstellen vom 1.11.1944.'
107. BAB R 13 I/ 618 'Ergänzung des Abkommens zwischen der Wirtschaftsgruppe und der Bezirksgruppe Nordwest vom März 1935', Art. 5a, p. 2.
108. Ibid.
109. Ibid., Art. 4, p. 1.
110. Ibid., Art. 5c, p. 3.
111. SAN, Rep. 502, VI KV-Anklage Interrogations R 48, Interrogation #321 'Vernehmung des Dr. J.W. Reichert, 18.11.1946', 7.
112. BAB R 13 I/ 601 Bd. 1. 'Reichert an den Verein deutscher Eisenhüttenleute, z. Hd. von Herrn Dr. Petersen, 18.6.1936'.
113. BAB R 13 I/241 'Krämer an Wirtschaftsgruppe Eisenschaffende Industrie, 2.12.1935'.
114. BAB R 13 I/461 'Niederschrift: Deutsche Stahlgemeinschaft GmbH 15.10.1937', 44 in BAB pagination.

115. R-WW, GHH Nachlass Paul Reusch 400101290/32b Guth's 'Vorschläge' attached to 'E. Poensgen an Guth, 22.2.1936'.
116. R-WW, GHH Nachlass Paul Reusch 40010290/32a 'Reusch an E. Poensgen 16.12.1934'.
117. SAN, Rep. 502, VI KV-Anklage Interrogations R 48, Interrogation #321A 'Vernehmung des Dr. J.W. Reichert, 3.1.1947', 8.
118. BAB R 13 I/241 'Krämer an Wirtschaftsgruppe Eisenschaffende Industrie, 2.12.1935'; R 13 I/241 'Niederschrift: Sitzung über die gesetzliche Neuregelung der Arbeit der Jugendlichen, 17.12.1935'; R 13 I 241 'Reichert an Krämer, 3.2.1936'.
119. BAB R 13 I/601 Bd. 1. 'Reichert an den Verein deutscher Eisenhüttenleute, z.Hd. von Herrn Petersen, 18.6.1936'.
120. BAB R 13 I/41 'Maulick an Reichert, 5.2.1937'.
121. R-WW, GHH Nachlass Paul Reusch 400101290/42 'E. Poensgen an Lange' forwarded to Reusch 18.8.1937'.
122. BAB R 13 I/ 617 'Süddeutsche Eisen- und Stahl-Berufsgenossenschaft an Wirtschaftsgruppe Eisenschaffende Industrie, 11.12.1935', 'Reichert an Süddeutsche Eisen- und Stahl-Berufsgenossenschaft, 15.2.1935'.
123. BAB R 13 I/617 'Süddeutsche Eisen- und Stahl-Berufsgenossenschaft an Wirtschaftsgruppe Eisenschaffende Industrie, 18.2.1935'.
124. BAB R 13 I/617 'Reichert an Süddeutsche Eisen- und Stahl-Berufsgenossenschaft, 18.2.1935' and 'Baare an Süddeutsche Eisen- und Stahl-Berufsgenossenschaft, 20.2.1935'.
125. '…man hätte müssen handeln mit dem Revolver in der Hand, um sich dann selbst umzubringen, indem man ins KZ wandert'. SAN Rep. 502, VI KV-Anklage Interrogations R 48, Interrogation #2197. 'Vernehmung des Jakob Reichert 14.5.1947', 9.
126. SAN Rep. 502, VI KV-Anklage Interrogations R 48, Interrogation #2197 'Vernehmung des Jakob Reichert 14.5.1947', 6.
127. BAB R 13 I/106 Bd. 28. 'Reichert an Fischer12.12.1933' and 'Reichert an Poensgen 8.12.1933'.
128. BAB R 13 I/106 'Aufzeichnung über die am 7. Dezember 1933 abgehaltene Sitzung des Hauptvorstandes und des Fachgruppenausschusses', 5.
129. BAB R 13 I/ 241 'Wirtschaftsgruppe Rundschreiben #779. 29.1.1936'.
130. Wolffsohn, *Industrie und Handwerk im Konflikt mit staatlicher Wirtschaftspolitik?* 274–75.
131. See, e.g., BAB R 13 I/ 240 'Baare an Bezirksgruppe, Verbände der Wirtschaftsgruppe, Empfänger des Rundschreiben 12.11.1935'.
132. BAB R 13 I/ 241 'Wirtschaftsgruppe Rundschreiben 1793 4.3.1936' and R 13 I/243 'Wirtschaftsgruppe Rundschreiben 11929 15.8.1938'.
133. BAB R 13 I/106 'Aufzeichnung über die am 7. Dezember 1933 abgehaltene Sitzung des Hauptvorstandes und des Fachgruppenausschusses', Draft of Reichert's *Jahresbericht*, 65, 67–68.
134. Reichert, 'Deutschlands Stellung in der Weltwirtschaft', 834–35.
135. BAB R 13 I/106 'Aufzeichnung über die am 7. Dezember 1933 abgehaltene Sitzung des Hauptvorstandes und des Fachgruppenausschusses', Draft of Reichert's *Jahresbericht*, 74.
136. For a discussion of this question see T. Mason. 1977. *Sozialpolitik im Dritten Reich: Arbeiterklasse und Volksgemeinschaft*, Opladen: Westdeutscher Verlag. See also R. Hachtmann. 2008. 'Labour Policy in Industry', in C. Buchheim (ed.), *German Industry in the Nazi Period*, Stuttgart: Franz Steiner Verlag; R. Hachtmann. 'Die Deutsche Arbeitsfront im Zweiten Weltkrieg', in D. Eichholz. 1999. *Krieg und Wirtschaft: Studien zur deutschen Wirtschaftsgeschichte 1939-1945*, Berlin: Metropol; T. Siegel. 1988.

'Rationalisierung statt Klassenkampf: Zur Rolle der DAF in der nationalsozialistischen Ordnung der Arbeit', in H. Mommsen (ed.), *Herrschaftsalltag im Dritten Reich*, Düsseldorf: Swann Verlag; Schneider, *Unterm Hakenkreuz*.
137. BAB R 13 I/106 'Aufzeichnung über die am 7. Dezember 1933 abgehaltene Sitzung des Hauptvorstandes und des Fachgruppenausschusses', Draft of Reichert's *Jahresbericht*, 59.
138. Ibid., 59, 61.
139. See, e.g., BAB R 13 I/ 602 'RWM Besprechung, 23.9.1938', 3, 10.
140. BAB R 13 I/602 'Aktenvermerk, Betr.: Broschüre des Hauptmann Schmidt, 'Kriegsgewinne und Wirtschaft', 5.10.1935'.
141. Ibid.
142. BAB R 13 I/ 601 'Reichert an E. Poensgen, 18.12.1936'.
143. BAB R 13 I/605 'RWM Besprechung, 4.6.1936', 7.
144. R-WW, GHH Nachlass Paul Reusch 400101290/32b 'Der Volkswirt, 3.7.1936' in Das neue Gesetz zum organischen Aufbau der deutschen Wirtschaft.
145. R-WW, GHH Nachlaß Paul Reusch 400101290/32a 'Guth an E. Poensgen, 'Exposé', 9.1.1935'.
146. Ibid.
147. BAB R 13 I/601 'RWM Besprechung 23.4.1937', 2.
148. See ibid. In this particular case, Poensgen was speaking in the context of the conflict over the double AVI-ZAV payments.
149. BAB R 13 I/605 'RWM Besprechung, 4.6.1936', 6.
150. BAB R 13 I/617 'Beiratssitzung, 27.2.1935'.
151. J. Reichert. 1936. *Nationale und internationale Kartelle*, Berlin: Junker und Dünhaupt Verlag, 47.
152. J. Reichert. 1935. 'Internationale Übersicht über die Kartellgesetzgebung' *Stahl und Eisen* 55(24) (13 June), 655.
153. J. Reichert. 1936. 'Ein Rückblick auf das zehnjährige Bestehen der internationalen Stahlverbände' *Stahl und Eisen* 56(48) (26 November), 1431.
154. J. Reichert. 1937. 'Aus Fachverein: Mitgliederversammlung der Wirtschaftsgruppe Eisenschaffende Industrie und Bezirksgruppe Nordwest', *Stahl und Eisen* 57(25) (24 June), 707.
155. R-WW, GHH Nachlaß Paul Reusch 400101290/32b 'Betr.: Das neue Gesetz zum organischen Aufbau der deutschen Wirtschaft', 4.
156. Reichert, 'Internationale Übersicht über die Kartellgesetzgebung', 655.
157. Reichert, *Nationale und Internationale Kartelle*, 49.
158. Ibid., 12.
159. Ibid., 9.
160. Ibid., 43.
161. Ibid., 53.
162. Ibid., 52.
163. Ibid., 53.
164. Reichert, 'Deutschlands Stellung in der Weltwirtschaft', 835.
165. J. Reichert. 1934. 'Die Handelspolitik der führenden Wirtschaftsvölker in der Nachkriegszeit', *Stahl und Eisen* 54(11) (15 Marz), 264; BAB R 13 I/106 'Aufzeichnung über die am 7. Dezember 1933 abgehaltene Sitzung des Hauptvorstandes und des Fachgruppenausschusses', Draft of Reichert's *Jahresbericht*, 55–56.
166. BAB R 13 I/106 'Aufzeichnung über die am 7. Dezember 1933 abgehaltene Sitzung des Hauptvorstandes und des Fachgruppenausschusses', 12. For a description of scrip and the ZAV see H. Ludmer. 1943. 'German Financial Mobilization', *Accounting Review* 18(1), 38; C. Kobrak. 2003. 'The Foreign-Exchange Dimension of Corporate

Control in the Third Reich: The Case of Schering AG', *Contemporary European History* 12(1), 36.
167. BAB R 3101 Anh/alt R 7 Anh. MCC/1 Office of the Military Government for Germany (US) Ministerial Documents Branch, Economics Division. APO 742. *Arbeitsgruppe Industrie, Eisen und Stahl* Berlin, 3.9.1946. 'Das Zusatzausfuhrverfahren (ZAV)', 2.
168. BAB R 13 I/106 'Aufzeichnung über die am 7. Dezember 1933 abgehaltene Sitzung des Hauptvorstandes und des Fachgruppenausschusses', Draft of Reichert's *Jahresbericht*, 56, 57.
169. BAB R 13 I/106 'Aufzeichnung über die am 7. Dezember 1933 abgehaltene Sitzung des Hauptvorstandes und des Fachgruppenausschusses', 16.
170. Reichert, 'Das neue Wettbewerbsgesetz der amerikanischen Eisen- und Stahlindustrie', 1031.
171. Ibid., 1032.
172. Reichert, 'Die Handelspolitik der führenden Wirtschaftsvölker in der Nachkriegszeit', 264.
173. Reichert, *Nationale und Internationale Kartelle,* 9.
174. BAB R 13 I/605 'RWM Besprechung, 4.6.1936', 5.
175. BAB R 13 I/241 'Reichert an die Mitglieder des Beirats und Geschäftsführer der Gruppen und Verbände, 8.3.1936'.
176. R 13 I/619 'Beschränkung der Ausfuhr, 11.6.1936'.
177. Reichert, 'Die Handelspolitik der führenden Wirtschaftsvölker in der Nachkriegszeit', 264.
178. BAB R 13 I/605 'RWM Besprechung, 21.3.1936', 4–5; R 13 I/605 'RWM Besprechung 14.5.1936', 4.
179. BAB R 13 I/605 'RWM Besprechung, 14.11.1934', 235–38 in BAB pagination.
180. BAB R 13 I/601 'Aufzeichnung über eine Besprechung mit Preiskommissar Goerdeler, 12.12.1934', 6.
181. BAB R 13 I/605 'Reichert an Köcke, 19.5.1936'.
182. M. Diehl. 2005. *Von der Marktwirtschaft zur nationalsozialistischen Kriegswirtschaft: Die Transformation der deutschen Wirtschaftsordnung 1933–1945,* Stuttgart: Steiner Verlag, 58.
183. Ibid. and BAB R 13 I/601 'Aufzeichnung über eine am 12. Dezember 1934 mit Herrn Oberbürgermeister Dr. Goerdeler im Reichskommissariat für Preisüberwachung geführte Verhandlung'.
184. BAB R 13 I/601 'Aufzeichnung über eine am 12. Dezember 1934 mit Herrn Oberbürgermeister Dr. Goerdeler im Reichskommissariat für Preisüberwachung geführte Verhandlung', 4, 7.
185. Ibid., 7.
186. BAB R 13 I/605 'RWM Besprechung, 12.12.1934', 7.
187. Ibid., 9–10.
188. Ibid., 8.
189. Ibid., 5; Dichgans, 'Stahl und Politik', 67–69; Diehl, *Von der Marktwirtschaft zur nationalsozialistischen Kriegswirtschaft,* 58.
190. BAB R 13 I/601 'Aufzeichnung über eine am 12. Dezember 1934 mit Herrn Oberbürgermeister Dr. Goerdeler im Reichskommissariat für Preisüberwachung geführte Verhandlung', 9.
191. BAB R 13 I/41 'Baare an Kiegel, 23.11.1935'.
192. SAN, Rep. 502, VI KV-Anklage Interrogations R 48, Interrogation #1454 'Vernehmung des Dr. J.W. Reichert, 18.6.1947', 9.
193. BAB R 13 I/605 'RWM Besprechung, 16.1.1936', 6.

194. BAB R 13 I/605 'RWM Besprechung, 6.2.1936', 2.
195. BAB R 13 I/605 'RWM Besprechung, 20.2.1936', 6.
196. Krupp had in fact indicated that he would submit to an independent arbitrator, and Poensgen carried this suggestion forward to Kiegel. BAB R 13 I/605 'RWM Besprechung, 4.6.1936', 5.
197. Ibid., 6.
198. Ibid.
199. BAB R 13 I/605 'RWM Besprechung, 20.2.1936', 2.
200. BAB R 13 I/601 'RWM Besprechung, 17.4.1837', 3; R 13 I/241 'Reichert an Kiegel, 8.2.1936'; R-WW, GHH Nachlass Paul Reusch 400101222/4 'Reichert an den Beirat der Wirtschaftsgruppe, 17.5.1935'.
201. BAB R 13 I/242 'Wirtschaftsgruppe Eisenschaffende Industrie, Rundschreiben #3381, 8.5.1936'.
202. BAB R 13 I/242 'Wirtschaftsgruppe Eisenschaffende Industrie, Rundschreiben #4877, 7.7.1936'.
203. Ibid.
204. BAB R 13 I/601 'RWM Besprechung, 17.4.1937', 2.
205. R-WW, GHH Nachlaß Paul Reusch 400101222/4 'Niederschrift über die Sitzung des Beirats der Wirtschaftsgruppe, 9.6.1936', 4.
206. BAB R 13 I/241 'Wirtschaftsgruppe Eisenschaffende Industrie, Rundschreiben #1777, 4.3.1936'.
207. See R. Puppo. 1989. *Die wirtschaftsrechtliche Gesetzgebung des Dritten Reiches,* Constance: Hartung-Gorre, 9–11.
208. See H.-E. Volkmann. 2003. *Ökonomie und Expansion: Grundzüge der NS-Wirtschaftspolitik,* Munich: R Oldenbourg, 103–31.
209. BAB R 13 I/601 'Niederschrift über die am 15. Juni 1937 im Amt für deutsche Roh und-Werkstoffe abgehaltene Besprechung', 2; R 13 I/242 'Reichs- und Preußischer Wirtschaftsminister an Wirtschaftsgruppe Eisenschaffende Industrie, 13.7.1936'; R 13 I/605 'RWM Besprechung, 4.6.1936'.
210. BAB R 13 I/242 'Reichs- und Preußischer Wirtschaftsminister an Wirtschaftsgruppe Eisenschaffende Industrie, 13.7.1936'.
211. BAB R 13 I/242 'Wirtschaftsgruppe, Rundschreiben #5527, 27.7.1936'.
212. Ibid.
213. Neebe, *Großindustrie, Staat und NSDAP 1930–1933,* 189; Broszat, *The Hitler State,* 164.
214. Hasselbach, *Autoritärer Liberalismus und soziale Marktwirtschaft,* 328, fn. 284
215. Pohl and Markner, *Verbandsgeschichte und Zeitgeschichte,* 319; 'Reuter (luth.) 1) Wolfgang Andreas, Unternehmeer' in Historischen Kommission bei der Bayerischen Akademie der Wissenschaften. 1982. *Neue Deutsche Biographie.* 21, Berlin: Duncker & Humblot, 464.
216. Pohl and Markner, *Verbandsgeschichte und Zeitgeschichte,* 319; BAB R 13 III/78 'Gemeinschaftsarbeit im Maschinenbau 15. November 1892 bis November 1942', 4.
217. See *Maschinenbau- der Betrieb: Organ der Arbeitsgemeinschaft der Deutschen Betriebsingenieure (ADB) & DIN Mitteilung des Deutschen Normenausschusses* 12(1), 1933.
218. O. Schweninger. 1933. 'Dienst der Technik/Organisation des Einsatzes der Arbeit und der technischen Mittel' *Maschinenbau* 12(9/10), 231–32; 'Betriebsingenieure an die Front'. 1933. *Maschinenbau* 12(15/16), 373.
219. Spoerer, *Von Scheingewinnen zum Rüstungsboom,* 172.
220. *The United States Strategic Bombing Survey, No. 55: Machine Tool Industry in Germany,* Equipment Division, 2nd edn, January 1947, 9.

221. Ibid.
222. Barkai, *Nazi Economics*, 175.
223. *The United States Strategic Bombing Survey, No. 54: Machine Tools and Machinery as Capital Equipment*, Table 16, 'Output and Domestic Sales of Machine Tools', 79.
224. Ibid., 21; Abelshauser, 'Kriegswirtschaft und Wirtschaftswunder', 513.
225. 'Maschinenstürmer'. 1934. *Maschinenbau* 13(3/4) , 64.
226. BAB R 13 III/78 'Gemeinschaftsarbeit im Maschinenbau 15. November 1892 bis November 1942', 5.
227. 'Maschinenstürmer', 64; Pohl and Markner, *Verbandsgeschichte und Zeitgeschichte*, 82.
228. Pohl and Markner, *Verbandsgeschichte und Zeitgeschichte*, 82.
229. Ibid.
230. Ibid.
231. Ibid., 83.
232. Ibid.
233. The documents used by Pohl and Markner demonstrate that Lange was in fact already a member of the Party (*Mitgliedsnummer* 2878730) at the time he was charged in early July 1934. However, as noted above, the documents used by these authors are no longer available. Neither the Bundesarchiv, Berlin Document Centre, nor the regional archives in Berlin have any record of Lange's party membership. Pohl and Markner relied on the records of a directors-level meeting for evidence of the charges against Lange, but these documents can no longer be located at the VDMA archive in Frankfurt. See Pohl and Markner, *Verbandsgeschichte und Zeitgeschichte*, 82.
234. Pohl and Lange, *Verbandsgeschichte und Zeitgeschichte*, 82–83.
235. Tooze, *The Wages of Destruction*, 100; 'Entries in the Account "National Trusteeship" Found in the Files of the Delbrueck, Schicker & Co. Bank', in International Military Tribunal. 1997. *Trials of the Major War Criminals before the Nürnberg Military Tribunals: Vol. 7 Pt. 1. Nürnberg Oct 1946–April 1949*. Buffalo, NY: William S. Hein. 567.
236. 'Entries in the Account 'National Trusteeship' Found in the Files of the Delbrueck, Schicker & Co. Bank' in *Trials of the Major War Criminals before the Nürnberg Military Tribunals*, 567.
237. Schneider, *Unternehmensstrategien zwischen Weltwirtschaftskrise und Kriegswirtschaft*, 200.
238. Ibid., 216–17.
239. BAB R 13 III/78 'Gemeinschaftsarbeit im Maschinenbau 15. November 1892 bis November 1942', 4.
240. BAB R 13 V/125 'Satzung der Wirtschaftsgruppe Elektroindustrie 23.5.1935' 11; R 12 I/ 214 'Reichsgruppe Industrie: Dienstverteilung in der Geschäftsführung 1.4.1934'.
241. Siemens A.G. Historisches Archiv (hereafter SHA) 49/LS 157 'an Zentralstelle für Verbandsangelegenheiten 29.9.1934' and 'Wirtschaftsgruppe Maschinenbau an die Mitgliedsfirmen 9.1.1935', 1–2.
242. Schneider, *Unternehmensstrategien zwischen Weltwirtschaftskrise und Kriegswirtschaft*, 202; BAB R 9 VIII/ 3 'Vorprüfungsstelle Maschinen- und Präzisionswerkzeuge an die Prüfungsstelle Maschinenbau 8.10.1938', 3.
243. Schneider, *Unternehmensstrategien zwischen Weltwirtschaftskrise und Kriegswirtschaft*, 201.
244. Ibid., 201–2.
245. BAB R 3101 Anh./alt R 7 Anh Mcc/1 'Office of Military Government for Germany (US) Ministerial; Documents Branch: *Das Zusatzausfuhrverfahren* (ZAV) 3.9.1946', 1.
246. BAB R 9 VIII/6 'Büro-Rundschreiben 7.7.1938'.

247. Siegel, 'Rationalisierung statt Klassenkampf', 175; Gehrig, *Nationalsozialistische Rüstungspolitik und unternehmerischer Entscheidungsspielraum*, 96.
248. BAB R 13 III/78 'Gemeinschaftsarbeit im Maschinenbau 15. November 1892 bis November 1942', 5; R 9 VIII/6 'Geschäftsverteilungsplan der Prüfungsstelle Maschinenbau 1.7.1938'.
249. Pohl and Markner, *Verbandsgeschichte und Zeitgeschichte*, 90.
250. BAB R 9 VIII/6 'An die Angestellten der Prüfungsstelle 8.3.1939'.
251. BAB R 9 XI/2 'Anschriften der Prüfungsstellen und Vorprüfungsstellen vom 1. November 1944', 1–2.
252. Schneider, *Unternehmensstrategien zwischen Weltwirtschaftskrise und Kriegswirtschaft*, 205.
253. SHA 49/LS 157 'Jacobi an Wirtschaftsgruppe Maschinenbau 10.4.1935'.
254. SHA 49/LS 157, 'Wirtschaftsgruppe Maschinenbau an Siemens & Halske, 16.1. 1936', 'Fachuntergruppe Präzisionswerkzeuge der Wirtschaftsgruppe Maschinenbau an Siemens & Halske, 11.3.1936', and 'Siemens & Halske AG, Wernerwerk an Wirtschaftsgruppe Maschinenbau, Betr.: Beitrag 2. Vierteljahr 1936'.
255. SHA 49/LS 157 'Siemens & Halske, AG. Wiener Werk an Siemens-Schuckert Wernerwerk, 7.4.1939' and 'Siemens & Halske AG. Wiener Werk an die wirtschaftspolitische Abteilung der S&H AG. und SSW AG. 11.5.1939'.
256. SHA 49/LS 157 'Siemens & Halske A.G. Wernerwerk an die wirtschaftspolitische Abteilung der S&H AG. und SSW AG. 11.5.1939'.
257. BAB R 13 V/226 'Lange an Hauptgruppe I, Reichsgruppe Industrie, 21.7.1936'.
258. BAB R 13 V/226 'Lange an Wirtschaftsgruppe Elektroindustrie, 24.7.1936' and 'Wirtschaftsgruppe Maschinenbau an Wirtschaftsgruppe Elektroindustrie, 5.11.1936'.
259. BAB R 13 V/34 'Wirtschaftsgruppe Maschinenbau (Free) an Wirtschaftsgruppe Elektroindustrie, 11.8.1937', 1; 'Braun an Sack, 11.8.1937', 1–7.
260. 'Betriebsingenieure an die Front', 373; Hans Fritz Sohns. 1936. 'Die geschichtlichen Voraussetzungen der Volkswirtschaft', *Maschinenbau* 15(17/18), 518.
261. Siegel and Freyberg, *Industrielle Rationalisierung unter dem Nationalsozialismus* 162, 167.
262. SHA 49/LS 157 'Wirtschaftsgruppe Maschinenbau an die Mitgliedsfirmen, 9.1.1935', 4.
263. Ibid., 3.
264. For discussion of the process of academic adaptation to Nazi economic ideas, see H. Janssen. 1998. *Nationalökonomie und Nationalsozialismus: Die deutsche Volkswirtschaftslehre in den dreißiger Jahren*, Marburg: Metropolis-Verlag and C. Kruse. 1988. *Die Volkswirtschaftslehre im Nationalsozialismus*, Freiburg: Rudolf Haufe Verlag.
265. BAB R 13 III/145b *Maschinenbau-Nachrichten* 1(30) (25 July 1935), 147; *Maschinenbau Nachrichten* 1(39) (26 September 1935), 190.
266. BAB R 13 III/145b *Maschinenbau-Nachrichten* (7) (February 1935), 39.
267. BAB R 13 III/145b *Maschinenbau-Nachrichten* (40) (3 October 1935), 195.
268. BAB R 13 III/145b *Maschinenbau-Nachrichten* (17 January 1935), 13 and *Maschinenbau Nachrichten* (42) (17 October 1935), 207.
269. BAB R 13 III/145b *Maschinenbau-Nachrichten* (9) (4 March 1937), 67.
270. BAB R 13 III/145b *Maschinenbau-Nachrichten* (18) (2 May 1935), 95.
271. BAB R 13 III/145b *Maschinenbau-Nachrichten* (13) (26 March 1936), 69.
272. BAB R 13 III/145b *Maschinenbau-Nachrichten* (44) (31 October 1935), 219.
273. Gehrig, *Nationalsozialistische Rüstungspolitik und unternehmerischer Entscheidungsspielraum*, 52; R 13 III/145b *Maschinenbau-Nachrichten* 3(1) (7 January 1937).

274. See G.D. Feldman, 'Financial Institutions in Nazi Germany: Reluctant or Willing Collaborators?' in F.R. Nicosia and J. Huener (eds), *Business and Industry in Nazi Germany*, New York: Berghahn Books, 31; A. Barkai. 1989. *From Boycott to Annihilation: The Economic Struggle of German Jews, 1933–1943*, William Templar, trans., Hanover: Brandeis University Press, 106.
275. SHA Ld 689 Bd. 2. 'Reichsgruppe Industrie an die Wirtschaftsgruppen, 13.10.1937' and 'Der Reichs- und Preußische Wirtschaftsminister, 1.12.1937'. For a description of the 'voluntary' and more limited forms of persecution of Jewish business in Germany between 1934 and 1937, see Barkai, *From Boycott to Annihilation*, 106.
276. R 13 III/145b *Maschinenbau-Nachrichten* 1(6) (7 February1935), 33–34.
277. Ibid.
278. BAB R 13 III/145b *Maschinenbau-Nachrichten* 1(5) (31 January 1935), 28; *Maschinenbau-Nachrichten* 1(26) (27 June 1935), 152; *Maschinenbau-Nachrichten* 2(1) (2 January 1936), 3.
279. BAB R 13 III/145b *Maschinenbau-Nachrichten* 1(8) (21 February 1935), 45.
280. BAB R 13III/145b *Maschinenbau-Nachrichten* 1(10) (7 May 1935), 87.
281. BAB R 13 III/145b *Maschinenbau-Nachrichten* 2(22) (28 May 1936), 112.

CHAPTER 3

Conflict and Coordination
Creating a National Socialist Economy

The National Socialist government's basic assumptions about race, power and violence led to dramatic changes in the German economy between 1936 and the outbreak of war in 1939. How powerful was the Nazi state, and what were its aims? The degree of authoritarian autarky achieved (or even pursued) by the National Socialist regime prior to the outbreak of war remains in dispute. Avraham Barkai in particular makes a convincing argument that despite its lack of intellectual or conceptual rigour, the NSDAP adopted a 'strain of antiliberalist nationalist etatism' prior to gaining power that it then attempted to implement to the fullest extent possible after 1933.[1] Richard Overy takes much the same approach but places it in the context of preparation for war.[2] Both these interpretations imply a preponderant influence of the state over the economy and, ultimately, entrepreneurs themselves. Overy in particular ties this fact directly to the conflict over the establishment of the Reichswerke Hermann Göring in 1937, in which he argues that 'heavy industry' as an interest group collided with, and was defeated by, the state.[3] This interpretation has been questioned by historians like Gerold Ambrosius, Christoph Buchheim and Jonas Scherner, who point out the contradictions between an increasingly directed economy and the fact that entrepreneurs retained private property as well as production and contract rights, which preserved a certain amount of business freedom within the Nazi economy.[4] However, the decision to prepare for war (or at least aggressively rearm) in 1936 substantially increased the role of the state in National Socialist Germany. Buchheim himself makes an exception for the iron and steel industry after the construction of the Reichswerke Hermann Göring in 1937, noting that this event represented a major intervention in the market economy.[5] However, rather than a notable exception or the first example of things to come, the establishment of the Reichswerke represented the articulation of tensions that had bubbled beneath the surface of the relationship between industry and the state since the very beginnings of the Third Reich.

The cornerstone of this process was the creation of the Office of the Four Year Plan in October of 1936, which was supplemented and further developed through a wide range of other measures. In an effort to create a Germany in the image of its own rather murky ideology, virtually every aspect of German life was 'coordinated' with the Party in an effort to make German institutions and organizations reflect the will of the regime. In the years leading up to the outbreak of the second global conflict in twenty years, this translated into a conscious attempt to create or at least prepare for a system to mobilize the entirety of the nation's resources for war. The different ideological positions Reichert and Lange developed from the very first days of the Nazi regime led to different kinds of engagement with this expanding regulatory structure in the Third Reich. While Reichert's reluctance to embrace National Socialism and his attempt to push the new regime towards adapting to his industry reflected both the tradition of his organization and the interests of iron and steel industrialists themselves, it clashed with the aims of the state, especially when it came time to deliver under the Four Year Plan. The result was an organization that was unable to function as either a regulative body or an effective lobbying group. Lange, on the other hand, was able to parlay his ideological conversion into ever more organizational and structural changes to his industry that reflected Nazi goals and methods. As a result, he was elevated to a position of exceptional importance in his own industry and in the German economy as a whole by the eve of war. This power not only allowed him to preserve and expand his own position but also to secure very tangible benefits for his members by integrating them into the machinery of the National Socialist state in a way that Reichert could not.

On 14 June 1937, the successor organization of the VDESI held its general membership meeting at the Stahlhof in Düsseldorf. The agenda, speeches and discussion at the meeting were riddled with the symbolism, priorities and overwrought melodrama of Nazi rhetoric. Ernst Poensgen led by warmly praising the *Führer* and optimistically looking forward to the security and self-sufficiency promised by the Four Year Plan.[6] The business manager of the North-West Group of the organization, Steinberg, followed with a shower of compliments for Hitler and the NSDAP, linking everything from social peace to the increased birth rate in the Ruhr to National Socialism.[7] Although Jakob Reichert's own address was a little more circumspect and Poensgen expressed some doubt about synthetic production programmes, the session not only closed with a Hitler salute but also sent Hitler a telegram with both a pledge of the iron and steel industrialists' commitment and a touching short poem for the *Führer* himself.[8] The iron and steel industry had, it would seem, wholeheartedly embraced National Socialism.

The public image presented during this event belied significant tensions between the German iron and steel industry and the Nazi state that broke out into a public conflict only a few short weeks after the meeting. Unlike the industrial organizations that had been absorbed into the fabric of the National Socialist state, the former VDESI had already lost much of its power, influence and authority. It was, moreover, increasingly regarded with suspicion and even contempt by the authorities in the Third Reich. In practical terms, Reichert and his organization's suspicions about National Socialism translated into their marked unwillingness to transform themselves into an arm of the ideological state, let alone embrace the interference of the Four Year Plan. Reichert and the old VDESI clung to the forms of organization and regulation they had developed throughout the preceding decades, making the organization of the iron and steel industry and its chief business manager objects of less and less interest to a state that was gearing up for war.

Aggressive rearmament had the potential to expand Reichert's power considerably. By November 1936, Schacht and the Ministry of Economics had made the leaders and chief business managers of the various *Wirtschaftsgruppen* responsible for oversight of the relevant cartels that regulated their industry.[9] This particularly significant responsibility in the heavily regulated iron and steel industry was especially important to Reichert. The establishment of the new organization likewise changed the direction of the old association's policies. Whereas Reichert had been a broker of deals between his members and a representative of the industry to the government and public, he was now expected to use the Wigru as an organ of the state. Thus, while Reichert pressured the Ministry of Economics to prevent the construction of a new hoop iron plant by Neunkirchner Eisenwerke in 1934 on the grounds that it interfered with private cartel agreements, two years later the RWM could instruct Poensgen and the Wigru to take a similar dispute in hand themselves as the responsible leaders of their industry.[10]

Nonetheless, the effective hierarchy in the regulation of iron and steel production was still far from clear. In theory, the *Wirtschaftsgruppe* was responsible both to the Ministry of Economics itself and to the Office of the Four Year Plan through its Oversight Office (*Überwachungsstelle*).[11] At the same time, each Wigru was affected by a variety of regulatory officials ranging from the Price Commissar through to transport and export authorities. In particular, Price Commissar Goerdeler's desire to hold down prices while avoiding any general price regulation across the industry created enormous administrative difficulties.[12] The regulative agencies of the Third Reich hoped to take advantage of the technical and administrative competence of people like Reichert, who maintained an up-to-date picture of production in his industry.[13] At the same time, their close association with national and international cartels allowed the association's staff to synthesize both quota levels and capacity for the regime.[14]

The *Wirtschaftsgruppe* was increasingly expected to intervene to track and regulate production and trade by reviewing and approving indirect export contracts, overseeing the Steel Works Association's regulation of direct exports and monitoring nonquota production destined for the shrinking private market.[15] The Wigru likewise acquired the authority to manage ore quota allotments.[16] Less impressively, the organization was made responsible for allocating secondary supplies like work boots and clothing to iron workers along with Christmas schnapps and other perks.[17] More importantly, the *Wirtschaftsgruppe* hoped to take advantage of its increased practical role in the machinery of the state to continue to represent its members' interests. Shortages of raw materials in particular were reported to the Wigru, which then went on to argue for a reallocation of resources before the Ministry of Economics and eventually the Office of the Four Year Plan.[18] To this end, the association solicited complaints, concerns and needs of its members that might be taken up later with the Ministry of Economics.[19]

However, success in this environment required a high level of engagement and cooperation with National Socialism, and Reichert remained ambivalent or even antagonistic towards other aspects of Nazi culture. Other groups went to considerable lengths to fit themselves into what had clearly become the dominant ideology in Germany. For instance, by 1938, Wirtschaftsgruppe Elektroindustrie in particular had already integrated Nazi cultural and physical activities into the life of the office by introducing DAF social events and physical exercises.[20] The Wirtschaftsgruppe Eisenschaffende Industrie did not encourage its own members to participate in similar practices. Rather, it left decisions like whether to allow Party or SS members the day off to attend the annual *Reichsparteitag*, for instance, to the firms themselves.[21] So far as possible, the Wigru in fact remained aloof from National Socialist culture, and from the relatively small changes that cost the association little but helped to accumulate political capital with the regime. Even after the war, Reichert was vague about his relationship to Nazi policies that did not directly impact his industry. He claimed, for instance, to have helped to support someone of mixed German and Jewish parentage (a so-called '*Mischlinge*') as late as 1944, but offered few details.[22] He likewise rather cryptically remarked that he had 'dared to criticize something once' but received only a 'sharp reprimand' (*großer Vorwurf*) for his trouble.[23] His own putative discomfort with the regime's actions was likewise relatively vague and unconvincing in the context of the postwar trials. He had, for instance, apparently 'observed with horror that, if the Germans themselves set about each other with cudgels, that they would not wear kid gloves when dealing with foreigners.'[24]

These differences with the regime extended into questions of the organization of both the national and international economy and clashed directly with the Third Reich's long-term foreign policy after 1936, partly by drawing on the example of events in the United Kingdom as a foil for the development of a state-led economy in Germany. In 1936 the reorganization and coordination of the British iron and steel industry had been placed in the hands of the newly formed British Iron and Steel Federation, an organization that Reichert later compared to the potential inherent in the Wirtschaftsgruppe Eisenschaffende Industrie.[25] The British federation assumed jurisdiction over cartel prices, approved new plant construction and employed its substantial 'stabilization fund' to direct the development of the industry.[26] Perhaps more to the point, the federation accomplished these tasks by relying on the 'moral obligations' of its members rather than the authority of the state. Reichert also found it 'noteworthy' that England did not resort to the 'public hand' for investment.[27] Germany, he thought, could 'learn something' from the English example.[28] To Reichert, it appeared that England had adopted ideas about the economy and industrial self-regulation that the German iron and steel industry had supported 'for years or even decades', and that Britons in general would now enjoy the results.[29] Reichert concluded that self-regulation was essential to German economic efficiency and even to a potential war economy.[30] He therefore urged his members to lobby the Ministry of Economics for maintenance of their own model of private voluntary self-regulation, like the AVI agreement with the finishing industry, despite the growing efforts to establish a centralized alternative.[31] More importantly, Reichert's way of extending these ideas to questions of international relations differed substantially from that of the increasingly aggressive Nazi state.

After 1945, both Reichert and Poensgen made much of the industry's supposed aversion to war. Poensgen argued that iron and steel industrialists in general (and not just in Germany) hoped that the International Steel Cartel would lead to a deeper international understanding.[32] Even as late as October 1939, Poensgen claimed that French, German and other industrialists were able to mix in a friendly way at an ISC meeting in Lüttrich.[33] Reichert's interrogators at Nuremberg were particularly interested in the iron industry's attitude towards an offensive war, and the former chief business manager was eager to demonstrate his members' innocence.[34] They had, Reichert argued, 'had their fill' of conflict in the previous war and had no interest in another.[35] Though Reichert was in favour of 'necessary defence' (and presumably the public spending that went with it),[36] he and his colleagues told themselves that 'the people would not be so stupid as to unleash a war', particularly with such a small store of iron laid up.[37] Poensgen himself, Reichert argued, had worked towards an international understanding and opposed, for instance, antagonizing the French by building too much in front of the Maginot Line.[38]

To be sure, these statements need to be taken with a large grain of salt and placed in the context of the postwar attempts to defend industry detailed by Jonathan Wiesen.[39] Neither Reichert nor his colleagues did much to prevent or oppose a war. His postwar defence of his industry also led him to exaggerate its opposition to war, leaving even dedicated Nazis like the businessmen Röchling and Zangen blameless despite his often bitter disagreements with these men.⁴⁰ However, Reichert's publications in the decade leading up to the war bear out his claim that he put a good deal of faith in methods other than brute force. It is not implausible that he believed that institutions like the International Steel Cartel (ISC) and the burgeoning relationship between German and English industrialists would lead to stability, as he claimed during his imprisonment.⁴¹ To a certain extent, this was the rational result of his experience in the Weimar years. Reichert had never given up his assumption that France was 'naturally' doomed to dependence on German heavy industry. However, the institutionalization of the relationship between the iron industries in a number of countries had softened some of the more aggressive aspects of his members' self-interest.

Right up until the eve of the Second World War, Reichert was convinced that only international agreements had prevented the collapse of his industry and offered a prospect of widespread peace and stability.⁴² In 1936, he asserted in his book *Nationale und internationale Kartelle* (National and International Cartels) that private international agreements had stepped into the role once filled by violence and conquest in international relations. Where victors had once imposed the redistribution of wealth and resources by the sword, the same ends could now be achieved through private self-regulation.⁴³ For him, an offensive war was out of date. Reichert waxed surprisingly romantic about the achievements of these private negotiations, arguing that they had not only ended the destructive 'price wars' (*Preisschleuderei*) that had plagued the industry, but also achieved a kind of industrial 'world peace' that could heal the political wounds left by the war.⁴⁴ The chief business manager also explicitly compared the private ISC to the failure of political summits like the London Conference.⁴⁵ This was a long way from the National Socialist vision of armed Darwinian conflict between states and peoples.

This turn towards private solutions to international conflict could be applied to more than just the French-German conflict. Reichert, who credited military spending as the source of Japan's economic recovery, speculated that Japanese dependence on the conquest and occupation of mainland China for its supply of ore was its Achilles heel.⁴⁶ As late as 1939, Reichert also seems to have argued against military expansion as economic policy in general. His personal papers contain the minutes of a lecture, given to the Trade Policy Committee of the Reichswirtschaftskammer in January of 1939, that includes an intriguing rejection of a trade and production policy based on conflict and subjugation.⁴⁷ In this document, Reichert employs his typically lengthy, broad historical perspective beginning with the Wends, Sorbs and Romans to argue against a German invasion or subjugation of south-eastern Europe.⁴⁸ 'The experience of 1,000 years of history' showed Reichert that 'a policy of national repression had failed to secure peace' in the German (or Austrian) relationships with the Hungarian, Czech, Croatian and Ukrainian peoples.[49] Economic relationships, on the other hand, had produced peace and prosperity for Germany in particular.[50] This relationship was based on economic reciprocity (albeit not entirely equal), in which Germans exchanged their industrial goods for agricultural produce.[51] This analysis depended on a certain degree of permanent backwardness in the east that was not unlike Nazi ideas about the region. But unlike the National Socialists, Reichert argued that German aims could only be achieved through private, peaceable, trade. In effect, he had begun to project the benefits of his own model of international cooperation in western Europe onto the east when he argued that private industry could succeed where violent state policy was doomed to failure. His ideas were unlikely to counteract the weight of Nazi ideas or rhetoric, but they did serve to alienate Reichert from the regime in significant ways. Taken together, these differences had serious practical results.

By early 1937, conflicts between the *Wirtschaftsgruppe* and the state were beginning to lead to Reichert's exclusion from important decisions. This became particularly clear when Reichert and Maulick met with Brinkmann in the Ministry of Economics to discuss the apparent disparity between export programmes.[52] At the time, the iron and steel industry was paying both export rebates under the old Weimar private AVI agreement with Lange and the finishing industry, and the new state-mandated export levies of the ZAV. Unsurprisingly, Reichert objected to paying both and hoped that the intrusive ZAV levy could be lifted in favour of payments under the private agreement.[53] Brinkmann not only rejected Reichert's suggestion but explicitly instructed him to drop the subject and suspend discussions with his members.[54] This, Brinkmann made clear, was a political issue that he would not allow to be poisoned by the petty interests of individual firms.[55] If this rebuke was not strong enough, Poensgen complained some days later that the Ministry of Economics representatives (particularly Brinkmann) had simply begun to avoid Reichert, refusing to meet or speak with him until important decisions like those associated with the export levy were already made.[56] For Poensgen, this debate in particular had stripped the state of all pretence of industrial self-regulation, and he threatened to remove himself from the process entirely.[57] The level of state involvement in private industry in iron and steel was, however, about to get much worse as the state set about regulating production in earnest.

The introduction of the Four Year Plan fundamentally changed the relationship between the iron and steel industry and the Third Reich. By 1936, business freedom and international trade were already so constrained that even the regime's own price commissar urged that Germany begin to open its borders in order to stimulate sustainable economic growth.[58] The decision to implement the so-called second Four Year Plan under *Reichsmarschall* Göring precluded any return to normal economic conditions once full employment had been achieved. Instead, it committed the German economy to gird the nation for war.[59] At the same time, it brought the German iron and steel industry into close contact with new and even more politicized facets of the National Socialist government, bringing the interests and ideology of the *Wirtschaftsgruppe* into open conflict with those of the state.

The difficulties associated with the adoption of the new plan were already apparent by the time the Wigru and Oversight Office met with Colonel Loeb of the Office for Raw Materials in January of 1937.[60] Loeb, a close associate of Hitler's personal economic advisor, Wilhelm Keppler, had been taken on at the Office of the Four Year Plan upon its inception.[61] He entered the discussion already extremely sceptical of the organizational abilities of the representatives of the iron and steel industry and believed that no reliable figures existed for iron production in Germany.[62] The industry's representatives bristled at this suggestion; Poensgen retorted that the German iron and steel industry was indeed very well organized and knew perfectly well what it had produced.[63] It is perhaps open to question whether the iron and steel organizations could have met the demands of the state without substantial changes, but their ability to cooperate was undoubtedly greater than in most industries. In the context of a discussion of steel shortages, Scheer-Hennings (of the Oversight Office, then under the auspices of the Ministry of Economics) re-emphasized the importance of the shortage of ore in Germany and expressed his frustration that the use of iron and steel had not been prohibited in construction.[64] This precipitated a sharp exchange between Reichert and Loeb about whether the authorities had in fact taken any effective measures to allocate iron in Germany.[65] Sufficiently browbeaten by Reichert's attack on the state's ability to regulate production and construction, the hapless Loeb relented and suggested that ore imports be raised to 50 per cent of raw materials in use. Reichert pointedly retorted that imports already constituted two thirds of production.[66]

This conflict was not just the beginning of a steep learning curve for Loeb, but more importantly an expression of the opinions and approach of the new Office of the Four Year Plan. This organization, and Göring in particular, were even less favourably disposed to tolerating protracted negotiation and foot-dragging than the Ministry of Economics had been. On 17 March 1937, Göring himself met with a number of economic associations including the RWM, the Raw Materials Office and Wirtschaftsgruppe Eisenschaffende Industrie in order to discuss iron and steel production in Germany.[67] This would, according to Göring, be 'perhaps the most important meeting in the context of the Four Year Plan'.[68] However, it would not be a particularly pleasant one for the iron and steel industry. Göring was very disappointed with German steel production and blamed the industry for the shortfall. He argued that the difficulty lay not in the shortage of ore that the iron and steel industry had bemoaned for some time, but rather in the lack of new furnace capacity.[69] Göring might have been forgiven for arriving at such a conclusion, as over the previous two decades Reichert and the iron and steel industry had taken pains to limit capacity in an effort to prop up prices. However, Göring also demanded a greater level of self-sufficiency in the German iron and steel industry.[70] It was, he emphasized, 'the duty' of German iron and steel industrialists to exhaust all options in order to increase production, regardless of cost.[71] Industrialists who put business expediency before national interest would, he warned, find things 'very uncomfortable' from now on.[72] This was not a very appealing prospect for an industry deeply concerned about its bottom line.

Although Göring had not yet settled on smelting iron for himself,[73] his meeting with Reichert and his colleagues demonstrated that the *Reichsmarschall* possessed a rather simplistic view of the industry. The complexity and cost of refining low-grade ore in particular was of little interest to him. Poor-quality ore, Göring thought, could simply be made into lower-quality steel to be used in products like bombs.[74] He amused, if perhaps not necessarily convinced, his audience with an anecdote about soldiers who sleep as well on cheap cots as on beds made from the 'finest wood', which was followed by a demand that industrialists abandon their belief that everything must be made from high-quality steel.[75] Even Röchling, by this time a committed National Socialist, was sceptical about Göring's demands and asked him to relax his expectations and allow more time for improvements.[76] Göring, however, saw increased production in iron and steel as simply a matter of willpower. The air fleet had already demonstrated what was possible, and it was up to the iron industry to make things happen rather than simply whine and complain.[77]

Almost three months later, the iron and steel industry still had failed to live up to the expectations of Göring or the regime in general. When representatives of the iron and steel, mining and nonferrous metal industries met with Colonel Loeb once again on 15 June, they found that he had only sharpened his criticism of the iron and steel industry since their last meeting.[78] Loeb not only shared Göring's scepticism about the capacity of the iron and steel industry but also accused industrialists of throwing away valuable iron and currency by over-exporting.[79] How, he wondered, could he be expected to tell Germans that they 'needed cannons, not butter' when German firms were sending their steel abroad?[80] Adding insult to injury, Loeb raised the ire of both Reichert and Poensgen when he suggested that Germany follow England's lead and retain steel for its own use, pushing international prices up in the process. Reichert judged this to be nonsense, pure and simple. He pointed out that the United Kingdom had actually exported more, not less, iron and steel in recent years. Göring's ideas in fact reflected the army's concerns about the loss of steel abroad, which were fundamentally irreconcilable with the Ministry of Economics' fears about declining exports. In either case, this had become a question of political aims rather than economic policy. Loeb maintained that his assertion was based on statements by Göring himself, who presumably knew the situation better than Reichert. This prompted Poensgen to step in to support his chief business manager.[81] When Loeb refused to back away from what was essentially a political argument, Poensgen exploded and launched an attack on National Socialist policies in general, arguing that it was foolish to say foreigners had forced prices up.[82] Unlike the German government, the U.K. state had nothing to do with setting prices. Exports, Poensgen noted, were important and needed to be supported.[83] Loeb remained unmoved and fell back on Göring's and Hitler's demands that rearmament be achieved using German products and materials.[84]

Despite Loeb's tactlessness and the now obvious conflict between ideology and economics in iron and steel, by the end of June Poensgen and the colonel had managed to arrive at a modus vivendi of sorts that would ensure a measure of independence for private industry. Rather than increasing capacity, the two men agreed to work together to maximize the use of existing plant in order to increase production by over three million tons per year, partly through greater exploitation of German ore.[85] Poensgen also used this agreement as a springboard to suggest to Göring deeper changes in policy that would decrease iron exports and reserves while placing the needs of the Wehrmacht above all other orders. In return, the regime would agree to pay real money, rather than foreign scrip or equivalents, for more foreign scrap and to allow the Steel Works Association to take responsibility for the allocation of available iron.[86] This would, in effect, place the traditional cartel at the centre of a system that more or less met the needs of the Nazi state while preserving the firms' independence and profits.

Poensgen's detente with Loeb was a clever piece of work that might have bridged the gap between the industry and the state, but it was too late: his efforts came to nothing. By the end of June, Göring had already determined to take the troublesome iron industry in hand and establish his own steel works to take advantage of the lower-quality German ore at Salzgitter.[87] This change in policy towards iron and steel industrialists was first manifested in the appointment of Colonel Hermann von Hanneken as General Commissar for Iron Production (*Generalbevollmächtigter der Eisenwirtschaft*) at the end of the month.[88] Until then, von Hanneken had functioned as chief of staff at the Army Ordinance Office (Heereswaffenamt).[89] His new position reflected the rapidly expanding influence that Göring and the Office of the Four Year Plan now had over more familiar organs of the state. Von Hanneken was also infinitely better suited to bring the iron and steel industry to heel than his predecessor. As Göring's personal deputy in iron and steel, von Hanneken was empowered to enforce decrees through the threat of a fine of up to 10,000 RM and the possibility of a jail sentence, to say nothing of the technical and personal difficulties that might befall a firm that crossed Göring.[90] In theory, responsibility for regulation of the iron and steel industry was to be shared between the Office of the Four Year Plan and the Ministry of Economics, so von Hanneken was cross-posted as an undersecretary and leader of his own department in the Ministry of Economics.[91] In practice, the RWM continued to manage most aspects of the iron and steel industry, but this remained subject to the approval and signature of the general commissar.[92] Regulations would then be enforced through von Hanneken's own office (*Reichsstelle*), which replaced the old Oversight Office (*Überwachungsstelle*).[93] This arrangement stood in sharp contrast to the regulation of the machine building industry, which would centralize power in Lange's hands the following year.

Although von Hanneken's new position did not convey the ultimate authority implied in his title, he possessed more direct power over the iron and steel industry than Loeb had ever enjoyed. He also possessed greater resolve (and less ham-handedness) than his predecessor. At his first meeting with the *Wirtschaftsgruppe* on 30 June, von Hanneken made it clear that the resources for the Four Year Plan simply had to be found. Excuses would not be accepted.[94] He was completely uninterested in Reichert and Poensgen's fears about using up German reserves in one go and demanded that up to 40 per cent of private orders be cancelled in order to meet state needs.[95] Von Hanneken was willing to bend in order to accommodate the 'free economy' as much as possible after the state's needs had been met, but it was clear that the new General Commissar was a different kind of representative than those Reichert and Poensgen had already come to know.[96] Von Hanneken was a man used to command and perfectly willing to subjugate the private economy to the needs of the state. Reichert later complained that whereas he had once faced the state as the representative of a powerful interest group, he now had to beg, protest and negotiate with von Hanneken – who nevertheless retained the last word.[97]

The appointment of von Hanneken, however, was not the end of the reform of the relationship between the iron and steel industry and the National Socialist state. At a meeting with representatives of the iron and steel industry on 23 July 1937, Göring announced his decision to build a state-run iron plant, the Reichswerke Hermann Göring.[98] This decision, he was careful to point out, was the result of the inadequacies of German iron and steel firms. Private industry had failed to meet the demands of the military in particular as a result of its unwillingness to smelt iron from low-quality ore.[99] Under these circumstances, only the state would be able to meet Germany's iron and steel needs.[100] The establishment of the *Reichswerke* would have far-reaching implications beyond the fact of new competition from the state. It would stand outside of the private regulatory bodies that the industry had created, and it remained unclear how it would be reconciled with international cartel agreements.[101] For the *Wirtschaftsgruppe*, this raised the spectre of unbridled expansion leading to an iron glut and collapse in prices similar to that which had followed the end of the Great War.[102] It also posed new threats to the private economy. Small and inefficient producers were to be gradually starved of ore and shut down, and industrialists would simply have to adapt to state priorities.[103] Göring also proceeded to introduce more threatening overtones into the state's iron policy. Opponents of the *Reichswerke* and reorganization scheme, he warned, would be treated as saboteurs.[104]

The German iron and steel industry was shocked by this announcement.[105] One month later, Poensgen was still incredulous that the state and military had seemed to have completely changed course in a matter of weeks.[106] In response to what industrialists saw as both the state's unreasonable intrusion into private business and an economically disastrous decision, Poensgen optimistically forwarded an English article on the subject to Göring. More practically, he also established a committee comprised of the managers Vögler, Wenzel, Daub and Reichert himself to produce a memorandum (*Denkschrift*) designed to change the *Reichsmarschall*'s mind.[107] Though this committee was theoretically dominated by industrialists associated with the United Steel Works and the powerful Vögler, the *Denkschrift* bore the hallmarks of Reichert's preoccupations from the very beginning. It is difficult to speculate on how much of the *Denkschrift* was written by Reichert alone, but he clearly took the lead in cobbling various arguments together into a single document.[108] The *Denkschrift* opened with the kind of heavily historicized argument that Reichert employed so often, reviewing the experiences of the iron and steel industry from the Hindenburg Plan through the Treaty of Versailles, *Ruhrkampf* and overproduction crisis.[109] Using Reichert's figures and analysis of the danger of overcapacity and production in the German iron and steel industry,[110] the document also outlined the industry's own research and planning for expansion as well as the important link between ore surplus and finished product.[111]

Under more normal political circumstances, Reichert's role as the representative of the iron and steel industry should have conferred tremendous authority on him at this juncture. The fact that the proposed *Reichswerke* threatened both business freedom and profits made it an ideal rallying point for iron and steel industrialists. Poensgen and the *Wirtschaftsgruppe* had already established a production plan that had gained the support of the Wehrmacht and seemed to meet the needs of iron and steel industrialists as well. Even some of the warmest proponents of the regime, like Vögler, thought Göring had gone too far. Finally, Minister of Economics Hjalmar Schacht supported the opposition and assured the industry that it could prevent the *Reichswerke* from ever being built.[112] This alignment of powerful forces was precisely the kind of circumstance in which Reichert could shine. However, the context of industrial politics had changed dramatically in the years since 1933. As noted above, the role of the successor to the VDESI had shifted, and its ability to act as an effective lobbying group had sharply declined. The public announcement of the establishment of the *Reichswerke* likewise made private industrialists the object of sharp criticism in the Nazi press in particular.[113] The role of the state had also changed substantially, and both Poensgen and Reichert were surprised to learn later that Göring had threatened several industrialists in a telegram shortly before the industry met to discuss the *Denkschrift* on 24 August.[114] Perhaps more importantly, it became increasingly clear to Reichert that any putative 'united front' in industry had collapsed long before the eventual demise of the opposition to the *Reichswerke* in late August. Nonetheless, he persevered for a surprisingly long time in his opposition to Göring's plans.

Politics and ideology undermined the iron and steel industrialist's position in the campaign against the *Reichswerke*. The extent of the industry's disunity became apparent when the controversy came home to Reichert after the second reading of the draft of the *Denkschrift* in Düsseldorf on 19 August.[115] As Poensgen was bedridden with a fever, Reichert found himself on his own as the discussion became increasingly divisive.[116] In general, iron and steel men, even including those most closely associated with the NSDAP, were dissatisfied with the policies of the regime. Even the dedicated Nazi Zangen discussed his own reservations with Reichert as the two men travelled together between von Hanneken's office and United Steel, going so far as to threaten to resign if the Steel Works Association did not regain control of the industry and reverse the intrusion of the state.[117] Even the setting of the meeting – the Düsseldorf *Stahlhof* – was significant. The building itself was a monument to the wealth, pride and power of the German iron and steel industry that had so long retained its prestige and independence. However, the reach of the Nazi state and ideology extended even into this symbolic seat of power. When Reichert arrived at the meeting, Zangen became visibly enraged upon being introduced to the contents of the *Denkschrift*.[118] In the course of the meeting and a subsequent dinner with Reichert, Krupp's Arthur Klotzbach and Klöckner, the opportunistic Flick likewise expressed his concern.[119] Both he and Klöckner argued that the memorandum was too negative, and that the industry could not afford to be seen as simply opposed to everything the regime did.[120] Röchling, unsurprisingly, not only opposed the *Denkschrift* but also actively tried to convince Schacht to back the construction of the *Reichswerke* from almost the moment it was announced.[121]

Not all of the participants in this meeting opposed Reichert. Höller of Buderus'sche Eisenwerke, for instance, was supportive, and Reichert later remembered that Wittke in particular had argued passionately in favour of the memorandum. These were, however, second-tier industrialists, and Flick and Zangen continued to attack the *Denkschrift* in telephone conversations with Reichert over the course of the following day.[122] Though both men, and perhaps even Röchling, might have been persuaded to sign if the demands in the *Denkschrift* were moderated and expressed interest in cooperating with a diminished *Reichswerke*, they rejected both the document's blanket opposition and Reichert's historicist argument.¹²³ Pressure on Reichert to alter the *Denkschrift* only increased over the course of the day as Otto Wolff entered the discussion to back Flick's criticism.¹²⁴ Even more ominously, Flick had already begun to speak to the authorities about the industry's opposition. Demonstrating surprising personal resolve in the face of opposition from some of his most powerful members, Reichert stubbornly refused to change the *Denkschrift* at so late a juncture. However, he finally bowed to at least one of Flick's demands and instructed Steinberg to organize a meeting in Düsseldorf on 24 August to put the matter to bed.¹²⁵

This meeting was a disaster for Reichert, Poensgen and the *Wirtschaftsgruppe*. It demonstrated that the industry could no longer hold itself aloof from National Socialist aims, whatever the position of the organization itself. Poensgen's pleas for a united front in the iron and steel industry and his assurances that Schacht supported their cause proved useless in a group that was already divided by both ideology and fear of the regime.¹²⁶ Röchling and Zangen, of course, spoke against the *Denkschrift* or indeed any criticism of a plant that bore the name of the *Reichsmarschall*.¹²⁷ For Röchling, the state was now clearly more important than private industry, and he demanded that his colleagues trust that the state had considered the issues carefully before making its decision.¹²⁸ Meyer likewise refused to stand against the regime.¹²⁹ Brüninghaus and Engel of the Neuenkircher Eisenwerke, however, took a more circumspect and practical view: both thought that the *Denkschrift* was simply a waste of time and that openly opposing the regime would get them nowhere, regardless of the accuracy of the document itself.¹³⁰ On the other side of the argument, Wittke of Dillinger Hüttenwerke and Lübsen from Reusch's GHH argued in favour of the statement while Haarman of the Klöckner-Werke found it shameful that the unity of the industry was collapsing so publicly over this issue.¹³¹ This effectively illustrated the three possible reactions to the regime: cooperation, quiet acceptance of a fait accompli and opposition. Reichert and the Wigru chose the latter.

Poensgen himself grew increasingly angry over the course of this discussion. He was particularly annoyed that so many firms had refused to commit their names despite widespread agreement that the contents of the *Denkschrift* were factually correct.¹³² This was, as far as he was concerned, a cowardly political concession rather than an economic position and had no place in the industry.¹³³ As it became apparent that no agreement could be reached, Poensgen (who was only just recovering) threatened to resign rather than 'ruin his health for the general good' of an industry that would not unify in the face of a common threat.¹³⁴ In an attempt to work out some kind of compromise between key players, Poensgen called for a break in the proceedings. While Röchling and Beyer discussed a compromise, Reichert tried to sway Klotzbach, who had essentially agreed with the contents of the *Denkschrift*, to lend his name.[135]

The inability to piece together a common response to the threat of the *Reichwerke* was proof positive of the weakened position of the successor to the VDESI in a state that was much more powerful and ruthless than any that had gone before. No compromise could be reached, Klotzbach did not sign, and the German iron and steel industry never produced a finished *Denkschrift*.[136] Lacking either 'political capital' or the power they had thought they commanded in the state, the *Wirtschaftsgruppe* representatives had few options but to lick their wounds and reconcile themselves to the new plant. Poensgen went so far as to tender his resignation to the Ministry of Economics, but it was refused.[137] The *Denkschrift* itself languished without the support of major industrialists, and responsibility for the hopeless opposition to the *Reichswerke* devolved to Reichert in September 1937 after he had published a substantial article in *Stahl und Eisen* extolling the superiority of the English system of self-regulation in iron and steel over the increasing interventionism of the German state.[138] Reichert thus effectively became the last public voice in the debate, but the battle was lost. In November Poensgen finally gathered together the documents related to the *Denkschrift* and closed the book on the initiative.[139]

As in Overy's analysis, Reichert referred to the disunity of the iron and steel industry in the face of the *Reichswerke* crisis as the end of the influence of heavy industry in Nazi Germany.[140] Rather than adapt or integrate into the increasingly regulated state, the Wigru took up its old oppositional position. The conflict, however, demonstrated the weakness of an industry that had shown itself to be a paper tiger in the face of National Socialist determination. The debate also helped to undermine the reputation of the *Wirtschaftsgruppe*. Under interrogation after the war, Reichert drew a direct connection between the *Reichswerke* debate and the scorn that the regime showed him in later years.[141] The debate also helped separate the wheat from the chaff in the eyes of the NSDAP. Whereas Reichert and Poensgen were left under a cloud of suspicion, Röchling and Zangen – the two principle opponents of the *Denkschrift* – went on to enjoy splendid careers in close cooperation with the regime.[142]

The fact that both Reichert and Poensgen believed that the iron and steel industry and the *Wirtschaftsgruppe* remained powerful enough to stand up to the National Socialist state as late as 1937 is a strong indication of their esteem for their industry, their faith in its power and their inability to master politics in the Third Reich. There is no evidence in the files of the *Wirtschaftsgruppe* that any of those involved in the creation of the *Denkschrift* worried that it would create a negative impression in the Nazi state that would come back to haunt them. Nor was this simply the act of a man constrained or guided by the structure or economics of the industry he represented. His own industry was in fact split and indecisive, but Reichert consistently sided with those most uncomfortable with the growing Nazi state. Indeed, as noted above, Reichert had flatly rejected attempts by some of his most important members, who were much closer to the regime than he was, to moderate the demands of the industry so as to make them more palatable. Even after the establishment of the *Reichswerke,* the Wigru continued to gripe about its form and role. Poensgen and Reichert themselves remained in negotiations over what their industry would be required to contribute in order to support the establishment of the new state-run plant.[143] As late as February 1938, Poensgen still hoped to make participation in the *Reichswerke* voluntary rather than compulsory.[144] At a time when Göring had secured control of both the Office of the Four Year Plan and the Ministry of Economics, Poensgen's hopes proved to be in vain.[145] The *Wirtschaftsgruppe* could do little to slow the construction of the *Reichswerke* save to drag its feet in supplying skilled labourers to man the new furnaces or attempt to block access to other materials and markets controlled by the network of self-regulation.[146] Although Reichert continued to regard the establishment of a state-run plant as a foolish economic blunder, he could not prevent it from pushing private firms out of markets, particularly after it had absorbed works in occupied territories.[147]

Though the Wigru had proved itself to be weaker than Reichert had assumed, he did little to take advantage of powers that the state actually offered him, which might have given him greater leverage in the new economy. The RWM and RGI had advised Reichert on several occasions that they expected the chief business managers of each business group, and Reichert in particular, to gather the various offices associated with preparing their industries for war into their own hands.[148] At the end of May 1937, the RWM instructed the *Wirtschaftsgruppen* to establish a mobilization commissioner (*MOB-Beauftragten*) with particular emphasis on wartime exports and imports.[149] Reichert took up this responsibility himself. However, the authorities remained suspicious enough about the structure of authority in the association that Reichert was forced to remind the RGI at least once that he had in fact accepted the position as they had hoped.[150] Reichert's approach to the appointment of a liaison between the *Wirtschaftsgruppe* and Ministry of Economics also proved frustrating. The Reich Chamber of Commerce in particular worried that the Wigru was dragging its feet in appointing a representative to work with the ministry.[151] When the association finally got around to appointing someone more than two months after the RWM had requested it, Reichert ignored the ministry's and RGI's requests that he take up the role himself and appointed Allan Haarman, director of the Klöckner-Werke, instead.[152]

The *Wirtschaftsgruppe* was also remarkably sanguine about its own potential growth following the first aggressive expansion of the regime. Reichert and the Wigru were willing to participate in the regime's aims at times, and the authorities later expressed their gratitude to Reichert for having furnished them with a *Wirtschaftsgruppe* employee, Spannagel, to help coordinate the absorption of Austria into the Reich.[153] However, Reichert and Wirtschaftsgruppe Eisenschaffende Industrie allowed the remaining cartels in their own industry to take the lead. By 17 March, von Hanneken had instructed the Wigru to investigate the productive and delivery capacity of the Austrian iron and steel industry in order to take it in hand.[154] By the end of April it appeared as though the *Wirtschaftsgruppe* would assume responsibility for the Austrian industry. Reichert had already begun to pedantically instruct his counterparts in Vienna on the importance of shrewd calculation of freight rates, for example, and entered into negotiations with von Hanneken and the RWM over an effective subsidy for the underperforming Austrian firms through favourable rates.[155] However, following the integration of Austrian firms into the Steel Works Association the following month, the Wigru backed away and left the administration of the new territory to the various associations, passing up another opportunity to expand its own influence in the process.[156] In each of these cases Reichert turned down opportunities offered (or even demanded) by the state that another man in his position could easily have exploited.

This reluctance to assume responsibility at the expense of the cartels also extended to the Wigru's approach to planning for the coming war. When faced with the choice, the successor to the VDESI would rather see the state assume responsibility for regulations that it opposed in general. Thus, when Solveen from the Ministry of Economics pushed the *Wirtschaftsgruppe* to assume a greater role in regulating contracts and delivery times in anticipation of more centrally planned war production, the Wigru, and Paul Maulick in particular, resisted this idea and instead suggested that von Hanneken himself take on this role.[157] Poensgen had even gone so far as to argue that von Hanneken should assume authority for almost all aspects of the iron and steel industry himself in order to avoid the confusion and delay of multiple offices.[158] Where it could, the Wigru likewise passed authority for a potential war-economy to the cartels. Steinberg and the North-West Group were willing to become more closely involved with government planning, but Reichert, who had been appointed to head the organization's Working Committee for the War Economy, pushed them into urging that the Ministry of Economics change as little as possible in the event of a war, and that any central planning be done by the Steel Works Association.[159] The same committee further pushed von Hanneken to bypass the Wigru entirely and work directly with the cartels and associations.[160] Remarkably, Reichert did not suggest to Poensgen that the *Wirtschaftsgruppe* take a direct role in the regulation of its firms in order to force an increase in production until after the invasion of Poland.[161]

Reichert's tendency to shrink from responsibility in what was clearly becoming a highly bureaucratized economy can be contrasted with not only Lange in the machine building industry but also Wilhelm Steinberg, the business manager of the Wigru's North-West Group, to demonstrate that Reichert in fact had a good deal of wiggle room in his relationship with the regime and his industry. Steinberg, a longtime associate of Poensgen, had taken over the management of the North-West Group following Schlenker's dismissal.[162] By 1938, he had become considerably more ambitious and adventurous than Reichert and knew a good opportunity when he saw it. On 3 September 1938, Steinberg went over Reichert's head and appealed to the Ministry of Economics to centralize mobilization planning and responsibility for iron and steel production in the west in one office under his own authority.[163] Reichert was not even notified of Steinberg's request until two days later.[164] The regional business manager had good reason to suspect that his own office could fulfil the role envisioned by the National Socialist government better than Reichert and the *Wirtschaftsgruppe*. News of Steinberg's competence and willingness to work with the authorities seems to have spread by 1938, and outsiders like Wiel, the leader of the Research Office for War Economy, actually already thought that Steinberg, rather than Reichert, was in charge.[165] Steinberg's association was also well placed to deal with both the authorities and cartels on practical matters, and by 1938 the Wigru branch office in Düsseldorf was working directly with the professional associations to regulate production.[166] Here was an example of a bureaucratic manager in the iron and steel lobby who was willing to take a different approach from that of the more intransigent Reichert.

Conversely, Reichert and the Wigru looked increasingly incapable of managing the industry. Only a few days after Steinberg's letter to the Ministry of Economics, von Hanneken made it plain that he wanted to integrate Reichert's organization into mobilization plans more fully, but frankly wondered if the Wigru had the staff and ability to meet the challenge.[167] Reichert's brother-in-law, Tosse, also had to defend Reichert's authority as the mobilization commissioner for the entire iron and steel industry when representatives of the RWM and United Steel threatened to usurp his position.[168] Even discussions in the RGI had begun to raise the possibility of establishing a new office to take over many of the duties of the Wirtschaftsgruppe Eisenschaffende Industrie in the event of war. In what was by now a rather shopworn argument, Reichert responded with marginal notes reiterating Economics Minister Funk's promise of self-regulation.[169] Reichert was also displeased by Steinberg's attempt to take on more responsibility. Despite his reluctance to take on the role in the first place, he made it clear to Steinberg that he was the mobilization commissioner and that lines of communication must lead through the chief business manager.[170] Reichert worried that the *Wirtschaftsgruppe* was already having trouble keeping its own duties out of the hands of the Chambers of Commerce.[171] Paradoxically, he also fretted that the North-West Group was far too involved in questions such as manpower and mobilization that properly belonged to the Chambers of Commerce themselves and the state more broadly.[172] For the moment, Steinberg backed down and assured Reichert that he had no desire to move beyond the confines of the old agreement between the Wigru and its North-West Group.[173] The issue, however, was far from settled.

Despite the Wigru's questionable efficacy as a centralized regulative body, some officials at the Ministry of Economics continued to hope that it could serve as an effective tool. Reichsbahnrat Förster in particular contrasted its putative centralized structure with that of the Chambers of Commerce and hoped to use it to deliver programmes, regulate the workforce and secure raw materials, along with other technical functions.[174] However, in light of Reichert's own reluctance, it was the North-West Group rather than the central office that was increasingly stepping up to work with the authorities on issues that affected iron and steel in general. Over the course of 1938 and 1939, both the Association of German Iron Manufacturers (VDEh) and several member firms (who also noted that Wirtschaftsgruppe Maschinenbau had already provided clear guidance while their own remained silent) turned to the Wigru for leadership in the continuing dispute over the financial and manpower demands made by the Reichswerke Hermann Göring.[175] Reichert, however, had passed the issue off to the North-West Group by August 1939.[176] At Steinberg's suggestion, the North-West Group and *Reichswerke* also collaborated on the establishment of a clearing office in Düsseldorf to coordinate the reassignment of workers from private firms to the state works.[177] Even the statistical committee, long the provenance of the central office in Berlin, began meeting in Düsseldorf and now included representatives of the North-West Group.[178]

It is therefore unsurprising that, when Reichert established a Working Committee for the War Economy in June of 1939, Steinberg was included as a member while the managers of other regional and technical groups were excluded.[179] Steinberg in fact arrived at the inaugural meeting armed with orders from the war economy inspector and insisted that regional groups like his own be included in central planning for a wartime economy.[180] Although other members of the committee opposed him, Steinberg continued to press his attack in late June.[181] On 30 June he sent sharp notes chastising Reichert for endangering the secrecy of war planning by circulating the minutes of the Working Committee on Economic Defence and requesting that he himself be made the deputy mobilization commissioner for iron and steel in Germany.[182] In July, Steinberg's case was strengthened when the RWM placed the North-West Group in a direct relationship with the regional economic defence department.[183] Following this, the regional manager dispatched a second letter to Reichert, asking once again to be made his deputy.[184] In a surprisingly blunt rebuff, Reichert responded by appointing the aging Baare as his deputy instead, conceding only that Steinberg might be consulted in Baare's absence.[185]

Incensed by Reichert's decision, Steinberg complained that Baare had no experience in these matters. To the baffled Steinberg, even Tosse would have been a better choice.[186] He had a point. Although Baare had been Reichert's right-hand man for decades, he did not seem to be up to the task and tended to bog meetings down with his pessimism and obstinacy.[187] In a clumsy effort to have his cake and eat it too, Reichert wrote to both the ministry and Steinberg, informing them that the manager of the North-West Group could be considered his deputy in matters directly related to the region, but that Baare was still to be consulted in more general questions.[188] An irritated Steinberg shot back that he was already the representative for regional economic planning and had intended, of course, to be made deputy for the iron industry as a whole.[189] While Reichert rather feebly claimed that there was little he could do to include Steinberg more fully, he began to relent, and the regional manager was drawn into more general discussions about the industry by early September.[190] Finally, following a statement by von Hanneken endorsing Steinberg's candidacy and the outbreak of war, Reichert relented and made Steinberg deputy for mobilization questions on 14 September.[191] However, in a memorandum circulated within the *Wirtschaftsgruppe*, Reichert was careful to assert that the relationship between the Wigru and its regional group would remain unchanged. Steinberg would assume independent authority only if communication with Berlin were to be cut, and Reichert expected to continue to be invited to the meetings of the North-West Group.[192] Nevertheless, Steinberg's incursions had demonstrated that it was indeed possible to reconcile iron and steel to some of the demands of the Nazi state and that many of Reichert's decisions reflected his own inclinations rather than the diktats of his members.

Further complicating Reichert's reticence and the increasing fractiousness of the *Wirtschaftsgruppe* was the iron and steel industry's unsatisfactory performance in the service of the state. Despite increases in production and the industry's own assertions that it could meet the demands of the state without the *Reichswerke*, the iron and steel industry remained unable to produce the necessary quantities of iron.[193] Surprisingly, Poensgen not only blamed the shortage on a lack of scrap but was also prompted to reverse almost twenty years of VDESI and Wigru policy to claim that his members desperately needed more capacity in order to satisfy the voracious appetite for iron and steel in Germany.[194] The iron and steel industry now found itself in an impossible position as it attempted to deliver approximately 6 million tonnes of finished product with only slightly over 4 million tonnes of iron contingent.[195] Von Hanneken, however, was mistrustful of the industry's motives and enraged at the thought of firms prioritizing lucrative private contracts over national needs.[196] This selfishness, rather than any failure of rationing or state policy, was the heart of the matter for von Hanneken. One year later, Solveen continued to reject

Poensgen and Reichert's complaints about reserves and the demands of the state. Indeed, he blamed the industry itself for hoarding and poor planning.[197]

As the *Wirtschaftsgruppe* seemed to demonstrate both unwillingness and inability to deliver, it became increasingly marginal in the regulation of the German economy. The Wigru continued to enjoy some real power over the iron and steel industry, doling out regular quotas of ore for furnaces and administering some discretionary reserves for emergencies and war production.[198] However, by 1939 many of the functions that Lange's organization fulfilled in machine building had been taken over by the state in iron and steel. Von Hanneken's Oversight Office (*Überwachungsstelle*) assumed responsibility for coordinating requests from firms in Austria and the Sudetenland.[199] Requests for structural iron in particular were to go through von Hanneken's organization rather than the Wigru or *Prüfungsstelle*.[200] By 1939 the *Überwachungsstelle* had likewise taken responsibility for the redistribution of unused quotas and contingent out of the hands of the *Wirtschaftsgruppe*, leaving Reichert to apologize for the increased delays that resulted.[201] Von Hanneken also made firms that were unable to make deliveries on time responsible to him and his organization rather than the Wigru.[202] At the same time, and taking his cue from Reichert and the *Wirtschaftsgruppe* itself, von Hanneken began to centralize control of some kinds and uses of iron as well as the distribution of wartime contracts in the hands of the Steel Works Association.[203] Von Hanneken used his authority to issue directives to the industry by beginning to restrict the use of iron in consumer products like heaters and stoves, while Brinkman in the *Überwachungsstelle* limited the production of steel pipes.[204] In contrast to the rapidly expanding Wirtschaftsgruppe Maschinenbau, Reichert was forced to dissolve his own technical group for iron and steel production under pressure from Funk.[205]

This decline in the authority of the *Wirtschaftsgruppe* over the industry itself was accompanied by a decline in the role of the association as a lobbying group. By late 1938, Reichert had begun to chastise firms for turning to the authorities themselves and asked them to continue to work through the Wigru again.[206] Some firms had even become confused about the actual role of the *Wirtschaftsgruppe* and assumed that the RGI was now responsible for things like sales tax rebates.[207] Even worse, the traditional relationship between the VDESI and the cartels (*Verbände*) began to break down. By the summer of 1938, the Wigru had to harass the cartels to keep them up to date on production and policy.[208] One year later, even the survival of these *Verbände* – which by now could hardly be called independent, private organizations – had come into question. Paul Reusch in particular resisted the continuance of a steel association that was less and less voluntary or cooperative and threatened to bring down what was left of the private self-regulation of the associations instead.[209] Over the course of his discussions with von Hanneken, Poensgen was forced to admit that he was unable to use his own position or the pressures traditionally employed by the VDESI to maintain the old *Verbände*. Thus he petitioned von Hanneken to step in himself to pressure or ultimately order Reusch to cooperate in their renewal.[210] Reichert and Poensgen likewise found themselves pushing an ambivalent von Hanneken to endorse the renewal of the International Crude Steel Association (IRG), an institution that Reichert continued to endorse even after Poensgen had begun to hesitate.[211] In any event, the changes wrought by the Third Reich had clearly already undermined international organizations substantially and prevented the close, private, international cooperation that Reichert had hoped for.[212]

In an extraordinary demonstration of how far the wishes of the *Wirtschaftsgruppe* had diverged from the state's prewar plans and demands, Reichert and Poensgen hoped that von Hanneken might be convinced to lift the system of rationing iron ore entirely as late as August 1939.[213] The regulation of raw materials would be unnecessary, if only 'certain offices' could be prevented from devouring iron supplies.[214] The gap between the state and the Wigru had grown wide indeed if the representatives of the German iron and steel industry could suggest a systematic deregulation of production on the eve of war. While von Hanneken was unsurprisingly sceptical, Solveen unreservedly rejected Reichert and Poensgen's assertion, blaming iron producers and bottlenecks in particular materials instead. The *Wirtschaftsgruppe* was not completely unsuccessful with von Hanneken. However, the concessions that it won, such as the easing and then lifting of restrictions on youth and female labour in the iron industry, owed more to economic necessity than to Reichert's efforts.[215] In any event, the Ministry of Labour took responsibility for disputes even in cases involving these concessions, leaving the Wigru on the sidelines as firms dealt directly with the state.[216] Reichert's own attempts to secure the iron and steel industry's exemption from the demand to supply the state and military with workers were fruitless, and Poensgen continued to worry about the firms' ability to produce at all in the event of war.[217]

By the last years of peacetime, the Wigru was increasingly aware that the Ministry of Economics' attempts to establish its own relationships with the firms themselves was a dangerous threat to both the *Wirtschaftsgruppe* and the associational system.[218] Reichert's regional and technical business managers were likewise concerned about the amount of paperwork their members were expected to fill out for the state.[219] Aside from any concerns that the firms' staff would 'choke' on red tape, much of the information demanded by the Ministry of Economics appeared to be more properly the provenance of the *Wirtschaftsgruppe* itself.[220] Although Reichert often worked with the ministry to produce questionnaires, the RWM increasingly drew up its own documents to be sent directly to iron and steel firms.[221] Von Hanneken appeared sympathetic, but paperwork was hardly a primary concern for the General, so Reichert was left making increasingly fruitless and irritating complaints.²²² Schmitt in particular had grown rather tired of Reichert's griping by 1939 and invited the firms to take the matter up with him in person.²²³ As a result of the ministry's efforts to sidestep the Wigru, Reichert (who had formerly exploited his own exclusive knowledge of production and business decisions as a negotiating advantage) found that he was forced to rely on ministry data about his own industry in the mobilization process.²²⁴

The successor to the VDESI was thus becoming a marginal player in a game with very high stakes. Although the firms themselves were generally able to accommodate the new regime and continue to produce, the organization that had represented the industry had changed substantially. Unlike Lange, who was willing to fundamentally change his principles and the function of his organization in order to integrate it into the Third Reich, Reichert and his organization had attempted to preserve the old structure of industrial self-regulation in the face of both an aggressive state and increasingly apathetic members. Consequently, both he and his organization came into increasing conflict with the state during the early years of the regime. By 1937, the NSDAP had had enough of this troublesome group and began to push the old organization towards the periphery as it planned for war.

This left Reichert and the Wirtschaftsgruppe Eisenschaffende Industrie in a precarious position. State authorities that had grown weary of opposition and foot-dragging from the iron industry cast an increasingly jaundiced eye at the Wigru and cut it out of the regulation of its own industry. The NSDAP had little interest in industrial organizations that were of questionable value to the regime. At the same time, the intrusion of National Socialist ideology and activity into the economy undermined the possibility of a united front in the iron and steel industry that had invested Reichert and his colleagues with authority and influence. Finally, the failure of the Wigru as a lobbying group in the new coordinated economy called its utility to the industry itself into question. As firms began to deal with other organizations and even with the authorities themselves, the *Wirtschaftsgruppe* became superfluous to them as well as the state. Reichert's strategy had failed. Rather than an independent institution representing a well-organized industry able to force the new regime in convenient directions, he was left with an organization that could neither lobby effectively nor regulate in the name of the state. In this respect, Reichert and the VDESI diverged sharply from the powerful, efficient and politically reliable organization that Karl Lange established before the invasion of Poland. In the crisis years that followed, the consequences of these two different strategies had profoundly different effects.

In contrast to Reichert, Lange pursued a policy of adaptation that yielded extraordinary results by the outbreak of war. At the beginning of November

1938, Göring appointed him to the position of commissar for machine building (*Bevollmächtigter für Maschinenbau*, BfM) under the Office of the Four Year Plan, in charge of a new Reich office (*Reichstelle*) attached to the Ministry of Economics.²²⁵ From this point on, Lange was recognized as the most important single regulator in the machine building industry. In addition to his ability to regulate production and distribution through subsidies, licences and the new rationing regime, Lange was now able to directly issue binding directives to the producers in his industry.²²⁶ This was a remarkable achievement for the chief business manager of the old VDMA. For the first time, the chief bureaucratic administrator was formally elevated above the industrialists who had occupied the presidency of the VDMA. Even in the context of other industries, Lange was surprisingly successful. Of the fifteen men appointed to similar positions by Göring between 1936 and 1942, Lange appears to have been the only association man named.²²⁷ Some of these, like Karl Crauch and Heinrich Koppenberg, were industrialists themselves; others, like Joseph Wagner and Wilhelm Meinberg, had had some experience in business before taking up positions in the administration of the economy.²²⁸ Still others, like Paul Walter, were simply party hacks or Nazi from the early days of the Party (*alte Kämpfer*) with an interest in a particular field, like the former National Socialist Motor Corps leader Adolf Hühnlein, who later became the *Beauftragte für den motorisierten Transport*.²²⁹ In this dubious company, Lange stood apart as the only representative of the old associational culture who had made the transition to the centralized National Socialist power structure.

He managed this extraordinary achievement by cementing his earlier adaptation to the regime in practical and useful ways. Lange, who was not only ideologically pliant but also adept at meeting the demands of the new regime, began to transform the old VDMA into an arm of the state that could oversee machine building in the Third Reich. This had two major effects. First, it solidified Lange's own position and assured the organization a place in the German economy. Second, Lange was also able to take advantage of the changes in industrial politics and National Socialist ideas about leadership to exert a much larger measure of control over his own industry and begin to tame his fractious members for the first time. Although this was a profound change in the structure of the machine building industry, it fit in nicely with the VDMA's long-time efforts at tighter organization. This had the effect of centralizing a remarkable level of authority in Lange's own hands, while also making Lange and his industry attractive to the regime as an effective regulatory body in an economy that was rapidly preparing for war.

Remade, the new VDMA bore significant fruit for both Lange and his industry. Unlike the real or imagined challenges to profitability faced by Reichert and the iron and steel industry throughout the regime, machine builders were able to exchange their former business plans and a large degree of their own autonomy for direct subsidies from the state. This was not a simple response to a change in government on the part of the old VDMA but a fundamental change in industrial organization that had already made Lange and his business group an important and trusted component of the machinery of the National Socialist state by the outbreak of war.

By 1939 Lange's endorsement of Nazi communitarian ideas had grown into outright condemnation of the 'capitalist thinking' of the past in favour of service to the community.[230] Indeed, shortly before the war 'liberal capitalist' had become dirty words even in the machine building industry, and Lange stepped in to deliberately complicate the takeover negotiations between the firms Gebrüder Boehringer and Frankenthal after Boehringer developed a reputation for traditional, competitive, ways of thinking.[231] This movement away from market competition was not necessarily bad for the firms themselves. The leader of Fachgruppe Werkzeuge, Dr Kappel, suggested that eliminating competition in the industry would allow the business group to finally direct production and consumption by manipulating prices of new or problematic machines.[232] This kind of price manipulation had simply not been possible in the old association with its embrace of liberal competition and represented a new level of regulation in an industry that still had access to a free market of sorts.

Lange's support of Nazi thought could take on a more sinister complexion as well. Given Lange and his own organization's earlier foray into racist politics, the regime's efforts to break the ties between German producers and Jewish business contacts came as no surprise to the representatives of the German machine building industry. Shortly after the Ministry of Economics communicated its intentions to the business groups, Lange and his organization instructed their members to find out if their foreign business representatives were Jewish or 'under Jewish influence'. However, the organization backed away from this position two years later, noting that it might be 'economically dangerous' for managers themselves to enquire too deeply into the race of their business partners.[233] By the end of 1938, the Wigru had established its own list of acceptable machine builders that excluded firms recognized as Jewish.[234] In any case, the *Wirtschaftsgruppe* made it clear that the 'elimination of the Jews from a firm's foreign sales organization [was] self-evident for a National Socialist-oriented manager'.[235] German machine builders were instead instructed to ensure that they employed or dealt only with Aryans, '*Reichsdeutsche*' (ethnic Germans) who had left Germany, or individuals with German roots.[236] The Wigru also made some attempts to couch the exclusion of Jewish trading partners in terms of fear of a more widespread backlash against supposed Jewish business practices. Citing the rise of anti-Semitism in Hungary in particular, the *Wirtschaftsgruppe* warned its members not to be caught on the wrong side of what they argued would be an inevitably anti-Semitic future.[237]

There were some loopholes in this increasing exclusion of Jewish firms and merchants from the machine building industry. The *Wirtschaftsgruppe* was willing to concede that some firms would simply have to put up with Jewish representatives for a time because of contractual difficulties.[238] However, the Wigru appeared less flexible than the Ministry of Economics itself. The ministry at least was willing to accept the pragmatic retention of foreign Jewish representatives in order to avoid a serious decline in sales. Lange and his organization were not.[239] Although it remained technically possible to trade with Jewish firms outside of Germany even into 1942, the *Wirtschaftsgruppe* admonished its members not to complain about the short-term difficulties of the expulsion of the Jews (*Entjudung*) of the German machine building industry's export concerns and to get on with the business of finding more suitable business partners.[240]

Compared to the representatives of their industry, machine builders themselves appeared rather less enthusiastic about the removal of non-Aryan business contacts. It was not easy for Lange's organization in Berlin to police a trading network that spanned the globe. Thus, despite the fact that *Wirtschaftsgruppen*'s control offices (*Prüfungsstellen*) were able to deny subsidies or licences to exporters who dealt with known Jewish merchants, the typewriter industry, for instance, still reportedly relied almost totally on Jewish merchants in the Balkans in 1940.[241] Even as late as 1942, a rather petulant representative of Shärfl's Nachfolger Machine Tools expressed impatience with the fact that the Wigru *Vorprüfungsstelle* had rejected his application to trade through Salgo in Budapest on the grounds that it was a Jewish firm. Arguing that Shärfl's had already established a long and successful relationship with Salgo, he reapplied in the hopes of being granted an exception.[242]

The ideological adaptation of the *Wirtschaftsgruppe* itself also extended to its relations with member firms, particularly after 1936. The export regime introduced in 1935 increased rationing of raw materials, particularly for export but also for scarce raw materials like hard rubber, and intruded on the autonomy of German machine building firms by definition.[243] The cost of administering the new organization also placed a considerable burden on its members. At the beginning of 1935, the *Wirtschaftsgruppe* introduced an interim contribution of 70 pfennig per worker and white-collar employee, and 35 pfennig for each apprentice.[244] These payments were supplemented by slightly higher separate payments to the relevant Wigru technical and subgroups. In 1937, the *Wirtschaftsgruppe* moved to simplify the various contributions of its members and centralize collection in the Wigru itself.[245] During this process, the association also shifted the basis for contributions from the number of workers employed to a percentage of sales.[246] Fachgruppe Machine and Precision Tools, for instance, settled on a rate of 0.4 per cent per 1,000 RM in sales.[247] The central *Wirtschaftsgruppe* itself charged 0.6 per cent per 1,000 RM for firms that were also subject to *Fach-* or *Untergruppen* payments and 0.8 per cent for firms that did not make payments to subordinate groups.[248] This seemingly modest rate in fact represented a substantial increase in costs for member firms. Siemens-Schuckert, for example, had already paid 2,477.39 RM to the *Wirtschaftsgruppe* and *Fachgruppen* for the first two quarters of 1937, but under the new schedule the firm was reassessed for the same period at 5,437 RM and thus was forced to remit a supplementary payment of 2,959.62 RM, more than double the fees formerly paid to the VDMA.[249] Moreover, contributions based on sales were elastic, so by the first quarter of 1938 Siemens-Schuckert was paying 3,813 RM per quarter.[250]

Lange's aggressive construction of a hierarchical structure within his own organization also extended to his relationship with other *Wirtschaftsgruppen*. Like so many other National Socialist policies, the establishment of the business groups created as many opportunities for conflict between rival offices and organizations as it did opportunities for effective administration of the economy.[251] In some industries the creation of the *Wirtschaftsgruppen* led to confusion and acrimonious negotiations between associations. The machine building industry in particular proved difficult to place amongst the variety of business groups that laid claim to aspects of production in industry. Some attempt was made to divide responsibility for branches of production amicably, as when Wirtschaftsgruppe Maschinenbau and Wirtschaftsgruppe Elektroindustrie met in October 1934 to assign various products rationally.[252] However, lengthy and occasionally bizarre arguments often determined how the German economy was administered as the stakes were raised during rearmament. Lange himself was capable of a surprising level of rapaciousness, for instance in asserting his authority over the production of horse wagons furnished with pneumatic tires, or common address plates – so long as the text of the plates had been completed.[253] In a long-standing dispute with Wirtschaftsgruppe Elektroindustrie over responsibility for industrial ovens, refrigerators and rail safety equipment, Lange shocked his counterparts in the electrical industry by treating the death of their own chief business manager as an opportunity to rewrite the terms of a tentative agreement the two men had reached several months before.[254] This feisty attitude towards his own jurisdiction made Lange a formidable force in the highly competitive Nazi economy.

Lange could meanwhile be surprisingly indifferent towards the business or technical arguments of firms or other *Wirtschaftsgruppen* when they conflicted with his aims for the organization. The electro-technical industry found this particularly frustrating, as Lange refused to recognize electrical machines as separate from his own jurisdiction.[255] He was similarly unmoved by concerns about profitability when they encroached on his own authority. This was even more problematic when it became apparent that an unknown number of mechanical screw tap, cutting tools and die producers that technically belonged to

Wirtschaftsgruppe Maschinenbau had been applying to the Business Groups for Wholesale Import-Export or Steel and Sheet Metal to take advantage of their better export subsidy levels.[256] Lange's representative in the Technical Group for Machine and Precision Tools, Paul Nordman, mixed administrative and efficiency concerns with a surprisingly emotional appeal to the traditions of the industry in an attempt to keep control over recalcitrant firms.[257] Lange, however, was more concerned with the effective control of costs and prices in the regulated economy of National Socialist Germany. He was also unwilling to share his own authority for business reasons, even when the Wholesale Import-Export *Wirtschaftsgruppe* offered to supplement the subsidies for particular firms or branches administered by Lange's Wigru in order to maintain their profitability.[258] Lange and his organization were likewise incensed to discover that Wirtschaftsgruppe Maschinenbau's reputation for thrift had led a number of other firms to turn to more generous organizations in the following years, and hoped to force them back into the fold.[259]

However, not all of the aims of the *Wirtschaftsgruppe* were incompatible with the traditional efforts of the old VDMA. Lange and his organization continued to push for comprehensive standardization and rationalization in the machine building industry, as they had done in the 1920s. This notoriously difficult undertaking had not met with much success under the Weimar Republic, so the Wigru began to turn to regulation where cooperation and persuasion had failed. Thus the organization was particularly pleased when the minister of economics demanded in November 1936 that the *Wirtschaftsgruppen* work towards standardization.[260] When the Reich Efficiency Board (Reichskuratorium für Wirtschaftlichkeit) was relaunched in April 1938, Lange shared the podium with the Gauleiter of the Bavarian Ostmark at its inaugural session.[261] After his anointment as BfM, Lange himself intensified the role of regulation in the rationalization process. This was given further impetus when both the RWM and Office of the Four Year Plan ordered the establishment of a new German Standardization Committee (Deutscher Normenausschuß) by September 1939.[262] In the period leading up to the war, however, these long-term goals of the organization also included regulations that were more than a little alarming to machine builders.

In July of 1939, Lange began to set production regulations that would reduce the total number of machine types produced in Germany. Mechanical presses in particular were restricted. Firms were normally permitted to produce no more than six machine types, but this could be increased depending on the scale of production: firms that delivered more than 150 presses weighing over 500 tonnes were allowed eight types, and those able to produce 300 presses or 1,000 tonnes could produce twelve.[263] With this centralization came a distinct unwillingness to support machine builders who remained sceptical of political interference. In April 1939, for instance, the National Socialist

Wilhelm-Gustloff-Stiftung proposed establishing a massive state-owned plant along the lines of the Reichswerke Hermann Göring for mass production of industrial lathes.[264] Affected German machine builders, led by the United Lathe Producers (Vereinigte Drehbankfabriken), took this suggestion very seriously and were no more enthusiastic about the construction of a state works than the iron and steel industry had been two years before.[265] Unlike Reichert, Lange was unwilling to confront the regime over the issue. Instead, he proposed a compromise solution in which a massive plant would be built with private funds but located in tiny Schlesen, east of Kiel, to address political concerns about depopulation rather than for business or efficiency reasons.[266] Unwilling to accept this, the firms of the Vereinigte Drehbankfabriken scrambled to increase their own production levels in order to diffuse the concerns raised by the Wilhelm-Gustloff-Stiftung.[267] Lange remained indifferent to their fears at best. He was similarly unhelpful to other branches of his industry that were facing conflicts with the state. The German typewriter producers, who had already given up any hopes of gaining sympathy from Lange and the *Wirtschaftsgruppe* for the problems their industry faced by 1935, were left to fend for themselves when they mounted an unsuccessful campaign against a mandatory 10 per cent reduction in the price of their products in 1938.[268]

Lange's adaptation to the regime likewise extended to his own position on the export of German machine goods. German exports in general declined considerably under National Socialism, due in part to the seductive profits of the armaments boom.[269] However, German producers also found themselves at a competitive disadvantage because of the inflated German currency, increased rationing of resources and cumbersome bureaucratic procedure that followed from National Socialist economic policies. This had an important impact on the machine building industry, which saw the value of exports decline from 43 per cent of sales in 1933 to 16.4 per cent by 1938.[270] Regardless, the Nazi state continued to depend on exports to a surprising degree in order to secure the foreign currency necessary to import raw materials in particular.[271] Lange and his colleagues thus found themselves in the curious position of advocating increased trade for reasons other than competitive advantage or profitability.

Unfortunately, the method that the association used to decide on allocating subsidies or rationed material through the ZAV remains obscure.[272] Nonetheless, it is clear that the *Wirtschaftsgruppe* took considerable pains to push machine builders to increase their foreign trade, and by 1937 the association was demanding that the technical groups take appropriate measures to increase exports.[273] This effort only intensified with the general economic downturn in 1938–39. Consequently, Lange (who by then had acquired significantly more power) instructed his control offices to reject domestic production requests that threatened to affect exports, and the Control Office for Office Machines

(Prüfungsstelle Büromaschinen) commanded its firms to leave enough free capacity in their plants to meet the equivalent of exports from 1937.[274] By the following year, firms were being instructed to report conflicts between local deliveries and exports to their Control Office so that the organization could participate in finding a solution.[275] Despite the continued focus on exports, this level of interference in firms' business practices was a far cry from the kind of free trade Lange had advocated in the 1920s.

Lange and the *Wirtschaftsgruppe* were also able to take advantage of the increasingly regulated environment in Germany to extend the function and reach of the association beyond the borders of the Reich. As both the Wigru and RWM increasingly put pressure on machine building firms to give up politically or racially unacceptable business contacts, the organization began opening its own offices abroad to service German producers. In January and November 1938, the *Wirtschaftsgruppe* opened international branch offices in both London and New York to serve as contact points for German machine builders and their customers.[276] Where it could not open its own offices, the Wigru became a kind of clearing house for international sales representatives by pushing firms to inform the organization of partners they had found that were acceptable to the regime. The *Wirtschaftsgruppe* could then put these representatives in touch with firms that had been unable to find their own politically suitable replacements.[277]

The *Wirtschaftsgruppe* was able to extend its influence much more directly after the *Anschluss* with Austria and invasion of the Sudetenland in 1938. As in other industries, the respective organizations of the two national machine building industries quickly reached out to each other in early 1938, and in April the Austrian Machine Building Association (Verband der Maschinenindustrie) and German *Wirtschaftsgruppe* exchanged pleasant telegrams congratulating each other on the success of the *Anschluß*.[278] However, only two months later Lange dispatched an employee of the Wigru, Paul Kathke, to take over the management of what would later become the Wigru's own branch office in Austria (Zweigstelle Ostmark der Wirtschaftsgruppe Maschinenbau).[279] This process was repeated in the Sudetenland. When the organization of the machine building industry there was first brought under German control, its old leader, Franz Bramsch, was allowed to retain his position, although German firms were instructed to drop the honorary Czech titles he had accumulated before the invasion.[280] However, Bramsch could not act independently, and to assist him the *Wirtschaftsgruppe* quickly sent its own representative, who was eventually replaced by Kathke himself.[281] These actions effectively brought the industry in the new territories under Lange's administration. They also gave an early indication of the VDMA's acceptance of the imperialist pretensions of the regime, which led Roth to identify industrial organizations with the Nazi state.[282]

Lange's success at adapting to National Socialism had a significant impact on his members, but by the latter part of the decade the machine building industry was benefiting directly from the regime's unorthodox economic policies as well. This was no simple exchange of support for immediate gains. The potential benefits of the new regime were not immediate or necessarily apparent in 1933, but by the end of the decade Lange had secured substantial advantages nonetheless. As noted above, the machine building industry was in fact relatively slow to recover from the economic crisis of the early 1930s or to benefit from National Socialist policies. In 1932, the industry as a whole was only producing at 28 per cent of 1928 levels and suffered from a substantial overcapacity problem.[283] Though production in Germany in general had returned to 1928 levels by 1935, the machine building industry did not recover until the following year. However, two years later, sales were more than 50 per cent higher than before the collapse of 1929.[284] While some firms were able to take advantage of the goals of the regime to fund the development of otherwise uneconomical product lines,[285] this success came primarily in the branches of the industry that were supported by both Lange and the regime itself. Spin-off from the armaments boom generated the most spectacular advances. Firms that produced for consumer goods markets, such as most textile, shoe and washing machine manufacturers, did relatively poorly throughout the period.[286] As the industry responsible for the machines needed to produce sophisticated modern weapons in particular, Lange's industry became one of the cornerstones of rearmament.[287] By 1938 the key milling machine sector, for instance, had increased its sales by 281 per cent over those of 1933, a figure exceeded only by agricultural machinery at 288 per cent, followed closely by construction machines at 255 per cent.[288] Actual production of machine tools in particular likewise increased from 61,104 tonnes to 253,558 tonnes in 1938.[289] Wanderer Werke AG, for example, saw its own profit balance increase dramatically. From just over one million marks by the end of 1933, it brought in 8,404,602RM in 1939.[290] Indeed, milling machines were significantly back-ordered by 1939: only 272,623 were delivered while 454,282 remained on order.[291]

While 'end user' rationing preserved a market of sorts for machines in Germany, this practice was distorted significantly by the activities of Lange's organizations. The administration of the ZAV in particular allowed the institutions of Wirtschaftsgruppe Maschinenbau to selectively subsidize export branches and even particular firms in the industry. As a result, the National Socialist regime created enormous opportunities for certain key sectors of machine construction. Machine tool exports remained below even 1933 levels by the end of 1935 at 65.9 million RM, but exports had reached 124 million RM by 1936 and peaked at 159.2 million in 1939.[292] Wanderer Werke AG alone reported earnings of 468,000 RM on exports in 1937, but without the subsidies provided by Lange's control offices, it would have suffered a 619,000 RM loss on the same sales. One year later, the value of subsidies for the firm was even greater at 1,358,361 RM in profits with the ZAV as compared to a loss of 659,400 RM without.[293] This staggering infusion of over three million marks into a single firm over two years highlights a substantial difference between the machine building and iron and steel industries. Without Lange's intervention German machine builders might still have benefited substantially from rearmament, but they would not have been able to compete as profitably in a still deeply troubled international market. Thus, while exports declined relative to domestic sales, even as late as 1943 exports themselves had increased in real terms to five times those of 1933.[294] As a national economic policy, this made very little sense. Producers of consumer goods might also have balked. However, for a substantial portion of the German machine building industry, Lange could now make a good business case for cooperation with the National Socialist government.

There is evidence to suggest that machine builders themselves saw Lange and his organization as a kind of insurance policy against less lucrative forms of intervention in their business. Producers were aware that Lange had managed to centralize a remarkable level of power over their industry.[295] However, rather than expressing alarm over this situation, some industrialists worried that Lange would remain unable to control the industry to the satisfaction of the Office of the Four Year Plan.[296] This reflected machine builders' fears that they might also be subject to some of the controls and interventions suffered by other sectors of the German economy and society. As noted above, lathe manufacturers were already unnerved by the suggestion that a state works might be established in their industry, even if Lange was indifferent. At the same time, suspicion was beginning to fall on the machine building industry for production bottlenecks in the armaments industry. The Office for Raw Materials in particular accused the machine building industry of not doing its share to fulfil the provisions of the Four Year Plan.[297] By the end of 1938, Zangen was using his new position as the head of RGI to assert that the machine industry, rather than iron and steel, was now the source of problems in production, implying that a lingering liberalism in machine building was the source of its inability to deliver.[298]

To a large extent, the machine builders' fears were vastly overblown. No one in a position of importance in the regime seems to have taken the suggestion that a *Reichswerke* be founded in the machine industry seriously. Indeed, the highly skilled, technically advanced industry could be easily reconciled with the 'modernizing' effects and ideas of the National Socialist regime described by Werner Abelshauser.[299] It was also much simpler to turn to Lange – especially after he had established a well-articulated, hierarchical, politically reliable organization – to keep the complex and fragmented machine building industry in line. However, aside from the economic benefits, Lange might indeed have provided a measure of protection for his members. Pohl and Markner in particular argue that a reluctant Lange consulted the *Wirtschaftsgruppen* advisory council before accepting the position of BfM. Fearing that they might do worse than their own chief business manager, his members advised Lange to accept the role in Göring's organization.[300] Even more intriguing is the fact that Lange ordered his own employees not to report machine builders' questionable activities to the authorities but instead to bring the information directly to him.[301] Unfortunately, it is not clear what sparked the demand or what Lange might have done with any information he received. It does, however, indicate that he might have been able to provide some measure of protection for his members. On the other hand, it also integrated Lange and his office into the surveillance structure of the regime.

Lange's willingness to hammer his organization into a shape acceptable to the National Socialist state thus had very tangible benefits for his industry. The chronology of this process is extremely important. Before the policies of the regime had become fully apparent, Lange developed the old VDMA into an organ that would be acceptable to National Socialism. He was then able to position the *Wirtschaftsgruppe* within the machinery of the Nazi state after 1936 in order to take full advantage of the benefits it eventually offered his industry from the inside. The consequences of Lange's efforts were that both he and his industry in general entered the Second World War in a markedly different position from that of the iron and steel industry. By 1939, the old VDMA and its chief business manager had transformed themselves from a liberal, politically moderate, free-trading organization representing a fractious and tenuously organized industry into a hierarchical regulative body that actively supported the National Socialist regime. Lange himself not only survived the transition to the Nazi state but expanded his own power and influence to a degree unequalled in German industrial politics. Upon the outbreak of hostilities, these changes to the structure and substance of regulation in the machine building industry would become enormously important. Lange could now offer a hierarchically structured industry that had already demonstrated its political and ideological reliability to the regime at a moment of crisis. The same could not be said for Reichert or the iron and steel industry, and this difference proved decisive in the years that followed the outbreak of war.

Notes

1. Barkai, *Nazi Economics*, 245, 247.
2. See Overy, *War and Economy in the Third Reich*, 179.
3. Ibid., 93.
4. Buchheim and Scherner, 'Anmerkungen zum Wirtschaftssystem des "Dritten Reichs"', 81, 83.
5. Ibid., 87.
6. Reichert, 'Aus Fachverein', 706.

7. Ibid., 707.
8. Ibid., 707, 709.
9. BAB R 13 I/619 'Beiratssitzung 9.7.1936'; SAN Rep. 502, VI KV-Anklage Interrogations R 48, 'Erklärung unter Eid, Reichert 3.7.1947', 4.
10. BAB R 13 I/ 602 'Reichert an den Reichswirtschaftsminister, 14.8.1934'; R 13 I/605 'RWM Besprechung 11.1.1936'.
11. Greer, *The Ruhr-Lorraine Industrial Problem*, 30.
12. BAB R 13 I/ 605 'RWM Besprechung 12.12.1934'.
13. BAB R 13 I/242 'Wirtschaftsgruppe Eisenschaffende Industrie Rundschreiben # 2892, 16.4.1934'.
14. BAB R 13 I/241 'Baare an Kiegel, 23.11.1935'.
15. BAB R 13 I/459 'Stahlwerksverband an die Mitglieder des Stabeisenverbandes 1.3.1937'; R 13 I/459 'Stahlwerksverband, Anweisung zur Anordnung Nr.22 'Auftragsregelung' 3.3.1937'.
16. BAB R 13 I/620 'Beiratssitzung 10.6.1938'.
17. SAN Rep. 502, VI KV-Anklage Interrogations R 48, Interrogation #323. 'Vernehmung des Dr. J.W. Reichert 18.11.1946', 10.
18. Ibid., 8.
19. BAB R 13 I/241 'Wirtschaftsgruppe, Rundschreiben #1777, 14, 3.1936'.
20. See BAB R 13 V/145 'Veranstaltung der NSG Kraft durch Freude, Vereinbarung über den Bezug von Theaterkarten, 4.1.1938'; R 13 V/145 'An alle Gefolgschaftsmitglieder der WEI und PEI, 18.9.1939'.
21. BAB R 13 I/243 'Wirtschaftsgruppe Rundschreiben 12043, 17.8.1938'.
22. Nürnberger Kriegsverbrecherprozess, MA Vernehmung des Dr. J.W. Reichert. Interrogation # 2197. 14.5.1947, 6.
23. Nürnberger Kriegsverbrecherprozess, MA Vernehmung des Dr. J.W. Reichert. Interrogation # 2221. 17.5.1947, 12.
24. 'Es schreckte mich besonders ab, zu beobachten, dass die Deutschen, wenn sie sich schon untereinander mit Knüppeln begegneten, auch nicht dem Ausland gegenüber wenigstens sozusagen "Handschuhe anzogen"', NSA Vernehmung des Dr. J.W. Reichert. Interrogation # 2197. 14.5.1947, 6.
25. J. Reichert. 1937. 'Die englische Eisen- und Stahlindustrie in Gegenwart und Zukunft: Nach den Ergebnissen einer amtlichen Untersuchung vom Jahre 1937', *Stahl und Eisen* 57(35) (2 September), 971.
26. Ibid., 972–73.
27. Ibid., 973; J. Reichert. 1936. 'Die Eisenwirtschaft im englischen Weltreich', *Stahl und Eisen* 56(10) (6 May 1936), 305.
28. Reichert, '*Die englische Eisen- und Stahlindustrie in Gegenwart und Zukunf*', 979.
29. Ibid., 978.
30. R-WW, GHH Nachlass Paul Reusch 400101290/32b 'Betr:. Das neue Gesetz zum organischen Aufbau der deutschen Wirtschaft', 5.
31. R-WW GHH Nachlass Paul Reusch 400101222/4 'Wirtschaftsgruppe Eisenschaffende Industrie "Streng Vertraulich" Zeichnung 629 R/Br., 8.3.1935'.
32. R-WW, GHH Nachlass Paul Reusch 400101290/42 E. Poensgen, 'Hitler und die Ruhrindustriellen: Ein Rückblick', 4.
33. Ibid.
34. SAN, Rep. 502, VI KV-Anklage Interrogations R 48, Interrogation #2197 'Vernehmung des Dr. J. W. Reichert, 14.5.1947', 3.
35. SAN, Rep. 502, VI KV-Anklage Interrogations R 48, Interrogation #2221 'Vernehmung des Dr. J. W. Reichert, 17.5.1947', 15.

36. SAN, Rep. 502, VI KV-Anklage Interrogations R 48, Interrogation #2226 'Vernehmung des Dr. J. W. Reichert, 21.5.1947', 7.
37. SAN, Rep. 502, VI KV-Anklage Interrogations R 48, Interrogation #2221 'Vernehmung des Dr. J. W. Reichert, 17.5.1947', 9.
38. Ibid.
39. Wiesen, *West German Industry and the Challenge of the Nazi Past,* 67–79.
40. SAN, Rep. 502, VI KV-Anklage Interrogations R 48 J.W. Reichert, 'Erklärung unter Eid, 7.7.1947', 9, 7.
41. SAN, Rep. 502, VI KV-Anklage Interrogations R 48, Interrogation #2197 'Vernehmung des Dr. J. W. Reichert, 14.5.1947', 8.
42. BAB R 13 I/42 'Aktenvermerk: Stahlwerksverbandssitzung, 2.2.1939'.
43. Reichert, *Nationale und Internationale Kartelle,* 37.
44. Reichert, 'Ein Rückblick auf das zehnjährige Bestehen der internationalen Stahlverbände', 1436; Reichert, *Nationale und Internationale Kartelle,* 39.
45. Reichert, 'Ein Rückblick auf das zehnjährige Bestehen der internationalen Stahlverbände', 1435.
46. J. Reichert. 1934. 'Japans Eisen- und Stahlindustrie in ihrer wirtschaftlichen Entwicklung', *Stahl und Eisen* 54(38) (20 September), 986.
47. It is difficult to definitively establish the authorship of this document. However, as it appears in the files of Reichert's *Handakten,* closely reflects his own ideas about industry in the west and is characterized by the deeply historicist arguments that Reichert tended to employ, it is reasonable to attribute it to him. See BAB R 13 I/615 'Geopolitische und historische Grundlagen deutscher Südostpolitik. Vortrag gehalten im Handelspolitischen Ausschuß der Reichswirtschaftskammer. Berlin, 17.1.1939', 141–61 in BAB pagination.
48. Ibid., 145.
49. Ibid., 161.
50. Ibid., 155, 160–61.
51. Ibid., 160.
52. BAB R 13 I/601 'RWM Besprechung, 17.4.1937'.
53. Ibid., 1.
54. Ibid., 2.
55. Ibid.
56. BAB R 13 I/601 'RWM Besprechung, 23.4.1937', 3–4.
57. BAB R 13 I/601 'RWM Besprechung, 23.4.1937', 2.
58. Tooze, *The Wages of Destruction,* 216–17.
59. Overy, *War and Economy in the Third Reich,* 185.
60. BAB R 13 I/601 'Niederschrift über die am 22. Jan. 1937 im Amt für Deutsche Roh- und Werkstoffe gehaltene Besprechung'.
61. Meyer, *Hitlers Holding: Die Reichswerke 'Hermann Göring,* 24, 74.
62. BAB R 13 I/601 'Niederschrift über die am 22. Jan. 1937 im Amt für Deutsche Roh- und Werkstoffe gehaltene Besprechung', 163 in BAB pagination.
63. Ibid., 164 in BAB pagination.
64. Ibid., 166 in BAB pagination.
65. Ulrich Hensler has demonstrated that iron and steel rationing was indeed problematic and largely driven by the demands of iron consumers. See U. Hensler. 2008. 'Iron and Steel Rationing During the Third Reich', in C. Buchheim (ed.), *German Industry in the Nazi Period,* Stuttgart: Franz Steiner Verlag, 57; U. Hensler. 2008. *Die Stahlkontingentierung im Dritten Reich,* Stuttgart: Franz Steiner Verlag.
66. Ibid., 167.

67. BAB R 13 I/601 'Der Arbeitskreis von Ministerpräsident Generaloberst Göring, 17.3.1937'.
68. Ibid., 116 in BAB pagination.
69. Ibid., 118 in BAB pagination.
70. Ibid., 117 in BAB pagination.
71. Ibid., 119.
72. Ibid., 119 in BAB pagination.
73. Meyer, *Hitlers Holding*, 76–77.
74. BAB R 13 I/601 'Der Arbeitskreis von Ministerpräsident Generaloberst Göring, 17.3.1937', 126 in BAB pagination.
75. Ibid., 125 in BAB pagination.
76. Ibid., 131 in BAB pagination.
77. Ibid., 132 in BAB pagination.
78. BAB R 13 I/601 'Zur Frage des direkten Eisenexports, 15.6.1937'.
79. Ibid., 157 in BAB pagination.
80. Ibid.
81. Ibid., 158.
82. Ibid., 159.
83. Ibid., 160–61.
84. Ibid., 161.
85. BAB R 13 I/597 'Bericht über die Verarbeitung deutscher Erze durch die Eisenindustrie im Rahmen des Vierjahresplanes', 185 in BAB pagination.
86. BAB R 13 I/597 'Poensgen an Ministerpräsident Generaloberst Göring, 29.6.1937'.
87. Meyer, *Hitlers Holding*, 76–77.
88. BAB R 13 I/601 'Niederschrift über die am 30.06.1937 bei Herrn Oberst von Hanneken (Heereswaffenamt) abgehaltene Besprechung', 144 in BAB pagination.
89. See Meyer, *Hitlers Holding*, 66; 'Hanneken, Hermann von, Militär' in Vierhus, Rudolph. 2006. *Deutsche Biographische Enzyklopädie (DBE)*. Munich: K.G. Saur. 4. 414.
90. Greer, *The Ruhr-Lorraine Industrial Problem*, 30.
91. Ibid., 33.
92. Ibid., 33–34.
93. Ibid., 34.
94. BAB R 13 I/601 'Betr.: Kontingentierungsfragen: Niederschrift über die am 30. Juni 1937 bei Herrn Oberst von Hanneken (Heereswaffenamt) abgehaltene Besprechung', 156 in BAB pagination.
95. Ibid., 145–46.
96. Ibid., 146.
97. SAN Rep. 502, VI KV-Anklage Interrogations R 48, Interrogation #323, 'Vernehmung des Dr. J.W. Reichert, 18.11.1946', 5.
98. BAB R 13 I/597 'Niederschrift über eine von Herrn Ministerpräsident Göring einberufene Sitzung am Freitag, den 23. Juli 1937', 170–75 in BAB pagination, here 170.
99. Ibid., 170 in BAB pagination.
100. BAB R 13 I/597 'Aktenvermerk über die Besprechung mit Ministerpräsident Göring am 12.8.1937', 268 in BAB pagination.
101. Ibid., 269.
102. BAB R 13 I/597 'Vertrauliche Besprechung bei Staatsrat Neumann, 5.8.1937', 275 in BAB pagination.
103. BAB R 13 I/597 'Aktenvermerk über die Besprechung mit Ministerpräsident Göring am 12.8.1937', 172 in BAB pagination.
104. Ibid.

105. Overy, *War and Economy in the Third Reich*, 99.
106. BAB R 13 I/597 'Betr.: Denkschrift betreffend Reichswerke, Niederschrift über die am 24. August 1937 im Stahlhof zu Düsseldorf abgehaltene Besprechung', 113 in BAB pagination.
107. BAB R 13 I/597 'Vertrauliche Besprechung bei Staatsrat Neumann, 5.8.1937', 276 in BAB pagination.
108. BAB R 13 I/597 'Reichswerke Denkschrift, 8.8.1937', 263–66 in BAB pagination.
109. BAB R 13 I/597 'Stichwörter für Denkschrift', 272 in BAB pagination; see also 'Fassung II, 19.8.1937', 234–36 in BAB pagination and 'Denkschrift, wie sie in der Stahlhofsitzung am 24.8.1937 zur Verlesung gekommen ist', 95–99 in BAB pagination.
110. BAB R 13 I/597 'Stichwörter für Denkschrift', 272 in BAB pagination; 'Fassung II, 19.8.1937', 236 in BAB pagination.
111. BAB R 13 /597 'Fassung II, 19.8.1937', 241–43 in BAB pagination; 'Stichwörter für Denkschrift', 272–73 in BAB pagination.
112. Overy, *War and Economy in the Third Reich*, 102.
113. Ibid.; BAB R 13 I/597 '*National-Zeitung*, 27.7.1937' and 'Eine neue Wirtschaftsepoche: Auszug aus der Zeitschrift "Reichswart" 31.7.1937', 126 in BAB pagination.
114. R-WW, GHH Nachlass Paul Reusch 400101290/42 E. Poensgen, 'Hitler und die Ruhrindustriellen: Ein Rückblick', 14; R 13 I/597 'Über die Vorgänge in Berlin am 20. und 21. August 1937', 4.
115. BAB R 13 I/597 'Über die Vorgänge in Berlin am 20. und 21. August 1937', 4; 'Steinberg an Reichert, 19.8.1937'.
116. Ibid.
117. BAB R 13 I/597 'Über die Vorgänge in Berlin am 20. und 21. August 1937', 1–2.
118. Ibid., 2.
119. Ibid.
120. Ibid.
121. Ibid., 3; Meyer, *Hitlers Holding*, 81.
122. BAB R 13 I/597 'Über die Vorgänge in Berlin am 20. und 21. August 1937', 3.
123. Ibid., 3–4.
124. Ibid., 4.
125. Ibid., 4.
126. BAB R 13 I/597 'Betr.: Denkschrift betreffend Reichswerke, Niederschrift über die am 24. August 1937 im Stahlhof zu Düsseldorf abgehaltene Besprechung', 106 in BAB pagination.
127. Ibid., 108–9 in BAB pagination.
128. Ibid., 112–13 in BAB pagination.
129. Ibid. 108 in BAB pagination.
130. Ibid., 110–11 in BAB pagination.
131. Ibid., 116 in BAB pagination.
132. Ibid., 107, 114 in BAB pagination.
133. Ibid., 107 in BAB pagination.
134. Ibid., 112 in BAB pagination.
135. Ibid., 116–17 in BAB pagination.
136. Ibid., 117 in BAB pagination.
137. R-WW, GHH Nachlass Paul Reusch, 400101290/42 Poensgen, 'Hitler und die Ruhrindustriellen: Ein Rückblick', 14.
138. BAB R 13 I/597 'D. Wenzel an Vögler, Goerens, Reichert, 18.9.1937'; Reichert, 'Die englische Eisen- und Stahlindustrie in Gegenwart und Zukunft', 969–79.
139. BAB R 13 I/597 'Reichert an E. Poensgen, 8.11.1937'.

140. See Overy, *War and Economy in the Third Reich*, 105 and SAN, Rep. 502, VI KV-Anklage Interrogations R 48, J.W. Reichert, 'Erklärung unter Eid, 7.7.1947', 5.
141. SAN, Rep. 502, VI KV-Anklage Interrogations R 48, Interrogation #1120, 'Vernehmung des Dr. J.W. Reichert, 4.2.1947', 18–20.
142. Donovan Archive, Cornell Law Library, 'Nuremberg Trials' vol. 17, Pt. 2 53.106 'Office of Strategic Services (OSS) Research and Analysis Branch, "Biographical Report, Zangen, William" #53, 106. 11.4.1945', 3 and 'OSS Research and Analysis Branch, "Biographical Report, Röchling, Hermann" 9.5.1945', 1.
143. BAB R 13 I/598 'Reichert an Meyer, 17.2.1938' and 'Reichert an Vereinigte Oberschlesische Hüttenwerke, 28.4.1938'.
144. BAB R 13 I/598 'Aktenvermerk, Betr.: Finanzierung der Reichswerke Hermann Göring', 246 in BAB pagination.
145. Overy, *War and Economy in the Third Reich*, 106.
146. BAB R 13 I/598 'E. Poensgen an Paul Pleiger, 17.8.1939' and SAN, Rep. 502, VI KV-Anklage Interrogations R 48, Interrogation #321, 'Vernehmung des Dr. J.W. Reichert, 18.11.1946', 13.
147. SAN, Rep. 502, VI KV-Anklage Interrogations R 48, 'Vernehmung des Dr. J.W. Reichert, 17.5.1947'; Overy, *War and Economy in the Third Reich*, 107–9.
148. BAB R 13 I/641 'Reichswirtschaftsminister an Reichert, 17.09.1937'; 'Reichsgruppe Industrie an die Wirtschaftsgruppen der RGI, 11.11.1937'; 'Reichsgruppe Industrie an Wirtschaftsgruppe Eisenschaffende Industrie, 30.11.1937'.
149. BAB R 13 I/641 'Reichswirtschaftsminister an die Heren MOB-Beauftragten, 27.5.1937'.
150. BAB R 13 I/641 'Baare an Reichsgruppe Industrie, 11.12.1937'.
151. BAB R 13 I/641 'Reichswirtschaftskammer an Wirtschaftsgruppe Eisenschaffende Industrie, 9.10.1937'.
152. BAB R 13 I/641 'Reichert an die Reichsgruppe Industrie, 22.11.1937'.
153. BAB R 13 I/ 602 'Büchmann an Reichert 16.9.1938'.
154. BAB R 13 I/606 'RWM Besprechung, 17.3.1938', 8.
155. BAB R 13 I/606 'RWM Besprechung, 24.4.1938', 5–6.
156. BAB R 13 I/42 Bd. 2 'Vereinbarung der ostmärkischen Stahle- und Walzwerke vom 11.5.1938'; R 13 I/243 'Wirtschaftsgruppe Eisenschaffende Industrie, Rundschreiben # 12462, 26.8.1938'.
157. BAB R 13 I/606 'RWM Besprechung, 11.10.1938', 6.
158. BAB R 13 I/602 'Niederschrift über die am 23.9.1938 im Wehrwirtschaftsstab und RWM abgehaltenen Besprechungen', 1.
159. BAB R 13 I/644 'Niederschrift über die am 20.6.1939 abgehaltene Sitzung in Düsseldorf der wehrwirtschaftlichen Arbeitsausschüsse', 112. In BAB pagination and R 13 I/645 'Steinberg an Reichert, 5.7.1939'.
160. BAB R 13 I/644 'Niederschrift über die am 20.6.1939abgehaltene Sitzung in Düsseldorf der wehrwirtschaftlichen Arbeitsausschüsse', 112 in BAB pagination.
161. BAB R 13 I/646 'Reichert an E. Poensgen, 6.9.1939'.
162. Weisbrod, *Schwerindustrie in der Weimarer Republik*, 178.
163. BAB R 13 I/656 'Steinberg an die RWM (Oberregierungsrat Geyer) 3.9.1938'.
164. BAB R 13 I/656 'Bezirksgruppe Nordwest an Reichert, 5.9.1938'.
165. BAB R 13 I/643 'Aufzeichnung über eine Aussprache bei der Verbindungsstelle für Schrifttum und Presse in Düsseldorf, 28.11.1938', 1–4.
166. BAB R 13 I/642 'Curtius an Reichert, 20.9.1938'.
167. BAB R 13 I/642 'Aktenvermerk, Betr.: Lieferprogramm, 6.9.1938'.
168. BAB R 13 I/642 'Abschrift (an Steinberg) 8.9.1938'.

169. BAB R 13 I/641 'Aktenvermerk: Sicherung des statistischen Meldewesens, 23.7.1938', 43 in BAB pagination.
170. BAB R 13 I/656 'Reichert an Bezirksgruppe Nordwest, 8.9.1938', 1.
171. Ibid., 2.
172. Ibid., 1.
173. BAB R 13 I/656 'Steinberg an Wirtschaftsgruppe Eisenschaffende Industrie, 15.9.1938'.
174. BAB R 13 I/643 'Aktenvermerk: MOB-Aufgaben der Wirtschaftsgruppe Eisenschaffende Industrie, 17.10.1938', 1.
175. BAB R 13 I/598 'Sächsische Gußstahlwerke Döhlen an Reichert, 21.4.1938', 'Vereinigte Oberschlesische Hüttenwerke an Reichert, 21.4.1938' and 'Verein deutscher Eisenhüttenleute an Reichert, 7.8.1939'.
176. BAB R 13 I/598 'Reichert an Verein deutscher Eisenhüttenleute, 8.8.1939'.
177. BAB R 13 I/598 '*Aktenvermerk, Betr.: Besprechung mit Arnold Rochall von den Hermann-Göring-Werk*, 15.8.1939' 92 in BAB pagination.
178. BAB R 13 I/ '*Aktenvermerk über die Sitzung des Statistischen Ausschusses*, 16.6.1939'.
179. BAB R 13 I/644 'Reichert an Gerwin, Maulick, Petersen, Schuerer, Steinberg 7.6.1939', 'Niederschrift über die am 20.6.1939 abgehaltene Sitzung in Düsseldorf der wehrwirtschaftlichen Arbeitsausschüsse', 100 in BAB pagination and 'Niederschrift über die Geschäftsführerkonferenz am 22.6.1939 in Düsseldorf', 31–32 in BAB pagination.
180. 'Niederschrift über die am 20.6.1939 abgehaltene Sitzung in Düsseldorf der wehrwirtschaftlichen Arbeitsausschüsse', 112 in BAB pagination.
181. Ibid.
182. BAB R 13 I/644 'Steinberg an Reichert, 30.6.1939' and R 13 I/656 'Steinberg an Reichert, 30.6.1939'.
183. BAB R 13 I/645 'Abschrift zu GBW 2/3943/39s, der Reichswirtschaftsminister an Bezirksgruppe Nordwest der Wirtschaftsgruppe Eisenschaffende Industrie, 18.7.1939'.
184. BAB R 13 I/656 'Steinberg an Reichert, 2.8.1939'.
185. BAB R 13 I/651 'Reichert an von Hanneken, 7.8.1939'.
186. BAB R 13 I/656 'Steinberg an Reichert, 8.8.1939'.
187. See BAB R 13 I/644 'Aktenvermerk über die Besprechung vom 9.6.1939 in RWM', 147–48 in BAB pagination.
188. BAB R 13 I/656 'Reichert an den Reichswirtschaftsminister, 29.8.1939' and 'Reichert an Steinberg, 29.8.1939'.
189. BAB R 13 I/656 'Steinberg an Verdeuteisen, 30.8.1939'.
190. BAB R 13 I/656 'Reichert an Steinberg, 2.9.1939', 'Reichert an Steinberg, 2.9.1939' and 'Steinberg an Tosse, 2.9.1939'.
191. BAB R 13 I/656 'Aktenvermerk: Stellvertretender MOB-Beauftragter Dr. Steinberg, 14.9.1939'.
192. Ibid.
193. BAB R 13 I/606 'RWM Besprechung 17.3.1938', 1.
194. Ibid., 2.
195. BAB R 13 I/606 'RWM Besprechung 11.10.1938', 1–4.
196. Ibid., 6.
197. BAB R 13 I/607 'RWM Besprechung, 10.8.1939', 3.
198. BAB R 13 I/243 'Wirtschaftsgruppe Eisenschaffende Industrie, Rundschreiben #14004. 29.9.1938', 'Wirtschaftsgruppe Eisenschaffende Industrie, Rundschreiben #16437, 11.11.1938' and R 13 I/244 'Reichert an alle Kontingentsempfänger, 18.2.1939' and R 13 I/646 'RWM an Wirtschaftsgruppe Eisenschaffende Industrie, 7.9.1939'.
199. BAB R 13 I/244 'Anordnung 38 der Überwachungsstelle 6.12.1938'.

200. BAB R 13 I/459 'Meldung an die Überwachungsstelle für Eisen und Stahl, Berlin', c. 1938.
201. BAB R 13 I/244 'Reichert an alle Kontingentsempfänger, 18.2.1939' and R 13 I/243 'Wirtschaftsgruppe Eisenschaffende Industrie, Rundschreiben #14004, 29.9.1938'.
202. BAB R 13 I/234 'Wirtschaftsgruppe Eisenschaffende Industrie, Rundschreiben #13063, 8.9.1938'.
203. BAB R 13 I/459 'Deutsche Drahtstahlwerke AG', Draft letter, n.d. and R 13 I/644 'RWM Besprechung 9.6.1939' 147–48 in BAB pagination.
204. BAB R 13 I/243 'Anklage zu Rundschreiben 10560 vom 20.7.1938' and R 13 I/244 'Dritte Anordnung über Beschränkung der Herstellung von Röhren aus Stahl oder dessen Legierungen vom 23.12.1938'.
205. BAB R 13 I/243 'Wirtschaftsgruppe Eisenschaffende Industrie, Rundschreiben #17441, 25.11.1938'.
206. BAB R 13 I/243 'Wirtschaftsgruppe Eisenschaffende Industrie, Rundschreiben #17482, 26.11.1938'.
207. BAB R 13 I/42 'Tosse an Vereinigte Stahlwerke, 21.11.1939'.
208. BAB R 13 I/243 'Wirtschaftsgruppe Eisenschaffende Industrie, Rundschreiben #11438, 4.8.1938'.
209. BAB R 13 I/607 'RWM Besprechung 21.3.1939', 1–2; 'RWM Bessprechung 12.11.1939', 1.
210. BAB R 13 I/ 'RWM Besprechung, 2.11.1939' 1., RWW, GHH Nachlass Paul Reusch 40010222/6 'Von Hanneken an Reusch, 3.11.1939' and 40010222/6 'Blank[?] an Reusch' nd. C26.9.1939'.
211. BAB R 13 I/606 'RWM Besprechung, 17.2.1938', 11. For Reichert's continued defence of private international agreements, see J. Reichert. 1939. 'Schrott im Außenhandel', *Stahl und Eisen* 59(11) (13 March), 325–30.
212. BAB R 13 I/606 'RWM Besprechung 11.10.1938', 11.
213. BAB R 13 I/607 'RWM Besprechung 10.8.1939', 3.
214. Ibid., 4.
215. BAB R 13 I/244 'Wirtschaftsgruppe Eisenschaffende Industrie, Rundschreiben #19506, 30.12.1938' and 'Abschrift: Verordnung über die Beschäftigung Jugendlicher in der Eisen- und Stahlindustrie, 20.1.1939'.
216. BAB R 13 I/ Wirtschaftsgruppe Eisenschaffende Industrie, Rundschreiben #19506, 30.12.1938'.
217. BAB R 13 I/243 'Wirtschaftsgruppe Eisenschaffende Industrie, Rundschreiben #11349, 4.8.1938' and R 13 I/602 'RWM Besprechung 23.9.1938', 2.
218. BAB R 13 I/644 'Aktenvermerk über die Sitzung des Statistischen Ausschusses, 16.6.1939', 100–101 in BAB pagination.
219. BAB R 13 I/644 'Niederschrift über die Geschäftsführer-Konferenz am 22.6.1939', 33.
220. BAB R 13 I/607 'RWM Besprechung, 21.3.1939', 1–2.
221. BAB R 13 I/643 'RWM Besprechung, 18.11.1938' and 'Wirtschaftsgruppe Eisenschaffende Industrie an Tosse, 15.12.1938'; R 13 I/607 'RWM Besprechung, 21.3.1939'.
222. BAB R 13 I/606 'RWM Besprechung, 10.2.1938', 185 in BAB pagination; R 13 I/644 'Aktenvermerk über die Sitzung des Statistischen Ausschusses, 16.6.1939', 100 on BAB pagination.
223. BAB R 13 I/607 'RWM Besprechung, 21.3.1939', 5.
224. BAB R 13 I/644 'Aktenvermerk über das Ergebnis der RWM-Besprechung vom 30.1.1939 in Düsseldorf', 178 in BAB pagination.
225. BAB R 13 III/140 Könemund/Sahm 'Lenkung der Maschinenproduktion: Anordnung des Bevollmächtigten für die Maschinenproduktion zur Rationalisierung der

Maschinenerzeugung und zur Auftragsregelung für Maschinenbauerzeugnisse. Sonderausgabe des Abschnitts 11 G des Sammelwerkes Eisen und Stahl' 1942, Verlag August Lutzeyer. 4; R 13 III/78 'Gemeinschaftsarbeit im Maschinenbau, 15. November 1892 bis 15. November 1942', 5.
226. BAB R 13 III/140 Könemund/Sahm 'Lenkung der Maschinenproduktion', 4–5.
227. R. Hachtmann and W. Süß. 2006. 'Kommissare im NS-Herrschaftssystem: Probleme und Perspektiven der Forschung', in R. Hachtmann and W. Süß (eds), *Hitlers Kommissare: Sondergewalten in der nationalsozialistischen Diktatur*, Göttingen: Wallstein Verlag, 9–10.
228. Lutz Budraß. 1993. 'Unternehmer im Nationalsozialismus. Der "Sonderbevollmächtigte des Generalfeldmarschalls Göring für die Herstellung der JU 88"', in Plumpe, Werner and Kleinschmidt (eds). *Unternehmen zwischen Markt und Macht. Apsekte deutscher Unternehmens- und Industriegeschichte im 20. Jahrhundert*, Essen: Schriften zur Unternehmens- und Industriegeschichte, 74, 76; 'Meinberg, Wilhelm, Politiker' in *Deutsche Biographische Enzyklopädie*, 6, 855.
229. Tooze, *The Wages of Destruction*, 415; *Deutsche Biographische Enzyklopädie*, vol. 5, 209; R. Hachtman and W. Süß. 2006. *Hitlers Kommissare: Sondergewalten in der nationalsozialistischen Diktatur*, Göttingen: Wallstein Verlag, 21.
230. BAB R 9 VIII/6 'Büro-Rundschreiben, 2.2.1939'.
231. A. Gehrig. 2002. 'Zwischen Betriebsinteresse und Lenkungswirtschaft: Drei mittelständische Unternehmer im "Dritten Reich"', in T. Größbölting and R. Schmidt (eds), *Unternehmerwirtschaft zwischen Markt und Lenkung: Organisationsformen, politischer Einfluß und ökonomisches Verhalten 1930-1960*, Munich: R. Oldenbourg Verlag, 107.
232. Bayerisches Wirtschaftsarchiv (hereafter BWA) F79 358 Schärfls Nachfolger Werkzeugmaschinenfabrik, München, 'Bericht über die Sitzung der Fachgruppe Werkzeugmaschine der Wirtschaftsgruppe Maschinenbau in Stuttgart am 4. 5. 1939', 6.
233. BAB R 13 III/145b *Maschinenbau-Nachrichten* 3(42) (21 October 1937), 244 and *Maschinenbau Nachrichten* 5(13) (30 March 1939), 67–68.
234. BAB R 9 VIII/6 'Büro-Rundschreiben Nr. 467. 1.12.1938'.
235. 'Die Ausmerzung der Juden aus der ausländischen Absatzorganization eines Betriebes ist für einen nationalsozialistisch eingestellten Betriebsführer eine Selbstverständlichkeit'. BAB R 13 III/145b *Maschinenbau Nachrichten* 5(13) (30 March 1939), 67–68.
236. BAB R 13 III/145b *Maschinenbau-Nachrichten* 3(42) (21 October 1937), 244.
237. BAB R 13 III/145b *Maschinenbau-Nachrichten* 4(51) (22 December 1938), 294; *Maschinenbau Nachrichten* 4(52) (29 December 1938), 300.
238. BAB R 13 III/145b *Maschinenbau-Nachrichten* 5(15) (13 April 1939), 77.
239. SHA LD. 689 Bd. 2., 'Der Reichs- und Preußische Wirtschaftsminister, 1.12.1937'.
240. BWA Shärfl's Nachfolger Werkzeugmaschinenfabrik, München, F79 357. 'Reisebericht 22.7.1942: Reise Berlin Bericht: Unterhandlung mit dem BFM', 8; BAB R 13 III/145b *Maschinenbau-Nachrichten* 5(15) (13 April 1939), 77.
241. Schneider, *Unternehmensstrategien zwischen Weltwirtschaftskrise und Kriegswirtschaft*, 221–22.
242. BWA F79 357. Schärfls Nachfolger Werkzeugmaschinenfabrik, München, 'Reisebericht 22.7.1942: Berlin Reisbericht : Unterhandlung mit dem BfM', 8.
243. Schneider, *Unternehmensstrategien zwischen Weltwirtschaftskrise und Kriegswirtschaft*, 210.
244. SHA 49/LS 157 'Wirtschaftsgruppe Maschinenbau an die Mitgliedsfirmen 9.1.1935', 1–2.

245. SHA 49/LS 157 'Wirtschaftsgruppe Maschinenbau, Rundschreiben Reihe I Nr. 37 5.5.1937'.
246. SHA 49/LS 157 'Auszug aus der Niederschrift über die ordentliche Beiratssitzung der Fachgruppe Maschinen- und Präzisionswerkzeuge am 9.7.1937'.
247. Ibid.
248. SHA 49/LS 157 'Wirtschaftsgruppe Maschinenbau, Rundschreiben Reihe 1. Nr. 94 21.9.1937'.
249. SHA 49/LS 157 'Siemens-Schuckert Wirtschaftspolitische Abteilung an Wirtschaftsgruppe Maschinenbau 21.10.1937'.
250. SHA 49/LS 157 'Wirtschaftsgruppe Maschinenbau 1Vj., 1938'.
251. The 'polycratic' nature of the Nazi state has been well documented. See Broszat, *The Hitler State*; I. Kershaw. 1993. '"Working Towards the Führer": Reflections on the Nature of the Hitler Dictatorship', *Contemporary European History* 2(2), 103–18; D. Rebentisch. 1989. *Führerstaat und Verwaltung im Zweiten Weltkrieg*, Stuttgart: Franz Steiner Verlag. For polycracy in economic life see Prollius, *Das Wirtschaftssystem der Nationalsozialisten 1933–1939* and O. Volkart. 2005. 'Wirtschaftspolitik und bürokratischer Wettbewerb im "Dritten Reich" 1933–1939', in T. Eger (ed.), *Erfolg und Versagen von Institutionen*, Berlin: Duncker & Humblot.
252. BAB R 13 V/219 'Wirtschaftsgruppe Elektroindustrie & Maschinenbau an Rud. Blohm 30.10.1934'.
253. BAB R 9 VIII/1 'Wirtschaftsgruppe Fahrzeugindustrie an die Wirtschaftsgruppe Maschinenbau 26.6.1939' and 'Abschrift. an die Prüfungsstellen Betr.: Organisatorische Zugehörigkeit der Hersteller von Address-platten. Behandlung der Z.A. Anträge 5.2.1936'.
254. BAB R 13 V/219 'Wirtschaftsgruppen Elektroindustrie und Maschinenbau an Rud. Blohm 30.10.1934'; R 13 V/34 'Wirtschaftsgruppe Elektroindustrie Geschäftsführung [illeg.] an Dr. Braun 16.8.1937' and 'Braun an Sack, 11.8.1937'.
255. BAB R 13 V/226 'Lange an Wirtschaftsgruppe Elektroindustrie, 21.2.1936'.
256. BAB R 9 VIII/3 'Wirtschaftsgruppe Groß- Ein- und Ausfuhrhandel, Abteilung Außenhandel, 13.12.1937', 'Prüfungsstelle Maschinenbau an die Prüfungsstelle für den Bereich der Fachgruppe Werkzeugindustrie, 10.1.1938', 'Prüfungsstelle Maschinenbau an Herrn Schäfer, 14.1.1938' and 'Prüfungsstelle für den Bereich der Wirtschaftsgruppe Eisen-, Stahl- und Blechwarenindustrie, 17.2.1938'.
257. BAB R 9 VIII/3 'Vorprüfungsstelle Maschinen- und Präzisionswerkzeuge an die Prüfungsstelle Maschinenbau, 8.10.1938'.
258. BAB R 9 VIII/3 'Prüfungsstelle Maschinenbau an die Prüfungsstelle für den Bereich der Fachgruppe Werkzeugindustrie, 21.12.1837' and 'Wirtschaftsgruppe Groß- Ein und Ausfuhrhandel an die Prüfungsstelle Maschinen- und Präzisionswerkzeuge, 13.12.1937'.
259. BAB R 9 VIII/4 'Vorprüfungsstelle Holzbearbeitungsmaschinen der Prüfungsstelle Maschinenbau an die Firma Gebrüder Leitz, 9.4.1940', 'Gebrüder Leitz an die Vorprüfungsstelle Maschinenbau, 11.4.1940', 'An die Wirtschaftsgruppe Maschinenbau, 18.4.1940' and 'Prüfungsstelle Maschinenbau an die Wirtschaftsgruppe Maschinenbau, Organizationsabteilung, 19.4.1939'.
260. Siegel and Freyburg, *Industrielle Rationalisierung unter dem Nationalsozialismus*, 206.
261. Schearer, 'The Reichskuratorium für Wirtschaftlichkeit', 599.
262. Siegel and Freyburg, *Industrielle Rationalisierung unter dem Nationalsozialismus*, 209.
263. BAB R 8 XVI/1 'BfM Anordnung über die Typenbereinigung von Schnellpressen, 20.7.1939'.
264. Gehrig, 'Zwischen Betriebsinteresse und Lenkungswirtschaft', 110–12.

265. Ibid., 89.
266. Ibid., 111–12.
267. Ibid., 89.
268. Schneider, *Unternehmensstrategien zwischen Weltwirtschaftskrise und Kriegswirtschaft*, 223, 214.
269. Siegel and Freyberg, *Industrielle Rationalisierung unter dem Nationalsozialismus*, 154.
270. Gehrig, *Nationalsozialistische Rüstungspolitik und unternehmerischer Entscheidungsspielraum*, 48.
271. Ibid., 75.
272. No policy documents have yet been identified that would shed light on this question. It may be possible to at least analyse the practical effects of such a policy by examining the requests and subsidy allotments of the member firms in a future research project. However, a curious filing system and the volume of fragmented information mean that uncovering this will require a massive investment of time as well as technical and mathematical skill. See also Schneider, *Unternehmensstrategien zwischen Weltwirtschaftskrise und Kriegswirtschaft*, 198.
273. Schneider, *Unternehmensstrategien zwischen Weltwirtschaftskrise und Kriegswirtschaft*, 206.
274. Ibid., 207, 209.
275. Ibid., 209.
276. BAB R 13 III/145b *Maschinenbau-Nachrichten* 4(1) (6 January 1938), 4; *Maschinenbau-Nachrichten* 4(44) (3 November 1938), 252.
277. BAB R 13 III/145b *Maschinenbau-Nachrichten* 4(48) (1 December 1938), 276; *Maschinenbau-Nachrichten* 4(52) (29 December 1938), 300.
278. BAB R 13 III/145b *Maschinenbau-Nachrichten* 4(15) (14 April 1938), 89.
279. Pohl and Markner, *Verbandsgeschichte und Zeitgeschichte*, 92; BAB R 9 VIII 'Rundschreiben Nr. 422 20.6.1938'.
280. BAB R 9 VIII/6 'Büro Rundschreiben 492 4.14.1939'.
281. Ibid.; Pohl and Markner, *Verbandsgeschichte und Zeitgeschichte*, 94.
282. K.H. Roth. 1999. 'Neuordnung' und Wirtschaftliche Nachkriegsplanung', in D. Eichholtz (ed.), *Krieg und Wirtschaft:Studien zur deutschen Wirtschaftsgeschichte 1939–1945*, Berlin: Metropol Verlag, 205.
283. Siegel and Freyburg, *Industrielle Rationalisierung unter dem Nationalsozialismus*, 153, 168.
284. Ibid., 153.
285. Scherner, *Die Logik der Industriepolitik im Dritten Reich*, 297.
286. Gehrig, *Nationalsozialistische Rüstungspolitik und unternehmerischer Entscheidungsspielraum*, 48.
287. Schneider, *Unternehmensstrategien zwischen Weltwirtschaftskrise und Kriegswirtschaft*, 16.
288. Siegel and Freyburg, *Industrielle Rationalisierung unter dem Nationalsozialismus*, 153.
289. BAB R 3101 Anh. Mcc/1 97 'Statistische Übersicht über den Absatz der deutschen Maschinenindustrie in den Jahren 1928–44, nach Maschinenart getrennt (in englischer Sprache).'
290. Schneider, *Unternehmensstrategien zwischen Weltwirtschaftskrise und Kriegswirtschaft*, 69.
291. Siegel and Freyburg, *Industrielle Rationalisierung unter dem Nationalsozialismus*, 165.
292. *United States Strategic Bombing Survey, No. 54: Machine Tools and Machinery as Capital Equipment*, Equipment Division, 2nd edn, January 1947, Table 16, 'Output and Domestic Sales of Machine Tools', 79. It should be noted that the figures on export

earnings that Richard Overy obtained from *Statistisches Jahrbuch* differ substantially from the ones used here but were not used for this comparison because they do not cover the period comprehensively. However, both sets of figures reflect the same general upward movement following the introduction of the ZAV in 1935. See Overy, *War and the Economy in the Third Reich*, 84.
293. Schneider, *Unternehmensstrategien zwischen Weltwirtschaftskrise und Kriegswirtschaft*, 69–72.
294. Gehrig, *Nationalsozialistische Rüstungspolitik und unternehmerischer Entscheidungsspielraum*, 48.
295. BWA F79 358 Schärfls Nachfolger Werkzeugmaschinenfabrik, München, 'Bericht über die Sitzung der Fachgruppe Werkzeug der Wirtschaftsgruppe Maschinenbau, 3.5.1939', 1–2.
296. Gehrig, *Nationalsozialistische Rüstungspolitik und unternehmerischer Entscheidungsspielraum*, 89–90 fn. 194.
297. SHA 49/LS 157 'Wirtschaftspolitische Abteilung, Betr.: Rundfrage der Fachgruppe Werkzeugmaschinen über die Produktionserhebung in Werkzeugmaschinen, 24.2.1938'.
298. BAB R 13 I/692 'Staat und Wirtschaft: Auszug aus einer Ansprache des neuen Leiters der Reichsgruppe Industrie, 2.11.1938', 2–3.
299. For a discussion of the technical and organizational modernizing effects of the regime, see W. Abelshauser, 'Modernisierung oder institutionelle Revolution?' See also H. Kaelble et al. (eds). 1978. *Probleme der Modernisierung in Deutschland: Sozialhistorische Studien zum 19. und 20. Jahrhundert,* Opladen: Westdeutscher Verlag; W. Abelshauser. 2003. *Kulturkampf: Der deutsche Weg in die Neue Wirtschaft und die amerikanische Herausforderung,* Berlin: Kulturverlag Kadmos. For a discussion on the state of research into technical development, see R. Stokes. 2008. 'Research and Development in German Industry in the Nazi Period: Motivations and Incentives, Directions, Outcomes', in Buchheim, *German Industry in the Nazi Period.*
300. Pohl and Markner, *Verbandsgeschichte und Zeitgeschichte,* 89–90.
301. BAB R 9 VIII/6 'Büro-Rundschreiben, Nr. 478. 4.2.1939'.

CHAPTER

4

Impotence
Jakob Reichert in the Nazi Wartime Economy

What might have happened to Reichert and the Wirtschaftsgruppe Eisenschaffende Industrie, had the war not intervened? He might have been more or less honourably shuffled out and into another occupation just as his old colleague Max Schlenker had been in 1933. He might even have been tolerated as a cantankerous anachronism in one of the many superfluous organizations in the Third Reich for some time to come, and perhaps even recouped some of his old influence later. The war might also have offered Reichert a chance of redemption in the eyes of the state. He had always been a nationalist and had gained extensive experience in production and regulation in the last war. He might easily have justified a closer relationship with the Nazi state as a defence of Germany in its hour of need rather than of the Party specifically. In the event, the crucible of war brought the conflict between Reichert, his organization and the National Socialist state to a head. He did make substantial efforts to involve the Wigru in the mobilization of the German economy for the war, but only on terms that the Nazi state could not accept. After initially committing himself to the war, he continued to emphasize the importance of private regulation over that of the state, a stance that was in line with both his own ideas and his memory of the previous war but far from the regime's vision of either the war effort or the peace that might follow. This made the temporary convergence of Reichert and the regime's efforts at the outset of the war an anomaly rather than a conversion to National Socialism. Perhaps more importantly, Wirtschaftsgruppe Eisenschaffende Industrie lacked basic infrastructure and expertise comparable to what Lange had built in the years leading up to the war that would enable it to regulate the industry in accordance with the demands of the state, even if Reichert had wanted to. Although Reichert made some attempts to compensate for this by wading into National Socialist policies and rhetoric more seriously for the first time, he was no more at home there than he had been in the previous years and quickly diverged from Nazi ideals and methods once again. In the end, after having established themselves as thorns in the side of the regime, neither Reichert nor his organization had any substantial 'political capital' to survive the changes that wracked the German economy as the war began to go badly for the Third Reich.

The war demanded that Germans from all walks of life contribute to the state in ways that would have been unimaginable in peacetime, and both the organizations examined here and the industrialists they represented were expected to meet this challenge. Beyond the immediate needs, demands and fears associated with war, the rapid expansion of the territory held by German armies also raised serious questions. What would the German and European economies look like when stability finally returned after the war? Even when Germany seemed to be poised on the brink of clear domination of Europe, this question went beyond the raw robbery and exploitation documented by Götz Aly, among others.[1] The Ministry of Economics and perhaps even Hitler himself looked forward to establishing an economic order that would chart a 'third way' between business freedom and the state control that had already expanded so rapidly.[2] This would draw the representative organizations of industry into a system that balanced private initiative with state needs, enforced the dominance of German firms and presumably rewarded firms and industries that were able to appreciate both aims.[3] While individual managers and industrialists undoubtedly had their own ideas about the relative emphasis between these two goals, this was a golden opportunity for an intrepid representative to prove his worth. Lange would lead his industry on the path towards reward in this putative postwar system. Reichert hoped to roll back the clock on the German economy and undo much of what the National Socialist government had done, even as it fought a murderous war on several fronts.

As a result, the National Socialist state began to ignore Reichert wherever possible and seek out more amenable administrators to confront the crisis. Over the course of the first three years of the war, Reichert and Wirtschaftsgruppe Eisenschaffende Industrie demonstrated that they were unable or unwilling to regulate their industry to the satisfaction of the regime. By 1942 this had become untenable, and the German economy in general was reorganized in a series of reforms culminating with Albert Speer's appointment as Minister for Armaments and Munitions, renamed Armaments and War Production in 1943. The changes he introduced were meant to turn the tide of war back in Germany's favour by harnessing the economy more fully.[4] In theory, the new systems were to be based on 'industrial self-responsibility'.[5] In practice, they relied heavily on businessmen's close collaboration with the aims, ideals and methods of the National Socialist state. Men like Röchling, Vögler or Zangen, who were willing to play the parts the Nazi state offered them, became the key regulators in German industry.[6] Men who were more hesitant, less useful or both were sidelined in this effort to mobilize the entirety of the nation's resources for war. This essentially removed Reichert from industrial politics in Germany. When this happened, he was of little use to even the men in his own industry and lapsed into insignificance while the war raged on around him. Reichert had spent decades defending the aims and ideas of the German iron and steel industry, but in the end this commitment mattered less than practical success. His obsolescence not only stripped him of his role and authority in the remaining years of the Third Reich but also followed him into the postwar period and his own final hours.

Despite the friction between Reichert, much of his industry and the National Socialist regime, the iron and steel men and their chief business manager threw themselves into the war effort with as much gusto as anyone else in Germany. Even Reichert, who had spent so much time pushing for fewer intrusions by the state, recognized that war was a different matter altogether and set aside some of his reservations about an interventionist state for the time being to meet the larger threat. Moreover, he had seen in the previous war how the imperial state had bungled the early efforts to mobilize industry in comparison to his own industry's ability to organize and direct production. Reichert hoped to avoid repeating the mistakes of the past and guarantee private industry the leading role in wartime production and, by extension, in the peace that would presumably follow. With the outbreak of war, the *Wirtschaftsgruppe* itself also grew in importance and theoretically took on additional responsibilities for carrying out the orders of the Ministry of Economics.[7] As the mobilization representative (*MOB-Beauftragter*) and chief business manager, Reichert was personally responsible for the iron industry's response to the war.[8] His own authority was also strengthened when the chief business manager of each *Wirtschaftsgruppe* was designated Representative for War Production (*Beauftragte für Kriegsaufbau*).[9] Reichert had seen it all before and was confident that the organization of his industry, if not perhaps its resources, was more than adequately prepared to meet the needs of the army during another massive conflict.[10] Under other circumstances his experience might have been valuable and useful, but as it turned out, it was too little, too late for the National Socialist regime at war.

The imminent and pressing needs of the war led Reichert to push Poensgen to involve the Wigru intimately in the business of its members for the first time in order to regulate the shift to wartime production.[11] This broad desire to pitch in during a period of crisis and the lingering memories of conflicts with the army twenty-five years before led directly to the establishment of the Gelsenkirchen Accord in early 1940, which brought together a committee of industrialists and army representatives to coordinate the switch to armaments that Zangen and Minister for Armaments Fritz Todt took up as a model for industry in general.[12] To facilitate a more formal working relationship, von Hanneken ordered iron and steel firms to begin to dissolve the 'secret' mobilization arrangements between individual firms and the Wehrmacht, opening the door to increased general oversight on the part of the Wigru.[13] Reichert's own connections and expertise were likewise made more openly available to the authorities. In the first year of the war, for instance, he met with Advisor (*Ministerialrat*) Schmitt in the Ministry of Economics to help put together a group of experts for 'Operation N', a programme designed to evaluate English production, develop bombing strategies and ultimately administer the British iron and steel industry following an invasion.[14]

Reichert and his *Wirtschaftsgruppe*'s contribution to the war effort also went beyond assistance in this kind of war planning as the state made increasing demands of them. For Wirtschaftsgruppe Eisenschaffende Industrie, this change meant that that the association was knitted closely into the regulative structure of the Third Reich for the first time. While the Ministry of Economics' offices (*Reichsstellen*) bore ultimate responsibility for the allocation of raw materials, working with the business groups and delegating some responsibility to them, the Reichsstelle Eisen und Stahl ruled in January 1940 that Reichert's organization would henceforth be responsible for assigning rations to its members. Thereafter, firms would submit assessments of their needs to the *Wirtschaftsgruppe*, which would then evaluate the broader demands of the industry.[15] Thus, rather than the lobby group or consultative body that it had tried to remain, the *Wirtschaftsgruppe* was now pushed to take on the full responsibility of a regulative body in the Third Reich in wartime.

This was followed by a series of other interventions into the wartime economy. In the first year of the war, the Wigru directed its members to submit detailed reports on the composition of their workforce in order to help manage the growing labour shortage.[16] As the crisis intensified, the *Wirtschaftsgruppe* took responsibility for ensuring that important plants were not shut down due to a lack of manpower.[17] By the beginning of 1942, it had established a rationalization committee to oversee the various associations responsible for more specialized products under the *Wirtschaftsgruppe*.[18] As the tighter rationing of a wide variety of products and activities made production more and more complicated, the Wigru also involved itself in less exalted occupations. For instance, in 1940 the association entered into negotiations with the Reich Office for the Leather Industry in order to secure a sufficient supply of safety boots for foundry workers.[19] Other subsidiary organizations were also obliged to turn to the Wigru to acquire or use certain products, as when the German Scrap Association sought Reichert's permission to use a new automobile to conduct inspections.[20] This willingness to be involved in regulating the German economy finally began to engage the *Wirtschaftsgruppe* in the managed economy in ways that the Nazi state had been demanding for years.

This new enthusiasm and effort did not go unnoticed by the regime. Von Hanneken, who had become more sympathetic as his association with the industry progressed, thanked iron and steel industrialists for their admirable response to the outbreak of war.[21] Moreover, he indicated that both Hitler and Göring themselves had expressed their gratitude and affirmed their trust in the industry during wartime.[22] This would have been welcome news to an industry and organization that had run so far afoul of the regime in the preceding years. However, the prosecution of a large-scale war required more than stopgap measures from an organization that had long dragged its feet in peacetime. Unlike Lange and his group, Reichert had not spent the preceding years situating himself and his organization at the centre of a hierarchical regulatory system. As a result, he found that however much he might want to take on even limited regulation of the industry during the crisis of the war, he lacked the real mechanisms to meet the regime's demands in a meaningful way, and his efforts quickly fell short of expectations. When this happened, the conflicts between the state and Wigru re-emerged in a more serious form.

In order to bring industrial firms in line with wartime production needs, the Ministry of Economics ordered Reichert's organization to increase the oversight of production and sales in the iron and steel industry.[23] Despite having appointed a new special inspector, Schmitt and the ministry likewise demanded that the Wigru take its members in hand over new construction projects in April 1940.[24] By the following month, a representative from the Ministry of Armaments informed Reichert that the authorities were in fact not at all satisfied with the effects of iron rationing under the Wigru.[25] Todt himself warned Reichert that the regime had already become deeply unhappy with the organization again, particularly with Poensgen's tendency to discuss and debate 'secret' issues so candidly inside the *Wirtschaftsgruppe*.[26] None of this pointed to an organization capable of aggressively mobilizing the industry in the way the authorities had envisioned.

The Wigru's poor performance was not entirely its own fault. Like leaders in most industries in Germany during the war, Reichert and his colleagues complained bitterly that state production plans changed too fast for any kind of effective regulation and production to keep up.[27] At the same time, Reichert was deeply frustrated that the Ministry of Economics refused to supply what he saw as the necessary raw materials, making it impossible to produce up to expectations.[28] Von Hanneken freely conceded that these capricious changes were 'political' decisions that reflected Göring's own plans, and Reichert grew increasingly concerned that the Wigru would simply never be able to meet the *Reichsmarschall*'s unrealistic expectations.[29] At the same time, in contrast to Lange, Reichert and the Wigru simply lacked much of the basic information necessary to make the kinds of decisions expected by the National Socialist government. In particular, the Wehrmacht often failed to include the Wigru in consideration of its construction or production plans, some of which defied all economic logic and cried out for the input of competent experts like Reichert.³⁰ The Reichswerke Herman Göring also simply refused to provide the Wigru with its own production figures, much less its plans.³¹

Notwithstanding these problems, many of the conflicts between Reichert, the *Wirtschaftsgruppe* and the Nazi state stemmed from the reservations of the iron and steel industry rather than the whims of the regime. To a certain degree, this was due to Reichert's pessimism about the war. In spite of his nationalism, he continued to doubt that the German armed forces would be able to guarantee the delivery of vital ore from Sweden through Narvik in particular.³² Indeed, during his interrogations after the war, he all but accused the Allies of having prolonged the conflict by failing to bomb this vital port from the beginning.³³ However, Reichert's disagreements with the authorities more often reflected the interests of his industry and limitations of an organization that still hoped to function as a lobby group or cooperative association rather than a regulative body. Even though the Wigru had been tasked with negotiating production and distribution in Luxemburg and Lorraine after they were overrun by German troops, Poensgen had simply given up by the end of July 1941, arguing that the Wigru simply lacked the capacity and authority to deal with the region.³⁴ Likewise, when the Ministry of Economics chastised the Wigru for delays in completing a survey of the iron and steel industry's workforce in preparation for another call-up for military service in 1941 (a survey already completed by the other business groups, including Lange's), Reichert complained bitterly about the effects the increased size of the army would have on the firms in his organization and threatened the minister with potential shutdowns.³⁵ The threat of having to mothball nonessential plants in fact motivated Reichert and the Wigru to oppose the Ministry of Economics more or less openly. Even at the beginning of the war the ministry found it necessary to forbid the organization from dividing up emergency allocations of material to prop up failing firms rather than employing them selectively in key plants.³⁶ When the ministry approached Reichert for advice on the planned shutdown of some plants to avoid an unpredictable crisis resulting from fuel shortages, the chief business manager simply refused to consider the question.³⁷ It was, he argued, just not possible to save any more fuel in the iron and steel industry. Besides, he pointed out, the *Wirtschaftsgruppe* really had no way of knowing the extent to which its members were engaged in vital war work.³⁸ Regardless of whether it demonstrated incompetence or resistance to regulation, the ministry was unmoved by this claim and ordered Reichert to conduct the survey, which would allow the ministry itself to determine a plant's value to the war effort.³⁹ Despite this, Poensgen continued to demand that ore be divided in a way that would prevent the shutdown of plants rather than maximize the use of important firms.⁴⁰ To officials, this began to look suspiciously like an attempt to protect the interests of the iron and steel industry rather than those of the state in a time of crisis.

Remarkably, Reichert and Poensgen continued to push for the liberalization of the German economy even in wartime. When faced with the problem of distributing reserves for production at the end of the first quarter of 1940, Poensgen rejected the idea of a centrally planned distribution by the *Reichsstelle* and instead pushed Todt to turn the reserves over to the merchants for distribution through the market, such as it was.[41] In a later discussion with Stellwaag of the armaments ministry, Reichert not only suggested that the Wehrmacht be forbidden from allocating orders, at least for a period of six to eight weeks, but also pushed Poensgen's suggestion that iron distribution in general be opened up to market forces.[42] Stellwaag was not entirely unsympathetic. Having written a study of the German economy in the First World War, he was favourably impressed by the ability of the associations of the iron and steel industry to meet war needs during that conflict.[43] Reichert assured him that these organizations were even better organized in 1940, and the two men agreed to explore the possibility of turning regulation over to private organizations in the future.[44]

Reichert and Poensgen were also deeply interested in salvaging what was left of the prewar economic order. Poensgen in particular expressed concern over the centralization of economic life and argued that regulation must be relaxed in order to leave industry free to meet the demands of the war.[45] Reichert, for his part, was concerned about the fate of the international Chambers of Commerce in Paris, and the Wigru was eager to revive the international cartels that had collapsed with the outbreak of war.[46] Strangely, the association continued to talk about integrating England into such a cartel despite the current political and military situation.[47] Furthermore, unlike the representatives of the RGI, neither Reichert nor Poensgen seemed to have considered using Germany's military success to force firms in other states to accept a cartel system regulated by the authorities in Berlin.

This reluctance to sacrifice the interests of some of his members for the war effort extended to the protection of the cartels and other associations of the iron and steel industry. The controversy over Reusch's reluctance to renew the marketing associations continued to plague the *Wirtschaftsgruppe* well into the war. Although most industrialists voted to extend the IRG in September 1939, both Poensgen's United Steel and Reusch's GHH (Gutehoffnungshütte) objected. Reusch even threatened to withdraw from the agreement entirely.[48] The fate of the remaining associations (*Verbände*) likewise remained in question, and Lübsen at least found the prospect of the continuation of existing quotas 'very bitter'.[49] In his eagerness to resolve the issue, von Hanneken asserted that a simple majority vote should be sufficient to extend the life of the association. This provoked a sharp rebuke from Reichert, who maintained that consensus must remain the primary goal, regardless of von Hanneken's ideas about the end of both the free market and voluntary associations.[50] This hardly reflected an authoritarian approach to wartime regulation. When Poensgen still failed to make any progress, von Hanneken resolved to send Reusch a personal letter offering him a chance to 'voluntarily' renew the *Verbände* before this was legislated.⁵¹ In a last effort to avoid direct intervention, von Hanneken empowered Poensgen to deal with the situation personally with the full backing of the Ministry of Economics.⁵² Reichert, for his part, seemed to have given up on both a negotiated settlement and the ability of the Wigru to push Reusch into accepting the renewal of the associations. He stayed behind after the meeting with von Hanneken to discuss the details of further regulations, although these were to be done by the state, not the Wigru.⁵³ Bowing to the mounting pressure, Reusch did in fact agree, and the associations were extended for another year.⁵⁴ Nevertheless, the continued existence of the marketing associations remained an open question until the reorganizations of 1942 rendered the question moot.⁵⁵

This unwillingness to upset the traditional role of cartels and other associations that had characterized the iron and steel industry extended to a defence of the independence of the firms themselves that, in the eyes of the Nazi authorities, appeared to be little more than a simple dereliction of duty. In the early days of the war, the larger RGI had attempted to establish a basis for the allocation of raw materials and production by compiling reliable production and capacity reports through the *Wirtschaftsgruppen*.⁵⁶ The Wigru ultimately refused to decide on the distribution of production and left it to the local industrial departments (*Industrieabteilung*) instead.⁵⁷ However, the fact that these decisions would be based on the Wigru's information and analysis potentially conferred considerable influence on Reichert and his colleagues that might have helped them secure a stronger position in the wartime economy. Yet the Wirtschaftsgruppe Eisenschaffende Industrie failed to take any steps to complete the task set for it by the RGI, much less to influence the decision-making process. When called to account in December, Tosse defended the Wigru's lack of progress by asserting that the association had concluded it lacked the necessary expertise and infrastructure. The decision, he thought, would be better left to the firms themselves.⁵⁸ Kessler and the RGI were clearly annoyed by this failure to carry out their directions and ordered the Wigru in no uncertain terms to get on with the job.⁵⁹

The real commitment of Reichert and the Wirtschaftsgruppe Eisenschaffende Industrie to the mobilization of the iron and steel industry in wartime thus became something of an open question, particularly in those circles that had looked on the industry with suspicion before the outbreak of hostilities. Reichert's attitude certainly reflected many of the interests of his industry, but these interests by no means precluded a more active role in the state or economy. This fact was dramatically demonstrated by the active intercession of the Wigru's most enterprising regional group (North-West) in order to secure benefits for the iron and steel men in its own region. As this group began to usurp much of the role of Reichert's office, the *Wirtschaftsgruppe* found itself confronted by a growing threat from its own subsidiary that demonstrated the consequences of Reichert's prewar policies.

After the outbreak of the war, the allocation of materials, distribution of production, granting of licences, employment practices and myriad other questions required the approval – or at least input – of local authorities.[60] Regional business offices (*Bezirkswirtschaftsämter*), industrial branches of Chambers of Commerce, armaments inspectors and *Gau* authorities became particularly important.[61] As a result, the regional representatives of the *Wirtschaftsgruppen* in Germany became vital to maintaining a smooth relationship on the ground. This was no simple task. Neither the state economic authorities nor the *Gau* boundaries necessarily coincided with Wigru regional divisions. In the case of the key North-West Group of the iron and steel industry, for example, three separate Chambers of Commerce theoretically administered the same area.[62] In an effort to maintain the authority of the regional groups, Steinberg turned directly to the RWM *Reichsstelle* for help. The regional group had, he argued, already established a close relationship with the regional business office (*Bezirkswirtschaftsamt*) in Düsseldorf, and he feared that the proliferation of local authorities would undermine its work.[63] Steinberg's group was therefore granted a special status that would allow it to operate with a large degree of independence.[64] In January 1940 the advisory council of the North-West Group had begun to sit jointly with the industrial office of the Düsseldorf Chamber of Commerce.[65] By April, this relationship was formalized as a working circle (*Arbeitsgau*), incorporating representatives of the authorities and the North-West Group of the Wigru under the auspices of the Chamber of Commerce.[66]

Consequently, the North-West Group of Reichert's association took on a wider set of duties during the war without him. It was responsible for reporting shortages, transport problems, changes in production and the mood and disposition of workers directly to the state authorities.[67] Steinberg was able to build on this relationship and enter into negotiations himself with the Armed Forces High Command (Oberkommando der Wehrmacht, OKW) about important issues like the employment of prisoners of war.[68] While Reichert balked at the plans to shut down some production lines or plants, Steinberg and the North-West Group entered into direct negotiations with the Ministry of Economics about shuttering less productive firms.[69] Steinberg also attempted to capitalize on these developments and lobbied Reichert to make him defence commissioner (*Abwehrbeauftragter*) in the north-west to fill in remaining gaps with the local authorities.[70]

As chief business manager of the North-West Group's relationship with the authorities, Steinberg went beyond questions that directly affected members in his own region. Like so many in German industry, he was deeply concerned about how the demands of the army affected his members' workforce, particularly after the regime began gearing up for the invasion of the Soviet Union.[71] Unlike Reichert, who could only complain about the voracity of the army, Steinberg was able to draw on his closer contacts to the regime to pursue a more technical process of protecting iron and steel workers from the draft. In early 1941, he first appealed to local military authorities to have iron and steel producers designated as a protected primary industry (*Grundstoffindustrie*).[72] When this effort failed, Steinberg became a key player in the larger effort to protect iron workers in general.[73] He began travelling to Berlin to participate in meetings between the Ministry of Economics and Wigru while his assistant, Wilhelm Salewski, entered into talks with the army command itself.[74] Steinberg achieved some successes, and was able to secure temporary protected '*Spezialbetriebe*' (special, or protected, firm) designations for a large number of his members.[75] When the iron and steel industry launched a new general effort to protect its workforce, it was Steinberg, not Reichert, who dispatched the request to the Ministry of Economics to have the entire industry protected under a special designation.[76] Although this was ultimately unsuccessful, Solveen promised Steinberg he would see what he could do about protecting more individual firms.[77]

In a more sinister development, the iron and steel industry dealt with the use and distribution of forced labourers through regional offices and authorities such as the organization's North-West Group and local Chambers of Commerce.[78] It should be clear that while this removed Reichert and his organization from direct administration of this gruesome business, it does not exactly absolve him from the sins of the regime. Reports from these organizations and state offices regarding the use of slave labour in general passed through Reichert's office, and the chief business manager could hardly have been in the dark about what was happening in Germany and elsewhere.[79]

Reichert's increasing irrelevance was likewise reflected in the growing importance of other associations in the regulation of the iron and steel industry. Orders or demands with the highest priority went directly to the relevant associations or, at best, to the Wigru branch office (*Zweigstelle*) in Düsseldorf. The central office in Berlin itself had virtually no contact with the Army High Command.[80] Reichert was also passed over when the administration of the occupied territories began to be divided up. Von Hanneken, seeking to extend the regulation of the iron and steel industry to newly occupied Poland, appointed the Steel Works Association, rather than the Wigru, to administer the new territory despite the objections of the Wigru's control office.[81] In the event, even this turned out to be overly optimistic. The General Government flatly refused to cede authority for iron and steel in the region to anyone else.[82] However, the fact that neither Reichert nor his Wigru had any role in this dispute is a telling symptom of their declining role.

Reichert's previous reluctance to engage in petty struggles over jurisdiction in the years leading up to the war likewise came back to haunt him. While Lange had worked hard to exert his own authority in sometimes dubious disputes with other organizations, Reichert had stood aloof. This became problematic when Lange claimed responsibility for partially worked steel that would eventually be turned into arms. It was particularly worrisome for firms that produced piping that would later be worked into rifle or artillery barrels. Despite Reichert's opposition, the Ministry of Economics ruled in June 1940 that these products would indeed be considered part of Lange's purview.[83] This deeply irked Reichert's members, particularly producers who were forced to pay the higher fees associated with Wirtschaftsgruppe Maschinenbau.[84] Some hoped to circumvent the ministry's decision by pushing Lange and his organization into some kind of compensation system along the lines of the AVI agreement.[85] Reichert, however, was not up to another conflict with either the ministry or Lange and pessimistically shut down any further discussion as useless.[86] As a result, the Wigru became not only an organization of questionable efficiency but also one threatened by the ambitions of competitor organizations in the highly fractious atmosphere of the National Socialist administration.

Throughout the first years of the war, Reichert did make some efforts to reconcile his organization with the National Socialist state, but these attempts were too little, too late. They were also too transparently self-serving. When speaking publicly, Reichert had begun to pick up the kind of rhetoric that so many employed in the Third Reich. Despite his earlier objections, he began to praise Hitler warmly for apparently having succeeded so brilliantly in war and having finally achieved autarky in iron and steel.[87] This, however, was publicly tempered by the chief business manager's doubts about the security of ore imports from Sweden, a concern that itself called into question the extent to which the regime had actually achieved autarky.[88] He also made a rather belated attempt to integrate the new regime into the older traditions of his industry by reaching out to trusted members of the regime. In particular Reichert and his staff, along with Zangen and Flick, made efforts to lure Paul Pleiger into the iron and steel marketing associations.[89] As the manager of Reichswerke Hermann Göring, Pleiger was one of the most important men in the Nazi economy at the time and had access to some of the highest levels of Party hierarchy. His participation in the iron and steel associations would form an important bridge to the regime. A large number of firms in Germany had behaved in a similar fashion, adding National Socialists to their board of directors or payroll in an attempt to harness their political connections.[90] This was, however, more of an attempt to catch the *Reichswerke* in the net of private negotiations than to heal the rift between Göring's representatives and the *Wirtschaftsgruppe*. In any case, neither Pleiger nor the *Reichsgruppe* had any interest in having their hands tied by the old regulatory bodies of the iron and steel industry.

Reichert was somewhat more successful in promoting the Wigru and its leadership within the National Socialist state, at least for a short time. He and his right-hand man Baare lobbied the authorities to recognize Ernst Poensgen with a service medal for his contributions to the war economy on the occasion of his eightieth birthday in an effort to raise the profile of his organization in the eyes of the Party.[91] Reichert not only succeeded in securing Poensgen the Adlerschild medal, but also convinced Minister of Economics Walther Funk to make an appearance at the birthday celebration to present the honour.[92] As it transpired, both Funk and General Thomas did indeed appear to sing Poensgen's praises as one of the economic leaders to whom the Wehrmacht owed its thanks.[93] Poensgen was, Thomas inexplicably asserted, a model of the *Führerprinzip* in action.[94] Even the DAF sent its congratulations to Poensgen and praised him for the good relationship between the Labour Front and business group.[95]

This celebration was a substantial public relations event for Reichert and the Wigru, and the chief business manager devoted a good deal of thought to it, going so far as to put pressure on his nephew at the newspaper *National-Zeitung* (who owed Reichert a sum of money) to cover the event in the right light.[96] For Reichert, this was not just an opportunity to honour the president of his association. He approached Poensgen's birthday celebration and the presentation of the medal as also an opportunity to push his own ideas about the state of the German iron and steel industry and lobby the regime for substantial changes. Leading up to the event itself, Reichert urged Funk to keep in mind certain issues that had gnawed at Reichert for years: the Treaty of Versailles and the overcapacity crisis of the postwar period. More to the point, he tried to push Funk to re-examine the price of iron, which had not changed since before the Nazis took power.[97]

The question of the cost of such a basic commodity as iron drew clear lines between the interests of the state and those of the industry itself. As noted in previous chapters, the potential for astronomical profits created by the armaments boom and iron shortage after years of overcapacity had been thwarted by the regime's demand for low-cost iron.[98] As a result, the basic price of iron and steel had remained frozen at 1932 levels throughout the Nazi period.[99] There were, to be sure, exceptions to this rule. Rebates, exemptions, subsidies and variable freight rates complicated the price of iron and steel. The *Reichswerke* in particular was able to take advantage of favourable freight rates or to simply ignore regulated prices as the war progressed.[100] The dispute over price was also affected by an image problem that the iron and steel industry continued to suffer during the war, being widely seen as a gang of rapacious profiteers. Poensgen was forced to tiptoe around the issue, arguing that although no one should make a profit during wartime, firms needed to be able to support themselves.[101] When the industry received a rebate to cover some of their increased costs during the war, Reichert was careful to launder the money through the Control Office to avoid the appearance of a subsidy to iron and steel men.[102]

Reichert, however, was particularly keen to secure an increase in the base price of iron and steel. He was emboldened in the first months of the war when von Hanneken met his complaints about rising costs with the suggestion that it was high time to raise the price.[103] In December of 1939, the chief business manager brought up the possibility of launching a campaign together with key industrialists to increase the price of certain types of iron. A number of firms were supportive, but Zangen spoke sharply against Reichert's suggestion and the matter was deferred.[104] In March of 1940 von Hanneken himself vetoed an increase in the price of iron.[105] Although Reichert and Poensgen were able to secure some freight changes and subsidies, the 'inner circle' of the iron and steel industry rejected any further attempt to raise basic prices in August 1940, and then again in September 1941.[106] Undeterred, Reichert tried to use the occasion of Poensgen's birthday and the laurels he was about to receive from the regime as a lever to secure the long awaited increase on his own. In the lead-up to Poensgen's birthday celebration, Reichert corresponded with Schmitt in the Ministry of Economics about Funk's projected speech. Throughout this process, the chief business manager urged the minister to bear in mind that the price of iron had not gone up since 1931 and to incorporate this into his speech.[107] To a certain extent, he was successful: Funk picked up and repeated Reichert's language about the frozen ore prices and dismissed any suspicion of profiteering on the part of the industry.[108] However, the economics minister also torpedoed the possibility of raising prices before the army had successfully carved out the required 'living space' for Germany.[109] Reichert would receive no price increase, and the matter seemed to have been definitively settled. As long as the regime needed iron and steel for its own aims, they would stay cheap. In the absence of any other compelling argument, Reichert was forced to bow to the will of the regime.

Unlike the more astute Lange, Reichert continued to hamstring his own lobbying efforts by persisting in a strong political stance on behalf of his industry as a whole in other areas as well. As noted above, the effects of the Treaty of Versailles had been a leitmotif, perhaps even an obsession, in Reichert's work and thought for two decades. He shared this obsession with much of the Nazi brass, but Reichert's concern was specifically focused on its effects on the iron and steel industry. He not only considered the Ruhr/Lorraine industrial system to be a more or less natural phenomenon but also continued to see the steel firms in Lorraine as the rightful property of German iron and steel industrialists.[110] The invasion of France, Holland and Belgium in May 1940 opened up an opportunity to address his long-standing complaints in a meaningful way. The Nazi authorities also recognized this fact, and Funk himself famously warned the Ruhr industrialists to 'repress any desire for annexation' in the region.[111] Curiously, even though this warning had been repeated to him personally on at least two separate occasions by both Zangen and von Hanneken and he himself had passed it on to his members, Reichert was later unable to recall it.[112] However, the dispute over the disposition of the firms in Lorraine and Luxembourg in particular demonstrated the gulf that had grown between the aims and long-term plans of the iron and steel industry and those of the regime.

As the conflict over the fate of the smelting capacity and minette found on Germany's western borders increased, Reichert came to play a key role in the clash between statist aims and the revanchist ideas of the German iron and steel industry. Both Göring and Paul Pleiger had their own plans for the iron and steel industries in the newly occupied territories.[113] They hoped to use these regions' resources and capacity to position the *Reichswerke* for domination of postwar iron and steel production at the expense of the Ruhr firms in particular.[114] By 1941, Paul Rheinlander had integrated these plans into a larger blueprint for a continental production system that would limit the activity of Reichert's members.[115] Although several firms had made important gains in the east, even industrialists of the stature of Krupp and Flick were frustrated by the limits the state placed on them.[116]

Even before the invasion of France, several major firms, including Krupp, Mannesmann and United Steel, had put forward their own claims to the plant and ore fields in Lorraine. However, these large companies (which also, improbably, claimed to speak for the smaller firms) hoped to avoid a hasty or instrumentalized division of the spoils by putting off a final decision about their distribution until the end of the war.[117] At the very least, they hoped to establish a private holding company to administer the firms in Lorraine and Luxembourg.[118] To defend what he described as his industry's strong legal and moral claims on the firms in Lorraine, Poensgen appointed Reichert to represent the Wigru and industry in further negotiations with the authorities.[119] The discussion did not go smoothly. In early July, Reichert clashed with the *Reichswerke* representative Paul Raabe, who advocated not only an expansion of the *Reichwerke* but also a strange suggestion that the newly acquired firms revert to the original families that had built them, rather than to the firms as corporate entities.[120] Reichert reacted rather strongly, arguing that claims to ownership should be handled under German estate law and revert to those firms that had inherited or purchased ownership rights.[121] He also openly expressed his concerns about the troubling appetite of the *Reichswerke*, something Göring's representative could hardly have failed to notice.[122] In an effort to push private claims, Reichert managed to arrange a meeting with Otto Steinbrinck, the chief steel representative of the German government in

Belgium, North France and Longwy, as well as Schmitt from the Ministry of Economics.[123] Reichert may have hoped that Steinbrinck could help him to reach out to the Nazi administration more effectively. Steinbrinck had once worked as Reichert's assistant in the VDESI during the Weimar years before joining Flick's management team, where he then helped to ingratiate the firm into the Nazi economy before leaving to take up an administrative position in the regime itself.[124]

Even leaving aside the question of the *Reichsmarschall*'s plans, determining legal claims to the plants in question was no easy task, and the ensuing discussion dragged on interminably. By early 1941 a joint committee, which included Reichert, had been assembled to represent industry and the state.[125] This body was charged with examining ownership as well as ore production, mine ownership and possible reparations to be appropriated by the Reich. Reichert was working at a distinct disadvantage. Acting on behalf of the *Reichswerke*, Raabe was able to outflank the chief business manager by having himself appointed Commissioner-General for Iron Ore Extraction (*Generalbeauftragter für den Eisenerzbergbau*) in Lorraine and Luxembourg, a position that allowed him to partly determine production in the region regardless of the ownership of the firms themselves.[126] Other industrialists were also able to draw on 'political capital' in a way that Reichert and the *Wirtschaftsgruppe* could not. Flick in particular, Reichert believed, was able to take advantage of his close relationship with Pleiger and the regime and did not need to concern himself with the Wigru's lobby efforts.[127] Röchling also used his support for the regime, particularly during the thorny debate over the *Reichswerke* in 1937, to bolster his own claims in the west. Given that he had not only committed himself to National Socialist causes but also lost old friends in the industry in the process, he warned that he would take it as a personal affront if he failed to gain the Rombach works in particular.[128] Although Röchling had a passable legal claim to the plant, he at least was able to bypass Reichert's ponderous technical arguments and appeal directly to the ideological state. Poensgen saw the danger of such a politicized debate. Fearing that the Wigru (and his own firm's) claims would be rejected on ideological or political grounds, he proposed 'sponsorship' (*Patenschaft*) of firms in Lorraine by German companies as a way of heading off the rapaciousness of the *Reichswerke*.[129] This idea was more or less taken up in the imposition of a 'Trusteeship' regime in 1942, but it by no means guaranteed that the legal claims of German firms would be considered later on.[130]

The final division of the plant trusteeships in the newly occupied territories in the summer of 1942 is difficult to assess. The *Reichswerke* took the lion's share of the spoils, claiming 1.4 million tonnes of productive capacity.[131] The Flick concern was well rewarded, and Röchling, Klöckner and the Neuenkirchener Eisenwerke profited as well.[132] United Steel Works (chaired by Poensgen) was pushed out of Lorraine entirely, although it gained important trusteeships in Luxembourg.[133] What to make of this? Proponents of the old Marxist 'state monopoly capitalism' thesis have taken this as clear evidence of the role of industry and big business in the Nazi state.[134] More circumspect and recent works have also seen the distribution of French plants and resources as a victory for the Ruhr industrialists in particular. However, others of the stature of Overy and Tooze have questioned the importance of the limited and potentially unstable trusteeships gained by German firms.[135] In any case, it is clear that the Wigru itself was deeply unsatisfied with the results at the time. Poensgen thought the Ruhr had been deliberately shut out, and Reichert continued to bicker with the authorities over the lack of legal niceties in the settlement of this question both in his capacity as chief business manager and as a member of the committee of experts established to observe production in the region.[136] Beyond this, the Wigru seems to have given up. This was a notable setback. Reichert had made complaints about the post-WWI settlement and its effects on the iron and steel industry a key part of his political and economic ideas for years. If he and the Wigru were unable to even deliver the plant that had been confiscated in 1918 now that it was in German possession once again, what use was he as a lobbyist?

Reichert's obstructionist approach to National Socialism had borne bitter fruit. This did not take the form of a spectacular clash with the authorities, open resistance to the regime or the dismantling of the Wigru and dismissal of Reichert. Rather, the National Socialist government simply ignored the chief business manager and his organization as the war progressed. This was evident both at home and abroad. The Governor General in Poland not only refused to involve the Wigru or any of its subsidiary organizations, but also appointed a merchant rather than a representative of the industry to be responsible for iron and steel in the region.[137] In the Reich, the development of what would eventually become an advisory council (*Beirat*) for the Ministry of Armaments proved even more disappointing. During the discussion phase, Reichert had put himself forward as a potential member and seemed to have assumed that Poensgen would be involved as a matter of course.[138] Yet when the committee was convened, both men were excluded. This was particularly irksome to Reichert, who discovered that the business managers of every other important business group (including Lange) had been invited.[139] Reichert was rapidly slipping into irrelevancy. Given the demands of the armed forces in a war that had already begun to go sour, the full mobilization of the iron and steel industry was of the utmost importance. While the National Socialist government might be perfectly willing to tolerate a degree of poor performance in its friends, it was hardly about to indulge the cantankerous and obstinate Reichert, and it finally took steps to master the irritating iron and steel industry during the general reorganization of 1942.

By the third year of the war, the iron and steel industry was simply not performing up to the expectations of the National Socialist state. Despite increased efforts to organize the industry on the part of Poensgen and Reichert and the infusion of scrap looted from occupied territories, production of raw steel actually fell to 1936 levels in 1940.[140] The next year, it declined another 11 per cent.[141] There were also some concerns about the quality of German iron and steel, particularly compared to that produced by the *Reichswerke*.[142] Already by 1941, Poensgen worried that he would be forced out of office to pave the way for a more clearly organized and hierarchical structure.[143] Even Reichert, a consummate 'association man' used to negotiating multiple layers of representation, thought the industry had become so confusing that it was difficult to allocate production for the war.[144] This failure and confusion had profound results. In the general reorganization efforts of early 1942, Speer and Göring fundamentally changed the iron and steel industry with their reforms. In the first months of 1942, Speer began his reorganization of the German economy by establishing a system of 'Main Committees' and 'Rings'.[145] Rather than any of the top administrators or industrialists of the old VDESI, the industrial manager Friedrich Noell was appointed leader of the new Hauptringe Eisen und Stahl.[146] This caused considerable consternation in the *Wirtschaftsgruppe*, and Reichert expressed his dismay at the fact that it was even unclear whom his organization was to be responsible to – the new body, the *Reichsgruppe* or von Hanneken.[147]

This situation was complicated further in the following months. In early 1942 the *Reichsmarschall* established a planning office for the steel industry under Hans Kehrl of the Ministry of Economics to oversee central planning, new materials and the workforce, among other things.[148] At the same time, Speer settled on the establishment of a national iron association, the Reich Iron Association (Reichsvereinigung Eisen, RVE), modelled on the body that had reorganized the coal industry.[149] The discovery that the regime intended to establish a single, centralized, hierarchical structure sent the Wigru, regional groups and a variety of marketing organizations scrambling for a response. They not only wondered naively why the regime seemed inclined to throw away a perfectly good and experienced organization like the *Wirtschaftsgruppe*, but also expressed alarm at the idea of a single man in control of the industry. In contrast, they reaffirmed their support for Poensgen and his style of leadership in the industry.[150] Even Röchling, who would later take over the new organization himself, expressed doubt that the regime would be able to find a man willing to take up the post.[151] Poensgen was not even sure that the rumours of the new organization were to be taken seriously and warned von Hanneken that the industry would not cooperate willingly.[152]

Speer proved to be in earnest, and the new RVE was established on 29 May 1942.[153] Although it functioned as an arm of the state, it was constructed as a private legal entity that, unlike the Wigru, was directly responsible for market regulation.[154] In theory, the RVE did not take over the old committees run by the *Wirtschaftsgruppe,* but these were obliged to carry out the wishes of the new organization.[155] In practice, the RVE dominated the old association, annexed much of the Wigru's office space and absorbed the most important divisions, like the statistics office.[156] While firms were still supposed to submit their needs to the Wigru, the *Hauptringe* and RVE would be the ones to assign production and contracts.[157] This new organization was also built with the *Führerprinzip* in mind.[158] Accordingly, Göring himself appointed Herman Röchling as President of the new RVE.[159] If all went well, Röchling was expected to consult with a *Präsidium* before making binding decisions. However, in case of disputes, Röchling was empowered to decide for himself.[160] The new president's powers in fact went considerably beyond this. In order to bring the organizations of the iron and steel industry together, Funk summarily dismissed Poensgen as leader of the Wigru and installed Röchling in his place only a few short months after the old leader had been so warmly praised and honoured by the regime.[161] Röchling was then further appointed as Commissar for Iron and Steel in the Occupied Territories (*Reichsbeauftragter für Eisen und Stahl in den besetzten Gebieten*), extending his personal reach far beyond that of the old Wigru.[162] At the same time, he was named leader of the Ring for Iron Production (Ringe der Eisenerzeugung), which centralized a considerable amount of power in his hands.[163] Despite Röchling's earlier reticence and his irritation about the division of the spoils of Lorraine, he took up his new role with relish. Recognizing that he would make few friends, Röchling informed iron and steel industrialists that his new organization would essentially be run on military lines. Although he might welcome advice, in the end he would give the orders.[164] Reichert later accused Röchling of simply acting as a dictator, arbitrarily distributing materials and orders, and although this reproach held an element of sour grapes the chief business manager did imply that Röchling was simply too self-absorbed to recognize that others might not see things the way he did.[165]

Curiously, the bureaucratic leadership of the new RVE remained undetermined for several months.[166] However, once the question was finally settled, Reichert found that he had been shut out. Rather than one of the functionaries of the iron and steel organization, the mining engineer Hans-Günther Sohl took up Reichert's position in the new RVE.[167] Chief Business Manager of the Main Ring for Iron Production (Hauptring Eisenerzeugung) Eugen Beck was also attached to the RVE to help oversee its day-to-day operation.[168] Some of the staff of the *Wirtschaftsgruppe* were transferred to the new organization, and Reichert's brother-in-law, Tosse, was made head of its Statistical Office.[169] There was also more continuity in the branch offices of the RVE, as Wilhelm Ahrens was transferred from the more compliant North-West Group, supported by Salewski as his assistant.[170]

By the end of 1942, the RVE had set up a series of branch offices in various regions of Germany, most notably in Düsseldorf, to deal directly with the firms themselves.¹⁷¹ By early 1943, the new organization also began to absorb the marketing associations that had defined the structure of the iron and steel industry for so many years and that Reichert had treated so deferentially. Under the direction of the Ministry of Economics, the Steel Works Association's purview was narrowed and the organization itself was relaunched as the Rolled Steel Association (Walzstahl-Verband).¹⁷² More importantly, the Crude Steel Association (Rohstahlgemeinschaft) was dissolved and replaced by the Iron and Steel Works Community (Eisen und Stahlwerksgemeinschaft) on 1 April 1943.¹⁷³ This new organization was directly subordinate to the RVE. Having thoroughly proved himself to the Party and regime, Zangen was made chair of the Iron and Steel Works Community, assisted by Scheer-Hennings of the *Reichsstelle*.¹⁷⁴ The new RVE also targeted the old Control Office and approached the RWM in 1942 to have it dissolved.¹⁷⁵ It managed to hold out for some time, but the organization was finally liquidated in the spring of 1944.¹⁷⁶

This fundamentally changed the relationship between iron and steel industrialists and their marketing organizations, vexed independent or self-assured men like Paul Reusch¹⁷⁷ and was a crushing defeat for Reichert. The industrialists in the organization had other irons in the fire. On top of his own work (and sustained power struggles) in United Steel, Poensgen continued to sit on the *Präsidium* of the RVE until mid 1944.¹⁷⁸ He was also able to shift his focus more towards the increasingly important regional authorities and was appointed Regional Commissioner for Main Committee IV: War Equipment (*Bezirksbeauftragter im Hauptauschuß IV: Wehrmachtsgerät*) in Wehrkreis VI in the Ruhr.¹⁷⁹ Wilhelm Steinberg of the North-West Group also left the Wigru at this point but was able to exploit the reputation he had built in the preceding years to redirect his career. Having cultivated contacts with the regime as well as with industrialists of various opinions about it, he was able to move into the management of United Steel with the support of both Poensgen and Flick, two industrialists who represented opposite approaches to the Nazi regime.¹⁸⁰ Reichert, however, had no political capital to spend, no effective influence in his industry any more and no business ventures to turn to. The chief business manager's more interesting tasks, like questions of price and the cartels, were taken out of his hands with no hope of their re-establishment.¹⁸¹ Even after the war the old chief business manager remained remarkably bitter about these years, complaining that he had virtually nothing to do and was forced to suss out work to keep himself busy.¹⁸²

With the establishment of the *Reichsvereinigung*, iron and steel production had finally been coordinated in the National Socialist sense into a clear hierarchy that obviated the need for an industrial diplomat like the aging Reichert. The *Wirtschaftsgruppe* did not disappear after the reorganization of 1942, but it led a ghostly existence in the shadow of the RVE from that point on. For a man who was used to being at the centre of a key industry speaking for powerful men, this subsidiary role was deeply distressing. Reichert himself suggested after the war that his organization was kept alive only to bolster Zangen's influence and to help pay the costs of operating the *Reichsgruppe*.[183] The same might be said of Röchling and the RVE's motives for tolerating Reichert's organization. The RVE was expensive; its executive predicted that it would require a budget exceeding that of the old Wigru by 325 per cent. Iron and steel industrialists themselves supplied the new organization with 343,615 RM in the first quarter of 1943, as opposed to 154,000 RM paid to all of the industry's various organizations in the previous year. In order to meet the voracious needs of the RVE, 70 per cent of the income of the Wigru was diverted to the RVE.[184] By 1944, the old *Wirtschaftsgruppe* collection system supplied 2,100,000 RM out of a total budget of 2,975,000 RM for Röchling's organization.[185]

Despite Reichert's diminished role, he was not being entirely truthful when he claimed to have had next to nothing to do after the establishment of the RVE. He was in fact quite busy and was, for instance, simply unable to find the time to visit his old friend and adviser Paul Reusch in the summer of 1943.[186] Even in the latter stages of the war Reichert travelled a surprising amount, particularly considering the prevailing conditions.[187] Over the course of the summer of 1943 alone, he was dispatched to Italy, Hungary and Romania to meet with local representatives of industry and exchange experiences.[188] However, the nature of his work had changed fundamentally. Under the new organization of the industry after 1942, Reichert was reduced to little more than an assistant or secretary. Although he continued to meet with Zangen and Röchling in the course of his duties, he no longer attended meetings with the higher echelons of the Nazi economic hierarchy as he had under Poensgen, and was literally reduced to taking notes at RVE meetings.[189] Most of his time, however, seemed to be taken up with research and writing. This had always been an important aspect of Reichert's career, but following the establishment of the RVE it dominated his professional life. By 1943 Reichert was working on a comparative analysis of the steel production of the Axis and Allied states. This resulted in a report that was intended to be a propaganda tool for the Reich to counter claims that the German iron and steel industry was in the same dire straits as in 1918.[190] However, though the Armaments Office (*Rüstungsamt*) was interested enough to have Reichert conduct this research for them, his own industry and the RVE were indifferent, and Reichert's report on the English iron and steel industry was cut from the agenda of the RVE/Wigru advisory council meeting of 6 June 1944 in the interest of saving time.[191] The powerful men who now directed iron and steel production in the Third Reich had more important things to worry about on the day of the Allied landing in France than the complex economic analysis of an aging functionary.

Reichert also undertook an extensive consideration of iron and steel production that was intended to be a surprisingly cool assessment of the problems posed by the growth of American iron manufacturing.[192] Indeed, as the Third Reich collapsed around him, Reichert's assumed that Germany and the world would look very much as they had during the Weimar years, an outlook that is difficult to square with Roth's portrayal of industrial organizations intimately involved in the development of a German imperium.[193] This work also reflected Reichert's indifference to the blind optimism encouraged by the regime and his own hopes for postwar economic policy. This was most obviously expressed when he was appointed to represent iron and steel as an expert witness to the Working Circle for Foreign Economic Questions (Arbeiterkreises für Aussenwirtschaftsfragen) in the spring of 1944.[194] He was joined by Lück, a protégée of Otto Ohlendorf at the Ministry of Economics who shared a good deal of Reichert's fears about the over-regulation of private industry.[195] In November, the chief business manager produced a secret memorandum on the future of the iron and steel industry in peacetime at the urging of the working circle and RGI.[196] Reichert was surprisingly realistic, even pessimistic, about the future borders of the Reich, but he was also very careful to use the opportunity to lobby the government once again to lift the regulations imposed on economic life in Germany.[197] Hitler, Reichert argued, had already promised in July of 1944 that he would restore private initiative in business after the war, and Reichert optimistically looked forward to a more open market.[198] When this section of his paper was deleted in the process of drafts, comments and revisions, the agitated chief business manager had to demand that it be reinserted.[199] If nothing else, Reichert's persistence is notable. However, by this point it was little more than empty talk, and even his own members and colleagues had little use for Reichert.

In February 1943, the Wigru and Verbindungsstelle Eisen, a body set up to examine historic economic questions in the iron industry, met together to form a working committee for coal and iron.[200] No representatives of the *RVE* bothered to participate.[201] Apparently acting on Hitler's orders, the group committed to completing a history of the iron and steel industry in Germany since the First World War. Reichert volunteered to write the history and to chair the committee itself.[202] His plan for the work was, at least in theory, surprisingly professional given the overheated rhetoric of the regime in wartime. He intended it to be a critical evaluation that would not 'sink into polemics' in its analysis.[203] It is impossible to judge whether Reichert followed through in his commitment to a 'scientific' work, as no drafts appear to have survived, but the evidence seems to suggest that it reflected his own concerns for the industry rather than those of the regime. His proposed outline was a rather prosaic affair that divided the work into three periods: 1918–32, 1933–39 and the war.[204] His focus also reflected his own longtime hobby horses and emphasized the revolution, Treaty of Versailles and postwar crisis, among other things, but it is not clear how these events were mobilized in any larger argument.[205] There is no indication that he intended to devote any time to the foreign aggression, finance capital or supposed Jewish conspiracies that dominated so much of the rhetoric of the period. To complete this history, Reichert hoped to draw on the work of up to 100 experts in the industry and in economic life in general.[206] This was a substantial undertaking, and a strangely academic one in the context of a world war that was already going very badly for Germany. It was also demanding too much from the industry. The committee responsible for the work expressed dismay about expending so many scarce resources on a work of history that would do little to affect the course of the war or the iron industry itself.[207] Reichert was thus instructed to avoid approaching younger experts whose skills and time were needed elsewhere, and instead to rely on older men and retirees.[208] In practice, Reichert did much of the work himself through to the end of the war, defeat and occupation.[209]

In effect, Reichert's career was over. He had once wielded the influence of the most powerful men in the German economy, but by 1943, at the age of fifty-eight, the chief business manager had been put out to pasture at the head of a collection of pensioners reminiscing about the old days of their industry. In contrast, his younger, more vibrant or useful colleagues continued to arm the nation in a desperate struggle. His obstinate attempts to guard the long-standing interests and aims of his industry had brought him into direct conflict with the state and prevented him from developing any sort of administration that would meet the demands of the regime, particularly in the emergency atmosphere of the war. Having failed the state, he was likewise of little use to his own members, who were left to their own devices and contacts. All the broad policy efforts Reichert had embarked on had proven futile. The Nazi state did not open up the iron trade to market (or even marketing association) forces, and the basic price of iron remained fixed. Worse, the expanding capacity that resulted from the demands of war and the opportunity for plunder were largely confined to the state-run Reichswerke Hermann Göring. Reichert had not even been able to persuade the state to return the plants that his members had lost in 1918. Many iron producers did indeed profit from the war, but this was due to their own connections and contracts with the regime, as in the case of firms like Krupp and Flick, or to diversification efforts to take advantage of industries that were more lucrative. United Steel in particular invested considerable hopes in Bochumer Verein as a kind of holding company for other forms of production.[210] At odds with the regime, unable to develop the kind of organization that could effectively regulate the German economy and of little use to his own members, neither Reichert nor the successor to the old VDESI were of much use to anyone.

This was not the result of any direct persecution from the Nazi state. No official, party member or organization decided to charge or punish Reichert in any open way for the difficulties he had made for the regime. He was not dismissed from his position, does not seem to have been personally threatened in any way and was certainly never confined to one of the many gaols or concentration camps that had become so common in Nazi Germany. However, he was eventually forced out of the position of influence that he had once enjoyed. Because this came in the form of a judgement by his own former members as much as the state, 1945 did not rescue Reichert from professional failure. The collapse of the Nazi state and its plans (vague though they might still have been) did not wipe the slate clean or clear the way for Reichert's return to prominence in the industry he had so doggedly defended. Instead, his state of obsolescence proved to be permanent and, in a very real sense, terminal. Even if the system that had rejected him was gone, his old members continued to look to functionaries who had made more successful collaborators with the Nazi government as the men who had the connections and expertise necessary to weather the post war crisis as well. Reichert no longer had the qualities and contacts that had made him so effective in the Kaiserreich and Weimar Republic, and was of less use to his members after the Second World War than the men who had collaborated with the regime more readily.

Immediately following the collapse of the Third Reich and beginning of the Allied occupation, Reichert attempted to carve out a place for himself in the new administration by drawing up an iron production plan of 55 million tonnes per year as an emergency measure to see Germany through the postwar period and supply a basis for reparations to the victorious powers.[211] He also prepared a second plan for the resumption of normal production and trade, which, on the advice of colleagues, he kept secret from the occupation authorities.[212] He was in any case far out of touch with the mood or decision-making process of the Allied powers, and was 'deeply shaken' by their decision to limit German production to 5.8 million tonnes per year, and perhaps by their unwillingness to take him seriously as an adviser.[213]

Reichert could also entertain little hope that his position in the Wigru would help him to re-establish his shattered influence and authority. In the spring of 1945, the *Wirtschaftsgruppen* were all dissolved and their assets made subject to confiscation by the occupation authorities.[214] This in effect formalized the devolution of power over the economy from the shattered remains of the central government to the regional organizations that had proven so much more willing than Reichert's to work with the regime. In this context, the initiative was seized by those best able to make use of it.[215] The Wigru's former North-West Group, which had much more readily tried to balance the interests of the industry with the demands of the state than Reichert had, reconstituted itself as the Nordwest-Gruppe der Deutschen Eisen- und Stahlindustrie under more or less the same management.[216] Following this most semantic of changes, the North-West Group not only resumed its old duties but also effectively took the place of a central industrial association until it helped to found the new Wirtschaftsvereinigung Eisen (WVE) on 31 August 1945.[217] Although it took great pains to stress that this new organization was in no way connected to the old National Socialist organizations, the WVE was in fact driven by the experience and competence of the men who had held prominent and responsible positions in the previous regime.[218] The two business managers of the new association, Salewski and Ahrens, were the same two men who had been taken up from the North-West Group into the Reichsvereinigung Eisen in 1942 and were able to make use of their roles in the National Socialist economy to survive the transition to a peacetime world. Salewski in particular moved directly from the management of the North-West Group into Reichert's old role as the head of the national association.[219] Reichert, confined to Berlin, out of favour with the new authorities and disconnected from the industry itself, was left to brood over the remains of the old *Wirtschaftsgruppe* and busied himself trying to secure pensions for his unluckier former employees.[220]

The old chief business manager did make some attempt to make the best of a bad job by branching out in Berlin. Reichert seems to have established himself as a minor economic adviser and trustee in Berlin, working with the municipal authorities. In this capacity he began developing a plan to make use of the vast quantities of scrap metal left by the war in the city.[221] He once again hoped to deal with the problem through private means rather than public authorities like those that had been created to handle gas and electricity.[222] He therefore proposed the establishment of a Scrap Working Group (Arbeitsgemeinschaft Schrott), with a central scrap depot located in Spandau or Schöneberg, that would serve as a model for a national association.[223] He had some success in winning others over to his new cause. Karl Lindeboom of the German Scrap Association (Deutsche Schrottgemeinschaft) supported him, and his colleagues made overtures to the Allied occupation authorities.[224] Reichert, however, was unsuited for this effort and lacked the expertise to set up a minor scrap empire. As the scheme matured, Lindeboom became aware of this as well. He thanked Reichert for his efforts but noted that the negotiations and details would be better left in the hands of someone with experience in the industry.[225] When this failed to deter him, Lindeboom made it plain that Reichert could neither be included in the negotiations any longer nor paid for his efforts.[226] Expertise and connections still counted in what remained of German economic politics, and Reichert no longer had either to offer.

Reichert's problems were compounded by the peculiar position of the iron and steel industry. The invading Allies blamed this industry in particular for both the rise of the Nazi party and the planning and prosecution of a war of aggression.[227] More importantly, because the often highly unreliable American intelligence authorities had ironically identified Reichert as 'one of the top leaders in the Nazi administration of German business',[228] he was arrested by the occupation authorities and dispatched to prison in Nuremberg on 26 August 1946.[229] His jailers soon came to realize that the ex-chief business manager was actually of little importance himself in the regime and used him chiefly as a source of information about the structure of the Nazi economic administration and the conduct of the industrialists with whom he had been in close contact.[230] To the increasing alarm of his wife, Reichert was held in rather uncomfortable circumstances for over a year before he was finally released on 4 October 1947.[231]

Despite the trials that a lengthy confinement indoors had inflicted on what had become a delicate constitution, Reichert returned to Berlin full of optimism that he would soon find a place in the iron and steel industry once again. He pinned his hopes on Hermann Reusch, the president of the new WVE and son of his longtime friend and mentor, Paul.[232] This was not as unreasonable as it might seem. Reichert himself had helped Lindeboom arrange to appoint a colleague as an adviser to the Scrap Association, despite the restrictions on former Nazi officials' participation in economic organizations and the individual's connection to the Party itself.[233] Steinberg himself emerged from prison the same year to embark on a successful career in the Ruhr in close collaboration with his former members and contacts there.[234] Reichert, after all, had never been a member of the Nazi Party and had come into conflict with the regime in many obvious ways. Reusch was becoming increasingly embroiled in a defence of heavy industry during the Nazi period, something that Reichert would once have been well suited to coordinate.[235] The occupation authorities were also often markedly willing to employ former expert functionaries in order to come to terms with the chaos of war and occupation. Given the size and importance of the industry, it seemed likely that Reichert might find useful work leading to his eventual rehabilitation. Ten years earlier, Reichert would have been the natural choice to coordinate the effort to put German industry back together again. He certainly would have been supported by iron and steel industrialists themselves.

However, too much had changed during the intervening period. Despite the fact that Salewski spoke very highly of his contributions to the industry after his death, Reichert was yesterday's man even before the end of the war and could no longer draw on a web of important and well-connected contacts, colleagues and informants.[236] As a lobbyist and bureaucratic manager who had been sidelined under National Socialism, by 1945 he was of little use to either the state or his industry and could play no significant role in the postwar order. As a result, Reichert's hopes proved vain. Early in the new year, Salewski (rather than Reusch) wrote to inform him that, owing to the restrictions on former officials under Law 52, he could find no work for him. To make matters worse, the chief business manager of the new iron and steel association noted that they were unable to pay him for his history of the industry that Reichert had continued to work on despite war, defeat, occupation and prison.[237] Reichert was devastated. His wife pushed him to find other work (he had two sons to support at the time, not to mention a substantial household), and former contacts stood ready to find him employment in other industries. But Reichert, made even more melancholy by the onset of a heart condition and, according to his wife, the death of a particularly well-loved household servant over Christmas, refused, and sank into an obstinate depression. Faced with defeat and personal redundancy, despairing of a return to the industry in which he had made his career and reputation, and unable to secure the contacts, information or respect that had characterized his work and underwritten his authority for decades, Jakob Reichert committed suicide on 17 January 1947.[238] Reichert had stood by the aims and interests he championed throughout his career, but the world had moved on, and his own industry valued success over fidelity. Having lost his place in his industry and economy during the last years of the war, Reichert was forced out of industrial politics in the new Germany and found his own way out of this world.

Notes

1. Aly, *Hitler's Volkstaat*.
2. L. Herbst. 1982. *Der Totale Krieg und die Ordnung der Wirtschaft: Die Kriegswirtschaft im Spannungsfeld von Politik, Ideologie und Propaganda 1939–1945*, Eichstätt: Deutsche Verlags-Anstalt, 127–50, esp. 150.
3. Ibid., 146–47.
4. Tooze, *The Wages of Destruction*, 550.
5. For Speer's own understanding of his policy of 'self-responsibility' see A. Speer. 1970. *Inside the Third Reich*, R. Winston and C. Winston, trans., New York: The Macmillan Company, 208.
6. Tooze, *The Wages of Destruction*, 561, 563, 571.
7. BAB R 13 I/646 'Richtlinien für die Zusammenarbeit zwischen staatlicher Wirtschaftsverwaltung und der Organization der gewerblichen Wirtschaft auf dem Gebiet der Kriegswirtschaft. 15.9.1939', 1.
8. Ibid., 2.
9. Kahn, *Die Steuerung der Wirtschaft durch Recht im nationalsozialistischen Deutschland*, 403.
10. BAB R 13 I/657 'Geheim! Kontingentsfragen 18.5.1940', 2.
11. BAB R 13 I/646 'Reichert an Poensgen 6.9.1939'.
12. Tooze, *The Wages of Destruction*, 352.
13. BAB R 13 I/646 'Reichsgruppe Industrie an MOB-Beauftragten 7.9.1939'
14. BAB R 13 I/692 'Peterson an Oberkommando der Wehrmacht, Abwehr Abteilung I 23.8.1940' and 'Aktenvermerk: Einsatz N 14.10.1940'; SAN Rep. 502, VI. KV-Anklage. Interrogations R 48 'Vernehmung des Dr. Jakob Reichert 28.9.1946', 1 and 'Vernehmung des Dr. Jakob Reichert 11.10.1946', 17.

15. BAB R 13 I/646 'Richtlinien für die Zusammenarbeit zwischen staatlicher Wirtschaftsverwaltung und der Organization der gewerblichen Wirtschaft auf dem Gebiet der Kriegswirtschaft. 15.9.1939', 3; S. Werner. 1991. *Wirtschaftsordnung und Wirtschaftsrecht im Nationalsozialismus*, Frankfurt a.M.: Peter Lang Verlag, 318–19.
16. BAB R 13/I 'Bezirksgruppe Nordwest an die Direktionen der Mitgliedswerke der Bezirksgruppe Nordwest 26.4.1940' and 'Baare an die Direktionen unserer Mitgliedswerke 6.5.1940'.
17. BAB R 13 I/654 'E. Poensgen an die Direktionen der Mitgliedswerke 23.4.1942'
18. BAB R 13 I/658 'Rationalisierung 14.2.1942'.
19. R-WW GHH, Nachlass Paul Reusch 4001214/2 'Wirtschaftsgruppe Eisenschaffende Industrie, Rundschreiben 6826/P/Rn 10.5.1940', 10.
20. BAB R 13 I/646 'Deutsche Schrottvereinigung an Wirtschaftsgruppe Eisenschaffende Industrie 26.9.1939'.
21. BAB R 13 I/672 'Betr.: Sitzung General von Hanneken am 14.3.1940', 1.
22. Ibid.
23. R-WW GHH Nachlass Paul Reusch 4001214/2 'Wirtschaftsgruppe Eisenschaffende Industrie, Rundschreiben 6826/P/Rn 10.5.1940'.
24. BAB R 13 I/607 'Niederschrift über die Besprechung am 25.4.1940 im RWM', 8.
25. BAB R 13 I/657 'Geheim! Kontingentsfragen 18.5.1940', 1.
26. BAB R 13 I/657 'Reichert an E. Poensgen 4.4.1940'.
27. BAB R 13 I/607 'Niederschrift über die am 19.10.1939 im RWM abgehaltene Besprechung', 4.
28. BAB R 13 I/32 'Niederschrift über die am 1.5.1942 im RWM abgehaltene Besprechung', 7.
29. Ibid.; R-WW Nachlass Otto Wolff, Abt. 72, Nr 285 Fasz. 1. N.d. (c. December 1939) 'Aktenvermerk: Witrschaftsgruppe Eisenschaffende Industrie'.
30. BAB R 13 I/657 'Niederschrift über die am 10.4.1940 im Munitionsministerium abgehaltene Besprechung', 2.
31. BAB R 13 I/607 'Niederschrift über die am 13.3.1940 abgehaltene Besprechung im RWM', 7.
32. BAB R 13 I/672 'Wenzel (Vstag) an Reichert 21.3.1940', 1; R 13 I/616 'Bund der Freunde der Technischen Hochschule München, 'Deutschlands und Europas Eisenversorgung' von Dr. J.W. Reichert', 1. For a discussion of the importance of iron imports through Sweden, see F. Petrick. 1989. 'Die Eisenerze Skandinaviens, der Erzhafen Narvik und die deutsche Kriegswirtschaft', in Eichholtz and Pätzold (eds), *Der Weg in den Krieg*; T. Munch-Petersen. 1981. *The Strategy of Phoney War: Britain, Sweden and the Iron Ore Question, 1939–1940*, Stockholm: Militahistorska fölaget; and J. J. Jäger. 1969. *Die wirtschaftliche Abhängigkeit des Dritten Reiches vom Ausland, dargestellt am Beispiel der Stahlindustrie*, Berlin: Berlin Verlag.
33. SAN Rep. 502, VI. KV-Anklage. Interrogations R 48 'Vernehmung des Dr. Jakob Reichert 17.5.1947', 5.
34. BAB R 13 I/652 'Aktenvermerk über die Besprechung der Leiter der Wirtschaftsgruppe Eisenschaffende Industrie, Poensgen, mit Herrn Unterstaatssekretär von Hanneken in RWM 25.7.1941', 2.
35. BAB R 13 I/608 'Niederschrift über die Besprechung im RWM 1.1.1941', 1–3.
36. BAB R 13 I/646 'RWM an Wirtschaftsgruppe Eisenschaffende Industrie 7.9.1939'.
37. BAB R 13 I/648 'RWM an Reichert 30.11.1939' and ' Reichert an E. Poensgen, Maulick, H. Poensgen, Steinberg 2.12.1939'.
38. BAB R 13 I/648 'Reichert an Reichswirtschaftsminister, 4.12.1939'.
39. BAB R 13 I/648 *'Reichert an die Direktoren unserer Mitgliedswerke,* 11.12.1939'.

40. BAB R 13 I/672 'Poensgen an Reichert, through to von Hanneken, 10.2.1940'.
41. BAB R 13 I/657 'Niederschrift über die am 10.4.1940 im Munitionsministerium abgehaltene Besprechung', 3.
42. BAB R 13 I/657 'Geheim! Kontingentsfragen 18.5.1940', 2.
43. BAB R 13 I/615 'Die deutsche Wirtschaft im Weltkrieg 1914–1918', summarized by Reichert; R 13 I/657 'Geheim! Kontingentsfragen 18.5.1940', 2.
44. BAB R 13 I/657 'Geheim! Kontingentsfragen 18.5.1940', 2–3.
45. R-WW GHH Nachlass Paul Reusch 4001214/2 'Niederschrift über die am 13.8.1940 in der RGI abgehaltene Besprechung', 5.
46. Ibid., 6–7, 3.
47. Ibid., 5.
48. BAB R 13 I/607 'Niederschrift über die am 19.10.1939 im RWM abgehaltene Besprechung', 1–2.
49. Ibid., 2.
50. Ibid., 1, 3.
51. R 13 I/607 'RWM-Besprechung 2.11.1939', 1 and R-WW GHH Nachlass Paul Reusch 400101222/6 'Von Hanneken an Reusch 3.11.1939'.
52. BAB R 13 I/607 'RWM-Besprechung 23.11.1939', 1.
53. Ibid., 2.
54. R-WW GHH Nachlass Paul Reusch 400101222/6 'Von Hanneken an Reusch 10.4.1941'.
55. BAB R 13 I/608 'Niederschrift über die Besprechung im RWM 18.3.1941', 2 and R-WW GHH Nachlass Paul Reusch 400101222/6 'Von Hanneken an Reusch, 10.4.1941'.
56. BAB R 13 I/648 'Aktenvermerk über die Besprechung in der RGI, 12.12.1939', 1.
57. Ibid., 5.
58. Ibid., 3.
59. Ibid., 3–4.
60. For a discussion of the role of local Party functionaries during the war, see G. Kratzsch. 1989. *Der Gauwirtschaftsapparat der NSDAP: Menschenführung, 'Arisierung', Wehrwirtschaft im Gau Westfalen-Süd. Eine Studie zur Herrschaftspraxis im totalitären Staat*, Münster: Aschendorff Verlag.
61. BAB R 13 I/646 'Richtlinien für die Zusammenarbeit zwischen staatlicher Wirtschaftverwaltung und den Organizationen der gewerblichen Wirtschaft auf dem Gebiet der Kriegswirtschaft 15.9.1939',2., Eichholtz II 180, and BAB R 13 I/648 *'Aktenvermerk über die Besprechung der RGI 12.12.1939',*2.
62. BAB R 13 I/648 'Aktennotiz Betr.: Wehrmachtsaufträge 19.12.1939'.
63. BAB R 13 I/646 'Steinberg an Kiegel (Reichsstelle) 18.9.1939'.
64. BAB R 13 I/648 'Aktennotiz Betr.: Wehrmachtsaufträge 19.12.1939'.
65. Übbing, *Stahl schreibt Geschichte*, 154.
66. BAB R 13 I/593 'Niederschrift über die Sitzung des Beirats der Industrieabteilung der Wirtschaftskammer Düsseldorf 22.4.1940'.
67. BAB R 13 I/589 'Lagebericht der Bezirksgruppe Nordwest der Wirtschaftsgruppe Eisenschaffende Industrie 6.4.1940', 173–81 in BAB pagination and 'Lagebericht der Bezirksgruppe Nordwest der Wirtschaftsgruppe Eisenschaffende Industrie 5.7.1940', 104–15 in BAB pagination.
68. BAB R 13 I/589 'Lagebericht der Bezirksgruppe Nordwest der Wirtschaftsgruppe Eisenschaffende Industrie 4.10.1940', 31.
69. BAB R 13 I/589 'Lagebericht der Bezirksgruppe Nordwest der Wirtschaftsgruppe Eisenschaffende Industrie 5.2.1941', 166 in BAB pagination.
70. BAB R 13 I/649 'Steinberg an Reichert 3.2.1940'.
71. Tooze, *The Wages of Destruction*, 432–33.

72. BAB R 13 I/652 'Steinberg an Wehrkreiskommando VI. Zu Hd. von Hern Oberstleutnant Heider 18.6.1941'.
73. BAB R 13 I/652 'Bezirksgruppe Nordwest an Reichert 24.6.1941', 'Tosse an Oberinspektor Ebert, RWM 11.7.1941', and 'Tosse an Bezirksgruppe Nordwest 17.7.1941'.
74. BAB R 13 I/652 'Tosse an Bezirksgruppe Nordwest 17.7.194' and R 13 I/653 'Steinberg an Reichert 13.10.1941'.
75. BAB R 13 I/653 'Steinberg an Reichert 3.9.1941'.
76. BAB R 13 I/654 'Steinberg an Ministerialrat Solveen, RWM 19.1.1942'.
77. BAB R 13 I/654 'Solveen an Steinberg 13.2.1942'.
78. BAB R 13 I/373 'Niederschrift über die Sitzung des Beirats der Bezirkschaftsgruppe Nordwest am Mittwoch, den 19. Nov 1941'.
79. See, e.g., BAB R 13 I/373 'Der Reichsminister für Bewaffnung und Munition 3.12.1941, Einsatz russischer Kriegsgefangener'.
80. SAN Rep. 502, VI. KV-Anklage. Interrogations R 48 'Vernehmung des Dr. Jakob Reichert 5.5.1947', 2.
81. BAB R 13 3101-15234 'von Hanneken an den Herrn Generalgouverneur- Bewirtschaftungsstelle für Eisen und Stahl für den Generalgouvernement Polens 9.12.1940' and 'RWM urschriftlich an das Referat V Export 8 im Haus 9.12.1940'.
82. BAB R 3101-15234 'an den Reichswirtschaftsminister 1) Vermerk, Betr.: Ausfuhr der Werke der eisenschaffenden Industrie in das Generalgouvernement 15.1.1941'.
83. BAB R 13 I/521 'Niederschrift über die Besprechung in Essen 6.3.1941', 1.
84. Ibid., 2.
85. Ibid.
86. Ibid., 5.
87. BAB R 13 I/616 'Bund der Freunde der Technischen Hochschule München, Deutschlands und Europas Eisenversorgung, Dr. J.W. Reichert', 1.
88. Ibid.
89. BAB R 13 I/621 'Besprechung im kleinen Kreis 15.8.1941', 1.
90. See, e.g., Degussa's actions in Hayes, *From Cooperation to Complicity*, 57 and the even more dramatic example of Siedersleben in U. Soénius. 2005. 'Im Auftrag des Reichswirtschaftsministeriums: Rudolph Siedersleben', in P. Danylow and U.S. Soénius (eds), *Otto Wolff: Ein Unternehmen zwischen Wirtschaft und Politik*, Munich: Siedler Verlag, 260.
91. BAB R 13 I/604 'Reichsgruppe Industrie, Rechtsanwalt Reusch an Baare 11.7.1941' and 'Zangen an Reichert 30.8.1941'.
92. BAB R 13 I/604 'Funk an Poensgen 17.9.1941', 'Reichert an Schmitt (RWM) 2.10.1941' and Unknown Newspaper Article Clipping, 13–14 in BAB pagination.
93. BAB R 13 I/604 Unknown Newspaper Clipping, 13–14 in BAB pagination.
94. Ibid.
95. BAB R 13 I/604 'DAF Fachamt Eisen und Metall, Zentralbüro Robert Kahlert an E. Poensgen 6.10.1941'.
96. This was ultimately unsuccessful, as the nephew was not permitted to work on the relevant article, which was in fact dealt with by the editors of the paper. BAB R 13 I /604 'Reichert an Jakob Reichert (*National-Zeitung*)' n.d. and 'Jakob Reichert (NZ) an Reichert, 11.9.1941'.
97. BAB R 13 I/604 'Reichert an Schmitt (RWM) 2.10.1941'.
98. Hensler, *Die Stahlkontingentierung im Dritten Reich*, 20.
99. AIZ OMGUS shipment 17, Box 243-1. Folder 3–5. 1945–6, Stahlwerksverband 'Organization of the Stahlwerksverband', 4.

100. W. Bopp. 2000. 'The Evolution of the Pricing Policy for Public Orders During the Third Reich' in C. Buchheim and R. Garside (eds), *After the Slump: Industry and Politics in 1930s Britain and Germany*, New York: Peter Lang, 154. For the business advantages that resulted from the *Reichswerke*'s highly problematic activities, see Meyer, *Hitlers Holding*; R. Overy. 1984. *Göring, the 'Iron Man'*, London: Routledge and Keegan Paul; H. Fiereder. 1983. *Reichswerke 'Hermann Göring' in Österreich, 1938–1945*, Vienna: Geyer; G. Wysocki. 1982. *Zwangsarbeit im Stahlkonzern: Salzgitter und die Reichswerke 'Hermann Göring' 1937–1945*, Braunschweig: Magni-Buchladen; and O. Rathkolb. 2001. *NS-Zwangsarbeit: Der Standort Linz der 'Reichswerke Hermann Göring AG Berlin' 1938–1945*, Vienna: Böhlau.
101. BAB R 13 I/672 'Betr.: Sitzung mit General von Hanneken am 14.2.1940', 8.
102. BAB R 13 I/621 'Niederschrift über die Besprechung im kleinen Kreis 14.3.1940', 40.
103. BAB R 13 I/607 'Niederschrift über die am 12.9.1939 im RWM abgehaltene Besprechung', 5.
104. BAB R 13 I/621 'Niederschrift über die Besprechung im kleinen Kreis am 14.12.1939', 107–8 in BAB pagination.
105. BAB R 13 I/672 'Betr.: Sitzung mit General von Hanneken am 14.3.1940', 3.
106. BAB R 13 I/607 'Niederschrift über die am 13.3.1940 abgehaltene Besprechung im RWM', 1; R 13 I/621 'Niederschrift über die Besprechung im kleinen Kreis 14.3.1940', 40; 'Niederschrift über die Besprechung im Kleinen Kreis 15.8.1941', 2; 'Niederschrift über die Besprechung im kleinen Kreis 30.10.1941', 1.
107. BAB R 13 I/604 'Reichert an Schmitt (RWM) 2.10.1941'.
108. BAB R 13 I/604 Unknown Press Clipping, 13–14 in BAB pagination.
109. Ibid.
110. SAN Rep. 502, VI. KV-Anklage. Interrogations R 48 'Vernehmung des Dr. Jakob Reichert, 18.11.1948', 11.
111. Eichholtz, *Geschichte der deutschen Kriegswirtschaft*, vol. 1, 163; Overy, *War and Economy in the Third Reich*, 325.
112. R-WW GHH 4001214/2 'Wirtschaftsgruppe Eisenschaffende Industrie, Rundschreiben G 1463 16.6.1940' and R 13 I/621 'Niederschrift über die Besprechung im kleinen Kreis 7.6.1940'.
113. BAB R 3101 33284 (alt R7 3284 Bd. 42) 'Abschrift: Zur Lage in den Westgebieten 19.7.1940'.
114. Overy, *War and Economy in the Third Reich*, 326–27, 336.
115. Ibid., 331.
116. Ibid., 325.
117. BAB R 13 I/621 'Poensgen an den Reichswirtschaftsminister' n.d. (c. March 1940).
118. Ibid.
119. BAB R 13 I/607 'E. Poensgen an Flick, Klöckner, Löser, Lübsen, Tagahrt, Zangen 27.6.1940'.
120. BAB R 13 I/602 'Reichert an Poensgen' n.d. (c. early July 1940), 134–35 in BAB pagination.
121. Ibid.
122. Ibid.
123. J. Gillingham. 1985. *Industry and Politics in the Third Reich: Ruhr Coal, Hitler and Europe*, London: Methuen, 142; BAB R 13 I/602 ' Reichert an Poensgen 6.7.1940' and R 13 I/692 'Reichert an Poensgen 6.11.1940'.
124. B. Grotto. 2008. 'Information und Kommunikation: Die Führung des Flick-Konzerns,

1933–1945', in J. Bähr et al. (eds), *Der Flick-Konzern im Dritten Reich*, Munich: R. Oldenbourg, 184–86.
125. BAB R 13 I/700 'Aktenvermerk: Lothringer Kommission 17.3.1941'.
126. SAN Rep. 502, VI. KV-Anklage. Interrogations R 48 'Erklärung unter Eid, Maßnahme betreffend Lothringen 7.7.1947', 1–2 and 'Vernehmung des Dr. Jakob Reichert 18.11.1946', 19; R. Overy. 1984. *Göring, the 'Iron Man'*. London: Routledge and Keegan Paul, 328. For a discussion of the internal administrative conflicts in industry in Lorraine, Luxembourg and North-Eastern France, see Gillingham, *Industry and Politics in the Third Reich*.
127. SAN Rep. 502, VI. KV-Anklage. Interrogations R 48 'Vernehmung des Dr. Jakob Reichert 18.11.1946', 13.
128. BAB R 3101/32262 'Röchling an von Hanneken 22.1.1941', 2–4.
129. SAN Rep. 502, VI. KV-Anklage. Interrogations R 48 'Vernehmung des Dr. Jakob Reichert 4.2.1947', 13.
130. BAB R 13 I/616 'Die Hüttenwerke im Minettegebiete, Belgien und Nordfrankreich July 1942'.
131. Overy, *Göring*, 328; BAB R 13 I/616 'Die Hüttenwerke im Minettegebiete, Belgien und Nordfrankreich Juli 1942'.
132. Ibid.
133. BAB R 13 I/616 'Die Hüttenwerke im Minengebiete, Belgien und Nordfrankreich Juli 1942'.
134. See Eichholtz, *Geschichte der deutschen Kriegswirtschaft, 1933–1945*, vol. 1, 53–63.
135. Overy, *War and Economy in the Third Reich*, 328–29; Tooze, *The Wages of Destruction*, 389.
136. BAB R 13 I/616 'Die Hüttenwerke im Minnengebiete, Belgium und Nordfrankreich July 1942'.
137. BAB R 13 I/43 Bd. 4. Heft 2. 'Auszug aus dem Verordnungsblatt des Generalgouvernements für die besetzten polnischen Gebiete, Nr. 11 21. 2.1940'.
138. BAB R 13 I/657 'Reichert an Hermann Poensgen 1.4.1940'.
139. Ibid.; BAB R 13 I/657 'Reichert an Reichsgruppe Industrie' 4.4.1940'.
140. Übbing, *Stahl schreibt Geschichte*, 154–5.
141. Ibid., 154.
142. L. Schwarz. 2000. 'German Technological Development During the 1930s: The Retrospective View of British Engineers and Scientists', in Buchheim and Garside, *After the Slump*, 141.
143. BAB R 13 I/621 'Niederschrift über die Besprechung im kleinen Kreis 15.8.1941', 2.
144. Übbing, *Stahl schreibt Geschichte*, 157.
145. E. Zilbert. 1981. *Albert Speer and the Nazi Ministry of Arms: Economic Institutions and Industrial Production in the German War Economy*, London: Associated University Presses, 108. See also J. Fest. 2001. *Speer: The Final Verdict*, Ewald Osers and Alexandra Dring, trans., London: Wiedenfeld & Nicholson.
146. BAB R 13 I/659 'Hauptringe Eisen und Stahl', 16.
147. BAB R 13 I/621 'Niederschrift über die Besprechung im kleinen Kreis 16.3.1942', 2.
148. Übbing, *Stahl schreibt Geschichte*, 161.
149. Tooze, *The Wages of Destruction*, 570.
150. BAB R 10 III/32 'Niederschrift über die am 1.5.1942 im RWM abgehaltene Besprechung', 1, 6.
151. Ibid., 2.
152. Ibid., 6.
153. BAB R 10/III/32 'Abschrift: Hauptabteilung R 1 29.9.1942', 1.

154. Ibid., 1, 4.
155. BAB R 10/III/32 'Vermerk, Betr.: Stellung der Zentralausschüsse 27.5.1942', 1.
156. BAB R 10 III/36 'Geschäftsverteilung und Mitglieder der RVE (Stand: April 1944)'.
157. BAB R 13 I/600 'Entwurf einer Vereinbarung Rohland-Kehrl über die Abgrenzung zum Planungsamt (Eisenplanung) und dem Hauptringe Eisenerzeugung bez. RVE und Hauptringe Eisenerzeugung January 1945' 138.
158. Werner, *Wirtschaftsordnung und Wirtschaftsrecht im Nationalsozialismus*, 372.
159. R 10 III/32 'Funk an Steinberg 1.6.1942'.
160. R 10 III/32 'Niederschrift über die am 1.5.1942 im RWM abgehaltene Besprechung', 3–4.
161. BAB R 13 I/640 'Funk an den Leiter der Wirtschaftsgruppe Eisenschaffende Industrie 30.5.1942'.
162. BAB R 10 III/33 'Berufung von Komerzienrat Dr. H. Röchling, Vorsitzender der RVE, zum Reichsbeauftragten für Eisen und Stahl in den besetzten Gebieten 18.6.1942'.
163. Ibid., 6.
164. BAB R 10 III/31 'Ausführung über die RVE in der Rede des Vorsitzenden Kommerzienrat Dr. H. Röchling vor dem Beirat der Bezirksgruppe südwest der Wirtschaftsgruppe Eisenschaffende Industrie 10.6.1942', 1.
165. SAN Rep. 502, VI. KV-Anklage. Interrogations R 48 'Vernehmung des Dr. Jakob Reichert 18.11.1946', 24.
166. BAB R 10 III/31 'Ausführung über die RVE in der Rede des Vorsitzenden Kommerzienrat Dr. H. Röchling vor dem Beirat der Bezirksgruppe Südwest der Wirtschaftsgruppe Eisenschaffende Industrie 10.6.1942', 8.
167. BAB R 10 III/32 'RVE Geschäftsführung', n.d.
168. BAB R 3101/32 247 'Anschriftenliste zum Organizationsplan des Hauptringes Eisenerzeugung'.
169. Ibid.
170. BAB R 10 III/36 'Geschäftsführung und Mitglieder der RVE (Stand: April 1944)'.
171. R-WW GHH Nachlass Paul Reusch 4001059/4 'Reichsvereinigung Eisen, Rundschreiben Nr. 8 Of/schi 19.12.1942'.
172. AIZ OMGUS Shipment 17 Box 243-1, Folder 3–5. 1945–6 Stahlwerksverband 'Organization of the Stahlwerksverband', 6.
173. BAB R 10 III/34 'Zangen an die Direktoren der Verbände 30.3.1943'.
174. Ibid.; Hensler, *Die Stahlkontingentierung im Dritten Reich*, 115.
175. BAB R 3101-15234 'RWM Aktenvermerk V. Ld 214583/42, 214476/42. 8.10.1942'.
176. AIZ Nürnberger Kriegsverbrecherprozess, MA 1555/18 NI 1983 Reichsvereinigung Eisen, 'Niederschrift über die gemeinsamen Sitzungen des Verwaltungsrats der RVE und des Beirats der Wirtschaftsgruppe Eisenschaffende Industrie, 20.6.1944', 5.
177. R-WW GHH 40010146/275 'Die eisenschaffende Industrie in der britischen Zone. Wirtschaftsvereinigung Eisen und Stahlindustrie. Düsseldorf, Juni 1946', 31.
178. R-WW GHH Nachlass Paul Reusch 400101222/4 'Niederschrift über die gemeinsamen Sitzungen des Beirats der RVE und der Wirtschaftsgruppe Eisenschaffende Industrie 20.6.1944', 2.
179. BAB R 13 I/659 'Aufstellung der Bezirksbeauftragten im Hauptausschuß IV Wehrmachtsgerät 12.3.1942'.
180. "Wilhelm Steinberg", *Stahl und Eisen* 8(84) (16 April 1984), 4.
181. SAN Rep. 502, VI. KV-Anklage. Interrogations R 48 'Vernehmung des Dr. Jakob Reichert 4.2.1947', 19.
182. Ibid.

183. SAN Rep. 502, VI. KV-Anklage. Interrogations R 48 'Vernehmung des Dr. Jakob Reichert 4.2.1947', 20.
184. R-WW GHH 4001059/4 'Vorlage: Betr.: Beitrag für die Reichsvereinigung Eisen, Abteilung G 1.2.1943'
185. R-WW GHH 400101222/4 'Niederschrift über die gemeinsamen Sitzungen des Beirats der RVE und der Wirtschaftsgruppe Eisenschaffende Industrie 20.6.1944', 4.
186. R-WW GHH Nachlass Paul Reusch 400101290/141 'Reichert an Reusch 1.4.1943' and 'Reichert an Reusch 21.8.1943'.
187. AIZ Nürnberger Kriegsverbrecherprozess, MA 1563/22 NG 1089 Jakob Reichert 'Office of the Council for War Crimes, APO 696 US Army Staff Evidence Analysis, Ministries Division, 'Pocketbook 1944 for daily entrances of Dr. Reichert'.
188. R-WW GHH Nachlass Paul Reusch 400101290/141 'Reichert an Reusch 21.8.1943'.
189. AIZ Nürnberger Kriegsverbrecherprozess, MA 1563/22 NG 1089 Jakob Reichert 'Office of the Council for War Crimes, APO 696 US Army Staff Evidence Analysis, Ministries Division 'Pocketbook 1944 for daily entrances of Dr. Reichert'; BAB R 3101/32023 'Zur Lage 28.9.1944', 110–11, in BAB pagination.
190. BAB R 13 I/675 'Reichert an Wirtschaftsgruppe Eisenschaffende Industrie und Rüstungsamt, Wehrwirtschaftsstab, 19.4.1943'.
191. R-WW GHH 400101222/4 'Niederschrift über die gemeinsamen Sitzungen des Beirats der RVE und derWirtschaftsgruppe Eisenschaffende Industrie 20.6.1944', 3.
192. BAB R 3101 Anh/alt R7 Anh MCC/1/272 'Zur Eisen- und Stahlwirtschaft der Welt' (c. 1944).
193. BAB R 13 I/616 'Reichert: Eisenausfuhr als Symptom' in Europa Kabel: Europäische Wirtschaftszeitung, 16.2.1945', 1; Roth, '"Neuordnung" und Wirtschaftliche Nachkriegsplanung', 205.
194. Herbst, *Der Totale Krieg und die Ordnung der Wirtschaft*, 352–54.
195. Ibid., 353, 267–68.
196. Ibid., 336.
197. Ibid., 376.
198. Ibid., 336.
199. Ibid.
200. R-WW GHH Nachlass Paul Reusch 400101290/141 'Niederschift über die Sitzung des gemeinsamen Ausschusses von Wirtschaftsgruppe Eisenschaffende Industrie und Verbindungsstelle Eisen für Vorkriegs- und Kriegsgeschichte der Eisenschaffenden Industrie am 17.2.1943', 1.
201. Ibid., 5.
202. Ibid., 1.
203. Ibid., 2.
204. R-WW GHH Nachlass Paul Reusch 400101290/141 'Vorläufiger Entwurf: Vorkriegs- und Kriegsgeschichte der deutschen Eisenschaffenden Industrie', 1–6.
205. Ibid.
206. R-WW GHH Nachlass Paul Reusch 400101290/141 'Niederschift über die Sitzung des gemeinsamen Ausschusses von Wirtschaftsgruppe Eisenschaffenden Industrie und Verbindungsstelle Eisen für Vorkriegs- und Kriegsgeschichte der Eisenschaffenden Industrie am 17.2.1943', 4.
207. Ibid., 2.
208. Ibid., 2.
209. R-WW GHH Nachlass Reusch 400101290/141 'Reichert an Reusch 1.4.1943'.
210. G. Seebold. 1981. *Ein Stahlkonzern im Dritten Reich: Der Bochumer Verein 1927–1945*, Wuppertal: Peter Hammer Verlag, 73–77.

211. BAB R 3101 Anh/alt R 7 Anh MCC/1/272 'Vorschläge für die künftige Versorgung mit Stahlerzeugnissen, J.W. Reichert', 5.
212. BAB R 3101 Anh/alt R 7 Anh MCC/1/281 'Reichert an von der Gablenz, 31.1.1946'.
213. BAB R 3101 Anh/alt R 7 Anh MCC/1/281, 'Skrodzki an Reichert, 29.1.1946'; 'Regionales Produktionszentrum: Die Schlüsselzahlen der deutschen Stahlindustrie ('Tagesspiegel)'; BAB R 3101 Anh/alt R 7 Anh MCC/1/282, 'Reichert an Ali Baron Ledersteger, 23.1.1946'.
214. R-WW Nachlass Otto Wolff, Abt. 72. Nr. 285. Fasz 4. 'Vermerk über die Mitgliederversammlung der früheren Bezirksgruppe Nordwest der Wirtschaftsgruppe Eisenschaffende Industrie in Düsseldorf [illeg. 1945]', 1.
215. See Wiesen, *West German Industry and the Challenge of the Nazi Past*, 56–59.
216. Ibid.
217. R-WW GHH 4001214/6 'Niederschrift über die Mitgliedsversammlung der Wirtschaftsvereinigung Eisen, 7.3.1946', 1.
218. Ibid.
219. Ibid.; and R-WW GHH 4001214/6 'Wirtschaftsvereinigung Eisen an die Direktoren der Mitgliedswerke 26.4.1948' and 'Nordwest-Gruppe, Düsseldorf 19.12.1945'.
220. R-WW GHH, Paul Reusch Nachlass, 40010290/141 'Reichert an Reusch, 7.2.1946'.
221. BAB R 3101 Anh/alt R 7 Anh MCC/1/282 'Wirtschaftsberater und Treuhänder Dr. J.W. Reichert und Gerhard Quandt an den Magistrat der Stadt Berlin, Abteilung Wirtschaft, 28.6.1946'.
222. Ibid.
223. BAB R 3101 Anh/alt R 7 Anh MCC/1/282 'Arbeitsgemeinschaft Schrott, J.W. Reichert, 21.8.1945' and 'Aktennotiz betreffend einere Besprechung über die Erfassung des Berliner Schrotts bei Herrn Direktor Kanofsky am 6.1.1946'.
224. BAB R 3101 Anh/alt R 7 Anh MCC/1/282 'Lindeboom an Petersen 4.2.1946' and 'Fritz Kanofsky an Reichert, 11.1.1946'.
225. BAB R 3101 Anh/alt R 7 Anh MCC/1/282 'Lindeboom an Reichert, 8.4.1946'.
226. BAB R 3101 Anh/alt R 7 Anh MCC/1/282 'Lindeboom an Reichert, 27.4.1946', 1–2.
227. AIZ OMGUS Shipment 17, Box 273-1, Folder 3–5, 1945–1946 Stahlwerksverband 'Secret Documents – to be kept in safe– Mr. Moser'; Wiesen, *West German Industry and the Challenge of the Nazi Past*, 54. See also N. Grunenberg. 2006. *Die Wundertäter: Netzwerke der deutschen Wirtschaft 1942 bis 1966*, Munich: Siedler Verlag, 39–64; K. Henke. 1995. *Die amerikanische Besetzung Deutschlands*, Munich: Oldenbourg; G. Hetzer. 1988. 'Unternehmer und leitende Angestellte zwischen Rüstungseinsatz und politischer Säuberung', in M. Broszat, K.D. Henke and H. Woller (eds), *Von Stalingrad zur Währungsreform. Zur Sozialgeschichte des Umbruchs in Deutschland*, Munich: Oldenbourg.
228. Donovan Archive, Cornell Law Library 53.057 OSS, Research and Analysis Branch. Biographical Report: Reichert, Jakob Wilhelm 16.5.1945', 1.
229. *Neue Deutsche Biographie*, vol. 21, 313.
230. This is evident from Reichert's first interrogation. Throughout his imprisonment, there was relatively little discussion of Reichert's own work, and although his written statements were often highly suspect, he could be quite candid during interviews under oath. See SAN Rep. 502, VI. KV-Anklage. Interrogations R 48.
231. *Neue Deutsche Biographie*, vol. 21, 313; R-WW GHH Nachlass Reusch, 40010290/141 'Margarete Reichert an P. Reusch, 11,8.1947', 1.
232. R-WW GHH Nachlass Reusch, 40010290/141 'Margarete Reichert an P. Reusch, 1.3.1948'.
233. BAB R 3101 Anh/alt R 7 Anh MCC/282 'Lindeboom an Reichert, 8.4.1946'.

234. "Wilhelm Steinberg" *Stahl und Eisen* 8(84) (16 April 1984), 4.
235. Wiesen, *West German Industry and the Challenge of the Nazi Past*, 56–59.
236. R-WW GHH 4001214/6 'Wirtschaftsvereinigung Eisen an die Direktoren der Mitgliedswerke! 26.1.1948'.
237. R-WW GHH Nachlass Reusch, 40010290/141 'Margarete Reichert an P. Reusch, 1.3.1948'.
238. Ibid.

CHAPTER 5

Indispensability
Karl Lange in the Nazi Wartime Economy

Whereas Reichert and the iron and steel industry appeared to have a considerable advantage over Karl Lange and the machine builders in 1933, the situation had been more or less reversed by the outbreak of hostilities in 1939. Lange's efforts over the preceding years provided the Wirtschaftsgruppe Maschinenbau with a solid basis to build on during the war that would at once satisfy the regime's expectations and meet the needs of member firms. Lange himself was central to this process, and he and his Wigru stepped smoothly into the war effort as it was imagined by the Nazi regime. His ideological identification was combined with a marked willingness to extend and intensify the regulation of his industry even further than he had during peacetime. When the regime sought integrate the machine building industry into its wartime munitions programme, it naturally looked to Lange as an administrator who could tie it to the new regime in war as well as in the peace that might follow. As a result, he was not only shielded from the reorganization that virtually ended Reichert's career, but was formally elevated above the businessmen in his industry to become leader of the Main Committee for Machines (*Hauptauschuß Maschinen*) under Speer.

Although this process implied a profound change for Lange and the old VDMA, he was able to use his new-found power to chart a course between the needs of the industry and those of the state. While he tightened regulation and market intervention in his industry in ways unimaginable in the Weimar years in order to mobilize the industry for the war effort, Lange was also able to continue to build on some of the traditions of the old organization, translating some of its aims and activities into new forms. This met the needs of both the state and his member firms. Consequently, Lange became virtually indispensable. Not only could the regime not think of dealing with his fractious industry without him, but the long-term profitability of his members themselves depended on Lange. This role as the key figure in the German machine building industry protected him during the last days of the Third Reich and carried over into the postwar period. At the very heart of the organization of his industry and its relationship to the governing authorities, Lange did not find himself abandoned by his members in the new era any more than during the war and was able to quickly re-establish himself in postwar Germany.

While Reichert threw himself into the war effort with the few resources left at his disposal, Lange was better able to integrate the ideals and prejudices of National Socialism into the rhetoric and actions of the machine building industry. This went far beyond insipid and fawning praise of Hitler or bilious Nazi rhetoric, although these certainly were present in the organization.[1] In his first annual address following the outbreak of war, for instance, the industrialist president Otto Sack parroted the regime's accusation that an aggressive enemy had forced a war on unwilling Germany, and *Maschinenbau-Nachrichten* circulated horror stories of innocent German citizens cast into internment camps by the Allied powers.[2] The Wigru also continued its anti-Semitic policy, pressing its own members to rid themselves of their remaining Jewish contacts abroad.[3] This was coupled with warnings about a predicted 'backlash' against Jews in other states and some of the legal difficulties of dealing with Jewish firms under the Third Reich.[4] Taken together, this formed a carefully developed, if irrational, argument for anti-Semitism in the machine building industry. To a certain extent, these efforts reflected the organization's failure to push its members away from these contracts. The Wigru was also embarrassed by the fact that its firms were deeply concerned that the invasion of Czechoslovakia would disrupt their business with Jewish firms there.[5] Curiously enough, even the machine building industry in the Reich proper continued to employ 214 Jewish workers as late as 1941 despite the efforts of the Wigru.[6] This, however, was in spite of Lange's efforts to push his members into officially sanctioned anti-Semitism.

Any study of the industrial organizations in National Socialist Germany immediately calls to mind questions about the role of men like Reichert and Lange in the horrors of the Holocaust and especially the use of slave labour. Lange's organization in particular worked with the Nazi state to identify and secure slave labourers from the ranks of Soviet prisoners of war.[7] By March of 1943, 59,000 forced labourers found themselves working in the machine building industry in Germany.[8] The business group also had some power to inspect firms that were using foreign or forced labour.[9] Although Lange's labour representative later claimed that machine builders treated their forced labourers well – or at least that the *Wirtschaftsgruppe* never received any reports of labourers who had become unfit for work – it seems highly unlikely that the organization would not have been well aware of the conditions in which slave labourers toiled, particularly when they were called upon to find replacements for the dead or dying.[10]

Lange was also careful to draw attention to his own role in the German war effort as well as the efforts of machine builders in general. As commissar for the machine building industry (BfM), he emphasized his members' importance in increasing both the rate and the quality of arms production and in the development of sophisticated modern weaponry.[11] Indeed, Lange's description of the products of his industry could be surprisingly lyrical, despite their bloody application.[12] He also linked these achievements directly to his own office.[13] It was, he argued, the result of his own efforts and those of his organization that provided the 'adaptability and hard work (*entschlossenes Zupacken*)' that allowed the machine building industry to deliver in a time of crisis.[14] Considerably more optimistic than the more sober-minded Reichert, Lange assured the regime that the German machine building industry was considerably ahead of its competition in almost every way. It could, he predicted, outperform both England and the United States and was in a good position to dominate the global market following the war.[15] Such a rosy view might have stretched the truth more than a little, but it was well in line with the almost pathological public overconfidence of so many in the regime.

This willingness to mirror even the worst ideology and expectations of the regime while at the same time asserting his own role closely reflected the strategies of adaptation that many followed in German enterprise and private life, particularly under the pressures of the war. However, as noted in the previous chapters, Lange's adaptation did not simply cloak business as usual in the machine building industry and its organization with the trappings of the National Socialist state. While Lange's own role and authority might have been important before the war, his efforts to structure his organization and position to match the demands of the state put him in a position of real power between 1939 and 1945. At the very beginning of the conflict, Lange and Sack made it clear to their members that they expected their full cooperation in the war effort.[16] This was backed by ever increasing levels of regulation and oversight that helped make the contribution of the machine building industry significant. As early as 7 September 1939 the *Wirtschaftsgruppe* began to extend its authority over its members by requiring that its firms go through the organization in order to deal with authorities like the Reich coal commissioner.[17] Lange's organization also quickly took responsibility for reviewing prewar machine orders to determine their suitability for wartime production and issuing new control numbers by the middle of November 1939.[18] This, however, represented little more than the application of Lange's prewar powers and did not satisfy the regime's demand for increased and planned production. Unlike Reichert and his organization, however, Lange and Wirtschaftsgruppe Maschinenbau still enjoyed the considerable confidence of the regime.

In order to bring the situation in hand, Minister of Economics Walther Funk was empowered to formally assume control over the construction, distribution and use of capital machinery in Germany on 11 December 1939.[19] Rather than exercise this authority himself or through the ministry, Funk delegated responsibility to Lange, effectively making him an arm of the RWM itself.[20] This new position did away with the last formal elements of a liberal market in the machine building industry by giving Lange direct control over the distribution and use of the products themselves when he officially took up his new responsibilities on 9 January 1940.[21] From this point on, Lange's orders were backed by an open-ended fine for disobedience.[22] In the event, this fearsome threat could be less devastating than his legal authority implied, and the courts quickly established a fine for disregarding Lange's orders on the production of agricultural machinery, for instance, at 1,000 RM.[23] This was a considerable sum, but it might well have been an acceptable price to pay. Nevertheless, the undetermined nature of the fine, to say nothing of Lange's other powers to harass recalcitrant firms, made the consequences of disobedience substantial. Indeed, for the remainder of the Third Reich, the Law for the Regulation of the Direction and Distribution of Machine and Apparatus Production of December 1939 underwrote Lange's authority in the machine building industry.[24] In January of 1940 a special commission (*Sonderauftrag*) from Göring himself was added to improve the repair and secondary use of agricultural machines.[25]

The old chief business manager of Wirtschaftsgruppe Maschinenbau had managed to assemble an impressive number of positions and responsibilities in the first months of the war. As Sack pointed out to his members, the titles held by the former bureaucratic manager of the old VDMA now included not only Chief Business Manager of the *Wirtschaftsgruppe*, but also Reich Representative (*Reichsbeauftragter*), Leader of the Control Offices, Mobilization Commissioner for the industry, Commissar for Machine Production (BfM) and Göring's Special Commissioner for Agricultural Machinery.[26] These were not simply honorific titles. Lange used this authority to enact 120 separate binding general orders in the following two years and to direct production policy in ways that could not have been imagined a decade before.[27]

Armed with his new authority, Lange began to establish a licensing regime that directly controlled the production of machinery rather than focusing on indirect management through material rations. Business in the machine building industry was now, Lange later asserted, not a question of profitability, but of regulating wartime production.[28] He thus introduced a series of forms required for production to proceed on 27 March 1940.[29] Beginning in April, all machines (with a few exceptions) would require a control number not only to acquire materials, but also to deliver the finished machine itself.[30] Important products, particularly machine tools (*Werkzeugmaschinen*) were to be overseen and approved through a complex order process.[31] A customer hoping to order a machine had to first approach an appropriate machine building firm to see if it could be built. A notice of intent (*Vormerkscheine*) would then be submitted to the appropriate rationing office for approval.[32] Following this, an order notice (*Meldescheine*) would be forwarded to Lange that included the specifications of the machine and the customer's needs, and also stated whether or not the machine type in question was already being produced by another firm.[33] This quickly evolved into a system that required the producers of virtually all machines to submit a series of forms to the BfM, depending on the kind of product and standing of the producer. Lange's office would then grant permission for production and allow the producer to order the necessary raw materials.[34] When the machine had actually been completed, another form was filed to notify Lange, who could then issue an F-Card (*F-Scheine*) that would permit delivery to the customer. Firms on the list of the best and most preferred plants (List 1) were permitted to deliver their products without an F-Card if all of the other appropriate paperwork had already been filed.[35] By April 1941, an agreement between Lange and the armaments ministry also required that producers submit a sworn statement (*eidesstattliche Erklärung*) that the machine in question would be used for essential war work and that any machines that it might replace were already in full use.[36] In theory, producers were still permitted to produce machines for civilian use, but this could only be undertaken after all war-related orders had been filled – if the necessary material was still available.[37]

Firms that failed to file the appropriate forms, receive permission or obtain the relevant cards and control numbers from Lange were simply not permitted to build.[38] This was no empty threat. By October 1941 Lange became aware that at least four hundred machine tool units had been produced without the forms that would generate an F-Card to allow delivery. Rather than pushing these producers to submit the missing forms or granting an amnesty, Lange used his authority to seize the machines for more appropriate dispersal.[39] When the BfM failed to receive shipment lists from a wide variety of other firms the following month, he likewise threatened to cut off the basic material rations of the tardy firms within eight days.[40] Lange also proved willing to assert his power over the distribution of machines when circumstances changed in his favour. On the very day that the German army invaded the Soviet Union, Lange seized all machine tools destined for delivery in Russia.[41] Two weeks later, he underlined his earnestness by sternly reminding unhappy members that factory owners would be held responsible for seeing that these machines were placed at Lange's disposal immediately.[42]

This stricter licensing system was accompanied by further intrusions into the activities of machine building firms through increasingly centralized production planning. Lange's elevation at the end of 1939 allowed him to influence the distribution of raw materials like iron and steel directly on the authority of the Ministry of Economics.[43] By February of 1940, he also demanded that all firms advise him of unused capacity in order to evaluate the distribution of production.[44] Firms likewise had to inform Lange if they planned to build a new type of machine or one that they had not produced in the past, and to justify their plans to his office.[45] To streamline production, he stepped up his decrees regulating the rationalization of production in his industry by limiting machine types, the variety of specifications and materials to be used for specific purposes. These orders were now backed up by the authority and threat of Lange's increased power.[46] By early 1942, these restrictions had become so specific, complicated and numerous that the Wigru began publishing new guidelines in booklet form.[47]

Lange was not simply content to live up to the regime's expectations within the borders of the old Reich. Instead, he used his new role to push his own authority beyond Germany. Despite the fact that, as a representative of the 'dynamic' exporting industry, Lange falls outside of most Marxist conceptions of industrial cooperation with the Nazi regime, the BfM embarked on regulating and systematizing the plunder of occupied states and the establishment of a 'new world order'.[48] At the same time, it is difficult to describe Lange as having been 'instrumentalized' in the sense described by Stefan Werner.[49] Instead, Lange helped to both legitimate and drive National Socialist aggression itself.

Although the former Czechoslovakia was formally separated from the administration of the Reich itself and the other occupied territories, Lange's representative in Prague and long-time colleague in the Wigru, Paul Kathke, was appointed Commissioner for Machine Production in Czechoslovakia (*Bevollmächtigter für Maschinenbauproduktion in Böhmen und Mähren*), establishing a close personal link to Lange.[50] He was even more successful in Poland. Even as the dust was settling in the newly occupied territory in early 1940, the Wigru instructed firms to report any representatives they had who were active in or near the region in order to establish an administrative presence in the General Government.[51] By May of 1941 at the latest Lange was able to appoint a representative in the General Government itself, Dr Hellmich, who identified firms in Poland that should report to the BfM in Berlin.[52] Shortly afterwards, machine building firms in Poland were instructed to follow the permission and licensing procedures he had established in Germany, and the Wigru began to oversee production in the occupied region.[53] This established a pattern to be applied in other territories overrun by the Wehrmacht, and Lange travelled to the western occupied territories to set things in order himself in the summer of 1940.[54] Lange demanded that Dutch firms also work through him and appointed Dr Bleik as his representative in the Netherlands.[55] He likewise retained a representative inside the occupation authorities in Belgium in order to tie the region to his own regulatory system.[56]

France was a tougher nut to crack.[57] Although he was not able to fully integrate occupied France into his organization, Lange did make substantial inroads west of the Rhine. Following the interruptions associated with the declaration of war and invasion, the Wigru satellite office (*Vertrauensstelle*) in Paris reopened in October 1940 under the direction of Gustav Scherdtmann.[58] Lange also maintained a representative in France acting for him as BfM. First this was König, then Hugo Heinz; however, they did not enjoy the same authority as their counterparts in other occupied territories.[59] In addition to this, Lange made use of Franz Rohman as his voice in the French military occupation authority.[60] Though this did not allow Lange to administer the region in quite the same way as the other occupied territories, his ties to the French machine building industry had important effects later on.

This network of representatives abroad allowed Lange to co-ordinate machine production in the occupied territories with that of the Reich. This became particularly important after Göring instructed the various control offices to look at transferring backlogged contracts abroad.[61] This attempt to disperse production could be used to benefit the more ambitious or predatory German firms. Unlike Reichert, Lange did not have to rely on an appeal to the authorities in Germany based on the aging legal claims of German firms displaced by the end of the First World War. Instead, the BfM could take advantage of his close relationship with the regime and the representatives he maintained abroad to step in and divide the spoils of war himself. As a result, Lange was able to grant 'trusteeships' that enabled German machine building firms to shift aspects of their production to suitably equipped French and Belgian firms in particular.[62] Lange was also able to use his position to regulate surviving trade relationships. Although the Ministry of Economics had suspended normal trade with the occupied territories in Norway, the Netherlands, Belgium and Serbia, Lange, as leader of the Control Office for Machine Building (Prüfungsstelle Maschinenbau), was able to evaluate the necessity of specific contracts or contacts and grant exceptions.[63] By the end of 1942, his permission was also required to order machines from outside the Reich.[64]

Lange had managed to follow the armies of the Reich into foreign territories in the first years of the war. This important achievement helped to consolidate his role as an indispensable component of the Nazi state and war economy and opened up the spoils of war to his own members. While iron and steel industrialists could expect little from Reichert and might even do better without him, machine builders in Germany were forced to work through Lange if they hoped to expand their business abroad. Lange also had the power to grant a substantial increase in capacity and customers to firms that appealed to him for help. On top of this, there is evidence to suggest that Lange had even grander plans in mind. In the past, he had often called on his members to defend the Nazi state to their foreign contacts and went to some lengths to provide them with suitable material. With the outbreak of the war, he asked that all firms with people abroad prepare reports on the business and economy in their operating region.⁶⁵ Thus the war effort of both the Wigru and the state had the use of his members as unofficial intelligence agents in a way that Reichert, for instance, had never suggested. Moreover, Lange's optimism about the future of the German economy seemed to spill over into high expectations for the army itself, and by the end of 1940 the BfM had already established an office for colonial questions in the Foreign Department of the *Wirtschaftsgruppe*.⁶⁶

Lange used the 'political capital' and power he had accumulated to expand his power considerably. In both Germany and the newly occupied territories he was able to establish a comprehensive regulatory system that harnessed the machine building industry for the war effort. This fit in well with National Socialist demands and had notable results. It also drew recognition from the regime, and in April 1941 Hitler and Todt granted Lange the War Service Cross, First Class.⁶⁷ In 1942, Hitler, Göring and Speer also sent their personal warm wishes to the Wigru on the event of the fiftieth anniversary of the establishment of the VDMA.⁶⁸ Lange had thus become the natural partner of both his industry and the regime, and unlike Reichert, his services could hardly be dispensed with during Speer's reforms of 1942.

Speer's professed commitment to appointing technical experts from within German business often had profound effects on the organization of German industry. Although the new organizations were tied to the older *Wirtschaftsgruppen*, Speer's notion of industrial 'self-responsibility' did not necessarily coincide with the traditional notion of self-regulation through the old bureaucratic organizations. Indeed, while Poensgen was being forced out of Wirtschaftsgruppe Eisenschaffende Industrie, a similar process occurred in Wirtschaftsgruppe Elektroindustrie: its old president was forced to resign to make way for a personal union with the leader of the new *Hauptringe*, Friedrich Lüschen, formerly the head of the board of directors at Siemens.⁶⁹ In the machine building industry, however, things were very different. Speer appointed Lange himself, rather than an industrialist or technician, as head of the new Main Committee for Machines (Hauptausschuß Maschinen).⁷⁰ As such, Lange took responsibility for eighteen special committees (*Sonderausschuße*), leading the committees for cellulose and textile machinery himself.⁷¹ Supporting these groups were 159 working committees and 4 working groups (*Arbeitsgemeinschaften*), including 21 subcommittees.⁷² Lange likewise appointed twenty-three regional representatives to coordinate with local authorities and three representatives for the occupied territories, solidifying his grip on both regional regulators and much of the occupied territory.⁷³

The new *Hauptausschuß* had no independent office or existence of its own. Instead it worked through the *Wirtschaftsgruppe*, and the Wigru staffed the positions o the new committees.⁷⁴ This formed the basic structure of Lange's organization until the end of the war, although some aspects of it were nominally changed or shuffled. At the end of 1943, the *Hauptauschuß* was split into three separate main committees, and Lange assumed responsibility for them all as the leader of Department for Machines and Machine Tool (Amtsgruppe Maschinen und Werkzeuge).[75] This, however, was short-lived; a year later the administrative structure of the machine building industry was collapsed back into a single main committee under Lange, leaving very little changed.[76] Lange's powers were further increased when the Ministry of Economics appointed him as BfM of Reichsstelle Maschinenbau on 1 November 1942, thus tying the responsibilities of the RWM offices in machine building directly to his person.[77] This gave him authority over the traffic of machine goods and allowed him to absorb some of the responsibilities for machined products or related parts from the Iron and Metal Office and Office for Technical Production (Reichsstelle Eisen und Metalle and Reichsstelle für technische Erzeugung).[78] This authority was further supplemented by the official assumption of control over the relevant cartels by the *Wirtschaftsgruppe* technical groups in early 1943, an event that Lange had worked towards for years.[79]

In 1941 Lange himself had already begun to reorganize the Wigru in order to adapt to its increased regulatory role. This was accomplished partly by funnelling virtually all activities through the Statistical Office.[80] He also began to shuffle his personnel; they had been somewhat diminished by the war but still numbered seventy expert staff, fourteen of whom were women in responsible positions, exclusive of support workers.[81] However, the changes of 1942 broke decisively with the interest group politics of the old VDMA. Lange, already the BfM, was formally elevated above the industrialists who had formerly presided over the organization of the industry. The nominal leader of the *Wirtschaftsgruppe*, Otto Sack, was brought into the new *Hauptauschuß*, but only as a subordinate of Lange in charge of the Special Committee for Machinery for the Food Industry (Ernährungswirtschaftsmaschinen).[82] By 1944, a number of other industrialists had been added to the Department for Machines and Machine Tool, but these men all remained subordinate to Lange, who was the only non-businessman in the group.[83] After 1942, Lange even began to forward names of men to the RGI to be designated as leaders of the technical groups, rather than relying on the relevant advisory councils or members to choose their own representatives as they had in the past.[84] He was also able to go further and have sitting leaders, such as Fritz Reuther of the Technical Group for Armatures and Machine Components removed for 'offences against the directives of the BfM'.[85] Lange likewise effectively ended the old VDMA practice of close collaboration with its stakeholders and excluded merchants from discussions of production and licensing questions.[86] This was, in effect, the triumph of the bureaucratic representative of the machine building industry over the industrialists themselves, who could no longer actively direct the policies of their industry.

The *Wirtschaftsgruppe* also became a surprisingly profitable undertaking during this period. Over the course of 1943, it amassed a total of 29 million RM in surplus ZAV export subsidy funds. This spectacular amount caused some consternation in the Ministry of Economics and led to a lengthy discussion to determine whether Lange's organization should in fact be allowed to keep the money.[87] The RWM was further concerned that the Wigru continued to charge relatively high contribution fees to its members despite this windfall.[88] Lange, for his part, rejected the idea of returning some of the surplus to his members as pointless. It would be better, he argued, to carry on with the Wigru's plans to use it to advance rationalization efforts, construct new offices to replace those destroyed by air raids and prepare to build further foreign branch offices after the war.[89] Admittedly, the Wigru had already reduced its fees for some firms by setting a general requirement of 1.3 RM per 1,000 RM in sales to cover all of the various organizations in the industry, although the motivation for this seems to have had little to do with their surplus funds.[90] In the end, the ministry did siphon 311,000 RM for the use of the vehicle industry, but apparently left the remaining fortune for Lange.[91]

Despite the fact that the Wigru was no longer even nominally run by industrialists and acted as a substantial tax collection office, there remained a degree of continuity with the activities of the old VDMA that helped Lange to draw his members into the system he was busy creating. This was particularly true in the case of the long-standing effort to effectively rationalize the industry and the organization's emphasis on the political power of sound accounting and good statistics. Rationalization in particular fit in very well with National Socialist demands during wartime. Throughout this period, Lange continued to issue a stream of orders regulating the number of machine types and technical specifications.[92] Efforts to push machine builders into particular types of products also took on increased importance under Speer's administration. Virtually all branches of production were at least nominally affected by Speer's attempt to increase production despite declining resources, but special emphasis was placed on the role of machine builders and the production of single-purpose machines that could save both men and material.[93] Lange immediately ordered his firms to evaluate their own ability to produce these machines. This had some effect, and rolling (*Glattwalzwerke*) types in particular were reduced from 70 to 6, extruders from 45 to 6, and a large number of other product types cut by at least half.[94] Despite this, Lange's success – not to mention his commitment – in trying to push the whole German economy away from traditional, more easily adaptable universal machines is questionable. Indeed, the large number of universal machines left in Germany at the end of the war still baffled U.S. authorities in particular. However, German producers had moved towards a hybrid that allowed for some flexibility in specialized, serial production, and more recent research indicates that the use of universal machines had declined substantially throughout the Nazi period.[95]

Although many machine builders remained highly sceptical of the American model of specialized shops producing single-purpose machines, Lange was able to force some change on reluctant members.[96] The firm Schärfls Nachfolger, for instance, was deeply grieved at being forced to reduce its number of products to one fifth of its prewar catalogue at great expense of time and money.[97] Other smaller individual firms felt powerful state pressure to reduce their product lines, and even the largest eighty-one machine building firms reduced their machine types from an average of 2.8 in 1938 to 2.4 in 1944.[98] Distribution of production itself was also affected by rationalization efforts. Lange reserved the right to favour more effective and reliable firms and proved more than willing to deny a plant permission to produce a machine that could be manufactured more efficiently elsewhere.[99] Even more extreme was Lange's threat to shut down less efficient or important firms in order to cannibalize their machine parks.[100] The BfM was also skilled at interpreting National Socialist demands to serve his organization's long-term goals. When Göring issued a general proclamation about reducing waste in industry, Lange quickly followed up with a series of directives forbidding machine builders to add decorative features or other 'frills' to their products.[101] Lange and his office also reviewed the actual production of his firms at year's end to ensure that their work continued to be suitable for the war effort.[102] He likewise forbade the production of prototypes or sample machines, forcing manufacturers to focus on proven production machinery.[103]

Apart from rationalization, Lange was able to adapt the old VDMA's focus on effective bookkeeping and statistics to bolster his position in the wartime economy. The VDMA had put considerable effort into standardizing its members' bookkeeping practices and deploying meticulously gathered statistics as a lobbying tactic. In the context of the war economy, Lange was able to use this expertise to exert the level of control the regime expected him to wield over his industry. In the very first days of the war, the *Wirtschaftsgruppe* demanded that its members continue to remit reliable statistics to the organization, despite the loss of many of the responsible employees to the army.[104] The Wigru also continued to push its firms to standardize their bookkeeping practices, which now was justified by the importance of centralized planning rather than the maximization of profitability.[105] By 1941, Lange ordered that virtually all communication between the Wigru and firms be funnelled through the Statistical Office, essentially giving it pride of place in the organization and ensuring the centralized management of information.[106]

The *Wirtschaftsgruppe*'s focus on increasingly detailed and intrusive statistics caused some consternation in the Siemens concern's Economic Policy Division, which worried that this was a prelude to a more fully centralized production and distribution system.¹⁰⁷ These fears were justified. The increasingly complex reporting procedures demanded information regarding products, weight, number of workers and types of machines ordered in order to calculate quota allotments.¹⁰⁸ By 1943, Lange and the Wigru had increased their demand for data considerably, characterizing statistics as the 'foundation for all planning'.¹⁰⁹ In the event, their emphasis on information also helped to keep the Wigru itself relevant in an increasingly complex regulatory system, as the committees and rings relied on the information provided by the *Wirtschaftsgruppe*'s Statistical Office and the management offices (*Bewirtschaftungsstellen*) attached to the various technical groups.¹¹⁰ By May of 1943, Lange had also begun to compile a catalogue of existing machines for possible redistribution.¹¹¹ Three months later, when his firms balked at this, he angrily demanded that they sign a pledge of their honesty and complete the relevant forms within one week.¹¹²

Although the aims and results differed, these efforts represented a strong degree of continuity in the machine building industry. Lange had begun to use his new-found power as BfM to give teeth to his long-standing effort to rationalize his industry in the face of recalcitrant member firms. As the situation grew increasingly desperate during the war, his focus shifted to some extent, yet he continued to push for the reduction of machine types and standardization of components that he had hoped for in the Weimar Republic. The means at his disposal, however, had changed substantially in the National Socialist state. A similar process occurred in the case of statistics. Lange was able to exploit the old VDMA's effective compilation and use of statistics to situate the *Wirtschaftsgruppe* as a vital aspect of the National Socialist economy. As a result, while Reichert fretted about the increasing amount of paperwork forced on his members by the regime, Lange could use the traditions of his organization and industry to his advantage in a new context. This may not have made wartime changes more palatable to certain of his members, but it did help to fit his once fractious industry into a complex network of regulation.

Whereas many of the projects undertaken by Lange and his organization were directly related to the priorities of the old VDMA, essential elements of the regulation of the industry during wartime were new. This was particularly true of the complex licensing system, which had been developed since 1940 to approve and allocate production but had already begun to outlive its usefulness. By January 1942 Lange announced his intention to create a new licensing system that would make the old reserve (*Vormerk*) system obsolete.¹¹³ By June a Machine Management Office (Maschinenbewirtschaftungsstelle) was established under Lange's authority in the Ministry for Armaments to look after the needs of high-priority consumers in the Wehrmacht and railroads.¹¹⁴ A comprehensive new licensing system was introduced for other products in the industry on 17 July.¹¹⁵ This was based on the previous *Vormerkscheine* system but moving towards an ever more complex system of oversight. From that point on all production required a 'permission certificate' (*Zulassungsscheine*) from one of the licensing offices (*Zulassungsstellen*) operated by the Wigru and its subsidiaries.[116] These offices, renamed management offices (*Bewirtschaftungsstellen*) by the end of the year, assessed whether or not the product in question was in fact necessary to the war effort and could not be obtained more easily elsewhere.[117]

In August this system was developed further in order to incorporate the system of oversight being introduced by Speer. After discussions with a suitable machine building firm, potential customers were compelled to seek approval from the regional *Rüstungskommando*. It would then pass through the technical or subsidiary technical groups to the Wigru's special committees.[118] The approval was then turned over to the 'ration management offices' (*Kontingentverwaltungsstellen*) that answered to Lange and was finally reviewed by either the Wehrmacht or Lange's Machine Management Office.[119] Officially, the entire process was overseen by the Ministry of Economics,[120] but by the following year the process also involved the control offices and ration holders, and by 1944, each finished machine had to be reassessed again before delivery.[121] Lange's reach extended to customers as well: by July 1944 relevant iron and steel rations to firms were earmarked only for the purchase of machines.[122] By the end of the war, properly completed and approved paperwork had to change hands a minimum of twenty-eight times in order to produce a single machine.[123] Lange's authority also covered repairs and the production of accessories in the machine building industry. By mid-1942 his members were required to assess the potential add-on needs of their customers and report this to the Wigru.[124] Repair reports for damaged machines were also compulsory, and replacement parts that exceeded 100 kg of rationed material were subject to the *Vormerkscheine* system.[125]

This complicated bureaucratic process caused considerable difficulties and in fact pushed other branches of the economy, particularly the Main Ring for Electrotechnical Production, to change their own protocols in order to adapt to Lange's.[126] However, the process was largely designed to take the act of production planning out of the hands of machine builders, who had been either unable or unwilling to calculate their own production in a way that fit in with Lange's or the regime's broader plans. The BfM was deeply irritated by the behaviour of some of his members, who had conflated the more theoretical 'global' rations that established the maximum production for each firm with the actual ration allocations that customers brought with them and then planned production based on double the amount of material that was actually available. Machine firms consequently found themselves short of the materials needed to cover orders they had already taken, and production was becoming dangerously backlogged. Orders from firms that were not directly connected to the Wehrmacht were given short shrift and –perhaps even more annoying to Lange – were told that the whole mess was the result of the double allocation of finite resources by his office.[127] The tightened *Vormerk* process would, Lange claimed, help to reduce waste both in the war effort in general and for the firms that had trouble calculating their own needs and production schedules.[128]

Lange was also capable of intervening more directly in what was left of the market for machines. As noted above, the BfM forbade the inclusion of 'frills' or the production of sample machines as part of his rationalization effort. To these were added more general rules about avoiding the purchase of new machines. Old machines were to be used up to the point at which continued production was endangered.[129] Producers were forbidden to order more complex machines that were flexible enough to be put to other uses in peacetime.[130] A machine exchange (*Maschinenausgleich*) was established to provide firms with used machines instead of new ones.[131] By the end of 1944, Lange had also established a centralized agency to distribute 'universal machines', although its use was not mandatory.[132] Taken together with the expanded licensing system, this concentrated effective control of the machine building industry overall in Lange's hands even as Reichert struggled to find meaningful work.

This power did not completely insulate Lange from the furious competition or spiteful squabbling that characterized much of the polycratic Nazi administration. Lange might be able to position himself as a *führer* in the National Socialist economy, but he was no dictator and did not have unlimited powers. It would be difficult to imagine Lange as able to keep any of the largest producers in Germany from completing their war-related production in particular. Larger firms could sometimes contract directly with state authorities under special conditions that would guarantee concessions or benefits, and machine builders were also adept at using the local or regional branches of Lange's organization to their own ends.[133] Speer's reforms of 1942 also laid a new level of administration over the old, sometimes creating as many disputes as efficiencies.[134] As a result, Lange continued to clash with other organizations – particularly the electrotechnical industry, with which it was necessary to continue negotiations.[135] The increasingly effective regulation of other industries likewise began to impact Lange's modest empire. The electrotechnical industry, for instance, ordered its members to annul all contracts for new machines that it did not consider to be directly related to the war effort, a move that clearly impinged on Lange's ideas about his own jurisdiction.[136] At the same time, the RWM Office for Iron and Metal began to tighten its own rules, limiting Lange and his members' access to materials.[137] By March 1944 the Wigru subsidiary Main Committee for Finishing Equipment (Hauptausschüsse Fertigungseinrichtung) had also been able to impose its own approvals process on the delivery of new machines.[138]

To this confusion of responsibility was added the pressing demands of the Wehrmacht itself. In June of 1942 the machine production for the Wehrmacht and Railroads was hived off from the rest of the machine building industry and thereafter handled by the Machine Management Office of the armaments ministry. Though this office was responsible to Lange, it was able to independently review orders for machines for direct arms production and rail use.[139] This was both a potential threat to Lange's office and an annoyance to his firms, many of which had great difficulty navigating the complex paperwork demanded by the Maschinenbewirtschaftungsstelle.[140] Speer himself was also able to advance or stall production priorities through this office, and the Wehrmacht could move particular machines up on production priority lists if it deemed them necessary.[141]

After the initial establishment of Speer's organization, its growth also continued to affect Lange. The first official order of business in the tortuous process of ordering new machines continued to be the local *Rüstungskommando* rather than Lange and his staff, linking the first step in production to Speer.[142] Lange also came to depend on the material allocations made by the Ministry for Armaments (now called Armaments and War Production) and forwarded his members' notices of intent (*Vormerkscheine*) on to Speer's ministry.[143] Although Lange negotiated regularly with Speer's head of armaments delivery, the arms ministry representative Walther Schieber harboured substantial misgivings about the efficiency of centralized planning in the Main Committee (*Hauptausschuß*) and suspected that machine builders were simply continuing to build what they wanted rather than what the state needed.[144] Speer's Central Planning Office (Planungsamt) also took over a measure of oversight of machine building by reviewing licence applications from Lange's members. This pushed Lange's assistants Gok and Fuchs into conflict with the office in the hopes of extracting more materials in spite of questionable applications.[145] Lange himself seems to have quarrelled with Speer over the latter's almost exclusive focus on end products, labouring to convince the minister of the importance of a wide variety of machines in the production chain.[146]

Speer's desperate attempt to reorganize and rationalize the administration of production in the last year of the war also helped to undermine the structure that Lange had carefully built since 1933. The division of the Main Committee for Machines in late 1943 into three separate groups under Lange's direction granted a certain degree of independence to the leader of Main Group for Finishing Equipment, Heinz Kiekebusch, in particular.[147] As an engineer, Kiekebusch had been active in several machine building firms before entering the War Economy and Armaments Office of the OKW in 1940. Kiekebusch was then taken on as the leader of the Finishing Equipment Office responsible for the vital machine tools in Lange's organization in 1943. That same year, he was elevated to leader of the newly formed Main Committee for Finishing

Equipment.[148] Before the new main committee was reabsorbed into Lange's office less than a year later, Kiekebusch's organization had taken on a key role in the production of this vital product. As the last office to examine and approve licence applications, this governed final delivery conditions.[149] Lange had laboured for the last decade to keep effective administrative authority invested in his person, and the development of competitors within his own fiefdom was a new experience.

These challenges should not necessarily be taken as evidence that Lange and his organization had passed their zenith or started on the same road to obsolescence as that travelled by Reichert. Competition and incursions on authority were endemic in the National Socialist regime, and Speer himself was constantly fending off or compromising with rivals.[150] Lange was subject to this same infighting, but his own experience in National Socialist politics allowed him to defend his own empire effectively. He remained, in the sardonic words of Schärfl's representative, one of 'the Greats' in the regime, at least from the perspective of machine builders.[151] From the beginning of Speer's ministry, Lange's office assured his members that he had Speer more or less in hand and that the *Reichsminister* could not possibly go much farther with his reforms.[152] More importantly, Lange found ways around some of the changes implied by Speer's reorganization and worked to keep real decision-making authority in his own hands. Despite the new licensing regime, for instance, Lange made it clear that firms could still deliver with the old licences as long as they obtained his permission first.[153] Although the Wehrmacht was able to speed up deliveries, Lange demanded that firms that entered into accelerated programmes also work through his office, assuring the BfM a role in the process.[154] Annoyed that other economic organizations were putting a 'rush' on certain products, Lange likewise forbade any production ahead of schedule without his own permission.[155] In July of 1942, he moved to limit the choices available to customer firms in order to keep decisions about production inside his own organization as much as possible.[156] By the beginning of the following year, he was cracking down on ration bearing firms (*Kontingentsträger*) that were overburdening some machine builders, leading to substantial confusion and delay.[157] Even as late as 1944, the primary responsibility for production licences lay with Lange's special committees.[158] In theory, firms that were dissatisfied with these decisions were to appeal directly to Speer's ministry.[159] In practice, however, firms tended to ask Lange to step in and reconsider the actions of his various subordinates or even Speer's organization.[160] Lange's own office also retained material and global-ration reserves that it could distribute to firms in trouble, regardless of the decisions of other offices involved in the licensing process.[161]

These attempts at regulating production more or less satisfied the demands placed on the machine building industry by the National Socialist state. The honours and titles Lange accumulated – to say nothing of his survival at the top of his administrative structure – are themselves a good argument for the regime's satisfaction with the old chief business manager. Beyond this, Germany's ability to meet its machine tool needs surprised U.S. authorities in particular, who had been convinced that Germany would be in the grip of an acute machine shortage by the end of the war.[162] The total output of machine tools and the machine industry in general did decline slightly throughout the war, and delivery delays increased from 13.8 months to 25.9. However, the total inventory of Germany's machine park almost doubled, increasing from 1.327 million units in 1938 to 2.266 in 1944.[163] The personnel of the American Strategic Bombing Survey were also puzzled that the German authorities were confident enough in their extant machine building capacity to transfer much of their production to strict munitions work.[164] Although this might have had more to do with immediate war needs and profitability, almost 44 per cent of machine building capacity had in fact been transferred to munitions by the end of the war.[165] Orders substantially exceeded deliveries, but this was largely the result of the over-ordering that was endemic in German industry throughout the war, and the former officials of the Wigru later maintained that these orders always exceeded actual needs and swore that the real demands of the war were met.[166]

It is difficult to thoroughly assess the attitude of machine builders themselves to Lange and his administrative empire. His members did not necessarily endorse all of his activities and decisions during the war, but there is little surviving evidence of open conflict between the BfM and machine builders over the structural changes to the industry. In part, this may be because they simply had little choice in the matter. Once the National Socialist regime was established, Lange was very careful to take advantage of the increasing regulation of the economy and society to assemble considerable power in his own hands. Some firms undoubtedly resented the increased regulation in the formerly independent and fractious industry. Mack of Schärfl's Nachfolger, for instance, complained bitterly about the level of bureaucratization achieved in the former VDMA and wondered what had happened to Hitler's promises about self-regulation and business freedom.[167] However, these complaints tended to be generalized concerns about the over-regulation of industry under the regime itself, rather than necessarily concerns about Lange in particular.

A number of firms also recoiled from the high dues charged by Lange's organization. Schärfl's in particular continued to pepper Lange with requests to remove aspects of their product line from his oversight well into the war.[168] Many firms took considerable pains to get around the constraints Lange had placed on them and, as in so many other industries in the Third Reich, tried to stockpile orders to guard against the whims of a capricious regime.[169] His members also irritated Lange by trying to avoid completion of the machine card-index that would allow him to reassign their own machines as the needs of the war effort demanded.[170] This reluctance was coupled with what the leader of the Technical Group for Sheet Metal Shears and Punches (Fachgruppe Blechscheren und Lochstanzen) characterized as a kind of passive resistance to rationalization.[171] Schärfl's is again an excellent example of a firm that was angered by the forced reduction of its catalogue.[172] However, this dissatisfaction did not prevent Lange from building an effective system of regulation.

There were good reasons for the relative ease in regulating the machine building industry. Despite a high level of oversight, Lange did not attract criticism for authoritarianism as Röchling did in iron and steel. Indeed, by the final year of the war the Wehrmacht complained that even Lange's oversight was not sufficiently 'dictatorial'.[173] Instead he was able to trade the loss of business independence for very tangible benefits. As in the Weimar years, Lange and his organization continued to work with their members to overcome technical and administrative difficulties, but this now meant navigating complicated regulatory systems rather than private import/export questions.[174] Lange was willing to at least consult his most efficient and trusted members before making decisions, as when he solicited their advice on the most effective way to distribute the machines he had confiscated as BfM.[175] His position also gave him unparalleled access to the authorities governing the German economy in wartime, which could work to his members' advantage.

Lange was likewise able to translate his former role as a lobbyist into active intercession in a way that Reichert could not. Firms in all branches of German industry suffered from a persistent manpower crisis that began in 1936 and only intensified as employees were called away from their workbenches and dispatched to the front. Lange went to considerable lengths to protect his own firms from these demands and enjoyed some success in the first years of the war. In February of 1940 he issued a warning to his members about local authorities that might seek to limit certain kinds of production in order to free up manpower. Firms that experienced difficulties were instructed to report to him.[176] By August of 1941, Lange had succeeded in having a representative from his own technical bureau placed on the local 'oversight' and 'combing-out' commissions to participate in the process of sorting essential workers from future soldiers.[177] Lange followed this with 'lengthy efforts and repeated negotiations' that eventually led to the designation of a number of firms as *OKW-Spezialbetriebe* that could be protected from demands on their workforces, transport and raw materials.[178] This did not cover all firms, but Lange was able to name the firms singled out for protection, considerably increasing his own importance to his members.[179] Lange also tried, though not entirely successfully, to prevent other authorities from poaching his members' employees or inspecting his firms without a representative from the *Wirtschaftsgruppe* present to intercede. These men reiterated Lange's right to be represented in local inspections, which had been granted by the Minister for Armaments Todt himself.[180] Lange continued to push the issue into 1942 and succeeded in having the head of the Army Office designate machine tool workers in general as technicians and builders, a semi-protected category, rather than labourers.[181] He was also able to convince the labour minister to issue orders compelling local authorities to exhaust all options to fill machine builders' needs.[182] This may have actually been of dubious value, as Lange continued to lobby both Göring and the army to exempt machine builders entirely from the draft and kept a close eye on the number of protected workers in his industry.[183]

Lange's position in the economic administration of the Reich also had a number of other very real business advantages for his members. Machine builders were able to make substantial new gains through the establishment of 'trusteeships' in the occupied territories. Lange himself arranged the trusteeships for members that would benefit from taking over French or Belgian firms. This gave his members access to not only their competitors' plant but their technical expertise and customer base as well.[184] German machine building firms were also able to put these trusteeships to their own uses by transferring less lucrative production abroad in order to concentrate on more profitable products (like tanks) at home, and then to transfer these contracts back into Germany in the later stages of the war.[185] Machine builders themselves were thus able to use the spoils of war to establish their firms in a position of competitive advantage when peace returned.[186]

German machine builders also saw their profits rise substantially as prices increased during the war. The number of machine building firms that entered into the profitable munitions industry during this period increased from 12.6 per cent in 1939 to 44.8 per cent in 1944, satisfying both the regime and the firms themselves.[187] Even more traditional machine building became increasingly lucrative as the war progressed. Total sales of machine tools, for instance, increased from 762.2 million RM in 1939 to 807.9 million RM in 1944 even as the total weight of machine production fell from 287,344 tonnes to 239,001 tonnes.[188] This was accomplished through substantial price increases in particular products. The price per unit of milling machines, for instance, increased from an average of 5,460 RM in 1939 to 7,650 by 1944.[189] The price increase in hammer and forge tools was even more dramatic, rising from 2,160 RM at the beginning of the war to 9,400 by 1944.[190] Despite the problems associated with the increased regulation of machine building, the fact that the industry was making more money by producing less was a powerful incentive to accept Lange's decisions. The BfM might have taken away much of its business freedom and centralized authority in his own hands, but increased regulation and hierarchical structures were hardly unique to the machine building industry. Every branch of production came under the authority of the state in one form or another. In the machine building industry, this process was carried out by a long-time representative of the industry itself who was able to secure for his members higher profits, opportunities for expansion and the technical modernization that the VDMA had sought during the Weimar Republic. This powerful justification for Lange's political plasticity allowed him to avoid alienating his members even as he curtailed their freedom of choice.

Perhaps Lange and the men he represented really did nurse long-term hopes of one day introducing liberal reforms to the Germany economy, or at least to their own industry, as they would later claim.[191] If so, they would not have to approach the regime as supplicants or penitents. Lange, as a 'leader' in the National Socialist sense who had shown his willingness to command where necessary, represented an industry that had demonstrated its political reliability and cast itself as a key component of the modern, rational economy that could deliver the power and prosperity the Nazis sought. He would be in a position to sit at the postwar bargaining table and shape the postwar world. Happily, the world that he had prepared for did not come to pass, for first the larger German empire and then the Nazi state itself fell to Allied troops. However, Lange did not go down with the regime he had grown so close to. Even though the structure he had spent so long building had now become a liability, Lange's central role in the endeavour had earned him respect and gratitude from his members that would carry him through into a new Germany.

The story of Lange and the machine building industry in the chaotic years that followed the end of the war is important, but it cannot be told here in the way it deserves. Nevertheless, the treatment Lange received at the hands of his members closely reflects the way his activities during the war were perceived by his industry. Machine builders' support for Lange's adaptation to the regime did not end in 1945. Instead, Lange led the attempt to integrate the organization into the new postwar order, despite the interruption of the Western Allies' rather short-lived attempt to purge the German economy and society of National Socialists. Machine builders were sufficiently pleased with their old chief business manager that he was carefully held in reserve until he was able to assume his duties once again. This was partly the result of Lange and his organization's compelling case for their own usefulness in the postwar period. The *Wirtschaftsgruppe* was particularly careful to emphasize the value of the well-developed relationships and infrastructure it had built in the Third Reich. Once again, Lange was able to rely on his statistical department. As the primary administrative body in the industry, the Wigru was in the unique position of being able to quickly and efficiently assemble the information necessary to assess and plan production in the reconstruction of Germany.[192] The Wigru likewise defended its own role in the Nazi state, arguing (rather implausibly), that Lange and his men had acted as the 'confidants' of the machine building industry rather than as an arm of the state.[193] The organization remained, it argued, a trusted tool of the industry that could protect it during the transition to capitalism and ensure that rationalization continued.[194] These efforts were aided by the fact that, unlike in iron and steel, the Allies had little enthusiasm for prosecuting the machine building industry.

Perhaps more importantly, Lange also had the foresight and good sense to leave Berlin. He had already begun to disperse the offices of his organization during the war to compensate for the damage sustained during air raids. As a result, several key bureaus, including the Statistics Office, had already moved to Thuringia.[195] After the war, the central office of the organization itself was moved to Bad Neuheim on the orders of U.S. forces.[196] As it became clear that the old *Wirtschaftsgruppen* would not be allowed to survive and responsibility devolved to local authorities, Lange fled to Düsseldorf, a city with easy access to 70 per cent of machine building production in the British occupation zone.[197] There he helped to found a new organization, the Business Association for Machine Building (Wirtschaftsverband Maschinenbau), and became its first chief business manager, serving under an industrialist president once again.[198] However, this first attempt to slip back into the pre-1933 structures was short-lived for Lange. Broader efforts to purge the old leaders of the Nazi economic administration finally forced him out by the end of the year.[199]

Lange could then easily have found himself abandoned in the wilderness like Reichert. The new organization appeared to carry on without him, and was refounded again as the Wirtschaftsverband Maschinenbau on 25 February 1946 in Berlin to represent the machine building industry in the British zone.[200] This organization took over the property and many of the responsibilities of the former VDMA/*Wirtschaftsgruppe*.[201] The situation was a little more confused in the American zone, which was now represented by the Verein Bayerischer Maschinenbau Anstalten, Vereinigung der Maschinenbauanstalten von Württemberg-Baden and Wirtschaftsvereinigung Maschinenbau in Groß-Hessen.[202] However, following the establishment of a unified American and British zone in January 1947, these various groups came together under an umbrella organization, the Working Group of Machine Building Associations (Arbeitsgemeinschaft der Verbände Deutscher Maschinenbau-Anstalten, AVDMA) on 7 December 1947.[203] This created a new national (or at least west German) system of representation in the machine building industry, albeit without Karl Lange.

Despite this unpromising start, Lange's position in the postwar period differed greatly from Reichert's. Whereas Reichert ended the war as a forgotten and powerless relic, Lange had been the key figure in the machine building industry and was at the centre of regulation and industrial politics. He had retained the respect and admiration of both the state authorities and his own members, and it was unthinkable that he not be involved in the industry in peacetime. When Lange left the new Düsseldorf Wirtschaftsverband Maschinenbau, this was made explicit by the association, and his successor, Herbert Stelter, was intentionally appointed as a stopgap 'Commissioned Chief Business Manager' (*Kommissarischer Hauptgeschäftsführer*) until Lange returned.[204] This same Stelter was then taken on as the chief business manager of the new AVDMA.[205] Throughout this period, the new organizations were careful to keep in contact with the former BfM.[206] Luckily for him, machine building did not capture the Allied imagination like the Ruhr iron masters, and Lange was not targeted by the occupation authorities in the same way Reichert was. Although he was held for a few days by the U.S. authorities and interviewed by the Strategic Bombing Survey, he was treated more like an expert witness to his industry's experience during the war than a prisoner.[207]

As a result, Lange remained closely involved with the representatives of his industry. This bore fruit when the old BfM cleared his denazification process, was classified in Group IV as a 'Fellow Traveller' in January 1948, and thus could be re-employed by his old association.[208] By August, Lange had been installed as chief business manager of the AVDMA, displacing Stelter.[209] By September 1949, his rehabilitation was complete. When the AVDMA dissolved itself to re-establish the old VDMA, Lange was unanimously elected as the new chief business manager once again.[210] Throughout the course of the founding meeting, the current president of the association explicitly connected Lange's role in the German economy during the Nazi period to his place in the postwar period. The old BfM, he argued, had stayed with the organization to the 'bitter end' in 1945. Lange had installed himself at the heart of the machine building industry, and anyone else at the head of the organization would have been 'unthinkable'.[211] The capable and adaptable Lange had survived another upheaval and could now get down to work in the new Germany that was emerging out of the destruction of the Nazi period.

Notes

1. See K. Lange. 1941. 'Deutscher Straßenbau und deutsche Straßenbaumaschinen: Eine Würdigung zum 50. Geburtstag Fritz Todts', *Der Vierjahresplan* 14(5), 744; K. Lange. 1941. 'Maschinenindustrie und Kriegspotential', *Der Vierjahresplan* 9(5), 510–13; K. Lange, 1940. 'Deutsche Maschinentechnik im Zeitgeschehen', *Der Vierjahresplan* 14(4), 594; R 13 III/ 145b Heft 6. *Maschinenbau-Nachrichten* 1 (4 January 1940).
2. BAB R 13 III/ 145b Heft 4 *Maschinenbau-Nachrichten* 1 (4 January 1940); R13 III/145b Heft 7, *Maschinenbau-Nachrichten* 3 (16 January 1940), 11, 12.
3. BAB R 13 III/ 145b Heft 7. *Maschinenbau-Nachrichten* 1 (2 January 1940), 4.
4. BAB R 13 III/145b Heft 6. *Maschinenbau-Nachrichten* 14 (4 April 1940), 55; *Maschinenbau-Nachrichten* 41 (10 October 1940), 180; and *Maschinenbau-Nachrichten* 48 (28 November 1940), 212.
5. BAB R 13 III/145b Heft 6, *Maschinenbau-Nachrichten* 14 (4 April 1940), 55.
6. BAB R 13 III/98 'Die Ergebnisse der Sondererhebung über Altersgliederung und UK-Stellung der im Maschinenbau tätigen männlichen Inländer, 24.3.1941'.

7. AIZ, München. Nürnberger Kriegsverbrecherprozess MA 1555, Rolle 1–47. NI 583 Translation of Document NI 583, Office of the US Chief of Council, 2; BAB R 13 I/373 'Der Reichsminister für Bewaffnung und Munition 3.12.1941', 5.
8. AIZ Nürnberger Kriegsverbrecherprozess MA 1555, Rolle 1–47. NI 583 Translation of Document NI 583, Office of the US Chief of Council, 3.
9. Ibid., 6.
10. Ibid., 6–7.
11. BAB R 13 III/140 Könemund and Sahm (eds). 1943. *Lenkung der Maschinenproduktion: Anordnung des BfM, Sonderausgabe des Abschnitts II G des Sammelwerkes Eisen und Stahl.* Verlag August Lutzeyer, 2; K. Lange. 1939. 'Werkzeugmaschinen als Grundlage der Produktionssteigerung' *Der Vierjahresplan* 19(3), 1134.
12. Lange, 'Deutsche Maschinentechnik im Zeitgeschehen', 594.
13. Ibid., 596.
14. Lange, 'Werkzeugmaschinen als Grundlage der Produktionssteigerung', 1134.
15. Lange, 'Maschinenindustrie und Kriegspotential', 511.
16. BAB R 13 III/145b Heft 4, *Maschinenbau Nachrichten* 36 (7 September 1939), 173.
17. SHA 49/LS 158 Bd. 15. 'Wirtschaftsgruppe Maschinenbau an unsere Mitgliedsfirmen, Rundschreiben Reihe 1 # 64. 7.9.1939'.
18. SHA 49/LS 159 Bd. 15. 'Wirtschaftsgruppe Maschinenbau an unsere Mitgliedsfirmen, Rundschreiben Reihe I # 80. 26.10.1939'.
19. 'Verordnung über die Lenkung und Verteilung der Maschinen- und Apparate-Erzeugung 11.12.939', in BAB R 13 III/140 *Lenkung der Maschinenproduktion: Anordnung des BfM*, 50.
20. 'Verordnung zur Durchführung der Verordnung über die Lenkung und Verteilung der Maschinen- und Apparate-Erzeugung 20.12.1939', in BAB R 13 III/140 *Lenkung der Maschinenproduktion: Anordnung des BfM*, 52.
21. SHA 49/LS 158 Bd. 15. 'Wirtschaftsgruppe Maschinenbau (Sack) an unsere Mitgliedsfirmen, Rundschreiben Reihe I Nr. 12.1.2.1940'.
22. 'Verordnung zur Durchführung der Verordnung über die Lenkung und Verteilung der Maschinen- und Apparate-Erzeugung 20.12.1939', in BAB R 13 III/140 *Lenkung der Maschinenproduktion: Anordunung des BfM*, 52; 'Funk an Lange', ibid., 54.
23. The National Adminstritive Court (*Reichsverwaltungsgericht*) in this case. R 13 III/145b Heft 8. *Maschinenbau-Nachrichten* 19 (8 May 1940), 75.
24. *Verordnung zur Durchführung der Verordnung über die Lenkung und Verteilung der Maschinen- und Apparate-Erzeugung.* See, e.g., R 13 III/64 'BfM: Anordnung über die Meldepflicht bei Aufnahme und Einstellung des Baues von Werkzeugmaschinen 27.5.1941'.
25. BAB R 13 III/140 *Lenkung der Maschinenproduktion: Anordnung des BfM*, 4.
26. SHA 49/LS 158 Bd. 15. 'Wirtschaftsgruppe Maschinenbau (Sack) an unsere Mitgliedsfirmen. Rundschreiben Reihe I. Nr. 12. 1.2.1940'.
27. BAB R 13 III/140 *Lenkung der Maschinenproduktion: Anordnung des BfM*, 4.
28. BAB R 13 III/44 'Erzeugungsplanung und Bedarfslenkung im Maschinenbau. Lenkungsbereich Maschinenbau. Statistisches Zentralreferat, Juli 1943', 3.
29. Ibid., 5.
30. SHA 49/LS 158 Bd. 15. 'Wirtschaftsgruppe Maschinenbau (Free) an unsere Mitgliedsfirmen. Rundschreiben Reihe I, Nr. 22. 29.3.1940', 2.
31. Ibid., 4.
32. Ibid., 12.
33. BAB R 13 III/64 'Anordnung über die Meldepflicht der Aufnahme und Einstellung des Baues von Werkzeugmaschinen 27.5.1941', 3.

34. BAB R 13 III/64 'Rundschreiben, Betr.: Meldscheine III/41 4.4.1941'.
35. Ibid.; BAB R 13 III/64 'An die Werkzeugmaschinenhersteller der Liste 1 und 2. 27.5.1941', 4.
36. BAB R 13 III/64 'An die den Meldescheine und Vormerkverfahren angeschlossenen Werkzeugmaschinenfabriken 23.4.1941'.
37. BAB R 13 III/64 'Bm/Nm X-X-100 Betr.: Lieferung von Werkzeugmaschinen für vordringliches Programm; Anordnung des Reichsministers für Bewaffnung und Munition vom 25.3.1941', 2.
38. SHA 49/LS 158 Bd. 15. 'BfM an alle Mitgliedsfirmen. Rundschreiben Reihe X Nr. 24. 13.3.1940', 2.
39. BAB R 13 III/64 'An die Werkzeugmaschinenhersteller der Liste 1, 20.10.1941'.
40. BAB R 13 III/64 'Betr.: Versandlisten für das III. Quartal 1941, 12.11.1941'.
41. BAB R 13 III/64 'An die Mitglieder der Fachgruppe Werkzeugmaschinen 22.6.1941'.
42. BAB R 13 III/64 'An die Hersteller der Werkzeugmaschinen 5.7.1941'.
43. SHA 49/LS 158 Bd.15 'BfM an alle Mitgliedsfirmen. Rundschreiben Reihe X Nr. 24, 13.2.1940', 1.
44. Ibid., 2.
45. BAB R 13 III/64 'Anordnung über die Meldepflicht bei Aufnahme und Einstellung des Baues von Werkzeugmaschinen 27.5.1941', 2.
46. See, e.g., BAB R 8 XVI/1 'BfM: Anordnung über die Typenbereinigung von Tiegeldruckpressen 10.2.1941'.
47. See BAB R 8 XVI/1 'BfM Anordnung über die Herstellung von Reibahlen 14.3.1942'.
48. For an example of this school, see Roth, '"Neuordnung" und wirtschaftliche Nachkriegsplanung', 205.
49. Werner, *Wirtschaftsordnung und Wirtschaftsrecht im Nationalsozialismus*, 608.
50. BAB R 9 VIII/6 'Büro-Rundschreiben Nr. 555, 25.4.1940' and 'Büro-Rundschreiben Nr. 614. 15.8.1941'.
51. SHA 49/LS 158 Bd. 15. 'Wirtschaftsgruppe Maschinenbau an unsere Mitgliedsfirmen. Rundschreiben Reihe I, Nr. 14. 12.2.1940', 3.
52. BAB R 8 XVI/4 'Amt des Generalgouverneurs für die besetztns polnischen Gebiete. Abteilung Wirtschaft, der Beauftragte des BfM. 2.5.1941'.
53. BAB R 8 XVI/4 'Der BfM, Betr.: Meldepflicht für die Verlagerung von Aufträgen' n.d.; 'Der Beauftragte der BfM an BfM 27.5.1941'; 'Wirtschaftsgruppe Maschinenbau an Herrn Dr. Hellmich, Amt des Generalgouverneurs, Abt. Wirtschaft, 12.7.1941'.
54. Pohl and Markner, *Verbandsgeschichte und Zeitgeschichte*, 97.
55. BAB R 8 XVI/4 'Der BfM, Betr.: Meldepflicht für die Verlagerung von Aufträgen 22.5.1941' and 'Dr. Bleik an der BfM, 1.11.1940'.
56. BAB R 13 III/67 'BfM an die Kontingentsverwaltungsstellen, 26.8.1942'.
57. For a discussion of the central role of the French economy in German military planning, see H. Homburg. 2003. 'Wirtschaftliche Dimensionen der deutschen Besatzungsherrschaft in Frankreich 1940–1944: Das Beispiel der elektrotechnischen Industrie', in Abelshauser, Hesse and Plumpe, *Wirtschaftsordnung, Staat und Unternehmen*, 183. See also A. Milward. 1970. *The New Order and the French Economy*, Oxford: Clarendon Press and W. Benz. 1990. 'Die Verlockung der französischen Ressourcen: Pläne und Methoden zur Ausbeutung Frankreichs für die kriegswichtigen Bedürfnisse und langfristigen Ziele des Reiches' in S. Marten (ed.), *La France et l'Allemagne en Guerre, September 1939–Novembre 1942*, Paris: Fondation pour les études de défense nationale, Institut d'histoire des conflits contemporains and Bundesministerium für Forschung und Technologie, Deutsches Historisches Institut Paris.
58. BAB R 13 III/146b Heft 6. *Maschinenbau-Nachrichten* 42 (17 October 1940), 183.

59. BAB R 9 VIII/6 'Büro-Rundschreiben Nr. 637 11.12.1941'.
60. BAB R 13 III/67 'BfM an die Kontingentträgerverwaltungsstellen 26.8.1942'.
61. BAB R 8 XVI/5 'Der Reichswirtschaftsminister, Betr.: Auftragsverlagerung an die Eisen und Metalle verarbeitende Industrie in dem besetzten westlichen Gebiet 18.10.1940'.
62. See, e.g., the discussion of Boehringer in France in Gehrig, *Nationalsozialistische Rüstungspolitik und unternehmerischer Entscheidungsspielraum*, 114ff.
63. BAB R 8 XVI/5 'Der Reichswirtschaftsminister an die Herren Leiter der Prüfungsstelle. Persönlich 30.8.1941'.
64. BAB R 13 III/44 'Erzeugungsplanung und Bedarfslenkung im Maschinenbau. Lenkungsbereich Maschinenbau, Statistisches Zentralreferat, Juli 1943'.
65. BAB R 13 III 145b Heft 4. *Maschinenbau-Nachrichten* 50 (21 December 1939), 240.
66. BAB R 9 VIII/6 'Büro-Rundschreiben Nr. 581 19.12.1940'.
67. BAB R 13 III/145b Heft #7, *Maschinenbau-Nachrichten* 17 (24 April 1941), 73.
68. BAB R 13 III/145b Heft 8, *Maschinenbau-Nachrichten* 47 (18 November 1942), 197.
69. SHA 49/LS 190 'Dir. H.C. Dr. Ingenieur Fr. Lüschen an die Mitglieder. 26.5.1942'; 'Hauptringe Elektrotechnische Erzeugnisse beim Reichsminister für Bewaffnung und Munition an die Mitglieder. 26.5.1942'.
70. BAB R 13 III/78 'Gemeinschaftsarbeit im Maschinenbau 15. November 1892 bis 15. November 1942', 5.
71. BAB R 13 III/112 'Organization der Hauptausschüsse Maschinen und Gliederung sämtlicher ihrer Haupt-,Sonder-, Spezialbesonder- und Arbeitsausschüsse bzw.-ringe 1943'.
72. Ibid.
73. Ibid.; Pohl and Markner, *Vebandsgeschichte und Zeitgeschichte*, 102.
74. AIZ. MA 1555, Rolle 1-47 NI 583 'Translation of Document 583, Office of the U.S. Chief of Council 'WVMA' signed by Dip Ing. Hans Kolberg. 21.8.1947' pg.1.
75. Pohl and Markner, 103., BAB R 13 III/112 '*Maschinenbau-Nachrichten, Amtsgruppe Maschinen und Werkzeuge im Reich für Kriegsproduktion*, 26.1.1944', 146-7 in BAB Schema.
76. Pohl and Markner, *Vebandsgeschichte und Zeitgeschichte*, 103.
77. BAB R 13 III/145b Heft 8. *Maschinenbau-Nachrichten* 45 (4 November 1942), 186.
78. 'Die Zuständigkeit des BfM für die Maschinenproduktion als Reichsstelle Maschinenbau. 26. Bekanntmachung über die Änderung der Zuständigkeit von Reichsstellen vom 7.11.1942', in BAB R 13 III/140 *Lenkung der Maschinenproduktion: Anordnung des BfM*, 62-70.
79. SAH 49/LS 160, 'Wirtschaftsgruppe Maschinenbau an unsere Mitgliedsfirmen! 16.3.1943'.
80. BAB R 9 VIII/6 'Lange an alle Stellen des Hauses. Büro-Rundschreiben Nr. 624. 19.9.1941', 1-3.
81. Ibid., Anlagen, 1-13.
82. BAB R 13 III/112 '*Organization des Hauptausschußes Maschinen und Gliederung sämtlicher ihrer Haupt-, Sonder-, Spezialbesonder- und Arbeitsausschüsse bzw. Ringe* 1943'.
83. BAB R 13 III/112 'Maschinenbau-Nachrichten, Amtsgruppe Maschinen und Werkzeuge im Reichsministerium für Kriegsproduktion 26.1.1944', 146-47.
84. BAB R 3101 9083 'RGI und das RWM, 17.12.1942 (Betr.: Leiterbestellung)' and 'Zangen an Düsterloh, 9.1.1943'.
85. BAB R 3101 9083 'Vermerk, Berlin 30.1.1943', 7 in BAB schema and 'Reichsstelle Eisen und Metalle, der Kommissarische Reichsbeauftragte [illeg] an den Reichswirtschaftsminister, z. Hd. Präsident Kehrl, 23.1.1943'.
86. BAB R 13 III/68 'Fachgruppe Werkzeugmaschinen der Wirtschaftsgruppe Maschinenbau an unsere Mitgliedsfirmen, 25.7.1944'.

87. BAB R 3101 9083 'Reichswirtschaftskammer an RWM 17.12.1943' and 'RWM an die Wirtschaftsgruppe Maschinenbau, 12.1.1944'.
88. BAB R 3101 9083 'Wirtschaftsgruppe Maschinenbau an das RWM, z. Hd. des Herrn Regierungsrat, Betr., 22.1.1944'.
89. BAB R 3101 9083 'Lange an die RWM, 12.6.1943'; BAB R 13 III/71 'Bericht der Wirtschaftsgruppe Maschinenbau über die Verwendung des Teilfertigungskontingents in NE-Metallen für Werkzeugmaschinen und holzverarbeitende Maschinen'; BAB R 13 III/293 *Maschinenbau-Nachrichten* (3.12.1943).
90. SHA 49/LS 160 'Wirtschaftsgruppe Maschinenbau an unsere Mitgliedsfirmen 16.3.1943', 1–2.
91. BAB R 3101 9083 'Reichswirtschaftsminister an Reichswirtschaftskammer, 17.5.1944'.
92. BAB R 8 XVI/1 'Rationalisierung und Leistungssteigerung in der Maschinenproduktion – Anordnungen und Zusatzanordnungen des Bevollmächtigten für die Maschinenproduktion [unvollständig] 1939–1943'.
93. BAB R 13 III/67 '*BfM, Betr.: Sondermaschinen für den Einsatz der Rüstungsindustrie*, 29.9.1942'.
94. BAB R 13 III/64 'Rationalisierung im Maschinenbau, 8.1.1942'.
95. Ibid.; *The United States Strategic Bombing Survey, No. 54: Machine Tools and Machinery as Capital Equipment*, Equipment Division, 2nd edn, January 1947, 35–36; A. Tooze. 2003. '"Punktuelle Modernisierung": Die Akkumulation von Werkzeugmaschinen im "Dritten Reich"', *Jahrbuch für Wirtschaftsgeschichte* (1), 84, 94.
96. Siegel and Freyberg, *Industrielle Rationalisierung unter dem Nationalsozialismus*, 276.
97. BWA, Schärfls Nachfolger Werkzeugmaschinenfabrik, München, F79 195 '*An die Fachgruppe Werkzeugmaschinen der Wirtschaftsgruppe Maschinenbau*, 16.4.1942' and '*An Hauptausschuß Maschinen beim Reichsminister für Bewaffnung und Munition, Sonderausschuß Werkzeugmaschinen*, 23.9.1942'.
98. V. Stöhr. 2000. '"Deutsche" Wege der Rationalisierung im Nationalsozialismus- dargstellt am Beispiel der sächsischen Maschinenbauindustrie', in T. Hänseroth and C. Krautz (eds), *Geschichte des sächsischen Werkzeugmaschinenbaus im Industriezeitalter: Beitrag der Tagung am 19. März 1998 in Dresden*, Dresden: Sächsisches Druckund Verlagshaus AG, 122; Siegel and von Freyberg, *Industrielle Rationalisierung unter dem Nationalsozialismus*, 216.
99. BAB R 13 III/68 'Fachgruppe Werkzeuge der Wirtschaftsgruppe Maschinenbau an unsere Mitgliedsfirmen, 25.7.1944'; BAB R 13 III/407 fol. 1. 'BfM i.A. an die Wirtschaftliche Forschungsgesellschaft GmbH, Hauptabteilung Fabriken, 13.7.1944'.
100. BAB R 13 III/44 'Erzeugungsplanung und Bedarfslenkung im Maschinenbau. Lenkungsbereich Maschinenbau. Statistisches Zentralreferat, Juli 1943', 8.
101. BAB R 13 III/64 'An die Hersteller von Werkzeugmaschinen von 4.2.1942'; 'Anordnung zur Vereinfachung der Bearbeitung und der äußeren Aufmachung von Werkzeugmaschinen von 4.2.1942'.
102. BAB R 13 III/64 'An die Vormerkscheinverfahren angeschlossenen Werkzeugmaschinenhersteller der Liste 1 und 2. 30.1.1942'.
103. BAB R 13 III/64 'Anordnung über das Verbot des Baues einzelner Arten oder Baumuster von Werkzeugmaschinen. 23.3.1942'.
104. SHA 49/LS 158 Bd. 15 'Free an die Wirtschaftspolitische Abteilung der Siemens und Halskewerke A.G., 8.9.1939'.
105. SHA 49/LS 157 'Zur Beachtung, da Änderungen aufgrund der Einführung des Kostenplanes für den Maschinenbau erfolgten, 24.6.1940'.
106. BAB R 9 VIII/6 'Lange an alle Stellen des Hauses. Büro-Rundschreiben Nr. 624, 19.9.1941', 3.

107. SHA 49/LS 159 Bd. 18. 'Wirtschaftspolitische Abteilung: Aktenvermerk, Betr.: Erhebung über Auftragsbestand und Produktionsverteilung im Rahmen der Wirtschaftsgruppe Maschinenbau, 19.11.1941'.
108. SHA 49/LS 159 Bd. 18. 'Wirtschaftsgruppe Maschinenbau: 'Berechnungsbogen für die Zuteilung der Eisenkontrollmarken für das II. Quartal 1942'.
109. BAB R 13 III/44 'Erzeugungsplanung und Bedarfslenkung im Maschinenbau. Lenkungsbereich Maschinenbau. Statistisches Zentralreferat, Juli 1943', 11.
110. Ibid., 7; BAB R 13 III/77 'Aufgaben der Bewirtschaftungsstelle Werkzeugmaschinenbau, 14.5.1943'.
111. BAB R 13 III/67 'Hauptausschuß Maschinen beim Reichsminister für Bewaffnung und Munition, der Leiter an die Vormerkscheinverfahren angeschlossenen Werkzeugmaschinenhersteller, 31.5.1943'.
112. BAB R 13 III/67 'Hauptausschuß Maschinen beim Reichsminister für Bewaffnung und Munition, der Leiter an die Vormerkscheinverfahren angeschlossenen Werkzeugmaschinenhersteller, 31.8.1943'.
113. BWA, Schärfls Nachfolger Werkzeugmaschinenfabrik, München, F79 195 'An die Firma Peddinghaus, 26.1.1943'.
114. BAB R 13 III/67 'Reichsminister für Bewaffnung und Munition, i.A. Dr. Merius, Rundschreiben an die Herren Leiter der Hauptausschüsse, Hauptringe, Sonderausschüsse und Sonderringe, 29.8.1942'.
115. SHA 49/LS 159 Bd. 18. 'Anordnung 1/42 des BfM über die Auftragsregelung für Maschinenbauerzeugnisse vom 17.7.1942'.
116. Ibid.
117. BAB R 13 III/67 'BfM an die Werkzeughersteller der Liste 1 und 2, Holzverarbeitungsmaschinenhersteller, 4.1.1943'; SHA 49/LS 159 Bd. 18. 'Anordnung 1/42 des BfM über die Auftragsregelung für Maschinenbauerzeugnisse vom 17.7.1942'.
118. BAB R 13 III/67 'BfM an die Kontingentsträger 4.1.1943' and 'BfM an die Vormerkscheinverfahren angeschlossenen Werkzeug- und Holzverarbeitungsmaschinenhersteller, 25.8.1942'.
119. BAB R 13 III/67 'Der BfM an die Vormerkscheinverfahren angeschlossenen Werkzeug- und Holzverarbeitungsmaschinenhersteller, 25.8.1942'.
120. BAB R 13 I/44 'Erzeugungs- und Bedarfslenkung im Maschinenbau. Jan. 1943'.
121. Ibid.; BAB R 13 III/68 'Hauptausschuß Maschinen an die Kontingentsverwaltungsstellen, 14.10.1944'.
122. BAB R 13 III/77 'Wirtschaftsgruppe Maschinenbaus Entwurf an die Kontingentsverwaltungsstellen, 22.6.1944'.
123. BAB R 13 III/77 'Aktennotiz: über die Besprechung in der Maschinenstelle, Betr.: Neuregelung des Vormerkscheinverfahrens am 3.4.1944. Anlage'.
124. BAB R 13 III/67 'Der BfM, Betr.: Kriegsmäßige Aufmachung und Ausstattung von Erzeugnissen des Maschinenbaus vom 26.2.1942' 20.6.1942.
125. SHA 49/LS 159 Bd. 18. 'Anordnung II/42 der BfM über die Durchführung der Ersatzteile und Reparaturdienste im Maschinenbau vom 17.7.1942'.
126. SHA 49/LS 190 'Hauptausschuß Nachrichtengeräte und Hauptring Elektrotechnische Erzeugnisse beim Reichsminister für Bewaffnung und Munition, 27.1.1943'.
127. BAB R 13 III/67 'Der BfM an die Kontingentsverwaltungsstellen <u>außer</u> Wehrmacht, Reichsbahn und Ausfuhr, 22.2.1943'.
128. BAB R 13 III/67 'Der BfM an dem Vormerkscheinverfahren angeschlossene Werkzeugmaschinen- und Holzverarbeitungsmaschinenhersteller, 14.9.1942'.
129. BAB R 13 III/67 'BfM an die Werkzeugmaschinenhersteller 9.9.1942', 2.
130. Ibid.

131. BAB R 13 III/67 'Der BfM an die Kontingentsverwaltungsstellen, 28.5.1942'.
132. BAB R 13 III/68 'Fachgruppe Werkzeugmaschinen der Wirtschaftsgruppe Maschinenbau an unsere Mitgliedsfirmen! 16.8.1944'.
133. J. Scherner. 2006. 'Das Verhältnis zwischen NS-Regime und Industrieunternehmen –Zwang oder Kooperation', *Zeitschrift für Unternehmensgeschichte* 51, 175. See also Schneider, *Unternehmensstrategien zwischen Weltwirtschaftskrise und Kriegswirtschaft*.
134. Fest, *Speer*, 136.
135. SHA 49/LS 190 'Hauptring Elektrotechnische Erzeugnisse beim Reichsminister für Bewaffnung und Munition an die Mitgliedsfirma der Fachabteilung 1 'Maschinen' der WEI 7.11.1942'.
136. SHA 49/LS 190 'Hauptring Elektrotechnische Erzeugnisse beim Reichsminister für Bewaffnung und Munition, der Leiter des Hauptrings an Betriebsführer, Leiter der Sonderausschüsse, usw. 23.5.1942'.
137. SHA 49/LS 159 Bd. 18. 'Neuordnung der Eisen- und Stahlbewirtschaftung: Anordnung I der Eisen und Stahl nebst Durchführungsbestimmung'.
138. BAB R 13 I/68 'Hauptausschuß Fertigungseinrichtung beim Reichsminister für Rüstung und Kriegsproduktion 7.3.1944'.
139. BAB R 13 III/67 'Reichsminister für Bewaffnung und Munition i.A. Dr. Merius, Rundschreiben an die Heren Leiter der Hauptausschüss, Hauptringe, Sonderausschüsse und Sonderringe, 29.8.1942'.
140. BAB R III/67 'BfM an die Hersteller von Werkzeugen und Holzverarbeitungsmaschinen 16.10.1942'.
141. BAB R 13 III/67 'BfM an dem Vormerkscheinverfahren angschlossene Werkzeugmaschinen und Holzverarbeitungsmaschinenhersteller, 14.9.1942', 3.
142. BAB R 13 III/67 'Der BfM an die Vormerkscheinverfahren angeschlossenen Werkzeugmaschin und Holzverarbeitungsmaschinenhersteller 25.8.1942', 2.
143. BAB R 13 III/293 'Der Reichsminister für Rüstung und Kriegsproduktion, i.A. Schinagel 1.11.1943'.
144. BAB R 13 III/77 'Aktennotiz: Über die Besprechung mit Herrn Fuchs und Frl. Gok über Neuregelung des Bewirtschaftungsverfahrens von 28.4.1944. 4.5.1944' and 'Der BfM als Reichsstelle Maschinenbau, Aktenvermerk über eine Besprechung in der Maschinenstelle, Betr.: Neuregelung des Vormerkscheinverfahrens am 3.4.1944, 4.5.1944', 1–2.
145. BAB R 13 III/71 'Hauptauschuß Maschinen (i.A. Fuchs und Gok) an Herrn Rechtsanwalt Cremer beim Planungsamt 20.11.1944' and 'Hauptausschuß Maschinen (i.A. Fuchs und Gok) an Herrn Rechtsanwalt Cremer beim Planungsamt, 12.12.1944'.
146. BWA, Schärfls Nachfolger Werkzeugmaschinenfabrik, München, F79 357 'Reise Berlin' n.d. (c. end of 1942), 3.
147. Pohl and Merkner, *Verbandsgeschichte und Zeitgeschichte*, 102; Gehrig, *Nationalsozialistische Rüstungspolitik und unternehmerischer Entscheidungsspielraum*, 200.
148. Gehrig, *Nationalsozialistische Rüstungspolitik und unternehmerischer Entscheidungsspielraum*, 200, fn. 30.
149. BAB R 13 III/77 'Der BfM als Reichsstelle Maschinenbau, Aktenvermerk über eine Besprechung in der Maschinenstelle, Betr.: Neuregelung des Vormerkscheinverfahrens am 3.4.1944. 4.5.1044, Anlage'; R 13 III/68 'Hauptausschuß Fertigungseinrichtung beim Reichsminister für Rüstung und Kriegsproduktion, 7.3.1944'.
150. See Fest, *Speer*, 193–219.
151. BWA, Schärfls Nachfolger Werkzeugmaschinenfabrik, München, F79 357 'Reise Berlin' n.d. (c. late 1942).

152. BWA, Schärfls Nachfolger Werkzeugmaschinenfabrik, München, F79 357 'Reisebericht, 22.7.1942', 9.
153. BAB R 13 III/64 'An die Werkzeugmaschinenhersteller der Liste 1 und 2, 20.4.1942'.
154. BAB R 13 III/67 'Der BfM an die Vormerkscheinverfahren angeschlossenen Werkzeugmaschinen und Holzverarbeitungsmaschinenhersteller 20.2.1943'.
155. BAB R 13 III/67 'Der BfM an die Versandlistverfahren angeschlossenen Werkzeugmaschinenhersteller, 24.11.1942'.
156. BAB R 13 III/67 'Der BfM an die Werkzeugmaschinenhersteller der Liste 1 und 2. 17.7.1942'.
157. BAB R 13 III/67 'Der BfM an die Werkzeugmaschinenhersteller der Liste 1 und 2, Holzverarbeitungsmaschinenhersteller 4.1.1943', 2 and 'Der BfM an die Kontingentsverwaltungsstellen außer Wehrmacht, Reichsbahn und Ausfuhr, 22.2.1943'.
158. BAB R 13 III/407 fol. 1. 'Hauptausschuß Maschinen beim Reichsminister für Rüstungs- und Kriegsproduktion, an Büro Transporteinrichtung, 6.4.1944'.
159. BAB R 13 III/67 'Der BfM an die Werkzeugmaschinenhersteller, 9.9.1942'.
160. BAB R 13 III/407 fol. 1. 'Maschinenfabrik Andritz AG an den BfM als Reichsstelle Maschinenbau, 27.1.1944'.
161. BWA, Schärfls Nachfolger Werkzeugmaschinenfabrik, München, F79 357 'Reise Berlin' n.d. (c. late 1942).
162. *The United States Strategic Bombing Survey, No. 54: Machine Tools and Machinery as Capital Equipment*, Equipment Division, 2nd edn, January 1947, 29, 33, 60, 15.
163. *The United States Strategic Bombing Survey, No. 55: Machine Tool Industry in Germany*, Equipment Division, 2nd edn, January 1947, 16, 33.
164. Ibid., 13.
165. Ibid., 62.
166. *The United States Strategic Bombing Survey, No. 54: Machine Tools and Machinery as Capital Equipment*, Equipment Division, 2nd edn, January 1947, 33.
167. BWA, Schärfls Nachfolger Werkzeugmaschinenfabrik, München, F79 357 Untitled document 'Erweiterung der Verfügung vom 28.5.1942', 'Besprechung beim Bevollmächtigten für die Maschinenproduktion 28.5.1942' and 'Reise Berlin, 22.7.1942'.
168. BWA, Schärfls Nachfolger Werkzeugmaschinenfabrik, München, F79 195 'An Firma Ferd. Peddinghaus, 26.1.1943'.
169. BAB R 13 III/67 'Der BfM an die Kontingentsverwaltungsstellen außer Wehrmacht, Reichsbahn und Ausfuhr 22.2.1943'.
170. BAB R 13 III/67 'Hauptausschuß Maschinen beim Reichsminister für Bewaffnung und Munition an alle dem Vormerkscheinverfahren angeschlossenen Werkzeugmaschinenhersteller, 31.8.1943'.
171. BWA, Schärfls Nachfolger Werkzeugmaschinenfabrik, München, F79 195 'Besprechung der Scheren- und Stanzfabriken in Hagen: W bezügl. der vom Ministerium für Bewaffnung und Munition geforderten Rationalisierung und damit Leistungssteigerung im Scheren- und Stanzenbau' n.d., 1.
172. BAB R 13 III/67 'An die Fachgruppe Werkzeugmaschinen der Wirtschaftsgruppe Maschinenbau, 16.4.1942'.
173. BAB R 13 III/66 'Vorschlag zur Vereinfachung des Bestellwesens von Werkzeugmaschinen. E. Paasch (Feldpost Nr. 08000) an Reichsminister für Kriegsproduktion 28.4.1944', 3.
174. BAB R 13 III/64 'Bm/Nm X-X 100, Betr.: Lieferung von Werkzeugmaschinen für vordringlich Programm: Anordnung des Reichsministers für Bewaffnung und Munition vom 25.3.1941', 1.

175. BAB R 13 III/64 'An die Firmen der Liste 1 und eine Auswahl von Firmen der Liste 2. 20.11.1941', 1–2.
176. SHA 49/LS 158 Bd. 15. 'Wirtschaftsgruppe Maschinenbau (Lange) an die Geschäftsleitung der Firma Siemens & Halske, Siemens Schuckert Werke AG, 23.2.1940'.
177. BAB R 9 VIII/6 'Lange an alle Stellen des Hauses. Büro-Rundschreiben Nr. 624, 19.9.1941', 5.
178. BAB R 13 III/64 'An die neuernannten OKW-Spezialbetriebe der Werkzeugmaschinen-Industrie, 13.11.1941'.
179. BAB R 13 III/64 'Firma...., Betr.: Ernennung zum OKW-Spezialbetrieb 23.1.1942' (blank form letter from Lange's office).
180. BAB R 13 III/64 'An die OKW-Spezialbetriebe der Werkzeugmaschinen, 19.11.1941' and 'Reichsminister für Bewaffnung und Munition an die Vorsitzenden der Prüfungskommission, 15.11.1941'.
181. BAB R 13 III/64 'An die [Engpasst] Werkzeugmaschinenfirmen, 21.1.1942', 1.
182. BAB R 13 III/64 'An die[Engpasst] Werkzeugmaschinenfirmen, 23.1.1942', 1.
183. BAB R 13 III/ 64 'An OKW-Spezialbetriebe der Werkzeugmaschinen-, Präzisionswerke-, Lehrenbau-, sowie Triebwerke- und Wälzlager Industrie laut besonderer Liste, 21.2.1942'.
184. Gehrig, *Nationalsozialistische Rüstungspolitik und unternehmerischer Entscheidungsspielraum*, 118.
185. Ibid., 119.
186. Ibid., 145.
187. *The United States Strategic Bombing Survey, No. 55: Machine Tool Industry in Germany*, Equipment Division, 2nd edn, January 1947, 62.
188. BAB R 3101 Anh/alt R 7 Anh MCC/1 97 'Machine Tools (*Werkzeugmaschinen*)'.
189. *The United States Strategic Bombing Survey, No. 55: Machine Tool Industry in Germany*, Equipment Division, 2nd edn, January 1947, 88.
190. Ibid.
191. BAB R 3101 Anh/alt R 7 Anh MCC/1/ 103 'Wirtschaftsgruppe Maschinenbau: Die Notwendigkeit des Wiederaufbaus der deutschen fachlichen Industrie-Organization, 18.8.1945', 5.
192. BAB R 3101 Anh/alt R 7 Anh MCC/1/ 104 'Wirtschaftsgruppe Maschinenbau (Bad Neuheim: Zum Wiederaufbau der deutschen Statistik 6.8.1945', 2–3.
193. BAB R 3101 Anh/alt R 7 Anh MCC/1/ 103 'Wirtschaftsgruppe Maschinenbau: Die Notwendigkeit des Wiederaufbaus der deutschen fachlichen Industrie–Organization, 18.8.1945', 5.
194. Ibid., 9–11.
195. Pohl and Merkner, *Verbandsgeschichte und Zeitgeschichte*, 103.
196. Ibid.; BAB R 3101 Anh/alt R 7 Anh MCC/1/ 103 'Wirtschaftsgruppe Maschinenbau: Die Notwendigkeit des Wiederaufbaus der deutschen fachlichen Industrie-Organization, 18.8.1945'.
197. Pohl and Merkner, *Verbandsgeschichte und Zeitgeschichte*, 114.
198. BAB R 3101 Anh/alt R 7 Anh MCC/1/ 272 'Siebert (Industrie verschiedener Eisen- und Stahlwaren an die Reichswirtschaftskammer) 29.11.1945'.
199. BWA, Schärfls Nachfolger Werkzeugmaschinenfabrik, München, F79 190 'Niederschrift über die Gründungssitzung des VDMA 4.9.1949', 3.
200. Pohl and Merkner, *Verbandsgeschichte und Zeitgeschichte*, 114.
201. Ibid.
202. Ibid., 114–15.
203. Ibid., 121.

204. Ibid., 114.
205. Ibid., 122.
206. BWA, Schärfls Nachfolger Werkzeugmaschinenfabrik, München, F79 190 'Niederschrift über die Gründungssitzung des VDMA 4.9.1949', 3.
207. Pohl and Merkner, *Verbandsgeschichte und Zeitgeschichte*, 112.
208. Ibid., 122.
209. BWA, Schärfls Nachfolger Werkzeugmaschinenfabrik, München, F79 190 'Niederschrift über die Gründungssitzung des VDMA 4.9.1949', 2.
210. Ibid.
211. Ibid.

Conclusion

The close comparison of two individuals can be a dangerous game. In the absence of broad sweeps of time and the levelling effects of demographic averages, less tangible facts like personality differences, health and even mood at crucial junctures can intervene in ways that make people and careers difficult to evaluate in historical perspective. To a certain extent, this is true in the case of Jakob Reichert and Karl Lange. Reichert was a deeply conservative and often obstinate man with strong ideas. While this helped to distance him from some of the radical ideas of the National Socialists, it also made him reluctant to change significantly to meet new challenges. Instead, he maintained an almost academic distinction between contemporary politics and policies as they existed, on the one hand, and those that he believed to be both correct and plausible on the other. He was unwilling to change his own ideas to suit the times and remained a cantankerous critic of many policies of both the republic and dictatorship. Lange was more mercurial. Throughout his career, he proved altogether more flexible and willing to compromise with a wide variety of interests. Indeed, Gerald Feldman and Ulrich Nocken went so far as to wonder whether Lange had any principles to speak of at all.[1] Whereas this seemed to make him a good citizen of the republic by allowing him to work with many different interests and ideals, it also helped him adapt to a much darker regime.

These basic personality differences played a large role in the course of these two chief business managers' careers, particularly when the new regime that began in 1933 forced them to choose what they could or could not bear. However, as Marx so famously pointed out, men might make their own history, but not in circumstances of their own making. As business managers, private bureaucrats, professional men and citizens of a state governed by a shockingly ruthless and violent party, each faced a set of constraints as well as choices. The interests of their industries, the men who dominated them, the pressures exerted by the state and their concern for their own jobs and status pulled these men in different directions at once. Taken together, they paint a bleak picture of a business culture that valued success more than anything else, even when it meant cooperation with an obviously violent, racist and repressive regime.

Neither Reichert nor Lange was a businessman himself, but each belonged to an elite group peculiar to German industry and shared in some of its travails. Beyond the initial turmoil of early 1933, the period of National Socialism did not result in dramatic turnovers in the management of German firms, which were generally able to adapt to the new regime.[2] In contrast, the period after 1945 saw more dramatic changes to the composition of the leading men in German industry.[3] This was particularly true in the case of the iron and steel industry, which in some cases saw all of its old managers swept away in the aftermath of the war.[4] The machine building industry, on the other hand, retained as much as 71 per cent of its old management elite.[5] To a certain extent, this was due to the high median age of managers in the iron and steel industry.[6] However, even younger managers in the branch were sacked or passed over after 1945.[7] Reichert's fate mirrors this demographic shift in the Ruhr in particular. As a conservative in the fullest sense, Reichert was closely associated with the fading older generation of managers and industrialists who had come of age in Imperial Germany. He thus appeared to belong to a different generation than the more dynamic Lange, despite the fact that they were very close in age. However, the importance of the role each man had played during the Third Reich in their postwar careers demonstrates an important continuity in German business history.

The options open to each man was circumscribed by the organization, structure and interests of his respective industry. As bureaucratic representatives of organizations composed of self-interested industrialists, Reichert and Lange were bound by the needs and wants of their members, but neither man was a puppet. More than one option was open to either man or industry at any given time. This was particularly true in the powerful and well-organized iron and steel industry. Although the institutions they erected constituted webs of organizations rather than clear hierarchies, they could be used to form remarkably unified and determined blocks under certain circumstances. Reichert was adept at harnessing his power as the chief business manager of the Verein Deutscher Eisen- und Stahlindustrieller to bolster his own authority in the industry and in the German economy as a whole, but it was ultimately based on the powerful men that he represented. Lange functioned in a different context. Although the machine building industry had established a similar organization in the Verein Deutscher Maschinenbau-Anstalten, his members remained more fractious, competitive and independent than Reichert's. While members of the VDESI hoped to regulate their economic relationships in order to achieve maximum profit, Lange's constituents favoured a liberal economic model and a limited role for regulation in their economic lives. Lange thus faced the challenge of forging a united block in spite of his members' misgivings, rather than manipulating a cooperative tradition. These differences in industry and organization had profound effects on the two business managers' careers and helped to determine some of the options open to them as they confronted political turmoil. Reichert had faith in the strength of his own industry; Lange was more used to negotiating a compromise solution.

Although Reichert was able to meet a wide variety of challenges in a career that spanned thirty-three years in industrial politics, he continued to fall back on the traditions and habits of the German iron and steel industry. While he and his members had no interest in an unregulated liberal economy, Reichert hoped to keep the state out of most aspects of iron and steel. After the collapse of the Kaiserreich, he even lost much of his faith in the power of protective tariffs, at least in the context of a popular democracy, and turned instead to the promise of self-regulation within his own industry, relying on the flexibility of overlapping organizations that allowed industrialists themselves to govern the process. His faith in industrial self-regulation grew into a romantic promise of peace and economic stability based on a 'natural' economy that inevitably favoured German iron producers. As a result, Reichert rejected any unwanted intervention in the economy as an unnatural 'political' intrusion that also clashed with the interests of the men he represented. In the context of the period following the First World War, this was problematic. Reichert rejected the international political settlements of the period out of hand and worked tirelessly to roll back the gains made by organized labour and the political left in 1918–19. By doing this, the chief business manager hoped to force the young republic to bow to the demands of an iron and steel industry that Reichert saw as the key to a successful state. This would also, of course, decrease the costs and increase the profits of the German iron and steel industry while giving the men he represented the right to make decisions both in their own factories and in the state as a whole.

This did not make Reichert a good citizen of the republic, even though he sat as an elected representative in the Reichstag. However, the fact that the ideas that he espoused reflected the interests and structure of his industry served to inoculate Reichert against the rising tide of extremism that outflanked him on the right. Even as many conservatives and others disappointed in Weimar democracy flocked to the NSDAP during the financial crisis of the early 1930s, Reichert clung to an older tradition of conservatism and the value he saw in industrial self-regulation. More than this, Reichert and many of his members actively tried to combat the rise of National Socialism amongst the traditional conservative elite, warning that it was a species of Marxism that would rob entrepreneurs of their autonomy, ruining the state and economy with nonsensical policies. Instead, he hoped that the failure of popular democracy would clear the field for industrial organizations that could effectively govern themselves and even set the foreign policy of the nation with minimal interference from any representative government.

Reichert failed, but even after the Nazi seizure of power in 1933, he remained highly suspicious of National Socialism. Although he moderated some of his views, Reichert refused to adopt the perspective of the new government or even instrumentalize Nazi beliefs in order to retain his authority in industrial politics or tap into the spoils offered by the new regime. Believing that the powerful iron and steel industry simply could not be ignored, Reichert instead tried to push the new regime towards his own views and policies, much as he had done in the Weimar Republic. This reluctance to embrace the ideology of the NSDAP translated into an unwillingness to transform the VDESI into an effective regulative body as the Wirtschaftsgruppe Eisenschaffende Industrie. As far as Reichert was concerned, the iron and steel industry had already developed ideal structures and organizations. All that remained to be done was to let these organizations fulfil their potential without the inconvenience of interference from the state. Reichert also carried the experiences of the early Weimar Republic with him and avoided trying to expand his own power even at times when the strength and demands of the state made his success much likelier. The result was that Reichert and the Wigru came into increasing conflict with an ever more impatient state, a situation that culminated in the establishment of a state-owned ironworks intended to circumvent independent iron and steel producers.

Although Reichert actively participated in the war effort on behalf of iron and steel, the consequences of his approach to the National Socialist regime had already come home to roost. He and his increasingly fractured industry were unable to meet the demands of a state that already suspected he was not really trying. When this happened, the state simply replaced his organization with one better suited to the National Socialist war effort. Reichert's authority and success had always hinged on his ability to manage and satisfy the powerful men of the iron and steel industry, and his relationship to the state reflected their wants and needs. Ironically, his defence of their interests and aims also resulted in his inability to deliver real benefits to his own members. Out of favour and out of step with an ideological regime, Reichert lost the contacts, respect and authority he had he once possessed in the apparatus of the state and economy. Having failed to even move towards a more centralized, 'coordinated' organization in the iron and steel industry, he was also unable to deliver benefits like those that Lange could distribute or to block, moderate or channel the state's demands in order to protect his own members. This rendered him incapable of fulfilling the demands of his own masters in industry. Virtually useless to either the state or iron and steel industrialists themselves, Reichert's power and authority vanished.

Lange's career took a very different path but also reflected the needs and wants of the industry he represented throughout the Weimar years. Where Reichert pushed for increased private regulation of the economy, Lange and his staff became leading proponents of open, liberal competition. At the same time, the dynamics of a technical industry that depended on flexibility and adaptation to survive was reflected in their approach to Weimar politics. Lange and his organization adapted so as to get the most out of prevailing conditions. The VDMA was willing to reach out to both the political left and right, acting as a bridge or mediator in the tense politics of the republic. By doing this, Lange hoped to ensure the profitability of his members and increase the role of the VDMA by acting as an indispensable aid to his industry. This willingness to compromise is the lifeblood of a democratic society, and Lange and the VDMA became models of a modern industrial organization in the Weimar Republic.

The onset of global economic collapse in 1929 left Lange and his organization in an uncomfortable position. In the charged and confused political atmosphere of Germany at the end of the Weimar Republic, the VDMA had few partners to reach out to. As a result, Lange and his assistants advocated an awkward mix of authoritarianism and economic liberalism that reflected the hopes of the machine building industry. This had the paradoxical effect of both contributing to the fall of the republic and antagonizing the supporters of National Socialism, leaving Lange and his organization dangerously exposed after the seizure of power in 1933. Lacking either the real or perceived power of the iron and steel industry, Lange was unlikely to be able to push the regime into policies acceptable to the machine building industry. Instead, he did what the VDMA had done in past crises: he looked for a workable compromise. Lange scrambled to drop ideologies that had become dangerous and embraced National Socialism openly. This allowed him to escape the purges of the early Nazi years and preserve his organization even as others were fired, driven into exile or worse. It also allowed him to begin building an organization capable of continuing much of the work of the old VDMA while channelling the spoils of the Nazi regime to his members. As Lange carefully accumulated the power and positions offered by the new regime in peace and in war, he became indispensable to the state and to German machine builders alike: the former relied on him to regulate a fractious industry; the latter to integrate them into the new regime in order to develop their business and maximize profits.

Compromising with the state enabled Lange to continue to secure tangible benefits for his industry. Like Höfgen in Klaus Mann's *Mephisto*, Lange was able to use the changes wrought by National Socialism to attain a level of success and prominence that he could never have achieved in the Wiemar Republic. In the process, he turned his back on the aims, ideals and colleagues he had once been close to, not to mention the broader moral consequences of the changes taking place in Germany. Unlike Höfgen, Lange's story does not close with a dire warning about a day of reckoning to come. He might have been an opportunist himself, but Lange also knew how to seize opportunities for his organization's members. Although many machine builders were unhappy with the course of the German economy under National Socialism and chafed under Lange's direction, the chief business manager had made himself indispensable by 1945. Machines could not be built and profits could not be made without the approval, contacts and expertise of Karl Lange. Consequently, Lange could not be simply ignored like Reichert. He was carried over into the leadership of the organization refounded to represent the machine building industry and took up his old duties until his death in July of 1955.[8]

Ideology and personality mattered during these tumultuous years, but their effects were often counterintuitive. As noted in the introduction and throughout this study, Reichert and his members have very often been cited as some of the ideological progenitors of the far right that gave birth to National Socialism. To be sure, Reichert and the NSDAP shared a number of negative ideas about democracy, the left and international relations. In this sense, he and the iron and steel industry contributed significantly to the collapse of the republic, particularly through their attacks on the SPD and moderate left. However, Reichert's obstinate conservatism also helped to distance him from Hitler and his party. Rather than embracing or supporting the upstart regime, Reichert and the VDESI stubbornly clung to their own vision of industrial organization and continued to believe that their role in an industrial economy allowed them to dictate policy to the state. The factories and villas of iron and steel industrialists might often have been draped in the flags and swastikas of the Nazi regime, but Reichert and the old VDESI continued to believe that they could make this new state see things their way. The National Socialists, for their part, were likewise deeply suspicious of an industry that excelled at regulating itself in order to ensure inflated prices in Germany. The outcome was that Reichert's fierce political conservatism backfired. Instead of reconciling himself to the new regime, he became increasingly isolated and confrontational.

Meanwhile, the experience of Lange and the VDMA demonstrates that the very spirit of compromise that allowed the machine building industry to adapt to the Weimar Republic so much better than iron and steel also facilitated its integration into the Third Reich. He was just as responsible as Reichert was for representing the wants and needs of his industry, but Lange, representing a weaker, less well-organized group, achieved his aims through a more circumspect policy of cooperation. When push came to shove, Lange was willing to dump much of the ideology of his organization and industry in order to compromise with the National Socialist state. The moderation and flexibility that made the VDMA so suitable for life in a democratic republic thus also helped to lead machine builders into cooperation with a murderously ideological regime. This is a chilling prospect, but it helps to explain why so many organizations that had no interest in National Socialism before 1933 integrated themselves into the Third Reich so quickly. Just as adept businessmen are able to adapt to meet the demands of changing market conditions, the highly competitive German machine building industry was able to adapt to make the most out of the Nazi state.

The effects of the relative strengths and organization of the two industries also point to noteworthy conclusions. The real power and prestige of the iron and steel industry in Weimar Germany did not translate directly into power in the new National Socialist regime. On the contrary, Reichert's faith that any new government would have to reflect and represent the interests of iron and steel as a matter of course proved to be a significant miscalculation. Believing that he and his industry would naturally have a place in the new regime, Reichert negotiated from what he believed to be a position of strength. In the event, the new Party proved more ruthless and indifferent to old economic interests and organizations than he had imagined. Profits, markets and the freedom of the entrepreneur were less important to the National Socialist regime than mobilizing for war, and Reichert's attempts to push policy on the regime cut him off from positions of real authority. The self-assurance that came with economic power in Weimar thus led to disenfranchisement in the Third Reich. The opposite was the case for Karl Lange and the German machine building industry. The chief business manager of the VDMA felt the weakness of his organization and industry keenly in 1933. Both he and his industry were targeted as enemies of the state the National Socialists hoped to create. Unlike Reichert, Lange could not assume that his industry's central role would allow him and his members to claw their way into the halls of power regardless of the regime. Therefore he moved quickly to reconcile himself and his organization with National Socialism in 1933. In this case weakness, not power, led to support for the 'national revolution'.

Jonathan Wiesen has ably illustrated the extent to which German industry and businessmen scrambled to demonstrate that they, too, were a kind of victim with no choice in a repressive regime but to collaborate.[9] This was often a self-serving, cynical ploy to escape the consequences of a lost war, but it was not a complete fabrication. If Buchheim and Scherner were right about the options open to men like Reichert and Lange, then their long-term effects brought these choices closer to Hayes and Termin's conceptions of coercion.[10] The enormous pressure the Nazi state could exert on individuals and industries sometimes took the form of slowly escalating demands that reduced the freedom to manoeuvre by degrees. Reichert and Lange were able to chart different paths through this period without immediate negative effects like dismissal or imprisonment, but the consequences of these choices and the values they demonstrate are disturbing. Reichert went to great lengths to represent the traditional structure, organization and role of the representatives of the iron and steel industry in the Third Reich. This eventually cost him his role in the German economy, his job and, though perhaps indirectly, his life. In the end, the iron and steel industry itself proved to be less interested in abstract or ideological aims than its chief business manager was. Once Reichert was no longer useful, his members all but abandoned him as they sought private accommodations with the Nazi government that would allow them to remain profitable, or at least solvent. When ideology failed, business trumped belief or even sympathy for a loyal servant. Few might shed many tears over the lonely suicide of a man who, after all, loyally represented a reactionary industry that managed to survive the regime and the war, but Reichert's experience points to the limits of the industrial lobby groups that had marked Imperial and Weimar Germany so deeply. Industrial firms, managers and representatives like Reichert and Lange were not forced to change or disband in the way that the trade unions and so many other groups in Germany were, but failure to work with the Nazi state carried very real consequences.

The actions of the machine builders tell a similar story, albeit from the other side of the coin. Lange's regulation of their industry and his willingness to give up on the liberal competition that had made them so successful had alienated a large number of machine builders who might have dropped him after the invading Allies had dismantled his organization and raised the possibility of open competition once again. He might also have been dismissed as a political liability in occupied Germany. This did not happen. Nothing succeeds like success, and Lange had managed to make himself indispensable to what remained of the machine building industry and the state, regardless of the direction in which he had taken the sector. When his former members looked back on Lange's career in the Nazi state, his success and that of his members, rather than the compromises made with a hateful and ultimately unsuccessful state, carried the day. Not only did collaborating not bar Lange from a position in the postwar economy, but it also facilitated his success in occupied and democratic Germany. In this sense, collaboration also offered substantial rewards, and not only just from the state itself. Colleagues, clients and contemporaries congratulated, rather than condemned, Karl Lange.

This study of the careers of Jakob Reichert and Karl Lange demonstrates the options open to industrialists and their representatives. While it might have been foolish to have openly opposed the policies of the regime, neither Reichert nor Lange was ever in any physical danger under National Socialism. At worst, they might have lost their positions and gone on to less lucrative or rewarding work, as Schlenker did after being removed from the leadership of the North-West Group of the VDESI. However, close collaboration with the regime and a willingness to integrate into the National Socialist state were seductive, whereas opposition was dangerous in ways that Buchheim and Scherner do not allow for. A cooperative stance allowed Lange to salvage his own position, preserve the VDMA and then, later, deliver all the benefits the new state could offer to his members. Although Reichert represented a very different industry with well-articulated goals and traditions, his own members ultimately expected the same results from him. The chief business manager of a major industrial association in Germany was ultimately judged on his ability to serve his member firms. When collaboration with a regime that opposed much of what they had stood for offered this chance to industrialists, they took it. Industrial representatives who failed to realize this were sooner or later cast aside in favour of those more willing to play along. Neither Karl Lange nor Jakob Reichert was an 'ordinary man'. They were important managers in a system dominated by much larger and ambitious personalities. Neither was faced with a direct question to kill or be killed, or to rescue or denounce, though the regime was more than willing to force such choices on its citizens or victims. When they did make their own choices, however, they found that their own peers and communities were more interested in their usefulness and success than in principle of any kind. Thus German industry became part of the coercion it later denounced. This itself is a kind of indictment of the industrial and business community in Germany under National Socialism, but it is also a sad and sobering reminder of our own capacity to overlook the broad consequences of personal interests and the small daily choices we are all called on to make from time to time.

Notes

1. Feldman and Nocken, 'Trade Associations and Economic Power', 433.
2. For an example of earlier studies of industrialists as a class see M. Broszat and K. Schwabe (eds). 1989. *Die deutschen Eliten und der Weg in den Zweiten Weltkrieg*, Munich: Verlag C.H. Beck. For more recent work see, e.g., Erker, *Deutsche Unternehmer zwischen Kriegswirtschaft und Wiederaufbau* and Joly, 'Kontinuität und Diskontinuität der industriellen Elite nach 1945', 58.
3. Joly, 'Kontinuität und Diskontinuität der industriellen Elite nach 1945', 58–59.
4. Stefan Unger's study of the Ruhr indicates that there was virtually a complete turnover in the management of iron and steel firms. This study, however, is based on a limited sample of 100 managers. See S. Unger. 2003. 'Die "Herren aus dem Westen" in den Jahren 1933 und 1945: Die personellen Konsequenzen der Errichtung und des Untergangs der nationalsozialistischen Diktatur für die Wirtschaftselite des Ruhrgebietes', in Abelshauser, Hesse and Plumpe, *Wirtschaftsordnung, Staat und Unternehmen*, 330.
5. Ibid.
6. Joly, 'Kontinuität und Diskontinuität der industriellen Elite nach 1945', 62.
7. Unger, 'Die "Herren aus dem Westen" in den Jahren 1933 und 1945', 332.
8. *Maschinenbau-Nachrichten* 9 (26 July 1955), 1.
9. Wiesen, *West German Industry and the Challenge of the Nazi Past*.
10. See Buchheim and Scherner, 'Corporate Freedom of Action in Nazi Germany: A Response to Peter Hayes'; Hayes, 'Corporate Freedom of Action in Nazi Germany'; Termin, 'Soviet and Nazi Economic Planning in the 1930s'.

Glossary
(German terms, firms, etc.)

Anschluß	German annexation of Austria in 1938
Bewirtschaftungsstellen	Management Offices
Fachgruppe	"Technical Group" for specific products or processes
F-Scheine	"F-Card" that permitted delivery to the customer
Führer	"Leader", or "The Leader" in the case of Hitler
Führerprinzip	"leadership principle" of the Nazi Party. This can refer to the dictatorship of Hitler or to the leadership position of other functionaries in an organization.
Gau	Nazi unit of regional administration.
Gleichschaltung	"Coordination", refers to the process of bringing virtually all aspects of life in Germany into line with the Nazi Party
Handlungsspielraum	Room for Manoeuvre, or for negotiation
Hauptausschuss	Main Committee
Kaiserreich	Imperial Germany
Machtergreifung	The "seizure of power" by the Nazi Party in 1933
Meldescheine	Order Notice
Osthilfe	"Help for the East". A Nazi charity.
Planungsamt	Speer's Central Planning Office
Prüfungsstelle	Control, or "pre-inspection" Office
Reichsstelle	"Federal Office". Refers here to offices attached to institutions like the Ministry of Economics in order to regulate certain aspects of the German economy

Ruhrkampf	The Ruhr occupation of 1923 and passive resistance campaign against mainly French troops.
Ruhrlade	A semiformal gathering of the most powerful iron, steel and coal men in the Ruhr Valley
Rüstungskommando	Armaments Command, or Inspectorate
Verbände	"Associations". Used to refer to the private marketing associations or specialized cartels used to regulate price and production in the iron and steel industry.
Vormerkscheine	Notice of intent or reserve for materials or production
Werkzeugmaschinen	Machine Tools
Wirtschaftsgruppe Eisenschaffende Industrie	Business Group Iron Industry
Wirtschaftsgruppe Maschinenbau	Business Group Machine Building

Bibliography

Archival Sources

Archiv des Instituts für Zeitgeschichte, München (AIZ)
    Albert Pietzsch; Industrieller und Wirtschaftsfunktionär; Präsident der Reichswirtschaftskammer; Nachlass 1874–1957.
    Nürnberger Kriegsverbrecherprozess, MA 1555/18 NI 1983 Reichsvereinigung Eisen.
    Nürnberger Kriegsverbrecherprozess, MA 1563/22 NG 1089 Jakob Reichert.
    OMGUS Shipment 17, Box 243-1, Folder 3–5. 1945–6 Stahlwerksverband.
Bayerisches Wirtschaftsarchiv, München (BWA)
    F79 195 Schärfls Nachfolger Werkzeugmaschinenfabrik
    F79 357 Schärfls Nachfolger Werkzeugmaschinenfabrik
    F79 358 Schärfls Nachfolger Werkzeugmaschinenfabrik
Bundesarchiv Berlin (BAB)
    R 8 XVI Bevollmächtigter für Maschinenproduktion als Reichsstelle für Maschinenbau. 1939–1945.
    R 9 VIII Prüfungsstelle Maschinenbau
    R 9 XI Prüfungsstelle Eisenschaffende Industrie
    R 10 III Reichsvereinigung Eisen
    R 12 I Reichsgruppe Industrie
    R 13 I Verein Deutscher Eisen- und Stahlindustrieller/Wirtschaftsgruppe Eisenschaffende Industrie
    R 13 III Wirtschaftsgruppe Maschinenbau 1872–1945
    R 13 V Wirtschaftsgruppe Elektroindustrie
    R 3101 Reichswirtschaftsministerium
    R 8099 Tätigkeit der VDMA in der Revolution. Industrie-Organisation (Reichsarbeitsgemeinschaft)
Donovan Archive, Cornell Law Library
    'Nuremberg Trials' Volume XVII, Pt. 2 53.106 'Office of Strategic Services, Research and Analysis Branch "Biographical Report, Röchling, Hermann" 9.5.1945,'
    'Nuremberg Trials' Volume XVII, Pt. 2 53.057 'Office of Strategic Services, Research and Analysis Branch. Biographical Report: Reichert, Jakob Wilhelm 16.5.1945'
    'Nuremberg Trials' Volume XVII, Pt. 2 53.106 'Office of Strategic Services, Research and Analysis Branch. Biographical Report: Zangen, William 11.4.1945'.
Siemens A.G. Historisches Archives, Munich (SHA)
    49/LD 689
    49/LS 157

49/LS 158
49/LS 159
49/LS 160
49/LS 190
49/LS 357
Staatsarchiv Nürnberg (SAN)
   Rep. 502, VI KV-Anklage/Interrogations R 48. Jakob Reichert.
Stiftung Rheinisch-Westfälisches Wirtschaftsarchiv zu Köln (R-WW)
   Historisches Archiv der GHH
   Nachlass Paul Reusch
   Nachlass Otto Wolff

Published Sources

Abelshauser, Werner. 2009. 'Eigennutz verpflichtet. Die Verantwortung des Unternehmers in der korporativen Marktwirtschaft', *Geschichte und Gesellschaft* 35(3), 458–76.
Abelshauser, Werner. 2002. 'Gustav Krupp und die Gleichschaltung des Reichsverbandes der Deutschen Industrie, 1933–34', *Zeitschrift für Unternehmensgeschichte* 47(1), 3–26.
Abelshauser, Werner. 1999. 'Kriegswirtschaft und Wirtschaftswunder: Deutschlands wirtschaftliche Mobilisierung für den Zweiten Weltkrieg und die Folgen für die Nachkriegszeit', *Vierteljahrshefte für Zeitgeschichte* 47(4), 503–38.
Abelshauser, Werner. 2003. *Kulturkampf: Der deutsche Weg in die Neue Wirtschaft und die amerikanische Herausforderung*. Berlin: Kulturverlag Kadmos.
Abelshauser, Werner. 2003. 'Modernisierung oder institutionelle Revolution? Koordinaten einer Ortsbestimmung des "Dritten Reiches" in der deutschen Wirtschaftsgeschichte des 20. Jahrhunderts', in Werner Abelshauser et al. (eds), *Wirtschaftsordnung, Staat und Unternehmen*, 17–40.
Abelshauser, Werner, Jan-Otmar Hesse and Werner Plumpe (eds). 2003. *Wirtschaftsordnung, Staat und Unternehmen: Neue Forschungen zur Wirtschaftsgeschichte des Nationalsozialismus*. Essen: Klartext Verlag.
Abraham, David. 1986. *The Collapse of the Weimar Republic: Political Economy and Crisis*, 2nd edn. New York: Holmes & Meier.
Abraham, David. 1980. 'Conflicts within German Industry and the Collapse of the Weimar Republic', *Past and Present* 88(August), 88–128.
Aly, Götz. 2005. *Hitler's Volksstaat: Raub, Rassenkrieg und nationaler Sozialismus*. Frankfurt a.M.: S. Fischer Verlag.
Bähr, Johannes. 2013. 'The Personal Factor in Business under National Socialism: Paul Reusch and Friedrich Flick', in Hartmut Berghoff, Jürgen Kocka and Dieter Ziegler (eds), *Business in the Age of Extremes*. New York: Cambridge University Press, 153–71.
Bähr, Johannes, Ralf Banken and Thomas Fleming. 2008. *Die MAN: Eine deutsche Industriegeschichte*. Munich: C.H. Beck
Bähr, Johannes, et al. (eds). 2008. *Der Flick-Konzern im Dritten Reich*. Munich: R. Oldenbourg.
Balderston, Theo. 1993. *The Origins and Course of the German Economic Crisis: 1923–1932*. Berlin: Haude & Spencer.
Barkai, Avraham. 1989. *From Boycott to Annihilation: The Economic Struggle of German Jews, 1933–1943*, William Templar, trans. Hanover: Brandeis University Press.
Barkai, Avraham. 1990. *Nazi Economics: Ideology, Theory, and Policy*. New Haven: Yale University Press.

Beck, Hermann. 2008. *The Fateful Alliance: German Conservatives and Nazis in 1933. The Machtergreifung in a New Light.* New York: Berghahn Books.
Benz, Wolfgang. 1990. 'Die Verlockung der französischen Ressourcen: Pläne und Methoden zur Ausbeutung Frankreichs für die kriegswichtigen Bedürfnisse und langfristigen Ziele des Reiches', in Stephan Marten, *La France et l'Allemagne en Guerre, Septembre 1939–Novembre 1942.* Paris: Fondation pour les études de défense nationale, Institut d'histoire des conflits contemporains and Bundesministerium für Forschung und Technologie, Deutsches Historisches Institut Paris, 435–48.
Berghahn, Volker, Stefan Unger and Dieter Ziegler. 2003. *Die deutsche Wirtschaftselite im 20. Jahrhundert: Kontinuität und Mentalität.* Essen: Klartext Verlag.
Berghoff, Hartmut, Jürgen Kocka and Dieter Ziegler (eds). 2013. *Business in the Age of Extremes.* New York: Cambridge University Press.
'Betriebsingenieure an die Front'. 1933. *Maschinenbau* 12(15/16)
Blaich, Fritz. 1979. *Staat und Verbände in Deutschland zwischen 1871 und 1945.* Wiesbaden: Franz Steiner Verlag.
Blumberg-Lampe, Christine. 1973. *Das Wirtschaftspolitische Programm der 'Freiburger Kreise': Entwurf einer freiheitlich-sozialen Nachkriegswirtschaft Nationalökonomen gegen den Nationalsozialismus.* Berlin: Duncker & Humblot.
Block, Jan. 1997. *Die Wirtschaftspolitik in der Weltwirtschaftskrise 1929 bis 1932 im Urteil der Nationalsozialisten.* Frankfurt a.M.: Peter Lang.
Böhret, Carl. 1975. 'Institutionalisierte Einflußwege der Verbände in der Weimarer Republik', in Heinz Joseph Varain (ed.), *Interessenverbände in Deutschland.* Cologne: Kiepenhauer & Witsch, 216–27.
Bopp, Wolfgang. 2000. 'The Evolution of the Pricing Policy for Public Orders During the Third Reich', in Christoph Buchheim and Redvers Garside (eds), *After the Slump: Industry and Politics in 1930s Britain and Germany.* New York: Peter Lang, 149–60.
Brady, Robert A. 1933. *The Rationalization Movement in German Industry: A Study in the Evolution of Economic Planning.* Berkeley: University of California Press.
Bräutigam, Petra. 1997. *Mittelständische Unternehmer im Nationalsozialismus: Wirtschaftliche Entwicklungen und soziale Verhaltnisweisen in der Shuh- und Lederindustrie Badens und Württembergs.* Munich: R. Oldenbourg.
Broszat, Martin. 1981. *The Hitler State: The Foundation and Development of the Internal Structure of the Third Reich,* John W. Hinden, trans. London: Longman.
Broszat, Martin, Klaus Dietmar Henke and Hans Woller (eds). 1988. *Von Stalingrad zur Währungsreform: Zur Sozialgeschichte des Umbruchs in Deutschland.* Munich: Oldenbourg Verlag.
Broszat, Martin, and Klaus Schwabe (eds). 1989. *Die Deutschen Eliten und der Weg in den Zweiten Weltkrieg.* Munich: C.H. Beck Verlag.
Browning, Christopher. 1993. *Ordinary Men: Reserve Police Battalion 101 and the Final Solution in Poland.* New York: Harper Perennial.
Brüning, Heinrich. 1970. *Memoiren: 1918–1934.* Stuttgart: Deutsche Verlags-Anstalt.
Buchheim, Christoph (ed.). 2008. *German Industry in the Nazi Period.* Stuttgart: Franz Steiner Verlag.
Buchheim, Christoph. 2001. 'Die Wirtschaftsentwicklung im Dritten Reich. Mehr Desaster als Wunder: Eine Erwiderung auf Werner Abelshauser', *Vierteljahshefte für Zeitgeschichte* 49(4), 653–64.
Buchheim, Christoph, and Redvers Garside (eds). 2000. *After the Slump: Industry and Politics in 1930s Britain and Germany.* New York: Peter Lang.
Buchheim, Christoph, and Jonas Scherner. 2003. 'Anmerkungen zum Wirtschaftssystem des "Dritten Reichs"', in Werner Abelshauser, Jan Ottmar Hesse, Werner Plumpe (eds),

Wirtschaftsordnung, Staat und Unternehmen: Neue Forschung zur Wirtschaftsgeschichte des Nationalsozialismus. Essen: Klartext Verlag, 81–98.

Buchheim, Christoph, and Jonas Scherner. 2009. 'Corporate Freedom of Action in Nazi Germany: A Response to Peter Hayes', *Bulletin of the German Historical Institute* 45(Fall), 43–50.

Buchheim, Christoph, and Jonas Scherner. 2006. 'The Role of Private Property in the Nazi Economy: The Case of Industry', *Journal of Economic History* 66(1), 390–416.

Budraß, Lutz. 1993. 'Unternehmer im Nationalsozialismus. Der "Sonderbevollmächtigte des Generalfeldmarschalls Göring für die Herstellung de JU88"', in W. Plumpe and C. Kleinschmidt (eds), *Unternehmen zwischen Markt und Macht: Aspekte deutscher Unternehmens- und Industriegeschichte im 20. Jahrhundert*. Essen: Bochumer Schriften zur Unternehmens- und Industriegeschichte, 74–89.

Chanady, Atilla. 1967. 'The Disintegration of the German National People's Party, 1924–1930', *Journal of Modern History* 39(1), 65–91.

Czichon, Eberhard. 1967. *Wer verhalf Hitler zur Macht? Anteil der deutschen Industrie an der Zerstörung der Weimarer Republik*. Cologne: Pahl-Rugenstein Verlag.

Danylow, Peter, and Ulrich S. Soénius (eds). 2005. *Otto Wolff: Ein Unternehmen zwischen Wirtschaft und Politik*. Munich: Siedler Verlag.

Dichgans, Hans. 1974. '100 Jahre Stahlwirtschaftliche Verbände', *Stahl und Eisen* 94(21) 994–1005.

Diehl, Markus. 2005. *Von der Marktwirtschaft zur nationalsozialistischen Kriegswirtschaft: Die Transformation der deutschen Wirtschaftsordnung, 1933–1945*. Stuttgart: Steiner Verlag.

Dlugoborski, Waclaw (ed.). 1981. *Zweiter Weltkrieg und sozialer Wandel*. Göttingen: Vandenhoek & Ruprecht.

Eichholtz, Dietrich. 1989. 'Das Expansionsprogramm des Finanzkapitals am Vorabend des Zweiten Weltkriegs', in Dietrich Eichholtz and Kurt Pätzold (eds), *Der Weg in den Krieg: Studien zur Geschichte der Vorkriegsjahre, 1935/36 bis 1939*. Berlin: Akademie Verlag, 1–40.

Eichholtz, Dietrich. 1969. *Geschichte der deutschen Kriegswirtschaft, 1933–1945*, vol. 1. Berlin: Akademie Verlag.

Eichholz, Dietrich. 1999. *Krieg und Wirtschaft: Studien zur deutschen Wirtschaftsgeschichte 1939-1945*. Berlin: Metropol.

Eichholtz, Dietrich. 1999. 'Ökonomie, Politik und Kriegsführung: Wirtschaftliche Kriegsplanung und Rüstungsorganisation bis zum Ende der "Blitzkriegphase"', in Dietrich Eichholtz (ed.), *Krieg und Wirtschaft: Studien zur deutschen Wirtschaftsgeschichte 1939-1945*. Berlin: Metropol Verlag, 9–42.

Eichholtz, Dietrich, and Kurt Pätzold (eds). 1989. *Der Weg in den Krieg: Studien zur Geschichte der Vorkriegsjahre, 1935/36 bis 1939*. Berlin: Akademie Verlag.

Erdmann, Karl Dietrich. 1978. *Die Kabinette Stresemann I und II*. Boppard am Rhein: Boldt.

Erker, Paul. 1999. *Deutsche Unternehmer zwischen Kriegswirtschaft und Wiederaufbau: Studien zur Erfahrungsbildung von Industrie-Eliten*. Munich: Oldenbourg Verlag.

Evans, Richard. 2004. *The Coming of the Third Reich*. New York: Penguin Press.

Fiereder, Helmut. 1983. *Reichswerke 'Hermann Göring' in Österreich, 1938–1945*. Vienna: Geyer.

Feldman, Gerald D. 2001. *Allianz and the German Insurance Business, 1933–1945*. Cambridge: Cambridge University Press.

Feldman, Gerald D. 2004. 'Financial Institutions in Nazi Germany: Reluctant or Willing Collaborators?' in Francis R. Nicosia and Jonathan Huener (eds), *Business and Industry in Nazi Germany*. New York: Berghahn Books, 15–42.

Feldman, Gerald D. 1997. *The Great Disorder: Politics, Economics and Society in the German Inflation, 1914–1924*. New York: Oxford University Press.
Feldman 2003. 'Historische Vergangenheitsbearbeitung: Wirtschaft und Wissenschaft im Vergleich', Max-Planck-Gesellschaft zur Förderung der Wissenschaften e.V. Präsidentenkommission 13, 'Geschichte der Kaiser-Wilhelm-Gesellschaft im Nationalsozialismus'.
Feldman, Gerald D. 1977. *Iron and Steel in the German Inflation, 1916–1923*. Princeton: Princeton University Press.
Feldman, Gerald D. 1984. *Vom Weltkrieg zur Weltwirtschaftskrise*. Göttingen: Vandenhoek & Ruprecht.
Feldman, Gerald D. 1974. 'Wirtschafts- und sozialpolitische Probleme der deutschen Demobilmachung 1918/19', in Hans Mommsen et al. (eds), *Industrielles System und politische Entwicklung in der Weimarer Republik: Verhandlungen des Internationalen Symposiums in Bochum vom 12–17. Juni 1973*. Düsseldorf: Droste Verlag.
Feldman, Gerald D., and Ulrich Nocken. 1975. 'Trade Associations and Economic Power: Interest Group Development in the German Iron and Steel and Machine Building Industries, 1900–1933', *Business History Review* 49(3), 413–45.
Feldman, Gerald D., and Irmgard Steinisch. 1985. *Industrie und Gewerkschaften 1918–1924: Die überforderte Zentralarbeitsgemeinschaft*. Stuttgart: Deutsche Verlags-Anstalt.
Fest, Joachim. 2001. *Speer: The Final Verdict*, Ewald Osers and Alexandra Dring, trans. London: Wiedenfeld & Nicholson.
Fletcher, Roger. 1984. 'Recent Developments in West German Historiography: The Bielefeld School and Its Critics', *German Studies Review* 7(3), 451–80.
Frei, Norbert. 2001. *Karrier im Zweilicht: Hitlers Eliten nach 1945*. Frankfurt: Campus Verlag.
Freyberg, Thomas von. 1989. *Industrielle Rationalisierung in der Weimarer Republik: Beispiele aus dem Maschinenbau und der Elektroindustrie*. Frankfurt a.M.: Campus Verlag.
Gall, Lothar (ed.) 2002. *Krupp im 20. Jahrhundert: Die Geschichte des Unternehmens vom Ersten Weltkrieg bis zur Gründung der Stiftung*. Berlin: Siedler Verlag.
Gall, Lothar, and Manfred Pohl (eds). 1998. *Unternehmer im Nationalsozialismus*. Munich: C.H. Beck.
Gall, Lothar et al. (eds). 1995. *The Deutsch Bank, 1870–1995*. London: Wiedenfeld & Nicolson.
Gaul, Claus-Martin. 2004. *Die industriellen Anlageinvestitionen und ihre Steuerung in Deutschland von 1933 bis 1939: Ein Beitrag zur Wirtschaftshistorischen Analyse des Verhältnisses von Politik und Ökonomie im Nationalsozialismus*. Hamburg: Verlag Dr. Kovač.
Gehrig, Astrid. 1996. *Nationalsozialistische Rüstungspolitik und unternehmerischerEntscheidungsspielraum: Vergleichende Fallstudien zur württembergischen Maschinenbauindustrie*. Munich: R. Oldenbourg Verlag.
Gehrig, Astrid. 2002. 'Zwischen Betriebsinteresse und Lenkungswirtschaft: Drei mittelständische Unternehmer im "Dritten Reich"', in Thomas Größbolting and Rüdiger Schmidt (eds), *Unternehmerwirtschaft zwischen Markt und Lenkung: Organisationsformen, politischer Einfluß und ökonomisches Verhalten 1930–1960*. Munich: R. Oldenbourg Verlag, 69–120.
Gerber, David. 1998. *Law and Competition in Twentieth Century Europe: Protecting Prometheus*. New York: Oxford University Press.
Gillingham, John. 1985. *Industry and Politics in the Third Reich: Ruhr Coal, Hitler and Europe*. London: Methuen.
Gladen, Albin. 1975. 'Probleme der staatlichen Sozialpolitik in der Weimarer Republik', in Heinz Joseph Varain (ed.), *Interessenverbände in Deutschland*. Cologne: Kiepenheuer & Witsch, 248–59.

Gluckstein, Danny. 1999 *The Nazis, Capitalism and the Working Class.* London: Bookmarks.
Gosewinkel, Dieter (ed.). 2005. *Wirtschaftskontrolle und Recht in der nationalsozialistischen Diktatur.* Frankfurt a.M.: Klostermann.
Greer, Guy. 1925. *The Ruhr-Lorraine Industrial Problem: A Study of the Economic Interdependence of the Two Regions and their Relation to the Reparation Question.* New York: The Macmillan Company.
Großbölting, Thomas, and Rüdiger Schmidt (eds). 2002. *Unternehmerwirtschaft zwischen Markt und Lenkung: Organisationsformen, politischer Einfluß und ökonomisches Verhalten 1930–1960.* Munich: R. Oldenbourg Verlag.
Grotto, Bernhard. 2008. 'Information und Kommunication: Die Führung des Flick-Konzerns, 1933–1945', in J. Bähr et al. (eds), *Der Flick-Konzern im Dritten Reich.* Munich: R. Oldenbourg, 165–294.
Grübler, Michael. 1982. *Die Spitzenverbände der Wirtschaft und das erste Kabinett Brüning: Vom Ende der Großen Koalition 1929/30 bis zum Vorabend der Bankenkrise 1931, Eine Quellenstudie.* Düsseldorf: Droste Verlag.
Grunenberg, Nina. 2006. *Die Wundertäter: Netzwerke der deutschen Wirtschaft 1942 bis 1966.* Munich: Siedler Verlag.
Hachtman, Rüdiger. 1989. 'Die Deutsche Arbeitsfront im Zweiten Weltkrieg', in D. Eichholz. 1999. *Krieg und Wirtschaft: Studien zur deutschen Wirtschaftsgeschichte 1939–1945,* Berlin: Metropol, 69–108.
Hachtmann, Rüdiger. 2008. 'Labour Policy in Industry', in Christoph Buchheim (ed.), *German Industry in the Nazi Period.* Stuttgart: Franz Steiner Verlag, 65–84.
Hachtmann, Rüdiger, and Winfried Süß. 2006. *Hitlers Kommissare: Sondergewalten in der nationalsozialistischen Diktatur.* Göttingen: Wallstein Verlag.
Hachtmann, Rüdiger, and Winfried Süß. 2006. 'Kommissare im NS-Herrschaftssystem: Probleme und Perspektiven der Forschung', in Rüdiger Hachtmann and Winfried Süß (eds), *Hitlers Kommissare: Sondergewalten in der nationalsozialistischen Diktatur.* Göttingen: Wallstein Verlag, 9–27.
Hänseroth, Thomas, and Carsten Krautz (eds). 2000. *Geschichte des sächsischen Werkzeugmaschinenbaus im Industriezeitalter: Beitrag der Tagung am 19. März 1998 in Dresden.* Dresden: Sächsisches Druck- und Verlagshaus AG.
Hartwich, Hans-Hermann. 1967. *Arbeitsmarkt, Verbände und Staat 1918–1933: Die öffentliche Bindung unternehmerischer Funktion in der Weimarer Republik.* Berlin: Walter de Gruyter.
Haselbach, Dieter. 1991. *Autoritärer Liberalismus und Soziale Marktwirtschaft: Gesellschaft und Politik im Ordoliberalismus.* Baden-Baden: Nomos Verlagsgesellschaft.
Hayes, Peter. 2009. 'Corporate Freedom of Action in Nazi Germany', *Bulletin of the German Historical Institute* 45(Fall), 29–42.
Hayes, Peter. 2004. *From Cooperation to Complicity: Degussa in the Third Reich.* Cambridge: Cambridge University Press.
Hayes, Peter. 1987. 'History in an Off Key: David Abraham's Second "Collapse"', *Business History Review* 61(3), 452–72.
Hayes, Peter. 1987. *Industry and Ideology: IG Farben in the Nazi Era.* Cambridge: Cambridge University Press.
Hayes, Peter. 2009. 'Rejoinder', *Bulletin of the German Historical Institute,* 45(Fall), 51.
Hayse, Michael. 2003. *Recasting West German Elites: Higher Civil Servants, Business Leaders and Physicians in Hesse between Nazism and Democracy: 1945–55.* New York: Berghan Books.
Helfferich, Karl, and Jakob Reichert. 1924. *Das Zweite Versailles.* Berlin: Deutschnationale Schriftvertriebstelle.

Henke, Klaus-Dietmar. 1995. *Die amerikanische Besetzung Deutschlands*. Munich: Oldenbourg Verlag.
Hensler, Ulrich. 2008. 'Iron and Steel Rationing During the Third Reich', in Christoph Buchheim (ed.), *German Industry in the Nazi Period*. Stuttgart: Franz Steiner Verlag, 53–64.
Hensler, Ulrich. 2008. *Die Stahlkontingentierung im Dritten Reich*. Stuttgart: Franz Steiner Verlag.
Herbst, Ludolf. 1982. *Der Totale Krieg und die Ordnung der Wirtschaft: Die Kriegswirtschaft im Spannungsfeld von Politik, Ideologie und Propaganda 1939–1945*. Eichstätt: Deutsche Verlags-Anstalt.
Hetzer, Gerhard. 1988. 'Unternehmer und leitende Angestellte zwischen Rüstungseinsatz und politischer Säuberung', in Martin Broszat, Klaus Dietmar Henke and Hans Woller (eds), *Von Stalingrad zur Währungsreform: Zur Sozialgeschichte des Umbruchs in Deutschland*. Munich: Oldenbourg, 551–91.
Hexner, Erwin. 1943. *The International Steel Cartel*. Chapel Hill: University of North Carolina Press.
Historischen Kommission bei der Bayerischen Akademie der Wissenschaften. 1982. *Neue Deutsche Biographie*. 13, Berlin: Duncker & Humblot.
Holtfrerich, Carl-Ludwig. 1982. *Alternativen zu Brünings Wirtschaftspolitik in der Weltwirtschaftskrise*, Frankfurter Historische Vorträge 9. Wiesbaden: Franz Steiner Verlag.
Homburg, Heidrun. 2003. 'Wirtschaftliche Dimensionen der deutschen Besatzungsherrschaft in Frankreich 1940–1944: Das Beispiel der elektrotechnischen Industrie', in Werner Abelshauser, Jan-Otmar Hesse and Werner Plumpe (eds), *Wirtschaftsordnung, Staat und Unternehmen: Neue Forschungen zur Wirtschaftsgeschichte des Nationalsozialismus*. Essen: Klartext Verlag, 181–201.
Hömig, Herbert. 2000. *Brüning: Kanzler in der Krise der Republik. Eine Weimarer Biographie*. Paderborn: Ferdinand Schöningh.
Horkheimer, Arnold J., and Frank C. Langdon. 1968. *Business Associations and the Financing of Political Parties: A Comparative Study of the Evolution of Practices in Germany, Norway and Japan*. The Hague: Martinus Nijhoff.
International Military Tribunal. 1997. *Trials of the Major War Criminals before the Nürnberg Military Tribunals: Vol. 7 Pt. 1. Nürnberg Oct 1946–April 1949*. Buffalo, NY: William S. Hein.
Jäger, Jörg-Johannes. 1969. *Die wirtschaftliche Abhängigkeit des Dritten Reiches vom Ausland dargestellt am Beispiel der Stahlindustrie*. Berlin: Berlin Verlag.
Jame, Harold. 1995. 'The Deutsche Bank and the Dictatorship, 1933–1945', in L. Gall et al. (eds), *The Deutsch Bank, 1870–1995*. London: Wiedenfeld & Nicolson, 277–82.
James, Harold. 1986. *The German Slump: Politics and Economics 1924–1936*. Oxford: Clarendon Press.
James, Harold. 2004. *The Nazi Dictatorship and the Deutsche Bank*. Cambridge: Cambridge University Press.
James, Harold. 2001. *Verbandspolitik im Nationalsozialismus. Von der Interessenvertretung zur Wirtschaftsgruppe: Der Centralverband des Deutschen Bank- und Bankiergewerbes 1932–1945*. Munich: Piper Verlag.
Janssen, Hauke. 1998. *Nationalökonomie und Nationalsozialismus: Die deutsche Volkswirtschaftslehre in den dreißiger Jahren*. Marburg: Metropolis-Verlag.
Joly, Hervé. 2003. 'Ende des Familienkapitalismus? Das Überleben der Unternehmerfamilien in den deutschen Wirtschaftseliten des 20. Jahrhundert', in Volker Berghahn, Stefan Unger and Dieter Ziegler (eds), *Die deutsche Wirtschaftselite im 20. Jahrhundert: Kontinuität und Mentalität*. Essen: Klartext Verlag, 51–74.

Joly, Hervé. 2000. 'Kontinuität und Diskontinuität der industriellen Elite nach 1945', in Dieter Ziegler (ed.), *Großbürger und Unternehmer: Die deutsche Wirtschaftselite im 20. Jahrhundert*. Göttingen: Vandenhoeck & Ruprecht, 54–73.
Jonas, Erasmus. 1965. *Die Volkskonservativen 1928–1933: Entwicklung, Struktur, Standort und staatspolitische Zielsetzung*. Düsseldorf: Droste Verlag.
Jones, Larry Eugene. 2009. 'German Conservatism at the Crossroads: Count Kuno von Westarp and the Struggle for Control of the DNVP', *Contemporary European History* 18, 147–77.
Jones, Larry Eugene, and Wolfram Pyta (eds). 2006. *'Ich bin der letzte Preuße'. Der politische Lebensweg des konservativen Politikers Kuno Graf von Westarp (1864–1945)*. Cologne: Böhlau Verlag.
Kaelble, Hartmut et al. (eds). 1978. *Probleme der Modernisierung in Deutschland: Sozialhistorische Studien zum 19. und 20. Jahrhundert*. Opladen: Westdeutscher Verlag.
Kahn, Daniela. 2006. *Die Steuerung der Wirtschaft durch Recht im nationalsozialistischen Deutschland: Das Beispiel der Reichsgruppe Industrie*. Frankfurt a.M.: Vittorio Klostermann.
Kershaw, Ian. 1993. *The Nazi Dictatorship: Problems and Perspectives of Interpretation*, 3rd edn. London: Edward Arnold.
Kershaw, Ian. 1993. '"Working Towards the Führer": Reflections on the Nature of the Hitler Dictatorship', *Contemporary European History* 2(2), 103–18.
Kim, Hak-Ie. 1977. *Industrie, Staat und Wirtschaftspolitik: Die konjunkturpolitische Diskussion in der Endphase der Weimarer Republik 1930–1932/1933*. Berlin: Duncker & Humblot.
Kirk, Tim (ed.). 2002. *Cassell's Dictionary of Modern German History*. London: Cassell.
Kobrak, Christopher. 2003. 'The Foreign Exchange Dimension of Corporate Control in the Third Reich: The Case of Schering AG', *Contemporary European History* 12(1), 33–46.
Köhler, Herbert W. 1974. *Die stahlwirtschaftlichen Organisationen im Jubiläumsjahr 1974: Ein Beitrag zum Selbstverständnis moderner Verbandstätigkeit*. Düsseldorf: Verlag Stahleisen.
Kolb, Eberhard. 2005. *The Weimar Republic*, 2nd edn, P.S. Falla and R.J. Park, trans. London: Routledge.
Kratzsch, Gerhard. 1989. *Der Gauwirtschaftsapparat der NSDAP: Menschenführung, 'Arisierung', Wehrwirtschaft im Gau Westfalen-Süd. Eine Studie zur Herrschaftspraxis im totalitären Staat*. Münster: Aschendorf Verlag.
Krüdener, Jürgen von (ed.). 1990. *Economic Crisis and Political Collapse: The Weimar Republic, 1924–1933*. New York: Berg.
Kruse, Christina. 1988. *Die Volkswirtschaftslehre im Nationalsozialismus*. Freiburg: Rudolf Haufe Verlag.
Kulla, Bernd. 1995. *Die Anfänge der empirischen Konjunkturforschung in Deutschland, 1925–1933*. Berlin: Duncker & Humblot.
Lange, Karl. 1932. 'Die Bedeutung der deutschen Fertigwarenausfuhr', *Maschinenbau: Wirtschaftlicher Teil* 11(11) (2 June), 81–82.
Lange, Karl. 1930. 'Bilanz der deutschen Handelspolitik 1925 bis 1929', *Maschinenbau* 9(1) (2 January), W1–W3.
Lange, Karl. 1931. 'Die deutsche Ausfuhr in der Weltwirtschaftskrise', *Maschinenbau* 10(1) (1January), W1–W2.
Lange, Karl. 1940. 'Deutsche Maschinentechnik im Zeitgeschehen', *Der Vierjahresplan* 14(4), 594–97.
Lange, Karl. 1941. 'Deutscher Straßenbau und deutsche Straßenbaumaschinen: Eine Würdigung zum 50. Geburtstag Fritz Todts', *Der Vierjahresplan* 14(5), 744–45.

Lange, Karl. 1931. 'Deutsch-österreichische Zollunion!' *Maschinenbau* 10(7/8) (16 April), W73.
Lange, Karl. 1932. 'Die Entwicklung des Welthandels', *Maschinenbau* 11(1) (7 January), W1–W3.
Lange, Karl. 1931. 'Handelsbilanz und Konjunktur', *Maschinenbau* 10(3) (5 February), W25–W26.
Lange, Karl. 1928. 'Industrie und Landwirtschaft', *Maschinenbau* 7(7) (5 April), 301–2.
Lange, Karl. 1941. 'Maschinenindustrie und Kriegspotential', *Der Vierjahresplan* 9(5), 510–13.
Lange, Karl. 1930. 'Schönheitsfehler der Handelsbilanz?' *Maschinenbau* 9(15) (7 August), W169–W170; also in *Wirtschafts- und Export-Zeitung* 25(28 July).
Lange, Karl. 1939. 'Werkzeugmaschinen als Grundlage der Produktionssteigerung', *Der Vierjahresplan* 19(3), 1133–34.
Lange, Karl. 1929. 'Wirtschaftsdemokratie oder organisierte Wirtschaftsfreiheit?' *Maschinenbau* 8(12) (20 June), 134–40.
Lange, Karl. 1929. 'Wirtschaftsdemokratische Irrtümer bezüglich der weiterverarbeitenden Industrie', in Deutsche Bergwerks-Zeitung (ed.), *Das Problem der Wirtschaftsdemokratie: Zur Düsseldorfer Tagung des Reichsverbandes der Deutschen Industrie*. Düsseldorf: Industrie Verlag und Druckerei A.G., 78–81.
Lange, Karl. 1930. 'Zum Thema: Bilanz der deutschen Handelspolitik 1925 bis 1929', *Maschinenbau* 9(3) (6 February), W25–W28.
Leckebusch, Roswitha. 1966. *Entstehung und Wandlung der Zielsetzung der Struktur und der Wirkung von Arbeitgeberverbänd*. Berlin: Duncker & Humblot.
Leopold, John A. 1977. *Alfred Hugenberg: The Radical Nationalist Campaign against the Weimar Republic*. New Haven: Yale University Press.
Ludmer, Henry. 1943. 'German Financial Mobilization', *Accounting Review* 18(1), 34–39.
Luntowski, Gustav. 2000. *Hitler und die Herren an der Ruhr: Wirtschaftsmacht und Staatsmacht im Dritten Reich*. Frankfurt a.M.: Peter Lang.
Maier, Charles. 1975. *Recasting Bourgeois Europe: Stabilization in France, Germany and Italy in the Decade after World War I*. Princeton: Princeton University Press.
Marten, Stephan. 1990. *La France et l'Allemagne en Guerre, September 1939–Novembre 1942*. Paris: Fondation pour les études de défense nationale, Institut d'histoire des conflits contemporains and Bundesministerium für Forschung und Technologie, Deutsches Historisches Institut Paris.
'Maschinenstürmer'. 1934. *Maschinenbau* 13(3/4)
Mason, Timothy. 1977. *Sozialpolitik im Dritten Reich: Arbeiterklasse und Volksgemeinschaft*. Opladen: Westdeutscher Verlag.
Mayer, Karl J. 2006. 'Kuno Graf von Westarp als Kritiker des Nationalsozialismus', in Larry Eugene Jones and Wolfram Pyta (eds), *'Ich bin der letzte Preuße'. Der politische Lebensweg des konservativen Politikers Kuno Graf von Westarp (1864–1945)*. Cologne: Böhlau Verlag, 189–216.
Meyer, August. 1999. *Hitlers Holding: Die Reichswerke 'Hermann Göring'*. Munich: Europa Verlag.
Milward, Alan. 1970. *The New Order and the French Economy*. Oxford: Clarendon Press.
Mommsen, Hans. 1999. *From Weimar to Auschwitz*, Philip O'Connor, trans. Princeton: Princeton University Press.
Mommsen, Hans. 1998. 'Konnten Unternehmer im Nationalsozialismus apolitisch bleiben?' in Lothar Gall and Manfred Pohl (eds), *Unternehmer im Nationalsozialismus*. Munich: C.H. Beck, 69–73.

Mommsen, Hans, et al. (eds). 1974. *Industrielles System und politische Entwicklung in der Weimarer Republik: Verhandlungen des Internationalen Symposiums in Bochum vom 12.–17. Juni 1973.* Düsseldorf: Droste Verlag.

Munch-Petersen, Thomas. 1981. *The Strategy of Phoney War: Britain, Sweden and the Iron Ore Question, 1939–1940.* Stockholm: Militahistorska fölaget.

Neebe, Reinhard. 1981. *Großindustrie, Staat und NSDAP 1930–1933: Paul Silverberg und der Reichsverband der Deutschen Industrie in der Krise der Weimarer Republik.* Göttingen: Vandenhoeck & Ruprecht.

Neumann, Franz. 1981. *Behemoth: The Structure and Practice of National Socialism, 1933–1944.* London: Longman.

Nicholls, A.J. 1994. *Freedom with Responsibility: The Social Market Economy in Germany, 1918–1963.* Oxford, Clarendon Press.

Nicosia, Francis R., and Jonathan Huener (eds). 2004. *Business and Industry in Nazi Germany.* New York: Berghahn Books.

Nocken, Ulrich. 1974. 'Inter-Industrial Conflicts and Alliances as Exemplified by the AVI-Agreement', in Hans Mommsen et al. (eds), *Industrielles System und politische Entwicklung in der Weimarer Republik: Verhandlung des Internationalen Symposiums in Bochum vom 12.–17. Juni 1973.* Düsseldorf: Droste Verlag, 693–704.

Nocken, Ulrich. 1979. 'Inter-industrial Conflicts and Alliances in the Weimar Republic: Experiments in Societal Corporatism'. Ph.D. dissertation, University of California, Berkeley.

Nolte, Ernst. 1963. *Three Faces of Fascism.* London: Weidenfeld & Nicholson.

Overy, Richard. 1984. *Göring, the 'Iron Man'.* London: Routledge and Keegan Paul.

Overy, Richard. 1994. *War and Economy in the Third Reich.* Oxford: Clarendon Press.

Parker, William. 1954. 'Entrepreneurship, Industrial Organisation, and Economic Growth: A German Example', *Journal of Economic History* 14(4), 380–400.

Parnell, Martin. 1994. *The German Tradition of Organized Capitalism: Self-Government in the Coal Industry.* Oxford: Clarendon Press.

Patch, William L. 1985. *Christian Trade Unions in the Weimar Republic, 1918–1933: The Failure of Corporate Pluralism.* New Haven: Yale University Press.

Patch, William L. 1998. *Heinrich Brüning and the Dissolution of the Weimar Republic.* Cambridge: Cambridge University Press.

Petrick, Fritz. 1989. 'Die Eisenerze Skandinaviens, der Erzhafen Narvik und die deutsche Kriegswirtschaft', in Dietrich Eichholtz and Kurt Pätzold (eds), *Der Weg in den Krieg.* Berlin: Akademie-Verlag, 279–98.

Pietzsch, Albert. 1933. 'Grundsätzliche Betrachtungen über Volkswirtschaft', supplement to *Der Arbeitgeber* 22(15 November).

Plumpe, Werner, and Christian Kleinschmidt (eds). 1993. *Unternehmen zwischen Markt und Macht: Aspekte deutscher Unternehmens- und Industriegeschichte im 20. Jahrhundert.* Essen: Bochumer Schriften zur Unternehmens- und Industriegeschichte.

Plumpe, Werner, and Joachim Scholtyseck (eds). 2012. *Der Staat und die Ordnung der Wirtschaft: Vom Kaiserreich bis zur Berliner Republik.* Stuttgart: Franz Steiner.

Pohl, Hans, and Johannes Markner. 1992. *Verbandsgeschichte und Zeitgeschichte: VDMA – 100 Jahre im Dienste des Maschinenbaus, Band I.* Frankfurt a.M.: Maschinenbau Verlag.

Pohl, Karl Heinrich. 1979. *Weimars Wirtschaft und die Außenpolitik, 1924–1926: Vom Dawes- Plan zum internationalen Eisenpakt.* Düsseldorf: Droste.

Priemel, Kim Christian. 2007. *Flick: Eine Konzerngeschichte vom Kaiserreich bis zur Bundesrepublik.* Göttingen: Wallstein Verlag.

Prollius, Michael von. 2003. *Das Wirtschaftssystem der Nationalsozialisten 1933–1939: Steuerung durch emergente Organisation und politische Prozesse.* Paderborn: Ferdinand Schöningh.
Pudor, Fritz. 1974. *Männer der frühere deutschen stahlwirtschaftlichen Verbände.* Düsseldorf: Verlag Stahleisen.
Puppo, Rolf. 1989. *Die wirtschaftsrechtliche Gesetzgebung des Dritten Reiches.* Constance: Hartung-Gorre.
Rathenau, Walther. 1918. *Die Neue Wirtschaft.* Berlin: Fischer Verlag.
Rathkolb, Oliver. 2001. *NS-Zwangsarbeit: Der Standort Linz der 'Reichswerke Hermann Göring AG Berlin' 1938–1945.* Vienna: Böhlau.
Rebentisch, Dieter. 1989. *Führerstaat und Verwaltung im Zweiten Weltkrieg.* Stuttgart: Franz Steiner Verlag.
Reckendrees, Alfred. 2000. *Das 'Stahltrust' Projekt: Die Gründung der Vereinigte Stahlwerke A.G. und ihre Unternehmensentwicklung 1926–1933/34.* Munich: Oscar Beck.
Reckendrees, Alfred. 1996. 'Die Vereinigte Stahlwerke A.G. 1926–1933 und "das Glänzende Beispiel Amerikas"', *Zeitschrift für Unternehmensgeschichte/Journal of Business History* 41(2), 159–86.
Reichert, Jakob. 1937. 'Aus Fachverein: Mitgliederversammlung der Wirtschaftsgruppe Eisenschaffende Industrie und Bezirksgruppe Nordwest', *Stahl und Eisen* 57(25) (24 June), 706–9.
Reichert, Jakob. 1931. 'Die Börsenbewertung führender in- und ausländischer Eisenaktien in den Jahren 1925 bis 1930', *Stahl und Eisen* 51(6) (5 February), 164–72.
Reichert, Jakob. 1932. 'Das britische Weltreich auf dem Wege zur Selbstversorgung mit Eisen und Stahl', *Stahl und Eisen* 52(45) (10 November), 1085–94.
Reichert, Jakob. 1929. 'Dawes-Plan-Erfahrungen und Young-Plan-Aussichten der deutschen Volkswirtschaft', *Stahl und Eisen* 49(43) (24 October 1929), 1553–58.
Reichert, Jakob. 1931. 'Deutsch-französische Aussprache über die Lage der deutschen Industrie', *Stahl und Eisen* 51(42) (15 October 1931), 1297–1299.
Reichert, Jakob. 1930. 'Die deutsche Wirtschaft unter dem Young-Tributplan', *Stahl und Eisen* 50(21) (22 May 1930), 730–736.
Reichert, Jakob. 1933. 'Deutschlands Stellung in der Weltwirtschaft', *Stahl und Eisen* 53(32) (10 August), 831–35.
Reichert, Jakob. 1936. 'Die Eisenwirtschaft im englischen Weltreich', *Stahl und Eisen* 56(10) (6 May), 297–305.
Reichert, Jakob. 1937. 'Die englische Eisen- und Stahlindustrie in Gegenwart und Zukunft: nach den Ergebnissen einer amtlichen Untersuchung vom Jahre 1937', *Stahl und Eisen* 57(35) (2 September), 969–79.
Reichert, Jakob. 1927. 'Die Festländische Rohstahlgemeinschaft', in *Weltwirtschaftliches Archiv: Chronik und Archivalien* 25. Jena: Gustav Fischer, 340*–72*.
Reichert, Jakob. 1934. 'Die Handelspolitik der führenden Wirtschaftsvölker in der Nachkriegszeit', *Stahl und Eisen* 54(11) (15 March), 261–64.
Reichert, Jakob. 1931. 'Die Hauptursachen der Arbeitslosigkeit und die Möglichkeit ihrer Überwindung', *Sonderdruck aus Ruhr und Rhein* 31(31 July). Offprint.
Reichert, Jakob. 1935. 'Internationale Übersicht über die Kartellgesetzgebung', *Stahl und Eisen* 55(24) (13 June), 653–57.
Reichert, Jakob. 1934. 'Japans Eisen- und Stahlindustrie in ihrer wirtschaftlichen Entwicklung', *Stahl und Eisen* 54(38) (20 September), 979–86.
Reichert, Jakob. 1930. 'Die Leistungsfähigkeit der deutschen Stahlindustrie', *Stahl und Eisen* 50(50) (11 December), 1744–49.

Reichert, Jakob. 1929. 'Die Löhne in der deutschen eisenschaffenden Industrie', *Stahl und Eisen* 49(7) (14 February), 214–21.
Reichert, Jakob. 1936. *Nationale und internationale Kartelle*. Berlin: Junker und Dünhaupt Verlag.
Reichert, Jakob. 1933. 'Das neue Wettbewerbsgesetz der amerikanischen Eisen- und Stahlindustrie', *Stahl und Eisen* 53(40) (5 November), 1031–34.
Reichert, Jakob. 1922. *Rathenaus Reparationspolitik: Eine kritische Studie*. Berlin: August Scherl.
Reichert, Jakob. 1919. *Rettung aus der Valutanot*. Berlin: Zeitfragen-Verlag.
Reichert, Jakob. 1936. 'Ein Rückblick auf das zehnjährige Bestehen der internationalen Stahlverbände', *Stahl und Eisen* 56(48) (26 November), 1430–36.
Reichert, Jakob. 1939. 'Schrott im Außenhandel', *Stahl und Eisen* 59(11) (13 March), 325–30.
Reichert, Jakob. 1931. 'Der Standpunkt eines deutschen Industriellen in französischer Betrachtung', *Stahl und Eisen* 51(49) (3 December), 1522–24.
Reichert, Jakob. 1932. 'Walzeisen-Weltmarktpreise und internationale Verbände', *Stahl und Eisen* 52(26) (30 June), 634–36.
Reichert, Jakob. 1934. 'Wiederaufstieg der deutschen Eisen- und Stahlindustrie im Jahre 1933', *Stahl und Eisen* 54(1) (4 January), 11–13.
Reichert, Jakob. 1931. 'Wirtschaftskrise und Eisenverbrauch', *Stahl und Eisen* 51(22) (28 May 1931), 671–75.
Reichert, Jakob. 1931. 'Wirtschaftssystem, Politik und Arbeitslosigkeit', *Der Arbeitgeber* 23(1 December), 572–75.
Roskill, Stephan (ed). 1972. *Hankey: Man of Secrets, Vol. II, 1919–1931*. London: William Collins Sons & Co.
Roth, Karl Heinz. 1999. '"Neuordnung" und Wirtschaftliche Nachkriegsplanung', in Dietrich Eichholtz (ed.), *Krieg und Wirtschaft: Studien zur deutschen Wirtschaftsgeschichte 1939–1945*. Berlin: Metropol Verlag, 195–220.
Shearer, Ronald D. 1997. 'The Reichskuratorium für Wirtschaftlichkeit: Fordism and Organised Capitalism in Germany, 1918–1945', *Business History Review* 71(4), 569–602.
Scherner, Jonas. 2008. *Die Logik der Industiepolitik im Dritten Reich: Die Investitionen in die Autarkie- und Rüstungsindustrie und ihre staatliche Förderung*. Stuttgart: Franz Steiner Verlag.
Scherner, Jonas. 2006. 'Das Verhältnis zwischen NS-Regime und Industrieunternehmen -Zwang oder Kooperation', *Zeitschrift für Unternehmensgeschichte* 51, 166–90.
Schlenker, Max. 1932. 'Aus dem Fachverein: Gesunde Wirtschaft im starken Staat', *Stahl und Eisen* 52(49) (8 December), 1226–28.
Schmädel, von Dieter. 1968. *Führung im Interessenverband: Probleme der innerverbandlichen Willensbildung*. Berlin: Dunker & Humblot.
Schneider, Michael. 1999. *Unterm Hakenkreuz: Arbeiter und Arbeiterbewegung 1933 bis 1939*. Bonn: Dietz.
Schneider, Michael. 2005. *Unternehmensstrategien zwischen Weltwirtschaftskrise und Kriegswirtschaft: Die Chemnitzer Maschinenbauindustrie in der NS-Zeit, 1933–1945*. Essen: Klartext Verlag.
Schneider, Michael. 1975. *Unternehmer und Demokratie: Die freien Gewerkschaften in der unternehmerischen Ideologie der Jahre 1918 bis 1933*. Bonn and Bad Godesberg: Verlag Neue Gesellschaft.
Scholtyseck, Joachim. 1999. *Robert Bosch und der liberale Widerstand gegen Hitler 1933 bis 1945*. Munich: C.H. Beck.
Schwarz, Leonard. 2000. 'German Technological Development During the 1930s: The Retrospective View of British Engineers and Scientists', in Christoph Buchheim and Red-

vers Garside (eds), *After the Slump: Industry and Politics in 1930s Britain and Germany*. New York: Peter Lang, 131–147.

Schweninger, Oskar. 1933. 'Dienst der Technik/Organisation des Einsatzes der Arbeit und der technischen Mittel', *Maschinenbau* 12(9/10), 231–32.

Seebold, Gustav-Hermann. 1981. *Ein Stahlkonzern im Dritten Reich: Der Bochumer Verein 1927–1945*. Wuppertal: Peter Hammer Verlag.

Siegel, Tilla. 1988. 'Rationalisierung statt Klassenkampf: Zur Rolle der DAF in der nationalsozialistischen Ordnung der Arbeit', in Hans Mommsen (ed.), *Herrschaftsalltag im Dritten Reich*. Düsseldorf: Swann Verlag, 97–149.

Siegel, Tilla, and Thomas von Freyberg. 1991. *Industrielle Rationalisierung unter dem Nationalsozialismus*. Frankfurt a.M.: Campus Verlag.

Silverman, Dan P. 1998. *Hitler's Economy: Nazi Work Creation Programs, 1933–1936*. Cambridge, MA: Harvard University Press.

Soénius, Ulrich. 2005. 'Im Auftrag des Reichswirtschaftsministeriums: Rudolf Siedersleben', in Peter Danylow and Ulrich S. Soénius (eds), *Otto Wolff: Ein Unternehmen zwischen Wirtschaft und Politik*. Munich: Siedler Verlag.

Sohn-Rethel, Alfred. 1987. *The Economy and Class Structure of German Fascism*. Martin Sohn-Rethel, trans. London: Free Association Books.

Sohns, Hans Fritz. 1936. 'Die geschichtlichen Voraussetzungen der Volkswirtschaft', *Maschinenbau* 15(17/18), 518.

Speer, Albert. 1970. *Inside the Third Reich*, Richard Winston and Clara Winston, trans. New York: The Macmillan Company.

Spoerer, Mark. 1996. *Von Scheingewinnen zum Rüstungsboom: Die Eigenkapitalrentabilität der deutschen Industrieaktiengesellschaften 1925–1941*. Stuttgart: Franz Steiner Verlag.

Stachura, Peter. 1983. *Gregor Strasser and the Rise of Nazism*. London: Allen & Unwin.

Statistische Gemeinschaftsarbeit Nordwestliche Gruppe des VdESI. 1933. *Statistisches Jahrbuch für die Eisen- und Stahlindustrie, 1933*. Düsseldorf: Verlag Stagleisen.

Statistisches Reichsamt. 1928. *Statistisches Jahrbuch für das Deutsche Reich*. Berlin: Verlag für Sozialpolitik, Wirtschaft und Statistik.

Statistisches Reichsamt. 1936. *Statistisches Jahrbuch für das Deutsche Reich*. Berlin: Verlag für Sozialpolitik, Wirtschaft und Statistik.

Stegmann, Dirk. 1975. 'Zum Verhältnis von Großindustrie und Nationalsozialismus 1930–1933: Ein Beitrag zur Geschichte der sog. Machtergreifung', *Archiv für Sozialgeschichte* 13, 399–482.

Stinnes, Eduard. 1979. 'A Genius in Chaotic Times: A Conversation between E. Stinnes and Andreas Kohlschütter of *Die Zeit*'. Bern: OFDAG, CH-3172 Niederwangen, 19.

Stöhr, Volker. 2000. '"Deutsche" Wege der Rationalisierung im Nationalsozialismus- dargstellt am Beispiel der sächsischen Maschinenbauindustrie', in Thomas Hänseroth and Carsten Krautz (eds), *Geschichte des sächsischen Werkzeugmaschinenbaus im Industriezeitalter: Beitrag der Tagung am 19. März 1998 in Dresden*. Dresden: Sächsisches Druck- und Verlagshaus A.G., 114–25.

Stokes, Raymond. 2008. 'Research and Development in German Industry in the Nazi Period: Motivations and Incentives, Directions, Outcomes', in Christoph Buchheim (ed.), *German Industry in the Nazi Period*. Stuttgart: Franz Steiner Verlag, 199–212.

Streb, Jochen. 2012. 'Das Nationalsozialistische Wirtschaftssystem: Indirekter Sozialismus, gelenkte Marktwirtschaft oder vergezogene Kreigswirtschaft?' in W. Plumpe and J. Scholtyseck (eds), *Der Staat und die Ordnung der Wirtschaft: Vom Kaiserreich bis zur Berliner Republik*. Stuttgart: Franz Steiner, 61–62.

Sutton, Eric (ed). 1937. *Gustav Stresemann: His Diaries, Letters, and Papers*, vol. 2. London: Macmillan.

Termin, Peter. 1991. 'Soviet and Nazi Economic Planning in the 1930s', *Economic History Review* 44(1), 573–93.
Thyssen, Fritz. 1941. *I Paid Hitler,* Cesar Saerchinger, trans. New York: Hodder and Stoughton.
Tooze, Adam J. 2003. '"Punktuelle Modernisierung": Die Akkumulation von Werkzeugmaschinen im "Dritten Reich"', *Jahrbuch für Wirtschaftsgeschichte* 1, 80-98.
Tooze, Adam. 2007. *The Wages of Destruction: The Making and Breaking of the Nazi Economy.* New York: Viking Penguin.
Trevarinus, Gottfried Reinhold. 1968. *Das Ende von Weimar: Heinrich Brüning und seine Zeit.* Düsseldorf: Econ Verlag.
Tribe, Keith. 1995. *Strategies of Economic Order: German Economic Discourse, 1750–1950.* Cambridge: Cambridge University Press.
Turner, Henry Ashby, Jr. 1985. *German Big Business and the Rise of Hitler.* New York: Oxford University Press.
Übbing, Helmut. 1999. *Stahl schreibt Geschichte: 125 Jahre Wirtschaftsvereinigung Stahl.* Düsseldorf: Verlag Stahleisen.
Ullmann, Hans-Peter. 1988. *Interessenverbände in Deutschland.* Frankfurt a.M.: Suhrkamp.
Unger, Stephan. 2003. 'Die "Herren aus dem Westen" in den Jahren 1933 und 1945: Die personellen Konsequenzen der Errichtung und des Untergangs der nationalsozialistischen Diktatur für die Wirtschaftselite des Ruhrgebietes', in Werner Abelshauser, Jan-Otmar Hesse and Werner Plumpe (eds), *Wirtschaftsordnung, Staat und Unternehmen: Neue Forschungen zur Wirtschaftsgeschichte des Nationalsozialismus.* Essen: Klartext Verlag, 321–337.
United States Strategic Bombing Survey. 1947. *No. 54: Machine Tools and Machinery as Capital Equipment,* Equipment Division, 2nd edn.
United States Strategic Bombing Survey, No. 55: Machine Tool Industry in Germany, Equipment Division, 2nd edn. January 1947.
Varain, Joseph (ed.). 1975. *Interessenverbände in Deutschland.* Cologne: Kiepenheuer & Witsch.
Verhandlungen des Reichstags: Stenographische Berichte und Drucksachen. 1930. Bd. 425. Druck und Verlag der Reichsdruckerei. 96. Sitzung. 26. Juni 1929. 2971–77.
Verhandlungen des Reichstags: Stenographische Berichte und Drucksachen. 1931. Bd. 427. Druck und Verlag der Reichsdruckerei 174. Sitzung. 27. Mai 1930. 5402–7.
Vierhus, Rudolph. 2006. *Deutsche Biographische Enzyklopädie (DBE).* Munich: K.G. Saur.
Volkart, Oliver. 2005. 'Wirtschaftspolitik und bürokratischer Wettbewerb im "Dritten Reich" 1933–1939', in Thomas Eger (ed.), *Erfolg und Versagen von Institutionen.* Berlin: Duncker & Humblot, 93–112.
Volkmann, Hans-Erich. 2003. *Ökonomie und Expansion: Grundzüge der NS-Wirtschaftspolitik.* Munich: R Oldenburg.
Volkmann, Hans-Erich. 1981. 'Zum Verhältnis von Großwirtschaft und NS-Regime im Zweiten Weltkrieg', in Waclaw Dlugoborski (ed.), *Zweiter Weltkrieg und sozialer Wandel.* Göttingen: Vandenhoek & Ruprecht, 87–116.
Weisbrod, Bernd. 1979. 'Economic Power and Political Stability Reconsidered: Heavy Industry in Weimar Germany', *Social History* 4(2), 241–63.
Weisbrod, Bernd. 1978. *Schwerindustrie in der Weimarer Republik: Interessenpolitik zwischen Stabilisierung und Krise.* Bielefeld: Peter Hammer Verlag.
Weiß, Hermann, and Paul Hoser (eds). 1989. *Die Deutschnationalen und die Zerstörung der Weimarer Republik: Aus dem Tagebuch von Reinhold Quaatz, 1928–1933.* Munich: R Oldenbourg Verlag.

Werner, Stefan. 1991. *Wirtschaftsordnung und Wirtschaftsrecht im Nationalsozialismus.* Frankfurt a.M.: Peter Lang Verlag.

Wiesen, Jonathan S. 2001. *West German Industry and the Challenge of the Nazi Past, 1945–1955.* Chapel Hill: University of North Carolina Press.

Winkler, Heinrich August. 1975. 'Unternehmerverbände zwischen Ständeideologie und Nationalsozialismus', in Heinz Joseph Varain (ed.), *Interessenverbände in Deutschland.* Cologne: Kiepenheuer & Witsch, 228–58.

Wiskott, Otto. 1929. *Eisenschaffende und eisenverarbeitende Industrie: Eine Untersuchung über die Verschiedenartigkeit ihrer Struktur und ihr gegenseitiges Verhältnis.* Bonn: Kurt Schroeder Verlag.

Wolffsohn, Michael. 1977. *Industrie und Handwerk im Konflikt mit staatlicher Wirtschaftspolitik? Studien zur Politik der Arbeitsbeschaffung in Deutschland, 1930–1934.* Berlin: Duncker & Humblot.

Wurm, Clemens. 1993. *Business, Politics and International Relations: Steel, Cotton and International Cartels in British Politics, 1924–1939.* Cambridge: Cambridge University Press.

Wysocki, Gerd. 1982. *Zwangsarbeit im Stahlkonzern: Salzgitter und die Reichswerke 'Hermann Göring' 1937–1945.* Braunschweig: Magni-Buchladen.

Ziegler, Dieter (ed.). 2000. *Großbürger und Unternehmer: Die deutsche Wirtschaftselite im 20. Jahrhundert.* Göttingen: Vandenhoeck & Ruprecht.

Zilbert, Edward. 1981. *Albert Speer and the Nazi Ministry of Arms: Economic Institutions and Industrial Production in the German War Economy.* London: Associated University Presses.

Zweig, Stephan. 1976. *Die Welt von Gestern: Erinnerungen eines Europäers.* Hamburg: Fischer Taschenbuch Verlag.

Index

Abelshauser, Werner, 5, 8, 141
Abraham, David, 4, 9
Ahrens, Wilhelm, 171, 177
Aly, Götz, 155
Ambrosius, Gerold, 110
Amtsgruppe Maschinen und Werkzeuge, 197
Armaments, 63–65, 87, 138, 140, 151, 156, 162, 165
Association of German Iron Manufacturers (Verein deutscher Eisenhüttenleute, VDEh), 77, 128
Association of German Iron and Steel Industrialists (Verein Deutscher Eisen- und Stahlindustrieller, VDESI), 2, 9, 12, 22, 24–5, 27, 29, 31, 33–4, 37–8, 48, 62–3, 65–6, 69–72, 78, 80, 84, 130–1, 221, 223, 225
  Budget, 31
  Membership, 7–8
  Organization, 22, 66
Association for Machine Building (Wirtschaftsverband Maschinenbau), 209
AVDMA, See Working Group of Machine Building Associations
AVI, See Working Group of the Iron Working Industry

Baare, Fernando Karl, 26, 78–9, 128–9, 165
Barkai, Avraham, 6, 110
British Iron and Steel Federation, 114
Browning, Christopher, 2
Brüning, Heinrich, 29, 30, 34–5, 36–7, 46
Buchheim, Christoph, 5, 6, 15, 110, 226–7

Business Association for Machine Building (Wirtschaftsverband Maschinenbau), 209
Business Group Electro-Industry (Wirtschaftsgruppe Elektroindustrie), 68, 94, 113, 136, 196
Business Group Iron Industry (Wirtschaftsgruppe Eisenschaffende Industrie), 62, 72–77, 79, 81–3, 84–7, 112–4, 116–7, 120–1, 123–32, 154–65, 167–74, 176, 223
  Budget, 73, 173
  Control Office (Prüfungsstelle), 73, 75
  Establishment, 62, 72
  North-West Group, 66, 73, 75, 76, 111, 126–9, 161–3, 171–2, 176, 177, 227
  Organization, 73–6
  Pre-Inspection Office (Vorprüfungsstelle), 76, 130
Business Group Machine Building (Wirtschaftsgruppe Maschinenbau), 62, 92–7, 134–40, 142, 189–92, 194–202, 205–6, 208, 209
  Anti-Semitism of, 96–7, 134–5, 190
  Budget, 95, 135–6, 145, 198
  Control Offices (Prüfungsstellen), 93–4, 135, 138–9, 140, 192, 195, 201
  Establishment, 62, 92
  Foreign Branch Offices, 139, 194–6
  Organization, 92–3, 197
  Pre-Inspection Offices (Vorprüfungsstellen), 93, 145
  Rationalization, 137, 194–6
Business Groups for Steel and Sheet Metal, 137

Index | 247

Business Group for Wholesale Import-Export, 137

Cartels, 2, 7–8, 22, 28–9, 37, 44, 47–8, 64, 70–1, 76–7, 79–87, 94, 112, 114–5, 119–20, 126–7, 130, 160–1, 172, 197
Catholic Center Party (Zentrum), 24, 36, 41
Chambers of Commerce, 46, 77, 125, 127–8, 160, 162–3
Commissar for Iron and Steel in the Occupied Territories, 171
Communist Party (KPD), 24, 29, 37, 41, 43, 66
Conservative People's Party (Konservative Volkspartei, KVP), 35, 66
Crude Steel Agreement (Internationale Rohstahlgemeinschaft , IRG), 29, 131, 160, 172

DAF, *See* German Worker's Front
DNVP, *See* German National People's Party
DVP, *See* German People's Party

Eichholtz, Dietrich, 63
Eisen und Stahlwerksgemeinschaft, 172
Export Policy, 43, 87, 90, 118
Export Promotion Procedure (Zusatzausfuhrverfahren, ZAV), 93, 116, 138, 140, 141, 198

Feldman, Gerald, 3, 8, 220
Fittings Association (Fittingsverband), 68–9
Flick Concern, 30, 168, 175
Flick, Friedrich, 10, 122–3, 164, 167, 168, 172
France, 1, 24–5, 27, 115, 166, 167, 168, 173, 194–5
Fröhlich, Friedrich, 38
Führerprinzip, 70, 72, 75, 165, 171
Funk, Walter, 36–7, 127, 130, 165–7, 171, 191–2

Gebrüder Boehringer (firm), 72, 96, 134
Gelsenkirchen Accord, 156
German Iron Federation (Wirtschaftsvereinigung Eisen, WVE), 177, 178

German Machine Builders' Association (Verein Deutscher Maschinenbau-Anstalten, VDMA), 2, 7, 9, 11, 14, 31, 38–49, 62–63, 88–92, 95–8, 133, 196, 199, 208, 220, 224, 225, 226
  Organization, 39, 40, 89
  Re-establishment, 210
  Statistical Office, 38, 40
German National People's Party (Deutschnationale Volkspartei, DNVP), 23, 25, 32, 33, 35–6, 49
German People's Party (Deutsche Volkspartei, DVP), 24
German Scrap Association, 157, 177
German Worker's Front (Deutsche Arbeitsfront, DAF), 67, 80, 81, 90, 113, 165
GHH, 123, 160
Goerdeler, Carl, 84–5, 112

Hanneken, Hermann von, 119, 120, 122, 126–7, 129, 130–1, 156–8, 160–1, 163, 166–7, 170
Haselbach, Dieter, 46
Hayes, Peter, viii, 5, 6, 226
Heinz, Hugo, 195
Hitler, Adolf, 3, 11, 21, 33–4, 36–7, 65, 67, 69, 70–1, 78, 81–2, 90–1, 96, 111, 117, 119, 155, 158, 164, 174, 190, 196, 205, 225
Horkheimer, Max, 3
Hugenberg, Alfred, 23, 32, 35

Imperial Germany (Kaiserreich), 8, 23, 25, 26, 39, 156, 176, 221, 222, 227
International Steel Cartel (ISC), 84, 114, 115
Iron and Steel Industry, 2–3,7–8, 10–14, 22–3, 25–31, 33–4, 37, 43–6, 62–78, 80–87, 93, 110–12, 114–24, 126–7, 129–31, 144n, 158–177, 180n, 201–2, 222–3, 225–7
  Capacity, 30–1
  Exports, 92
  Production, 7, 31, 117–8, 129
  Profits, 63, 64–5, 69

Kastl, Ludwig, 31, 66, 68, 88
Kathke, Paul, 139, 194

Index

Kehrl, Hans, 170
Kershaw, Ian, 62
Kiegel, 75, 83–6
Kiekebusch, Heinz, 203–4
Kim, Hak-Ie, 24
Klöckner (Firm), 125, 168
Klöckner, Florian, 85, 122–3
KPD, *See* Communist Party
Krupp (Firm), 85, 122, 167, 175
Krupp, Alfried, 11, 106n, 167
Krupp, Gustav, 66
KVP, *See* Conservative People's Party

Lampe Delta, 1
Lange, Karl, 2–4, 6–15, 21–2, 28, 39–49, 62–3, 65, 71–2, 75–79, 88–98, 107n, 111, 116, 120, 126, 130, 132, 133–42, 154–5, 158–9, 164, 169, 189–210, 220–228
    Appointment as BfM, 133
    Appointment as Chief business Manager, 39, 210
    and early Conflict with National Socialism, 48, 90–91
    and Drafted Workers, 206–7
    Early Life, 39
    and Economic Democracy, 45
    and Liberalism, 3, 11–2, 21, 40–2, 43, 46–9, 89, 90, 95, 134, 208, 221, 224, 227
    on Organized Economic Freedom, 47
    and the Political Left, 41–2
    Post War, 208–10
    Production Regulations, 137, 139, 192–3, 200–1
    and Speer Re-Organization, 196–204
    and War Service Cross, 196
Langnamverein, 33–4, 66
Law for the Preparation of the Organic Construction of the Economy, 72
Law for the Regulation of the Direction and Distribution of Machine and Apparatus Production, 192
Lindeboom, Karl, 177, 178
Loeb, Fritz, 117–120
Lüschen, Friedrich, 196

Machine Building, 7–8, 10, 38–9, 41, 44, 89, 90, 93, 148, 150, 190, 195, 208, 199, 203, 205, 207

Electrical Machines, 136
Exports, 44, 80, 148
Extruders, 98
Hammer and Forge Tools, 207
Lathes, 138, 141
Machine Tools, 44, 90, 135, 140, 192–3, 205, 207
Mechanical Presses, 137
Milling Machines, 140, 207
Profits, 63, 79, 140–1, 207
Rolling Machines, 31, 72, 77, 98
Typewriters, 7, 92, 135, 138
Universal Machines, 7, 26, 199, 202
Machine Management Office (Maschinenbewirtschaftungsstelle), 200, 201, 203
Main Committee for Machines (Hauptauschuß Maschinen), 189, 196, 203, 189
Main Ring for Iron and Steel (Hauptringe Eisen und Stahl), 170
Mannesmann, 167
Maschinenfabrik Augsburg-Nürnberg (MAN), viii, 11, 14
Ministry for Armaments and Munitions, later Armaments and War Production, 155–6, 158, 160, 169, 173, 193, 200, 203, 207
Ministry of Economics (RWM), 29, 46, 68, 72–6, 83–4, 86–7, 89 96, 112–4, 116–8, 120–21, 124–8, 131, 133–5, 155–8, 161–6, 168, 170, 172, 174, 191, 193, 195, 197–8, 201
Ministry of Labour, 131

Nazi Party, 21, 36, 59, 62, 66–7, 177–8
Nocken, Ulrich, 8, 220
Noell, Friedrich, 170
Nordman, Paul, 137
North-West Group of the German Iron and Steel Industry (Nordwest-Gruppe der Deutschen Eisen- und Stahlindustrie), 22–3, 66, 73, 75–6, 111, 126–9, 161, 162–3, 171–2, 176–7, 227
NSDAP, *See* Nazi Party

Office of the Four Year Plan, 74–5, 77, 111–113, 117, 119–20, 125, 133, 137, 141
Ordoliberalism, 46

Organic Economy, 13, 21, 70, 72, 80, 94
Overy, Richard, 5, 110, 124, 159

Pleiger, Paul, 34, 164, 167, 168
Poensgen, Ernst, 11–12, 34, 48, 66, 70–81, 84–7, 106n, 111–2, 114, 116–127, 129–31, 151, 156, 158–61, 165, 166–73, 196
Price Commissar, 74, 76, 80, 84, 111–12, 116

Raabe, Paul, 72, 167, 168
Rationalization, 30, 31, 41, 137, 157, 194, 198, 199, 202, 206, 209
Reich Association of German Industry (Reichsverband der deutschen Industrie, RdI), 8, 22, 31, 42, 46, 66, 68, 89
Reich Iron Association (Reichsvereinigung Eisen, RVE), 170–4
Reichert, Jakob, 2–15, 21–39, 40, 42–3, 46–9, 62–89, 91–2, 94, 96–8, 111–33, 138, 142, 164–79, 189–91, 195–6, 200, 202, 204, 209–10, 220–8
   and Authoritarianism, 3, 24–5, 31–2, 34, 70
   and Conflict over Pietzsch, 66–8
   and Conflict with Steinberg, 127–9, 161–3
   and Division of firms in Alsace-Lorraine, 166–9
   Early Life, 22
   Entry into the War, 114–5
   and Establishment of RVE, 171–2
   Historical Work, 174–5
   on International Cooperation and Cartels, 28–9, 30, 37, 64, 80, 82–4, 102, 113–6, 131, 160
   on Natural Economy, 12, 21, 26–7, 29, 32, 37, 47, 80, 115, 166, 122
   and Opposition to National Socialism, 12, 23, 35–8, 78–9, 80, 130
   and Opposition to Reichswerke, 121–125
   Political Career, 23, 35–6, 42
   Post War, 176–9
   Suicide, 179, 227
Reich Group Industry (Reichsgruppe Industrie, RGI), 68, 73, 79, 81, 84, 85, 92, 94, 125, 127, 130, 141, 160–1, 174, 197

Reichskuratorium für Wirtschaftlichkeit, 137
Reichswerke Hermann Göring, 6, 110, 120–22, 125, 128–9, 138, 159, 164–5, 167–8, 170, 175
Reparations, 23, 24, 27, 32–3, 168, 176
Reusch, Hermann, 178
Reusch, Paul, 9, 11, 22, 23, 32, 130, 131, 160–1, 173
Reuter, Wolfgang, 46, 89
Reuther, Fritz, 197
RGI, *See* Reich Group Industry
Rheinlander, Paul, 167
Ring for Iron Production (Ringe der Eisenerzeugung), 171
Röchling, Herman, 10, 114, 118, 132–4, 155, 168, 170–3, 206
Rolled Steel Association (Walzstahl-Verband), 172
Rohman, Franz, 195
Roth, Karl Heinz, 139
Ruhr Crisis, 24, 27, 28
Ruhrlade, 8, 123
Rüstow, Alexander, 40, 42, 46, 48, 89
RVE, *See* Reich Iron Association

Sack, Otto, 89, 190–2, 197
Salewski, Wilhelm, 163, 171, 177, 178
Schacht, Hjalmar, 75, 83, 87, 91, 112, 121, 122–3
Scherdtmann, Gustav, 195
Scherner, Jonas, 6, 110, 226, 227
Schieber, Walther, 203
Schleicher, Kurt von, 35, 46
Schlenker, Max, 33, 66, 73, 154, 227
Schmitt, Heinrich, 132, 157, 158, 166, 168
Scholtyseck, Joachim, 11
Scrap, 76, 119, 129, 157, 160, 177
Shärfl's Nachfolger Machine Tools, 199, 204–6
Siemens & Halske, 94
Siemens, 196, 199
Siemens-Schuckert, 136
Silverberg, Paul, 42, 66, 88
Slave Labour, 163, 190
Social Democratic Party (Sozialdemokratische Partei Deutschlands, SPD), 23, 24, 41, 42, 43, 66, 69, 225

Sohl, Hans-Günther, 171
Soviet Union, 5, 45, 163, 193
Speer, Albert, 14, 155, 170, 189, 196, 198, 201–4
Spoerer, Mark, 6, 63, 89
Springorum, Fritz, 33, 66, 72
State Monopoly Capitalism, (STAMOKAP), 3, 169
Stegmann, Dirk, 4
Steinberg, Wilhelm, 73, 76, 111, 123, 126–9, 162–3, 172, 178
Steinbrinck, Otto, 167–8
Stresemann, Gustav, 3, 24, 34

Termin, Peter, 3, 5, 10
Thyssen, Fritz, 32–3, 37, 38
Todt, Fritz, 156, 158, 160, 196, 207
Tooze, Adam, 169
Tosse, Werner, 127, 129, 161, 171
Treaty of Versailles, 24, 31–2, 121, 165, 166, 175
Treviranus, Gottfried, 35–6

VDESI, *See* Association of German Iron and Steel Industrialists
VDMA, *See* German Machine Builders' Association
Vereinigte Stahl-Werke, 7, 121, 168

Vögler, Albert, 8, 10, 11, 31–2, 121, 155

Wanderer Werke AG, 140
Westarp, Kuno von, 23, 35–6
Wiesen, Jonathan, 4, 114, 226
Wigru, *See* Business Groups
Wilhelm Grillo (firm), 1
Wirtschaftsgruppe Eisenschaffende Industrie, *See* Business Group Iron Industry
Wirtschaftsgruppe Maschinenbau, *See* Business Group Machine Building
Wolff, Otto, 123
Working Group of the Iron Working Industry (Arbeitsgemeinschaft der eisenverarbeitenden Industrie, AVI), 29, 43, 44, 114, 116, 164
Working Group of Machine Building Associations (Arbeitsgemeinschaft der Verbände Deutscher Maschinenbau-Anstalten, AVDMA), 209–10
WVE, *See* German Iron Federation

Young Plan, 27, 31–3, 53, 91

Zangen, Wilhelm, 10, 33, 115, 122, 123–4, 141, 155–6, 164, 166–7, 172–3
ZAV, *See* Export Promotion Procedure

www.ingramcontent.com/pod-product-compliance
Lightning Source LLC
Chambersburg PA
CBHW072149100526
44589CB00015B/2149